Travel Agency Operations

Wayne A. Steinberg

and the Editors

of the

International Institute of Travel

Prentice
Hall

Toronto

Canadian Cataloguing in Publication Data

Steinberg, Wayne A., 1949–
      Travel agency operations

ISBN 0-13-027245-0

1. Travel agents. 2. Tourist trade. I. International Institute of Travel. II Title.

G154.S734 2001a   338.4'791   C00-930767-2

ISBN 0-13-027245-0

Vice President, Editorial Director: Michael Young
Executive Editor: David Stover
Marketing Manager: Sophia Fortier
Signing Representative: Sherry Zweig
Associate Editor: Susan Ratkaj
Production Editor: Julia Hubble
Copy Editor: Lu Cormier
Production Coordinator: Peggy Brown
Page Layout: Janette Thompson (Jansom)
Interior Design: Julia Hall
Cover Design: Monica Kompter
Cover Image: Digital Vision

1 2 3 4 5   05 04 03 02 01

Printed and bound in Canada

Contents

Preface

INTRODUCTION

This book is intended to be much more than a review of how a travel agency operates. It is also an overview of each of the areas in which a travel agent is assumed to have some degree of expertise in the sale of travel products and services. Some agents and agencies will, of course, specialize in the sale of certain types of products and services, and they will need particular expertise in those areas.

Generally, however, a successful travel agency will need to have on-hand agents who are conversant with a broad range of travel products and services. This book uses descriptions and examples of products to help the reader understand the processes involved. In some cases, samples of typical products available have been replicated; in other cases, real-life examples have been used.

An attempt has been made, where possible, to mention the major players in each sector of the Canadian travel marketplace. Although there are many similarities between the types of travel products and services available inside and outside Canada, the book is based exclusively on the Canadian experience. It does not seek to cover the suppliers in any detail who are not selling in the Canadian market, although some specific foreign examples may appear from time to time.

Each chapter of this book examines a particular aspect of a travel agency business. Exercises have been included to assist with review of the chapter content. The reader should also, when possible, apply the information found in this book to currently available travel products and promotional material. Try to have a look at some of the brochures available in your own local market.

Tourism is a multifaceted field with abundant career opportunities. I am a lawyer by profession, and I have worked for a number of years in the travel industry as in-house counsel with the International Institute of Travel. During that time, I have been able to learn much about this industry through its instructors and staff. I hope that you will be inspired by this book to find your own niche in this growing industry.

Text Contents

The first two chapters offer a general introduction to tourism and the travel industry. Chapter 1 introduces the types of travel agencies and the services provided, and includes an overview of the travel distribution system. Chapter 2 covers some of the basic information you will need to know about working in a travel agency, including where to get information, the use of preferred suppliers, currency exchange, and travel brochures.

The majority of the book examines specific travel products in detail. Most of these chapters include industry terminology and booking procedures; many also have examples of pricing. Chapter 3 deals with the advanced booking charter (or ABC) air carriers. Chapter 4 examines the accommodation sector of the industry and the use of industry hotel guides. Chapter 5 takes an in-depth look at car rentals: the types of rentals and insurance alternatives. You'll find out what questions to ask to get the right product for your client. The Canadian, U.S., and European passenger rail systems are all reviewed in Chapter 6. Chapters 7 and 8 look at motorcoach and sea transportation, respectively. Each section gives a general overview of the industry and the terminology used. Chapter 9 covers booking land arrangements with a wholesaler. Chapter 10 handles inclusive tour charters, while Chapter 11 reviews booking independent tours.

The next few chapters cover some of the broader aspects of travel matters, which you will also need to know in order to work in the travel industry. Chapter 12 looks at travel insurance, including the various types available, insurance waivers, changes, and cancellations. Chapter 13 considers the special needs traveller, with a review of features important to each group. Chapter 14, travel and the law, reviews some of the important aspects of legal liability and protection from legal action. And Chapter 15 reviews travel documents and other travel requirements (such as health, currency, and customs) when travelling to different locales.

The four appendices offer more specific information in several areas. Appendix A gives examples of agency forms that may be useful to you. Appendix B highlights some specific worldwide accommodations. Appendix C, Sea Transportation, lists ferries, freighters, cruise lines, and ports. And in Appendix D, you'll find an extensive list of Canadian and U.S. tour operators.

Acknowledgments

This book is the result of an ongoing effort on the part of many individuals over a number of years. It was originally designed as a textbook for the Travel Agency Operations course offered by the International Institute of Travel, one of Canada's largest travel training organizations. My thanks to the staff, and, in particular, the instructional staff of the Institute, both past and present and at all of its locations. Without your assistance this book would not have been possible. A special thank you to Robert Quilter, an instructor at the Toronto campus, for his invaluable contributions to this project; to Rudolph Nareen, president of the Institute; and to those who reviewed the draft and made helpful comments and suggestions.

I would also like to thank the following companies for allowing us to make use of their material in the preparation of this book: Amtrak, Astor Travel Services, Avis Inc., Cahners Travel Group, Canadian Travel Press, Choice Hotels International, Cruise Lines International Association, International Airline Publications, Rail Europe, Thomas Cook Publishing, Via Rail, and Voyageur Insurance Company.

Thanks also to the staff at Pearson Education Canada for their contribution to this project, specifically to David Stover and Susan Ratkaj, and to Lu Cormier for her assistance with the editing of the manuscript. If I have missed anyone, it was unintentional.

Wayne A. Steinberg, B.A., LL.B.

1

The Tourism Industry

"Travel Agency Operations" covers much more than this book title might at first suggest. The operation of a travel agency encompasses the sale of a wide variety of travel products and services, and the travel agency plays a major role in the tourism industry as it has evolved. Travel agencies rely heavily on tourism and, of course, tourism depends on tourists. So what exactly do we mean by the terms *tourism* and *tourist*?

Tourism. The industry that includes transportation, feeding, lodging, and entertainment of tourists.

Tourist. A temporary visitor who travels to a location other than where he or she resides for a variety of reasons, including leisure and recreation, study, business, family commitments, or to attend a convention.

THE HISTORY OF TOURISM

Humankind is by nature curious of the unknown. Even the earliest records of history indicate this interest in exploration. Indeed, we can trace the history of the human race through its famous travellers such as Marco Polo and Christopher Columbus.

We continued this pursuit of the unknown throughout our history, and travel took many forms: from travel on land by foot, horseback, or camel, to travel on water by canoe or ancient sailing ship. Our more modern modes of transportation include the railroad, cruise ship, jet plane, automobile, and motorcoach.

Over time, as we took up these various modes of travel and as increasing numbers of people were both willing and financially able to travel, it became inevitable that certain individuals would go into the business of providing travel services to the public. The first travel agent was probably Thomas Cook, who arranged the first known organized tour by rail in 1841 in England. It was a 12-mile (19-kilometre) journey to a nearby town for a temperance convention. "Cook's Tours" of the continent of Europe, personally escorted by Mr. Cook himself, soon became fashionable for the wealthy. That modest beginning was the foundation of Thomas Cook & Son, today one of the largest travel organizations in the world. Now throughout the world, even in the smallest village, a local travel agent can easily be found.

The mid-nineteenth century travel agency focused predominantly on rail transportation and on steamships for intercontinental travel. The twentieth century saw the beginning of the jet age, starting in the 1950s. Gradually the jet replaced the ship as the primary mode of transportation and opened the door to mass tourism. Tourism is probably the largest employer in Canada today, and Canadians have proven to be among the world's greatest travellers. With the introduction of new facilities, new destinations, and improvements such as larger and more elaborate cruise ships and larger and faster airplanes, the travel industry can be expected to continue its spectacular growth.

THE REASONS WE TRAVEL

Why Are More People Travelling?

Below are some of the reasons more people are travelling:
- Rising disposable income after providing for the necessities of life;
- Shorter working time and increased time for leisure;
- Earlier retirement;
- Technological advances, especially the jet plane;
- Declining costs;
- Higher educational qualifications among the travelling public.

Can you think of any others?

_____

_____

_____

Why Do People Travel?

There are many reasons to travel. Following is a list of some of the main reasons, but obviously this is not an exhaustive list. If you can think of other reasons, add them in the space below.
- To relax; for example, a beach holiday to Jamaica;
- To visit a country of origin; for example, the recent immigrant who goes back on a visit;
- To attend special cultural events, such as the Jazz Festival in Spoleto, Italy, the Mardi Gras in New Orleans, or the Winter Carnival in Quebec City;
- To experience different lifestyles, such as going on a work-related sabbatical abroad;
- To see special historic or cultural sites, such as Carnegie Hall in New York City, the Kremlin in Moscow, the Citadel in Quebec City, the Eiffel Tower in Paris, or the Opera House in Sydney, Australia;
- To attend theatre, such as Broadway productions in New York, West End productions in London, or the Shaw Festival in Niagara-on-the-Lake, Canada;
- To attend sporting events, such as the Daytona 500 automobile race, the Queen's Plate horse race, the World Cup soccer tournament, or a tennis match at Wimbledon;

- To visit museums or art galleries, such as the Louvre and the D'Orsay Galleries in Paris, the Prado in Madrid, the Hermitage in St. Petersburg (formerly Leningrad) or the Metropolitan Museum of Art in New York City;
- To gamble, such as a junket to Las Vegas or Atlantic City, a visit to the Monte Carlo casino, or a cruise on a gambling riverboat on the Mississippi River;
- For a honeymoon to destinations such as Niagara Falls or the Pocono Mountains;
- To visit natural wonders, such as the Grand Canyon, the Arctic glaciers in Alaska, the fjords of Norway, or wildlife in Kenya;
- To take ecological tours to areas where the plant and animal life is at risk from development, such as the rainforests of Brazil and Costa Rica;
- To visit theme parks, such as Universal Studios, Disney World, Canada's Wonderland, or Euro-Disney;
- To shop at one of the many shopping destinations, such as New York's Fifth Avenue, Maine's outlet stores, the West Edmonton Mall (one of the world's largest), or London's Oxford Street;
- For religious pilgrimages, such as travelling to Mecca, attending the Oberammergau Passion plays, or visiting the Vatican and St. Peter's Basilica or the Shrine at Lourdes;
- For education, such as a year at Oxford University or an art school in Cuernavaca, Mexico;
- For health reasons, such as a visit to the Florida spas, a stay at the thermal baths at Carlsbad, or a winter visit by the asthma sufferer to Arizona;
- For business travel;
- To try out new destinations on the "cutting edge" of the travel industry (Jet-Set travel);
- To attend conventions or conferences.

Add any other reasons you can think of here:

_____

_____

_____

_____

_____

_____

_____

_____

_____

With so many different reasons to travel, it is not surprising that a broad variety of travel agencies exist, some specializing in particular types of travel.

THE TRAVEL DISTRIBUTION SYSTEM

The Travel Distribution System provides a framework in which the various components of the industry can be examined. The traveller or tourist is serviced by the travel agency that, in turn, is serviced by the tour operator and other travel suppliers. The chart below sets out the components.

> **Tour Operator/Travel Supplier**
> ↓
> **The Travel Agency**
> ↓
> **The Traveller**

Category	Supplier	Example
Transportation	Scheduled airlines	Air Canada
	Charter airlines	Air Transat
	Railways	Via Rail
	Bus companies	Greyhound
	Car rental companies	Hertz
	Airport ground transportation companies	Pacific Western Transportation
Accommodation	Hotels	Hilton
	Resorts	Sandals
	Villas, vacation homes	Tryall, Jamaica
	Bed and breakfasts	Napa Inn, CA
	Campgrounds	Cinnamon Bay, U.S. Virgins
	Condominiums/apartments	Reef Club, FL
Tours	Package tour operators (ITC)	Sunquest
	Independent tours (FIT)	Holiday House
	Cruise lines	Carnival Cruises
	Escorted tours	Trafalgar
Destination Management	Local sightseeing	Gray Line
	Tour guides	Step-on Guides
	Ground operators	Supertravel, U.K.
Other Suppliers	Travel insurance	Voyageur
	Attractions	Busch Gardens
	Bon voyage gifts	Flowers arranged through local florists or directly through tour operators
	Theatre tickets	Keith Prowse
Miscellaneous	Tourist boards	British Tourist Authority

THE TRAVEL AGENCY

What Is a Travel Agency?

A travel agency is a sales office that sells to customers many of the various components of travel (transportation, accommodation, sightseeing, car rentals, etc.). These items are offered to the agent by travel suppliers in return for a commission paid by the supplier or wholesaler. As an agent of the supplier or wholesaler, the agency is an intermediary between the supplier/wholesaler and the client.

The travel agency is a service business and relies on the following factors for its success:

• **Travel agency reputation**—word-of-mouth advertising;

- **Conventional advertising**—radio, TV, direct mail, newspaper ads;
- **Repeat clients;**
- **Convenience of location/hours**—the agency may be selected because it is located close to the client's home or business, or its hours of operation may be very convenient for the client. Travel decisions are often made in the evening or on weekends, so convenience is important.

Why Use a Travel Agent?

The answer to this question is best given through an example. Assume that a couple seeks information about a cruise. Without the services of an agent, they would have to call a dozen or so cruise lines, wait to receive brochures in the mail, and then spend many hours trying to decide which cruise would be best for them.

And without the agent, thousands of suppliers would need their own representatives and staff to get the attention of potential travellers for direct bookings. The booking process would become a nightmare for consumers and suppliers alike.

Following are some reasons customers say they use travel agents:

- Helps to get the most value for money;
- Assures the highest quality accommodation and other services;
- Provides objective opinions;
- Helps to ensure a trouble-free trip (by dealing with reputable suppliers and by anticipating problems so that they can be resolved before departure);
- Provides someone to call when things go wrong.

Ten Reasons Why a Local Travel Agent Is Well Worth It

1. The service is free! At no extra cost, the client receives the personal attention of a local travel agent who is dedicated to ensuring that the customer's business and pleasure trips give the best value for the money. The client gets the service he or she expects, and the agent gets paid through commissions from the airlines, hotels, and other service providers. (Note: Some agencies do charge service fees.)

2. Your agent will provide the most up-to-date information, can guide you through the maze of daily changes, and can even save you money in the process.

3. Your local travel agent will know the best places to discover and the ones worth avoiding.

4. Time is money, and your local agent will save you time by preparing your itinerary and making all the telephone calls needed to get information and to make reservations.

5. Your local agent will understand and make suggestions for everything that will be necessary for the whole trip, including transportation to/from destinations, hotels, cars, sightseeing, shopping, and all of the other details that help a trip run smoothly.

6. Your travel agent will guide you through the tough choices: charters vs. scheduled carriers, car rental options, fare specials, family travel packages, choice of tour operators, etc. And a travel agent will always work to get you the best deals because his or her reputation is on the line.

7. Seasonal price swings are an agent's year-round specialty. Knowing when to go and where to go at the best price can make a huge difference in your travel plans and costs.

8. Your travel agent has many resources available such as brochures and videos to help you get a "feel" for where you want to go.

9. Your travel agent is someone who knows you and the things that make you a satisfied customer. And when you have a travel problem, it's comforting to know you have someone to call for help.

10. When you use a travel agent, you're supporting local business and boosting your local economy.

Types of Agencies

Travel agencies may be classified in the following ways:

Small. Owner/manager operated with one or two staff; caters to the independent traveller; operates on a word-of-mouth basis with little or no advertising; may not be automated.

Medium. Staff of eight to ten; a blend of commercial and vacation travellers; small scale advertising and some automation.

Large. Either a single office with dozens of staff, or various branch offices; may employ specialists; has more extensive advertising; often fully automated with its own in-house computerized accounting system, and fully computerized reservation and ticketing systems.

Franchise. (Current examples are Uniglobe and Goliger's Travel.) Manager operated, using the name, reputation, advertising, and promotion of the franchisor in exchange for a royalty payment based on sales volume. The franchisor also assists in designing a marketing plan and in negotiating rates with suppliers. Other aspects of the franchised agency (franchisee) are independently operated.

Cooperative or consortium. (Current examples are Giants and Intra Travel.) An arrangement between a group of otherwise fully independent agencies to obtain benefits of large-scale advertising and increased sales volumes. Generally they have agreements with suppliers for special rates or higher levels of commission. They may also assist in making arrangements with computer companies, ticket wallet printers, uniform suppliers, or staff trainers.

Chains and associated offices. (Current examples are American Express, Thomas Cook, and Carlson Wagonlit.) A company with a large number of agencies in several countries, using standardized systems and sales methods, and advertising extensively on a national basis, relying on reputation and buying power for business.

Categories of Agency Business

There are pluses and minuses when dealing with various kinds of clients. Travel agencies may deal with one or more of the following types of business:

Commerical or corporate travel. Business accounts, which also tend to lead to repeat business and to vacation travel for the business staff; fewer problems in collection of charges than for pleasure travel; profit depends on high volume, which often pays small commissions (often only air transportation is booked); requires frequent changes, which increase labour costs; requires more favourable credit terms and additional services such as free ticket delivery.

Pleasure or leisure travel. Arrangements for holiday travel; requires more knowledge of product and imagination on the part of the counsellor, but pays higher commissions (although competition for leisure travel is fiercely competitive).

Ethnic travel. Movement of specific ethnic groups from and to their country of origin; often dependent on the agency's location near an ethnic area and on an individual counsellor's reputation within that ethnic community.

Group travel. Travel by a number of people together who are using the same transportation, accommodation, and other facilities, in order to obtain bulk-buying power. This type of travel can be further subdivided into these five categories:

1. **Special interest.** Travel for a particular hobby, sport, or cultural event.
2. **Religious pilgrimages.** Tours by a particular religious denomination to a particular event (such as Christmas in Bethlehem) or landmark (such as Notre Dame Cathedral in Paris).
3. **Sales conferences.** Travel to a common location, used by a business to introduce new sales techniques and personnel to its staff; the conference is held in a location away from their normal office and home routines.
4. **Convention travel.** Travel to a destination for a common purpose such as an annual meeting of a professional, service, or fraternal organization (for example, the Lions Club or the Canadian or American Bar Association).
5. **Sales incentives.** Travel used to increase sales as an incentive to the staff of a business or to attract new customers (for example, travel prizes may be offered in a contest entered by prospective customers).

Services Provided

There are differences in the types of services provided by a travel agency, depending on the type of business in which it specializes:

Commercial or Corporate Travel

- Booking scheduled flights, including seat assignment and special meals, according to the corporate accounts policy;
- Arranging car rentals;
- Booking hotels according to the corporate accounts policy;
- Booking limousine services for executives;
- Making vacation arrangements for company executives;
- Providing documentation (issuing tickets, boarding cards, and itinerary, and packaging the materials in a ticket wallet). Large agencies often have a separate ticketing department.

    While the above items are common to all corporate travel agencies, some other possible services include the following:

- Ticket delivery;
- Service from coast to coast (through agency chain);

- Meetings with company's travel coordinator to plan travel services;
- Management reports on travel arrangements;
- Duplicate copies of itinerary for home or office;
- Newsletter for corporate clients;
- Hotel corporate rate program;
- Corporate credit cards for payment;
- Special fares;
- Car rental program;
- Travel insurance under one policy for all corporate staff (for example, an annual policy);
- Discounts for leisure bookings by corporate staff;
- Advanced automation used by agency to ensure best fares;
- Boarding cards provided with tickets;
- Discounts for airport limousine and airport parking;
- Airline tickets issued according to corporate policy (for example, there may be corporate policies restricting the use of first-class travel or dealing with how "Frequent Flier" points are to be allocated).

Pleasure or Leisure Travel

- Booking charter and scheduled flights;
- Arranging tour packages, cruises, tours, car rentals, hotels, etc.;
- Providing documentation (tickets, vouchers, etc.);
- Providing videos and various tour and cruise brochures;
- Issuing insurance policies;
- Consulting in person or on the phone;
- Researching possible destinations and activities;
- Preparing a newsletter;
- Arranging for tourist cards and visas.

Ethnic Travel

- Offering specialized travel products or services where suitable;
- Supplying passport/visa application forms and notarization;
- Providing services of wiring funds, faxing, and messaging;
- Researching and observing religious/ethnic requirements (for example, no travel on the Sabbath for Orthodox Jews).

Group Travel

- Arranging flights from a variety of cities across the country to a meeting location, and issuing the tickets;
- Escorting the group to assist with the smooth operation of the event and to solve any problems on-site;
- Booking hotel rooms, suites, etc. for guests arriving on different days;

- Booking meeting rooms (including coffee and tea for breaks) and audio visual equipment;
- Arranging local sightseeing and transfers by chartering buses and hiring guides;
- Arranging local event tickets for theatre, attractions, or sporting activities;
- Planning dining events such as barbecues, banquets, or theme meals with entertainment;
- Arranging sporting activities such as golf tournaments, tennis, sailing, fishing;
- Researching all of the above activities.

The Travel Counsellor's Role

While not intended to be a comprehensive list, the following are all part of the travel agent's normal responsibilities:

- Operating office equipment including postage meters, copiers, adding machines, typewriters, reservations and ticketing equipment;
- Composing letters; assembly and storage/retrieval of client files;
- Handling cash, preparing deposits, and requisitioning or issuing cheques;
- Familiarity with Bank Settlement Plan (BSP) requirements and completion of all reports;
- Knowledge of geography and ability to read maps and atlases;
- Product knowledge and keeping up to date on travel industry manuals and brochures;
- Counselling and sales skills;
- Telephone skills;
- Coping with stress and with client complaints;
- Research skills;
- Knowledge of ticketing and fare rules and forms.

A recent poll asked travel agents how they would break down their day-to-day responsibilities in providing services and in fulfilling their other requirements as travel agents. This information reveals the main tasks of an agent:

Consulting/customer service	38%
Sales	27%
Processing/reservations/tickets	24%
Marketing	3%
Management	3%
Training	2%
Other	3%

Employment Opportunities in the Travel Industry

Type of Service	Job Description
Travel agency	Cruise agent only
	Corporate travel agent
	Vacation sales
	Customer service (call centre)
	Destination specialist
	Outside sales representative
Consolidator	Airline ticketing
Tour operator or wholesaler	Customer service/reservations
	Sales and/or marketing
	Destination representative
	Ticketing department
	Operations
Group organizer or meeting planner	Group leader/tour guide
	Sales
	Program planner
	Operations (ticketing, etc.)
Tour guide	Tour guide
Airlines	Reservation agent
	Sales
	Ground agent
Cars	Car rental sales agent
Hotel	Front desk
	Reservations
	Sales
Sales office	Represent a cruise line or hotel chain

THE TRAVEL SUPPLIERS/WHOLESALERS

Travel suppliers and wholesalers work in a variety of areas, as follows:

Transportation. Airlines, railroads, buses, shipping, car rental, etc.;

Accomodation. Hotels, timeshares, resorts, guesthouses, condominiums, etc.;

Tour operators and guides;

Insurance companies.

MAJOR TRAVEL ASSOCIATIONS

There are many travel industry associations. Depending on the nature of the agency's business, membership in one or more of these organizations may be useful to keep up with changes in the industry and to have a say in how the industry should deal with issues of mutual concern to travel professionals. Some of the associations are listed here:

ACTA—Alliance of Canadian Travel Agents. This association of travel agencies and various travel suppliers and wholesalers is engaged in promotion and consumer protection, and acts as a lobby group for travel issues.

ASTA—American Society of Travel Agents. This U.S. association of travel agencies serves a function similar to that of ACTA in Canada.

CITC—Canadian Institute of Travel Counsellors. This association administers formal education programs and sets industry standards.

CLIA—Cruise Lines International Association. This association of cruise shipping companies promotes the cruise line industry and provides education.

PATA—Pacific Asia Travel Association. This association of tour operators and travel agencies specializes in the Pacific Asia area.

SACA—South and Central America Information Office. This association of tour operators and travel agencies specializes in South and Central America.

CTO—Caribbean Tourism Organization. This association of tour operators and travel agencies specializes in the Caribbean islands.

MPI—Meeting Planners' International. This association is made up of companies who plan and conduct meetings. They provide education and opportunities for networking among members.

SITE—Society of Incentive Travel Executives. This society consists of companies and individuals that organize and conduct incentive travel trips.

UFTAA—Universal Federation of Travel Agents' Association. This global federation of travel agents' associations represents the interest of travel agents internationally.

AIRLINE REGULATORY AGENCIES

In addition to travel industry associations, which are all voluntary organizations, there are a number of other bodies involved in the regulation of the travel industry in Canada and internationally. Following are some of these organizations:

ATC—Air Transport of Canada. A national service organization for Canadian commercial air transportation.

CTC—Canadian Transport Commission. The governing body for scheduled air carrier operations in Canada.

DOT—Department of Transport. This U.S. government department has responsibility for protecting the consumer regarding airline travel.

MOT—Ministry of Transport. The government department in Canada that licenses pilots and air traffic controllers, provides safety rules and regulations, and operates Canadian airports, air traffic control centres, and control towers.

CAB—Civil Aeronautics Board. Now a part of the DOT, this body handled requests for fare approvals in the U.S.A up to 1985.

FAA—Federal Aviation Administration. The government body in the U.S.A. that is responsible for air safety requirements, control tower personnel, and testing/licensing of pilots.

NTSB—National Transportation Safety Board. A U.S. body that makes safety recommendations to the FAA and investigates air transportation accidents.

IATA—International Air Transport Association. A nongovernmental body of the world's scheduled airlines, it ensures a common set of standards worldwide.

TEN COMMANDMENTS FOR TRAVELLERS

1. Thou shalt not expect to find things as thou has them at home...for thou has left thy home to find things different.

2. Thou shalt not take anything too seriously...for a carefree mind is the beginning of a fine vacation.

3. Thou shalt not let the other tourists get on thy nerves...for thou art paying good money to enjoy thyself!

4. Remember to take only one-half the clothes thou thinks thou needs...and twice the amount of money!

5. Remember thy passport so thou knowest where it is at all times...for a man without a passport is a man without a country!

6. Remember if thou were expected to stay in one place, thou would have been created with roots!

7. Thou shalt not worry. He who worrieth hath no pleasure...few things are fatal!

8. Thou shalt not make thyself too obviously Canadian. When in Rome do somewhat as the Romans do!

9. Thou shalt not judge the people of a country by the one person with whom thou hast had trouble!

10. Remember thou art a guest in every land...and he that treateth his host with respect is treated as an honoured guest.

● *EXERCISES*

1. Describe some personal attributes that would make someone a good travel agent.

   _____

   _____

2. Describe some of the services a travel agent might be able to provide for clients seeking to do the following:

   a. See a play on Broadway.

      _____

      _____

   b. Take a pilgrimage to Lourdes.

      _____

      _____

   c. Play blackjack in Atlantic City.

      _____

      _____

   d. Attend the Olympic Games in Sydney, Australia.

      _____

      _____

   e. Purchase emeralds in Colombia.

      _____

      _____

   f. Be seen with the "beautiful people" on the French Riviera.

      _____

      _____

   g. Visit the Amazon jungle.

      _____

      _____

3. What are the different reasons why people may choose a particular travel agency over its competitors?

   _____

   _____

   _____

   _____

   _____

2

Working in a Travel Agency

We already examined some of the duties of a travel agent in the first chapter. In this chapter, we will look at industry identification, continuing education, and some of the other things you need to know if you intend to work as a travel agent.

TRAVEL INDUSTRY IDENTIFICATION CARD

Other than pointing to your diploma or certificate hanging on the wall of your office, how can you identify yourself as someone who is involved in the industry? In Canada, ACTA issues the Canadian Travel Industry ID Card as a means of personal identification that is recognized by the travel industry worldwide. In the U.S.A., ASTA issues an ASTA Membership Card.

A growing number of airlines and hotels, in particular, are concerned about the cost to their companies of unauthorized access to travel industry benefits and will require the card when checking in. As you may know, one of the advantages of working in the industry is that there are many industry benefits (such as reduced fares and accommodation).

In addition, all travel agents are provided with business cards by their agency to give to their clients, suppliers, and other industry personnel.

CONTINUING EDUCATION AND TRAINING

Your need for training does not end with the completion of a travel and tourism course at a qualified educational institution but continues throughout your career. Courses are offered by a wide variety of educators, including travel industry bodies like ACCESS. Many companies—including various suppliers, wholesalers, and some large travel agencies—will also maintain an in-house series of continuing education programs.

You may increase your knowledge after your education is complete by taking part in some of the following activities.

- **Seminars.** Tourist boards and tour operators provide information seminars on their destinations.
- **Trade shows.** These are intended for the travel industry only and are offered by various regions or countries.
- **Specialist training.** A number of countries such as Australia and Holland, and corporations like Walt Disney Company, provide intensive instruction that may include travel information, videos, and exercises.
- **CITC and CLIA.** These associations provide skills upgrading courses. They also provide the opportunity to be officially recognized by the industry and the public by offering the following designations after completing selected courses.

CTC	Certified Travel Counsellor	(CITC)
CTM	Certified Travel Manager	(CITC)
ACC	Accredited Cruise Counsellor	(CLIA)
MCC	Master Cruise Counsellor	(CLIA)

- **Familiarization trips (FAM) and agent specials.** These allow the travel agent to personally visit destinations and learn firsthand about the hotels, sights, food, and other sales features at little or no cost. These trips are sometimes paid for by the agency that employs you.

  (Note: Educational trips are not holidays. Since time is limited, the itinerary may be quite hectic.)
- **Product launch** by a tour operator.

INDUSTRY INFORMATION

Sources of Information

To be effective, a travel agent must have access to an incredible amount of information, and you may require help from time to time to stay informed. It is impossible, though, to keep fully up to date about every destination. Therefore, agents use sources of information such as the following:

1. Talk to your colleagues.
2. Talk to past clients when they return from their travels to learn about the ship, hotel, etc.
3. Tourist boards may supply general brochures on a destination.
4. Visit the local library—most libraries have travel sections.
5. Contact sales reps from the airlines, tour operators, cruise lines, and other industry suppliers.
6. Obtain newsletters and information sheets from your suppliers.
7. Read trade and consumer newspapers and magazines.
8. Obtain travel agent reference guides published by tourist boards and tour operators with information on where to book various products and the benefits to your clients.

9. Use an airline computer system (for example, Apollo or SABRE) not only to handle flights but also to book cars, hotels, resorts, limousines, lei greetings in Hawaii, show tickets in London, etc.

10. Use the Internet and CD-ROMs.

11. Watch videotapes.

12. Use agency guides such as the *OAG Flight Guide, Hotel and Travel Index*, etc.

13. Read brochures provided by tour operators.

Trade Papers

Listed below are some of the travel industry trade papers that cover news, updates, destination reports, marketing ideas, and job openings.

Canada	U.S.A.
Travelweek Bulletin	*Tour & Travel News*
Canadian Traveller	*Travel Weekly*
Canadian Travel Press	*Recommend*
Travel Courier	*Travel Trade*
Meetings & Incentive Travel	*Travel Counselor*
	Meetings & Conventions

Consider subscribing if your agency doesn't already receive these useful resources.

Personnel Guide to Canada's Travel Industry

Published twice a year, *The Personnel Guide to Canada's Travel Industry* lists all the travel agencies, tour operators, airlines, and cruise lines operating in the Canadian market.

The listings generally include the name of the company, address, phone and fax numbers, and number of staff. A version is also available on computer disk.

MONEY MATTERS

Foreign Currency

If you work in a travel agency, you need to have some basic understanding of foreign currency and in what form clients should take money on their travels. When travelling outside of Canada your clients may wish to carry some or all of the following:

- Travellers cheques (for travel to Europe, these are available in European currencies or in Euros)
- Local currency
- Credit card
- Canadian or U.S. cash

List some places where your clients can exchange money when travelling.

_____

_____

_____

When clients are travelling outside Canada, you may well need to convert costs into or from the foreign currency. You therefore need to be familiar with exchange rates.

Exchange Rates

When quoting prices, you will normally quote your client's trip in Canadian or U.S. funds. However, on occasion you may have to convert foreign amounts to Canadian or vice versa.

Assuming the current Canada–U.S. exchange rate is

USD 1.00 = CAD 1.40
(USD = U.S. dollars; CAD = Canadian dollars)

calculate the following:

USD 1,268.00 = CAD _____

CAD 497.00 = USD _____

Bank Buy Rate (BBR) is the exchange rate that a bank quotes to buy any currency. But the exchange rates actually used are normally slightly higher than this rate to allow the currency changer to make a profit.

Commissions

The travel agency acts as the "agent" on behalf of its suppliers by promoting, selling, and handling the paperwork for the products sold and, in turn, the agency is paid a commission for the effort. (However, by law, an agent is able to bind its principal to provide the service as sold, and therefore a principal/agent relationship can have serious consequences to a travel agency and a travel agent if, for example, there is misrepresentation to the client.)

Commission rates are negotiated and therefore vary depending on sales, but the list below gives you a general idea of the commission levels:

Scheduled airlines	5–8% + overrides*
Charter airlines	10–15%
Tour operators	10–15%
Cruise lines	10–15%
Car rental companies	5–10%
Hotels	8–10%
Travel insurance	20–44%

*Overrides are bonuses paid by the supplier for achieving certain sales performance levels.

Sales amounts that are commissionable are known as *gross rates*. The gross rate less the commission provides what is known as a *net rate*.

In some situations, travel suppliers may place their product on sale at a reduced rate, and this is commonly known as a *sell off*. These rates may be gross (offer a commission) or net (in which case you must add your markup).

Some agencies also now charge service fees for consulting time, changes to tickets, services with low markups (rail tickets for example), etc. This trend is increasingly likely as more and more companies (particularly airlines) lower commissions in order to cut costs. Some airlines may even pay no commissions, and flights on those airlines must therefore be booked directly with the airline rather than through a travel agent.

Form of Payment

Agencies receive payments for services from their clients by one of the following methods:

Cash—includes traveller's cheques and money orders. Depending on the source of the product sold, payment could be in Canadian or U.S. funds.

Cheques—perhaps from corporate accounts or repeat clients. Whether the agency accepts cheques from new clients will depend on the agency's policy. Most agencies have a policy that restricts or prohibits accepting cheques from new clients, especially if it is close to the departure date.

Credit cards—the most common type of payment, although not all tour operators accept each of the major cards. Some agencies will require a credit card form to be filled out and signed by the client. For regular customers, an agency may simply keep a credit card number and a sample signature on file. (Note that the tour operator or airline is the merchant and you—as the merchant's agent—are responsible for obtaining credit card approvals on their behalf. Don't forget to get all credit card payments approved by the card issuer.)

PREFERRED SUPPLIERS

It is impossible for a travel agent to know everything about all tour operators. However, most travel agencies deal only with four or five major tour operators and three or four cruise lines. These are known as *preferred suppliers*.

Listed below are some of the benefits of a preferred supplier relationship:
- Higher commission levels;
- Confidence in the product you sell (because you know it well);
- Sufficient copies of supplier brochures and other sales material always on hand;
- Invitations to seminars, information sessions, and FAM trips;
- Sales support available in case of problems.

Preferred suppliers should be chosen after considering the following:
- Popularity of the product line. This will depend on the market your agency serves;

- Breadth of appeal of the product. Does the product attract many customers or is it so specialized that it appeals only to a select few?
- Availability;
- Their sales representatives. Are they accessible and knowledgeable, and do they offer in-house backup if needed?
- Sales and marketing policies;
- Are they agent-friendly?
- Tenure and experience of the personnel. Do you often have to explain everything over again to new people?
- Revenue potential;
- Marketing support.

TRAVEL BROCHURES

Features

The travel brochures issued by suppliers are the major sales tool used by agents. Below are some of the common features of a travel brochure:

Opening Section
- Index of contents;
- General information about the company and perhaps a grading system for its products;
- Add-on airfares to the gateway cities;
- Any special rates for seniors, children, etc.;
- Local stopover hotel at the gateway cities.

Destination Pages
- Destination descriptions;
- Information on the hotels, cruise ships, etc., or an itinerary of the tour;
- Pricing information.

Terms and Conditions
- Deposit information;
- Cancellation information;
- How changes are handled;
- Travel insurance options explained;
- Age restrictions defined (for example, for what ages are child fares and benefits included?).

Back Cover
- Travel agent's stamp to be affixed.

Ordering a Supply of Brochures

Brochures are usually printed twice a year by tour operators that offer year-round tours and once a year by most other suppliers (for example, cruise lines or specialty products such as skiing holidays).

Brochures may often be ordered from one supply source. For example, most major tour operators and cruise lines in the Toronto area store their brochures with either Alltours (ICS Logistics) or Watts, who supply the agents with re-order cards. They generally visit each travel agency and tour operator on a daily basis to pick up cheques for the tour operators and to drop off brochures, tickets, and trade newspapers. They are an excellent and inexpensive means of sending travel-related material back and forth among the various travel companies involved in a client file.

Filing Brochures

If your agency has a display rack, only the preferred suppliers' brochures should be exhibited. Not every brochure on every destination needs to be displayed.

Keep your own copy of the preferred suppliers' brochures at your desk, and attach any comments about the featured hotels.

General office brochures should be filed as follows:

- A large supply of preferred brochures kept readily available;
- One or two each of other brochures filed by destination (clients normally ask for information by destination/region rather than by company);
- Specialty files kept by activity for skiing, adventure holidays, golf, etc.

PACKAGING/PRESENTATION

Presentation is very important to effective selling. For example, you can prevent giving a client a ticket with mistakes simply by checking the ticket when it comes in. Once tickets are received at the agency, review the contents to ensure they are complete and then discuss the details with the client.

Documents from the cruise lines and escorted tour operators are often quite elegant and may include flight bags, books, and other special items. Some agencies may supply tickets to their clients in the agency's jacket rather than the ticket jacket supplied by the operator (normally for airline tickets).

● *EXERCISES*

1. a. Where might you suggest a client go to obtain foreign currency before leaving for a trip to Europe?

    _____

    b. Where might the client obtain currency after arriving in Europe?

    _____

2. What is the normal commission paid to a travel agency on most tour packages?

    _____

3. Suggest some ways a representative from a tour operator could assist the travel agent?

    _____

    _____

    _____

4. If you wanted to learn more about corporate meetings in Canada and the U.S.A., which two magazines should you read?

    _____

    _____

5. Assume the following exchange rates:

0.48 pounds sterling	=	CAD $1.00
5.70 Hong Kong dollar	=	CAD $1.00
0.73 U.S. dollar	=	CAD $1.00

    What is the equivalent of CAD 2,345.00 in the following currencies?

    Pounds sterling_____

    Hong Kong dollar _____

    U.S. dollar_____

    If the Canadian dollar is worth 1.382 to the U.S. dollar, what is the equivalent of USD 962.78 in Canadian currency?

    _____

6. Choose the correct answer for each of the following questions:

    a. A FAM trip is
    1. a specially packaged trip for families who travel together;
    2. a trip arranged for family members of a travel agent;
    3. a trip arranged for travel agents to personally visit and learn about a destination.

b. An override is

1. an extra mileage charge imposed by an airline for longer than normal travel routings;
2. a bonus paid by a supplier in addition to normal commission;
3. a flat fee paid to travel agents, which replaces commission.

c. Travel Courier is

1. a travel industry trade publication;
2. a domestic land-based courier company specializing in delivery of travel industry–related material;
3. an air service used to deliver travel documents from one country to another

d. CTC is

1. the initials of a Canadian government–sponsored program (Come to Canada) designed to attract foreign tourists;
2. a non-accredited designation as a corporate travel counsellor;
3. a Certified Travel Counsellor who has completed selected industry courses.

7. A client has booked a trip with a tour operator from a travel brochure picked up at your agency. Due to the illness of one of the passengers, the client wants to cancel. Where would you get the cancellation information?

_____

_____

3

Advanced Booking Charters

Airplanes have become the single most important means of transportation to move people from place to place, and air travel today is the foundation upon which modern travel agencies are built.

On the one hand, airlines offering scheduled flights, for the most part, operate under IATA rules and regulations. International air travel is also subject to bilateral treaties between countries as well as national government rules and regulations.

On the other hand, nonscheduled, or charter, flights do not typically have the same type of restrictions as may apply to IATA member airlines. These *advanced booking charters*, or *ABCs*, are not governed by IATA rules and therefore each charter airline sets its own rules, subject to any overriding governmental requirements. There is normally only one class of service (although some offer large seats as an option), and both meal and bar service are typically included in the price.

Charter flights are normally seasonal, with limited dates of travel and departure times. They are usually only available for the most popular destinations at the most popular times of the year (for example, London or Amsterdam in the summer, or Florida in the winter), and these flights usually require a stay of at least one week.

It is important to differentiate ABCs from charter class fares, which are a type of fare offered by a scheduled airline. An airline that offers charter class fares will offer a limited number of seats at that rate. Booking conditions, however, are similar to the booking conditions for ABCs.

The following are some charter airlines in Canada:

- Skyservice
- Air Transat
- Royal Airlines
- Canada 3000
- Canair (Western Canada only)

    What are some typical charter destinations?

Summer: _____

Winter: _____

Charters are not for everyone. To decide whether they are appropriate for your clients, consider these advantages and disadvantages of ABCs, and add any others that come to mind.

MAJOR ADVANTAGES OF USING AN ABC

1. It is cheaper than paying full fare on a scheduled carrier.

2. Tickets are issued by the airline, not the travel agent.

3. Commissions are generally higher than on scheduled flights.

4. _____

5. _____

6. _____

MAJOR DISADVANTAGES OF USING AN ABC

1. They usually operate at less convenient times of the day than scheduled airline flights.

2. There is less frequent service than on a scheduled carrier.

3. No advance seat selection is typically offered. (However, recently some charter airlines offer advance seat selection for an extra fee.)

4. There is less variety of fares than on scheduled carriers.

5. Tickets on ABCs are 100% nonrefundable, whereas scheduled carriers often permit cancellations if a client pays a penalty.

6. There is an increased risk of ticket error since the travel agent does not issue the ticket.

7. _____

8. _____

9. _____

Note: Since each ABC sets its own rules, you must carefully check the airline's terms and conditions in its brochure for such information as booking requirements, deposit details, and when final payment is required.

PRICING A CHARTER FLIGHT

Charter flights are priced one way only, so you need to add together the cost of both the *outbound* flight (to the destination) and the *inbound* flight (return trip). Below is an example of ABC pricing:

ABC Pricing Between Toronto and Amsterdam

From Toronto   From Amsterdam

Tuesdays—May 07 to October 15   **Wednesdays**—May 08 to October 16
Fridays— May 03 to October 25   **Saturdays**—May 04 to October 26
Thursdays—June 27 to September 12   **Fridays**—June 28 to September 13

Toronto to Amsterdam	Adult	Senior	Child	Amsterdam to Toronto	Adult	Senior	Child
May 01 – May 09	269	249	229	May 01 – May 17	270	250	230
May 10 – May 23	289	269	249	May 18 – May 31	290	270	250
May 24 – June 20	319	299	279	June 01 – June 28	320	300	280
June 21 – July 04	349	329	309	June 29 – July 12	350	330	310
July 05 – August 22	369	349	329	July 13 – September 02	400	380	360
August 23 – September 05	349	329	309	September 03 – September 13	350	330	310
September 06 – September 26	319	299	279	September 14 - October 11	320	300	280
September 27 – October 10	319	299	279	October 12 – October 18	320	300	280
October 11 – November 02	279	259	239	October 19 – November 03	290	270	250

Infants under 2 years old (at date of completion of travel) travel free but do not occupy a seat • Child (2 to 15 years old) • Senior (60 years old and over)
• NOT INCLUDED: Canadian Navigational Surcharge: $30; Dutch Taxes: $22. • Flight schedules are subject to change without notice.

Using the table above, the following fares would apply for one adult, one senior, and one child leaving Toronto on June 3 and returning from Amsterdam on August 2:

	Adult	Senior	Child
Toronto to Amsterdam	$319.00	$299.00	$279.00
Amsterdam to Toronto	400.00	380.00	360.00
Subtotal	719.00*	679.00*	639.00*
Dutch taxes	22.00	22.00	22.00
Selling price	$741.00	$701.00	$661.00

* Includes navigational surcharge of $30 round trip.

Some Considerations When Pricing an ABC

Below are some things to consider when pricing an ABC.

- **Child fare.** What are the ages specified for children?
- **Senior fare.** What is the minimum age requirement?
- **"Open jaw."** Is the client able to fly into one city and return from another (for example, fly into Amsterdam and return from Frankfurt)?
- **Days of operation.** Most charters operate only a few days of the week, and times may vary.

- **Seating.** Some charters offer wide/big/club seating as well.
- **One-way option.** One-way tickets may be available; however, the price is higher than the half fare listed above (which assumes a round trip).

BOOKING A CHARTER FLIGHT

An ABC flight cannot be booked directly with the airline but instead must be handled through a tour operator (contacted by phone or through your airline computer system). However, certain charter airlines work closely with specific tour operators (for example, Signature Vacations generally uses Canada 3000; Sunquest uses Skyservice).

If booking at the last minute (less than two weeks prior to departure), clients will have to pick up the tickets from the tour operator desk at the airport.

CONSOLIDATORS

A consolidator is a wholesaler that distributes large amounts of airline inventory on certain scheduled airlines travelling to certain markets.

Some examples of Canadian consolidators are

- Skylink
- Network
- CTI Carriers

Choose one or two "preferred" consolidators as you would pick a preferred tour operator. In deciding your preferred consolidators consider the following details:

- Which airlines and parts of the world does the consolidator service?
- Some consolidators hold blocks of seats and therefore may be able to offer seats when airlines and computers show the space as sold out.
- A consolidator may not be able to offer seat selection.
- Changes to a consolidator ticket may be difficult. (Check the rules as they may differ among airlines.)
- Fares are low and will vary among consolidators. Some offer net rates and some offer commissionable rates.
- The consolidator—not the travel agent—issues the ticket.
- Some consolidators are both wholesalers and retailers, and a travel agency may end up competing with them.

EXAMPLE OF A CONSOLIDATOR'S RATE SHEET
(Net Rate for Agents Only)

Europe	From	Africa	From	South America	From
Amsterdam	470	Abidjan	1560	Buenos Aires	1230
Athens	700	Accra	1350	Lima	760
Budapest	690	Cairo	900	Rio De Janeiro	1230
Copenhagen	480	Dar es Salaam	1460	Sao Paulo	1230
Frankfurt	530	Dakar	1360	Montevideo	1230
Glasgow	410	Harare	1510	El Salvador	850
Istanbul	750	Johannesburg	1350		
Larnaca	700	Kano	1350		
St. Petersburg	860	Lilongwe	1560	Indian Subcontinent	From
London	370	Lagos	1210	Bombay	1275
Manchester	370	Lusaka	1560	Colombo	1170
Moscow	740	Nairobi	1360	Calcutta	1185
Milan	690			Dhaka	1285
Munich	495			Delhi	1075
Paris	470	Middle East	From	Karachi	1185
Prague	690	Amman	950	Katmandu	1430
Rome	690	Abu Dhabi	1260	Madras	1425
Vienna	575	Bahrain	1300		
Warsaw	680	Dahran	1260		
Zurich	575	Beirut	1060	Australasia	From
		Damascus	950	Auckland	1920
		Doha	1260	Brisbane	1920
Far East	From	Jeddah	1260	Melbourne	1760
Bangkok	1100	Kuwait	1350	Perth	1920
Hong Kong	1000	Muscat	1260	Sydney	1760
Kuala Lumpur	1130	Tehran	1350		
Jakarta	1210				
Manila	1020				
Seoul	1090				
Singapore	1130				
Taipei	1000				
Tokyo	1070				
Osaka	1130				

Prices are subject to change without notice.

Following is a sample calculation of a consolidator's fare based on the rate sheet provided.

Toronto to Frankfurt published price		$678.00*
Consolidator rate	$530.00 net	
Markup (use 10% for example)	53.00	
Total consolidator price	583.00	583.00*
Savings for your client (published fare minus consolidator price)		$95.00

* Taxes are extra

ABC AND CONSOLIDATOR REQUIREMENTS

The following information may be required to book an ABC or consolidator ticket, either through the computer reservations system or directly with the tour operator:

1. Client name(s) and title(s)—Mr., Mrs., Ms., etc.—and ages (if a senior or a child);
2. Number of people in the party who will be travelling, plus names and titles of those in addition to the clients;
3. Client's home phone number;
4. Dates required for travel and preferred time of day for travelling (are they flexible?);
5. Form of payment to be used (and credit card approval, if paying by credit card);
6. Special requests (for example, wheelchair passenger, salt-free or kosher meals);
7. Confirm whether cancellation insurance is required.

When making the reservation be sure to check any rules or restrictions regarding the tickets, obtain a confirmation or booking number, and note the name of the agent.

● EXERCISES

Referring to the ABC pricing chart earlier in this chapter, complete the following exercises, and include all taxes in your calculations.

1. A passenger, age 16, wants to fly to Amsterdam from Toronto, departing the last Thursday in August and returning on the first available flight after September 15 (which happens to be on September 16). Complete a costing for this client.

    _____

    _____

2. The sister of the above passenger, age 15, wants to accompany the client on the trip. What would her flights cost?

    _____

    _____

    _____

    _____

    _____

    _____

3. A single mother who is 20 years old wants to fly to Amsterdam with her six-month-old baby. What will be the cost of the mother's ticket only, for travel departing Toronto on June 15 and returning July 12?

    _____

    _____

    _____

    _____

    _____

    _____

4. The above passenger's father is a Dutch citizen, age 75, and he would like to fly back with her to Toronto on July 12. He will return to Amsterdam on August 5. Complete a costing for this passenger.

    _____

    _____

    _____

    _____

    _____

    _____

4

Accommodation

Providing accommodation to the traveller dates back to biblical times. The earliest inns were small and privately operated. They usually provided both accommodation and food to the travellers, as well as fresh horses (most early land-based travel was on horseback). Generally the inn was owner-operated and the facilities were basic.

It was not until the Industrial Revolution in Europe that these inns began to take on the shape of a modern hotel. Many of Europe's deluxe city hotels have their beginnings in this era, and they catered to the wealthy travellers who were embarking in ever greater numbers on a "grand tour" of Europe. With the advent of the railroad and then the motor vehicle, travel gradually increased to the point where it was no longer the privilege of the wealthy, and over time an extensive network of all types of overnight accommodation was developed.

Leisure travel soon spread from Europe into North America, and the twentieth century witnessed the construction of an extensive road network supported by hotels and motels. Prices were directed at the average person and as time went on the accommodations would become increasingly luxurious. Also, the twentieth century produced the concept of chain hotels (for example, Howard Johnson and Holiday Inn). They used standardized systems to increase efficiency, and computerized reservations systems were developed to reduce costs. There is now a growing interdependency with various other sectors of the travel market that are also involved with accommodation. For example, in Canada, the railroads have purchased hotels, and elsewhere airlines have done the same.

TYPES OF ACCOMMODATION

There are a wide variety of products available, depending on the client's wishes, the destination selected, and the price range. The choice extends from the simplest guest house to the fanciest resort.

Bed and breakfast, or guesthouse—provides a private room in a private home; usually includes breakfast.

Youth hostel—inexpensive student lodging (for example, university residences when not in session and the YMCA).

Pension—the European equivalent to a bed and breakfast.

Parador (Spain) or pousada (Portugal)—government-run small hotel, which may be basic to deluxe; typically located in castles, palaces, or old monasteries in tourist areas. (These hotels are very popular and must be booked as much as a year in advance for prime dates.)

Cottage—small, self-contained unit that typically includes kitchen facilities; usually located away from city centres, often near a lake or campground.

Villa—self-contained unit, usually larger and more deluxe than a cottage; typically located in a quiet location by itself.

Apartment or condominium—a unit in a complex, rented either from a management company (apartment) or the unit owner (condominium), with kitchen facilities, and often without maid service included; generally located in a residential neighbourhood. Apartments may be studio (one room with a couch that converts to a bed in a combined living/bedroom space), or have separate living space and bedrooms (typically between one and three bedrooms).

Motel—usually smaller in size than a hotel, typically located near an expressway; free parking; more modest facilities and cost than hotels.

Hotel—generally a large-scale complex that caters to business travellers and the wealthier vacation traveller. It is often multistorey and located near city centres or close to tourist attractions or transportation facilities; has luxurious decor and extensive facilities; may include room service, parking (often indoor and for a fee), concierge, and a dining room; may be chain owned; often part of a centralized computer reservation service.

Suite hotel—rooms with a bedroom and a separate living area, and usually also includes additional sleeping accommodation on a folding couch; may or may not have a kitchen.

Resort—a type of hotel, usually sited on a vast property, often scenically located and isolated. The following varieties of resorts are available:

   a. **Summer resort**—found where summer climates are warm, often near lakes or mountains (for example, the Muskoka Lakes region in Ontario, Sunshine Coast in B.C., and the Catskills in New York State).

   b. **Winter cold resort**—found in areas where winter sports predominate (for example, Vail in Colorado, Banff or Jasper in Canada, and Val D'Isere in France).

   c. **Winter warm resort**—cold weather escape, such as Florida or Mexico.

   d. **Year-round resort**—area where the climate suits both summer and winter facilities (for example, Whistler, B.C., Hawaii, and the Rocky Mountains).

Most of the above accommodations do not include kitchen facilities, but an *efficiency* contains a small kitchen, usually with a refrigerator, stove, and sink, as well as pots, plates, and utensils.

Room Types

STUDIO	A single room unit, combining a bedroom and living room in the same space, and with a sofa-bed (couch that folds out into a bed).
SUITE	One or more bedrooms, together with a separate living room area, usually found in hotels.
JUNIOR SUITE	A larger room than typical, with a sitting area separated from the bedroom.
EFFICIENCY OR SELF-CATERING	A room that includes kitchen facilities.
ADJACENT ROOMS	Two or more rooms close to, or opposite, each other.
ADJOINING ROOMS	Two or more rooms located side by side, without connecting doors between them.
CONNECTING ROOMS	Two or more rooms located side by side, with connecting doors between them.
DOUBLE	A room containing one double bed, intended for two persons.
DOUBLE DOUBLE	One room with two double beds.
TWIN	A room containing two single beds; intended for two persons.
TRIPLE	A room containing beds for three persons.
QUAD	A room containing beds for four persons.
SINGLE	A room containing a bed for one person.
QUEEN ROOM	A room containing a queen size bed.
KING ROOM	A room containing a king size bed.
HOSPITALITY SUITE	A suite of rooms, usually in a hotel, used for entertaining (for example, a reception or a meeting).
CABANA	A hotel room located near a pool or beach; also refers to a small room (often tented) used for changing clothes or for protection from the sun.
LANAI ROOM	A hotel room with a patio, balcony, or porch.
PARLOUR OR SALON	A sitting room.

Other Accommodation Terms

RUN OF THE HOUSE   The same rate is charged for any room, regard-
                           less of where it is located.

ROLLAWAY BED   A portable bed (often a fold-up bed on wheels)
                           provided at an additional charge, for an extra
                           person occupying the room.

SERVICE CHARGE,   A fee paid to waiters and other hotel staff for
GRATUITY, OR TIP   service provided. It may be included as a fixed
                           amount or percentage added to the bill (also
                           known as *service compris*); or it may not be
                           included and at the option of the guest (also
                           known as *service noncompris*).

VAT OR GST   A government tax added to the cost of goods
                           and services (Value Added Tax in Europe and
                           Goods and Services Tax in Canada).

Hotel and Meal Plans

A LA CARTE   Menu with individually priced items.

TABLE D'HOTE   Menu with a full-course meal provided at a
                           fixed price (with few or no choices offered).

EUROPEAN PLAN (EP)   A hotel rate that includes accommodation only
                           (no meals).

CONTINENTAL PLAN (CP)   A hotel rate that includes both accommodation
                           and continental breakfast (a light breakfast
                           consisting of a beverage of coffee, tea, milk, or
                           juice, plus toast, breakfast roll, or croissant).

AMERICAN PLAN (AP)   Same as full pension (American term).

BERMUDA PLAN (BP)   A hotel rate that includes a full breakfast; usu-
                           ally offered by small hotels or bed and break-
                           fasts.

BREAKFAST PLAN (BP)   Same as Bermuda plan.

DEMI-PENSION   A hotel rate in Europe, with accommodation,
                           breakfast, and one other daily meal included.

HALF BOARD   Same as demi-pension.

MODIFIED AMERICAN PLAN (MAP)	Same as demi-pension (American term).
FULL PENSION	A hotel rate in Europe, with accommodation and three daily meals included.
FULL BOARD	Same as full pension.
SEMI-INCLUSIVE	A price that includes most features specified in the brochure.
ALL-INCLUSIVE	A price that includes all features (usually hotel room, meals, and entertainment); may or may not include liquor, taxes, tips, and extras.
SUPER/ULTRA ALL-INCLUSIVE	A price that includes everything.

Examples of "All-Inclusives"

Club Med—over 120 "villages" located in more than thirty-two countries; mainly oriented to adults but also includes "family villages."

Sandals—10+ hotels in four countries (Jamaica, Antigua, St. Lucia, and Barbados); most are couples oriented.

Elegant Resorts—very luxurious; located in Jamaica (Round Hill, Half Moon, Tryall, and Trident); includes a single-fee vacation plan that offers dine-around options at the other properties.

Superclubs—Jamaica (for example, Hedonism II and Couples Ocho Rios).

Captain Bluff—Antigua.

Jumby Bay—Antigua.

Meridien Club—Turks and Caicos.

Petit St. Vincent Resort—Grenadines.

CLASSES OF HOTELS

There has been a long-standing difficulty in classifying hotels, since the standards differ vastly from country to country. What would be considered a "five-star" or luxury hotel in China would certainly be different from a five-star hotel in the United States, for example. The World Tourism Organization (W.T.O.) has therefore recommended a five-class system, as outlined below:

W.T.O. System	Other Grading Systems		
1. Luxury class—hotels of great luxury	*****	or	Deluxe
2. First class—hotels of very great comfort	****	or	Superior
3. Second class—hotels of great comfort	***	or	Moderate
4. Third class—hotels of good comfort	**	or	Standard
5. Fourth class—hotels of average comfort with at least ten rooms	*	or	Budget

Certain countries have a government-rated system for hotels. France, for example, uses a system of one through five stars (similar to the W.T.O. system), with one star being basic and five stars being the most luxurious.

Canadian tour operators perform their own grading, and therefore ratings among different operators may vary for the same hotel. Some tour operator grades are based on facilities only, while others include service levels as well.

List below some examples of hotel services or facilities that would be important to consider when looking for accommodation for a client:

Hotel Services

_____

_____

_____

_____

_____

_____

Hotel Facilities

_____

_____

_____

_____

_____

_____

HOTEL INSPECTION TRIPS

As a travel agent, you are encouraged to take part in hotel inspection trips, in order to perform your own gradings. Listed below are some of the reasons why you might want to perform your own gradings:

- It is easier to sell a hotel you know and have seen.
- You can discover if it is suitable for a particular type of client.
- In some cases you may negotiate rates.

Example: Your clients plan to visit the Bahamas, and the Paradise Island Fun Club looks great in most tour operator brochures. However, when you visited the hotel the previous month, you discovered that the beach is lined with signs warning guests not to swim in the sea because of the danger of sharks. You also noted that the rooms overlook the commercial harbour with freighters and tankers, etc. You recommend a different hotel to your clients. Had you not inspected the hotel, your clients may have been unhappy with their holiday and blamed you for not warning them about the accommodation.

What to Look for During an Inspection

A lot of basic information can be obtained from hotel brochures, for example, the number of rooms. But other particulars can only be determined firsthand. Below are some of the things to look for when you plan an on-site inspection:

- What types of people does the hotel cater to (families, couples)?
- What are the key selling points of the property?
- Is it clean (check ashtrays, washrooms, closets, etc.)?
- Does the property have any unique features?
- Is it in good shape (lampshades, rugs, etc.)?

Make sure that you check all of the following areas of the property:

- Lobby (first impression to guests)
- Restaurants
- Function/meeting space
- Guest rooms (bottom and top categories)
- Recreational facilities

On a hotel inspection trip you will want to see much more than just a sample room. Keep written notes for yourself of what you found and what your general impressions were. These notes are important sources of information for your clients once you return to the office.

RATES

When pricing accommodation, there are a number of factors to consider, including the following:

1. Scale of luxury (see the "Classes of Hotels" section above);
2. Room size;
3. Location (ocean front is more expensive than garden view, for example);
4. Whether the room has an in-suite shower (especially in some of the older European properties where this is not always the case);
5. Season of travel (summer will be high season in Amsterdam or Paris and winter will be high season in Florida and Barbados);
6. What meals, if any, are included;
7. Number of persons.*

* Normal rates are based on double occupancy and, unless otherwise stated, it is assumed that one person will pay a single supplement; in a room with three or more persons each will normally pay a reduced rate.

Although per-night rates are typically quoted, there may be a minimum stay required. Generally rates quoted will be exclusive of all taxes. Service charges may also be added, especially in Europe, to cover a gratuity for the hotel staff. In North America, the gratuity is normally left to the discretion of the client. Note that agents' commissions are calculated on the room rate only, and not on taxes or service charges. Also, commissions are not deducted from deposits collected by a travel agent from a client. Rather, payment is made directly to the hotel in full, and the hotel is then expected to pay a commission back to the agent.

Group Rates

Many hotels and other suppliers of accommodation will be prepared to negotiate a cheaper rate for group bookings than is normally available for individual accommodation. It may also be possible to negotiate other features in the group rate, depending on the supplier. For example, meals may be included when they would not normally be provided for the standard rate.

Child Rates

In North America, two children 18 years of age and under (verify ages with the hotels) are permitted to stay free of charge, provided they share the room with two adults. In Europe there is normally a charge for children staying in the room.

RESERVATIONS

The following methods are available to the travel agent when booking accommodation:
- Call the hotel directly (often there is a toll-free number).
- Call a local representative of the hotel (for hotels located outside of North America).
- Call central reservations for the major hotel chains.
- Use the agency's computer reservation system.
- Use a fax or telex.
- Call a tour operator.

Most hotels will require credit card details in order to guarantee a booking. Otherwise, the reservation will automatically be cancelled if the customer has not checked in by a certain time of day (often 6:00 p.m.). The hotel may require a deposit, and the deposit may equal the cost of staying a minimum number of nights. This is especially common in resort areas.

Most of the world's major hotels are included in computer reservations systems used by travel agencies, providing instant confirmation of booking. Those not listed will require at least 24 to 72 hours for a confirmation after receiving a booking by fax or telex.

Be sure to note the date of your call and the name of the person you spoke with. Also obtain a confirmation number from the hotel for the booking. Verify that the hotel will pay a commission to the agent for the booking (be aware that many smaller properties do not pay commissions).

Some hotels' rates are published on a net basis, which does not include commission, but even when commission is excluded from the rate quoted, hotels will often pay a small commission (say 5%) for group or convention bookings. The normal commission rate for accommodation is 10%.

Information Supplied to a Hotel

The following information will need to be supplied to the hotel when making a hotel reservation:
1. Date and time of arrival;
2. Number of nights required;
3. Client's full name, and names and ages of children;
4. Type of accommodation required;

5. Any special requests (for example, connecting or ocean front rooms);

6. Name of travel agency, IATA number, and name of travel agent;

7. Form of payment if making a deposit;

8. Frequent traveller number for a corporate account;

9. Means of arrival, and whether the hotel is providing transportation from a pick-up point (such as the airport).

Also check what is included in the rate (for example, a meal plan, service charges, taxes). If the hotel is in another country, confirm which currency is used for their room quote (it may be the local currency or U.S. dollars).

Payment for Hotel Stays

Three types of payment methods are available, as follows:

1. Cash

2. Credit card

3. Prepaid voucher—applies in particular to hotels booked through tour operators (see p. 55 for additional examples.)

Sample Hotel Voucher

ASTOR TRAVEL SERVICES 1240 Bay Street, Suite 302 Toronto, Ontario M5R 2A7 CANADA	DATE	CONFIRMED BY	
PLEASE PROVIDE OUR CLIENT(S)	PARTY OF	WITH THE FOLLOWING SERVICES	
COMMENCING TERMINATING NO. NIGHTS EXP ARRIV TIME		VIA SPECIAL REMARKS	
TO			
RATE PLAN EP MAP AP DEPOSIT PAID AMOUNT DATE DEPOSIT PAID		BY _____	
1. CLIENT INTRODUCTION YOUR UTMOST COOPERATION IS REQUESTED TO SATISFY OUR CLIENTS. CLIENTS WILL SETTLE IN FULL FOR SERVICES RENDERED AT TIME OF DEPARTURE.			

Reprinted courtesy of Astor Travel Services

While hotel bookings normally only require a credit card to guarantee the reservation, if the hotel is arranged through a tour operator, payment in full is required in advance (although there may be a deposit paid first, and then final payment later). When a tour operator is used (and this is an exception to the normal rule), the agent's commission can be deducted from the client's final payment if payment was made by a cheque payable to the travel agency. However, if the final payment was made on the client's credit card, the full payment should be sent to the tour operator and a commission cheque will be sent back.

Upon receipt of full payment, the tour operator will issue a hotel voucher to the agency, which in turn will give it to the client to be exchanged directly at the hotel for accommodation.

Hotel Booking Terms

CHECK-IN	Procedure used by each hotel to register guests upon arrival, to secure payment arrangements, and to assign rooms.
CHECK-OUT TIME	The time of day by which the guest is required to vacate the room on departure in order to avoid extra charges (varies from late morning to mid-afternoon).
DAY RATE	A reduced occupancy rate for day use only of room (usually between 8:00 a.m. to about 6:00 p.m.).
DEPOSIT	A prepayment of part of the room rate in order to hold the reservation (may or may not be refundable in the event of cancellation).
EXTRA PERSON CHARGE	The added cost of another person in the room beyond the basic number already included in the regular room rate (usually two persons are included in the rate advertised).
INCIDENTALS	Extra charge for items not included in the regular room rate (liquor, bar snacks, room service, laundry, and some or all phone calls).
MASTER ACCOUNT	An overall bill, used in group travel (usually by pre-arrangement), that includes all room charges (including meeting rooms) but not individual guest incidentals, which are charged directly to the individual.
PRE-REGISTRATION	Pre-arranged registration of guests and room assignment, used in group travel to save check-in time.
RACK RATE	A retail rate that appears in the hotel's own publications, but is not necessarily the cheapest rate available.
SERVICE CHARGE	A charge, based on a percentage of a hotel bill (typically 10% to 15%), used to pay tips to hotel

	staff (common in Europe and in all-inclusive accommodation in North America).
GUARANTEED ROOM	A reserved room for which payment is certain (often prepaid or paid by credit card) irrespective of whether the room is used.
RUN OF THE HOUSE	The same rate is charged for any room, regardless of where it is located, but location is chosen by the supplier.
TRADE DISCOUNT	A discounted rate made available to qualified travel industry personnel (generally requires some industry ID and pre-arrangement).
NO SHOW	A cancelled reservation due to failure of the guest to check in by the required arrival time in the reservation.

Cancellation

The hotel's rules for cancellation must be carefully followed. If the hotel reservation was booked directly and guaranteed with a credit card, the client will be charged for one night's accommodation unless cancelled by a specified time (as with confirmations, be sure to get a cancellation number, the name of person whom you spoke with, and the date of your call). If the booking was made through a tour operator, there may be a cancellation penalty in any event, depending on the terms and conditions of the tour package.

Hotel Personnel

The following is a list of some of the key personnel who work in hotels. A travel agent will deal with many of these people at various times.

GENERAL MANAGER	Responsible for overall supervision of all departments and activities.
RESIDENT MANAGER	The on-site manager takes on duties assigned by the general manager.
ASSISTANT MANAGER	Assists the general manager and the resident manager in supervisory duties.
FRONT OFFICE MANAGER	Supervises front desk staff who handle reservations, information, and guest registration.
CONCIERGE	Arranges tours and reservations and handles general inquires.

WORLDWIDE ACCOMMODATION

Major Hotel Chains

Best Western International	Omni Hotel
Clarion Hotel	Outrigger Hotel
Comfort Inn	Park Inn
Days Inn	Penta Hotel
Econo Lodge	Princess Hotel
Embassy Hotel	Quality Inn
Fairmont Hotel	Radisson Hotel
Friendship Inn	Ramada Inn
Four Seasons	Red Lion Hotel
Guest Quarters	Ritz Carlton Hotel
Hilton Hotel	Rodeway Inn
Holiday Inn	Shangri-La Hotel
Hyatt Hotel	Sleep Inn
Inter-Continental Hotel	Sonesta
ITT Sheraton Hotel	Stouffer Hotel
Kempinski Hotel	Super 8
Loew's Hotel	Trust House Forte
Marriott	Vagabond Inn
Meridien	Westin Hotel
Nikko Hotel	Wyndham Hotel
Oberoi Hotel	

See Appendix B for samples of U.S. golf resorts, tennis resorts, spa hotels, dude ranches, and casino hotels. Also included are lists of Caribbean all-inclusive resorts, and deluxe hotels of the world.

REFERENCE MATERIAL

The following publications may be useful to travel agents to obtain information about accommodation:

Hotel and Travel Index—published quarterly; lists hotels, motels, resorts, and hotel representatives.

Official Hotel Guide—four-volume directory of a large number of hotels and resorts worldwide.

CTG Business Travel Planner—published quarterly in North American and Worldwide editions; lists hotels, transportation services, and other destination information.

Star Service—updated monthly with detailed matter-of-fact descriptions of top hotels.

Hotel and Motel Redbook—annual publication; lists primarily U.S. properties.

Mobil Tour Guide—U.S. hotels and motels.

Michelin Guides—Excellent resources for Western European hotels and restaurants and for some other destinations.

Fodor's, Frommer's, Lonely Planet, Berlitz, and many other travel books, published on a country-by-country, area-of-the-world, or themed basis.

Hotel chain brochures from Sheraton, Hilton, etc.

Government Tourist Office publications.

Hotel representatives' lists and manuals.

Tour operator brochures.

CD-ROM, Internet sources.

Apollo and SABRE computer reservations systems offer extensive listings of hotels, bed and breakfasts, and other types of accommodation. (These are two of the most popular systems in Canada, but there are a number of others used worldwide.)

Special guides such as the *Caribbean Gold Book*.

PRICING EXAMPLES REPLICATED FROM HOTEL BROCHURES: SUN 'N SAND HOTELS, OAHU

(All hotels are located on Beachside Row, near the Beach!)

Sun 'N Sand Beach Tower
220 Beachside Row, Honolulu
(390 Rooms)

Room Type	Winter Rate	Summer Rate	Spring/Fall Rate
Standard	$110.00	$100.00	$90.00
City view	120.00	110.00	100.00
Partial ocean view*	130.00	120.00	110.00
Full ocean view*	140.00	130.00	125.00
Efficiency			
Standard[†]	115.00	105.00	100.00
City view[†]	125.00	115.00	110.00
Partial ocean view*	145.00	135.00	130.00
Studio Efficiency[‡]			
Standard	135.00	135.00	135.00
Partial ocean view	175.00	175.00	175.00

Family plans available

* Maximum 2 persons
[†] Maximum 3 persons
[‡] 1 to 3 persons

Sun 'N Sand Ocean View
260 Beachside Row, Honolulu
(375 Rooms)

Room Type	Winter Rate	Summer Rate	Spring/Fall Rate
Standard	$100.00	$90.00	$85.00
Moderate	110.00	100.00	95.00
Efficiency*			
Standard	105.00	100.00	95.00
Moderate	115.00	110.00	105.00
Studio Efficiency†			
Standard	130.00	130.00	130.00
Moderate	140.00	140.00	140.00

Family plans available

* Maximum 2 persons
† 1 to 3 persons

Sun 'N Sand Hawaiian Palace
241 Beachside Row, Honolulu
(430 Rooms)

Room Type	Winter Rate	Summer Rate	Spring/Fall Rate
Standard	$100.00	$90.00	$85.00
Moderate	110.00	100.00	95.00
Efficiency			
Standard	105.00	100.00	95.00
Moderate	115.00	110.00	105.00
Studio	130.00	130.00	130.00
Studio Efficiency			
1 bedroom	140.00	140.00	140.00

Family plans available

Standard room: maximum 2 persons
Efficiency: maximum 3 persons
Studio: maximum 4 persons
Suite efficiency: maximum 5 persons
Studio and suite efficiency rates apply for 1 to 4 persons

Sun 'N Sand Island Paradise
250 Beachside Row, Honolulu
(266 rooms) — Opened spring 1997

Room Type	Winter Rate	Summer Rate	Spring/Fall Rate
Standard	$100.00	$90.00	$85.00
City view	110.00	100.00	95.00
Park view	120.00	110.00	105.00
Moderate	120.00	120.00	120.00
City view deluxe	130.00	130.00	130.00

Family plans available

**EXAMPLES OF HOTEL DESCRIPTIONS REPLICATED FROM TOUR BROCHURES:
SUNJET HOLIDAYS; NEGRIL BEACH, JAMAICA HOTELS**

Tropic Beach Villa

Beachfront studios, 2- and 3-bedroom cottages, and a deluxe 3-bedroom villa (for 6 to 10 persons); includes a cook, serene atmosphere, idyllic setting.

Features/facilities

- Air conditioning (some units)
- Ceiling fans
- Equipped kitchens/kitchenettes
- Library
- Daily maid service
- Gymnasium
- Beach bar
- Water sports available nearby (by arrangement)
- Discos/beach parties nightly nearby
- Tennis and squash nearby
- Groceries available nearby
- Restaurants within a five-minute walk

Ocean Spray Hotel

20 cozy rooms, each with en suite bath, located in the centre of Negril's famous seven-mile beach with crystal clear waters.

Features/facilities

- Air conditioning
- Colour TV
- Maid service
- Telephone
- Beach bar
- Oceanside dining restaurant
- Night time entertainment available nearby
- Beach
- Sailing/windsurfing/snorkelling/scuba diving/parasailing
- Sightseeing tour (by arrangement)
- Groceries available nearby

Peacock Villas

Located on nine landscaped acres, filled with fruit trees and flowers, and adjoining 1,000 feet of beachfront, this property is all-inclusive and offers 1-, 2-, and 3-bedroom villas that still maintain their original rustic charm; new showpiece superior hotel room and spacious 1-bedroom suites also now available.

Features/facilities

- Air conditioning
- Living/dining areas (villas)
- Kitchens (villas)
- Maid/cook
- Pool
- Jacuzzi
- Restaurant
- Beach bar
- Nightly entertainment information available
- Duty-free shop
- Exercise room
- Tennis
- Beach
- Water sports available
- Sightseeing tours (by arrangement)

Negril Surfside

Seaside villa/hotel, ideal for groups of two to twelve, with only eight individually furnished rooms, each with a private sea-view balcony.

Features/facilities

- Air conditioning/ceiling fans
- Satellite TV
- King size waterbeds
- Stocked bar
- Soft drink, beer, mixtures
- French wines, California champagnes
- Room service
- Full menu on request
- Restaurants/groceries within a 5-minute drive
- Daily maid service
- Complimentary breakfast daily
- Jacuzzi/hot tub
- Private sea access
- Sundecks
- Fresh juices and vegetables

EXERCISES—Using Hotel Brochures

Hotel chain brochures and tour operator brochures will provide costing information for various hotel properties. While formats will vary, it is important to understand how to decipher these brochures. Two fictitious examples can be found in the preceding pages: namely, Sun 'N Sand Hotels, Oahu, and Sunjet Holidays, Jamaica Hotels.

Referring to the Sun 'N Sand Hotels material, please answer the following questions:

1. Which of the hotels is new? _____

2. Where is it located? _____

3. What is the cost of a moderate room per night? _____

4. A couple want to take their 30-year-old daughter on holiday to Honolulu next January. The Sun 'N Sand ocean-view studio efficiency rooms have been recommended by their neighbour. What is the total cost of the room for the three people for a seven-night stay (excluding taxes and service charges, if any)? _____

   _____

5. a. Another couple are planning a summer holiday, spending three nights in Honolulu en route to visiting Hong Kong. They insist on guaranteed full ocean view. Which Sun 'N Sand Hotel do you recommend?

   _____

   b. What is the total cost of the room (excluding taxes and service charges, if any) for their stay?

   _____

Referring to the hotel descriptions in the Sunjet Holidays, Jamaica Hotels material in the preceding pages, please answer the following question:

1. Six clients would like to go to Jamaica for Christmas. They would like to be on the beach, with water sports and a Jacuzzi available. Which property offered by Sunjet Holidays would you recommend and why?

   _____

   _____

EXERCISES—Hotels

Please use the extracts from the various hotel guides provided at the end of this chapter to answer the following questions. (Note that the *Official Hotel Guide* was formerly called the OHRG.)

1. *Official Hotel Guide*—Airport Plaza Hotel, St. John's, Newfoundland

    a.   Is this hotel accessible to the handicapped? _____

    b.   How far from the airport is this hotel? _____

    c.   What is the toll-free number for this hotel offer? _____

    d.   Does the hotel accept Diner's Club cards? _____

    e.   What is the cost of a double room with bath? _____

    f.   What tax is applied to the bill? _____

    g.   What is the commission rate? _____

2. *Official Hotel Guide*—Paris, France

    A passenger needs a Paris hotel for five nights commencing tomorrow. The client would like a suite in a deluxe hotel. Refer to the selections from the *Official Hotel Guide* to answer the following questions.

    a.   Which hotel would you book? _____

    b.   How much per night would it cost? _____

    c.   What is your commission? _____

    d.   Where is the hotel located? _____

    e.   If the client wishes to reserve a room for a meeting, how many people can be invited? _____

    f.   Prepare a hotel voucher based on the highest suite rate (vouchers can be found on the following pages.)

Blank hotel vouchers for confirming bookings and a car/hotel voucher are located at the end of this chapter on pages 55 and 56.

3. *CTG Business Travel Planner*

   Your clients wish to go to Tucumcari, New Mexico. How would you advise
   them to get there? _____

   _____

   a. If they wish to stay near the highway, which accommodation would you
       recommend? _____

   b. What is the area code and phone number for this hotel?

   _____

4. *Star Service*—Gritti Palace, Venice

   a. When do groups book this hotel? _____

   b. Who represents the hotel? _____

   c. What information do you have about the bar? _____

   _____

   d. When was the hotel built and what was its original use?

   _____

5. *Choice Hotels International*—Pensacola Beach, Florida

   a. Which property is closest to the airport? _____

   b. How many rooms does this hotel have? _____

   c. What is this hotel's toll-free number? _____

   d. What points of interest are nearby? _____

   _____

Official Hotel Guide

PORT-AUX-BASQUES
☎ Country Code: 1

•Port-aux-Basques Hotel
50 Rooms

1 High St, PO Box 400 **POST CODE:** A0M 1C0 **PHONE:** (709)695-2171 **FAX:** (709)695-2250
Moderate First Class Family-oriented Motor Hotel (1959) situated 2 km from Marine Atlantic Ferry Terminal - Rooms with private bath, phone, radio & color cable TV (premium channel) - Rooms for nonsmokers - Wheelchair access - Limited Room Service - Family Restaurant - Cocktail Lounge - Banquet & Meeting Room to 80 - Free Parking - Fishing, boating & water sports nearby - Renovations in 1997
RATES: EP SDWB CAD 55-63 ($35-41) EAP 5 (3) - Max rates Jul 1-Sep 30 - Tax 15% **COMM:** R-04 CREDIT CARDS: AE DC DIS ENR JCB MC VISA
RESERVATIONS: CRS: Sabre

ST. JOHN'S
☎ Country Code: 1

Served by ST. JOHN'S AIRPORT (YYT), 5 miles northwest of St. John's

•Airport Plaza Hotel
100 Rooms

Airport Rd, PO Box 21142 **POST CODE:** A1A 5B2 **PHONE:** (709)753-3500 **FAX:** (709)753-3711
Superior Tourist Class Commercial Motor Inn (1973) located ½ km from airport - 9 km from downtown & train station - Rooms with private bath, phone, radio & color cable TV - 3 Suites - Rooms for nonsmokers - Wheelchair access - Room Service - Dining Room - Coffee Shop - Cocktail Lounge - Convention Facilities to 300 - Concierge - Laundromat - Free Parking - Winter & water sports nearby - Renovations in 1996
RATES: EP S/DWB CAD 68-80 ($44-52) Ste 110 (71) EAP 6 (4) - Tax 15% - Ste rates avail **COMM:** R-10 CREDIT CARDS: AE DC DIS ENR MC VISA
RESERVATIONS: Toll-Free: (800)563-2489 **E-Mail:** csc@cityhotels.ca **Internet:** http://www.cityhotels.com

•The Battery Hotel & Suites
125 Rooms

100 Signal Hill Rd **POST CODE:** A1A 1B3 **PHONE:** (709)576-0040 **FAX:** (709)576-6943
First Class Quiet Six-story Hotel (1963) situated on Signal Hill, overlooking the harbor & city - 8 km from airport - Rooms with private bath, phone & remote-control color cable TV - 23 Suites with separate bedroom & kitchen area - Rooms for nonsmokers - Wheelchair access - Room Service - Dining Room with panoramic view - Cocktail Lounge - Meeting Facilities to 300 - Business Services - Heated Indoor Pool - Whirlpool & Sauna - Dry Cleaning - Free Parking - Renovations in 1997
RATES: EP SWB CAD 89-109 ($57-70) D/TWB 99-135 (64-87) Ste 1-2BR 120-175 (77-113) EAP 10 (6) - Max rates May 1-Oct 31 - Tax 15% **COMM:** R-10 CREDIT CARDS: AE DC ENR MC VISA **TD:** Reduced rates
RESERVATIONS: Toll-Free: (800)563-8181 **CRS:** Sabre **E-Mail:** battery@nfld.com **Internet:** http://www.netfx.iom.net/battery

•Best Western Travellers Inn
88 Rooms

Kenmount Rd **POST CODE:** A1B 3P9 **PHONE:** (709)722-5540 **FAX:** (709)722-1025
Moderate First Class Attractive Motor Inn (1962) located at TransCanada Highway's entrance to city, ½ mile from shopping mall - 5 miles from airport - Rooms with private bath, phone & color cable TV - Rooms for nonsmokers - Limited wheelchair access - Room Service - Dining Room & Lounge - Meeting Room to 100 - Outdoor Heated Pool - Free Parking - Renovated 1991
RATES: EP SWB CAD 79-89 ($51-57) D/TWB 89-99 (57-64) EAP 10 (6) - Tax 15% **COMM:** R-10 CREDIT CARDS: AE DC DIS ENR MC VISA
RESERVATIONS: REPS: BW CKS **Toll-Free:** (800)528-1234 **CRS:** Sabre, Worldspan **Internet:** http://www.bestwestern.com

•Delta St. John's Hotel & Conference Centre
276 Rooms

120 New Gower St **POST CODE:** A1C 6K4 **PHONE:** (709)739-6404 **FAX:** (709)739-1622
Superior First Class Impressive, Harborview Hotel (1987), centrally located near shopping district - 10 km from airport - Rooms with private bath, climate control, phone (bath extension), radio & remote-control color cable TV (premium channel, movies); some with data ports - 9 Suites - Executive Floor - Rooms for nonsmokers - Wheelchair access - Restaurant - Lounge & Pub - Convention Facilities to 1100, banquet-style - Business Center - Fitness Center with indoor heated pool, sauna & whirlpool, aerobics & exercise room - 2 Squash Courts - Concierge - Free Parking - Renovations in 1997
RATES: EP S/D/TWB CAD 150-165 ($97-106) Ste 275-550 (177-355) EAP 15 (10) - Tax 15% **COMM:** R-10 CREDIT CARDS: AE DC DIS JCB MC VISA **TD:** 50%
RESERVATIONS: REPS: UI DEL **Toll-Free:** In US (800)563-3838 **CRS:** Amadeus, Apollo, Galileo, Sabre, Worldspan **Internet:** http://www.deltahotels.com

•Holiday Inn
186 Rooms

180 Portugal Cove Rd **POST CODE:** A1B 2N2 **PHONE:** (709)722-0506 **FAX:** (709)722-9756
First Class Four-story Hotel (1966) in park-like surroundings, adjacent to provincial Legislature & the University - 3 km from airport - Rooms with bath, climate control, phone, data port, remote-control color cable TV & coffee maker - 4 Suites - Rooms for nonsmokers - Wheelchair access - Restaurant - Lounge - Meeting Facilities to 800 - Outdoor heated Pool - Free Parking - Golf & water sports nearby - Renovations in 1996
RATES: EP S/DWB CAD 99-155 ($64-100) Ste 175 (113) EAP 10 (6) - Max rates May 1-Sep 15 - Tax 18% **COMM:** R-10 CREDIT CARDS: AE CB DC DIS ENR JCB MC VISA **TD:** 50% TA
RESERVATIONS: REPS: CKS HOL **Toll-Free:** (800)HOLIDAY **CRS:** Sabre, Worldspan **Internet:** http://www.holiday-inn.com

•Hotel Newfoundland
301 Rooms

Cavendish Sq, PO Box 5637 **POST CODE:** A1C 5W8 **PHONE:** (709)726-4980 **FAX:** (709)726-2025
Superior First Class Downtown Hotel (1982) constructed on the site of the original Newfoundland Hotel, overlooking the Narrows near historic Fort William - Within walking distance of commercial district - 5 km from airport - Rooms with climate control, private bath, minibar, phone, radio, color cable TV (premium channel) with video player & city of harbor view - 19 Suites - 5 Minisuites - Concierge Floor - Rooms for nonsmokers - Wheelchair access - Evening Turndown - 24-hour Room Service - 2 Restaurants - Lounge - Atrium - Meetings to 1000 - 24-hour Full-service Business Center - Indoor Pool & Sauna - Fitness Center - Racquetball Court - Gift Shop - Hair Salon - Free Parking - Renovations in 1997
RATES: EP S/D/TWB CAD 109-599 ($70-386) EAP 20 (13) - Tax 15% - Ste rates avail **COMM:** R-10 CREDIT CARDS: AE DC DIS ENR JCB MC VISA **TD:** 50% TA
RESERVATIONS: REPS: CKS CPH SNR **Toll-Free:** (1800)441-1414 **CRS:** Abacus, Amadeus, Apollo, Fantasia, Galileo, Gemini, Sabre, Worldspan **Internet:** http://www.cphotels.ca

•Prescott Inn
18 Rooms

19 Military Rd **POST CODE:** A1C 2C3 **PHONE:** (709)753-7733 **FAX:** (709)753-6036
Intimate Bed & Breakfast Inn (1986) set in building dating from 1897 - Situated 2 blocks from the harbor, near restaurants & shops - 3 miles from airport - Guest rooms fitted with period furnishings, original artwork, radio & color cable TV; some with semi-private bath - 6 Suites with kitchen - 4 Apartments - Rooms for nonsmokers - Meeting Room to 10 - Free Parking - Renovations in 1996
RATES: BB S/DWB CAD 45-105 ($29-68) EAP 15 (10) - Tax 12% - Apt & Ste rates avail **COMM:** R-10 CREDIT CARDS: MC VISA **TD:** 10-30%

•Quality Hotel by Journey's End
162 Rooms

2 Hill O' Chips **POST CODE:** A1C 6B1 **PHONE:** (709)754-7788 **FAX:** (709)754-5209
Superior Tourist Class Modern Hotel (1990) situated downtown, 1 km from St. John's Memorial Stadium & 4 km from airport - Rooms with climate control, work table, phone (free local calls), clock radio & remote-control color cable TV (movies); some with data port - Rooms for nonsmokers - Wheelchair access - Licensed Restaurant overlooking harbor - Free Parking - Convenient location for sightseeing
RATES: EP S/DWB CAD 85-125 ($55-81) EAP 8 (5) - Tax 19.84% **COMM:** R-10 CREDIT CARDS: AE DC DIS ENR MC VISA
RESERVATIONS: REPS: CCQ **Toll-Free:** (800)228-5151 **CRS:** Apollo, Sabre, Worldspan

•Hotel St. John's
105 Units

102 Kenmount Rd **POST CODE:** A1B 3R2 **PHONE:** (709)722-9330 **FAX:** (709)722-9231
Tourist Class Comfortable Apartment Hotel (1975) located 6 km from downtown, 9 km from Confederation Building & 11 km from airport - Rooms with phone, data port, radio & remote-control color cable TV - 28 fully equipped efficiency units - 6 Suites - Rooms for nonsmokers - Room Service - Restaurant & Cocktail Lounge - Meeting & Banquet Room to 150 - Laundry/Dry Cleaning - Valet Service - Free Parking - Pets permitted - Shopping nearby - Fishing trips & sight-seeing tours arranged - Renovations in 1995
RATES: EP SWB CAD 69-76/74-80 ($45-49/48-52) D/TWB 76-83/78-86 (49-54/50-55) Ste 79-86/86-94 (51-55/55-61) EAP 7 (5) - Max rates Jun 1-Sep 30 - Tax 19.84% - Effcy rates avail **COMM:** R-10 CREDIT CARDS: AE DC DIS ENR MC VISA **TD:** 5%
RESERVATIONS: Toll-Free: (800)563-2489 **E-Mail:** csc@cityhotels.ca **Internet:** http://www.cityhotels.ca

STEPHENVILLE
☎ Country Code: 1

•Holiday Inn
47 Rooms

44 Queens St **POST CODE:** A2N 1M5 **PHONE:** (709)643-6666 **FAX:** (709)643-3900
First Class Modern Hotel (1993) situated adjacent to shopping center - ½ mile from city center or airport - Comfortable rooms with air conditioning, minibar, coffee maker, phone, data port & remote-control color cable TV (movies) - 2 Suites - 36 Rooms for nonsmokers - Wheelchair access - Room Service - Restaurant & Lounge - Meeting & Banquet Facilities to 200 - Hair Salon - Free Parking - Geological site nearby - Skiing, golf & tennis in area - Renovations in 1996
RATES: EP S/DWB CAD 110-120 ($71-77) Ste120-130 (77-84) EAP 8 (5) - Tax 15% **COMM:** R-10 CREDIT CARDS: AE DC DIS MC VISA **TD:** 50% TA
RESERVATIONS: REPS: HOL **Toll-Free:** (800)HOLIDAY **CRS:** Sabre, Worldspan **E-Mail:** holinn.sville@nf.sympatico.ca **Internet:** http://www.atlific.com

White's Hotel/Motel
31 Units

14 Main St **POST CODE:** A2N 2Z5 **PHONE:** (709)643-2101 **FAX:** (709)643-3307
Superior Tourist Class Small Motor Inn (1955) located downtown, 2 miles from Stephenville Airport - Rooms with bath, heat control, phone, radio & color cable TV - 20 Efficiency Units - Bridal Suite - Rooms for nonsmokers - Wheelchair access - Limited Room Service - Dining Room - Cocktail Lounge - Meeting Room to 24 - Free Parking - Renovations in 1995
RATES: EP SWB CAD 55 ($35) D/TWB 60-75 (39-48) Ste 85 (55) EAP 6 (4) - Tax 19.84% - Effcy rates avail **COMM:** R-00 CREDIT CARDS: AE CB DC ENR MC VISA

Official Hotel Guide

Champs-Elysees - Spacious rooms with traditional decor, private bath & shower, hair dryer, phone, radio, color cable TV & minibar - Connecting Rooms & 3 Suites - 24-hour Room Service - Meeting Room to 6 - Laundry/Dry Cleaning Service - Parking (charge) - Renovations in 1995
RATES: EP S/D/TWB FRF 950-1500 ($162-256) Ste 1500-2000 (256-341) EAP 200 (34) - SC incl COMM: R-08 CREDIT CARDS: AE DC EC ENR JCB MC VISA
RESERVATIONS: REPS: UI EMA MKH Toll-Free: in US (800)221-6509 CRS: Amadeus, Apollo, Sabre, Worldspan

•MARIGNAN ELYSEES, WESTIN DEMEURE HOTELS

DELUXE   Map A, Dot 174

12 rue de Marignan (F-75008)
Phone: 1-40-76-34-56   Fax: 1-40-76-34-34   Telex: 644018
Affiliation: Westin Hotels & Resorts   73 Rooms   Comm: R-10

Description/Location: Contemporary Hotel (1991) housed in a 19th-century neo-Gothic building with Art Deco facade -- Situated off the famous Champs Elysees, within walking distance of the Arc de Triomphe and the Eiffel Tower

Accommodations: Air-conditioned rooms, each with color cable TV (24-hour news channel), direct-dial phone, minibar, individual safe, hair dryer and bathrobe; some with large terrace offering superb views of the Eiffel Tower -- Duplex Suites with sitting room and tea/coffee making facilities -- Floor for nonsmokers -- 24-hour Room Service -- Evening Turndown Service -- Complimentary daily newspapers

Facilities/Services: Restaurant supervised by renowned chef -- Lounge and Bar -- Meeting Facilities accommodating up to a maximum of 110 persons -- Secretarial Services available -- Concierge -- Guest Laundry and Dry Cleaning Service -- Babysitting -- Foreign Exchange -- Multilingual Staff -- Valet Parking

Rates: European Plan
Single/Double with Bath......................................FRF 2000-2550 ($341-435)
Duplex Suite 2800 (478)
SC & Tax incl -- Corporate rates available -- Credit Cards: AE DC JCB MC VISA

RESERVATIONS:
Reps: WIH -- Toll-Free: In US & Canada (800)WESTIN-1;
in UK (0800)282-565; in Germany (0130)852662;
in Japan (outside Tokyo) 0120-39-1671; in Tokyo (813)5423-4811
CRS: Amadeus, Apollo, Galileo, Sabre, Sahara, SystemOne & Worldspan

•Hotel Massenet   41 Rooms   Map A, Dot 175
5 bis, rue Massenet POST CODE: F-75116 PHONE: 1-45-24-43-03 TELEX: 640196 F FAX: 1-45-24-41-39
Superior Tourist Class Pleasant 7-story Hotel (1930) with limestone & glass exterior, situated in residential area located near Rue de Passy & the Eiffel Tower, 5 minutes from Bois de Boulogne Park - 2 km from Montparnasse train station & 15 km from Orly Airport - Rooms with bath, direct-dial phone, radio, color TV & minibar - Wheelchair access - Elevator - Bar - Garden - Pets permitted - Parking (charge) - Renovated 1992
RATES: CP SWB FRF 535-715 ($91-122) D/TWB 740-840 (126-143) EAP 180 (31) - SC & Tax incl COMM: R-10 CREDIT CARDS: ACC AE DC EC ENR JCB MC VISA
RESERVATIONS: REPS: IHO Toll-Free: In US (800)528-1234

•Mayfair Hotel   52 Rooms   Map A, Dot 176
3, rue Rouget-de-Lisle POST CODE: F-75001 PHONE: 1-42-60-38-14 FAX: 1-40-15-04-78
Moderate First Class Pleasant, Traditionally Styled Hotel (1900) in 6-story building situated in the heart of the business quarter, near the Tuileries Gardens, Faubourg Saint-Honore & the Place de la Concorde - 45 minutes from airports - Soundproof, air-conditioned rooms with private bath, hair dryer, direct-dial phone, radio, color cable TV, minibar & in-room safe - Wheelchair access - Bar - Renovations in 1998
RATES: CP SWB FRF 1288 ($220) D/TWB 1415-1655 (241-282) EAP 308 (53) - SC & Tax incl COMM: R-08 CREDIT CARDS: AE DC EC JCB MC VISA TD: 30% TA
RESERVATIONS: REPS: UI EEX EUC JCB CRS: Worldspan

•Mercure Hotel Paris Porte de Versailles   91 Rooms   Map A, Dot 177
69, blvd Victor POST CODE: F-75015 PHONE: 1-44-19-03-03 TELEX: 205628 F FAX: 1-48-28-22-11
Moderate First Class Modern 7-story Hotel (1976) located in Left Bank neighborhood, opposite Paris Expo & 10 minutes from Eiffel Tower - 5 km from Montparnasse train station & 15 km from Orly Airport - Soundproof rooms with climate control, bath, hair dryer, phone, radio, remote-control color cable TV (movies, premium channels) & minibar - Rooms for nonsmokers - Wheelchair access - Restaurant & Bar - Meetings to 250 - Parking (charge) - Renovations in 1997
RATES: EP SWB FRF 890-1200 ($152-205) D/TWB 970-1280 (166-218) Ste 1500 (256) - SC & Tax incl - Ste rates avail COMM: R-08 CREDIT CARDS: AE DC EC MC VISA TD: 50%
RESERVATIONS: REPS: RSN Toll-Free: in US (800)221-4542 CRS: Galileo, Sabre, Worldspan Internet: http://www.hotelweb.fr

•Mercure Hotel Ronceray-Paris Opera   130 Rooms   Map B, Dot 178
10, blvd Montmartre POST CODE: F-75009 PHONE: 1-42-47-13-45 TELEX: 283906 F FAX: 1-42-47-13-63
Moderate First Class Contemporary Hotel (reopened in 1989) housed in a building dating from 1860 - Situated in the heart of the business district, near the Opera & within walking distance of shopping & the Palais Royale - 10 km from Orly Int'l Airport - Soundproof rooms with high ceilings, private bath or shower, phone, radio, color TV & minibar - 1 Suite - 12 Duplexes - Rooms for nonsmokers - Bar - Meetings to 320 - Business Services Center - Parking (charge) - Restaurants in area - Renovations in 1998
RATES: EP SWB FRF 650-890 ($111-152) D/TWB 690-930 (118-159) Ste 1400-1600 (239-273) - SC incl COMM: R-08 CREDIT CARDS: AE CB DC EC MC VISA
RESERVATIONS: REPS: UI EEX RSN Toll-Free: (800)221-4542 CRS: Sabre, Worldspan Internet: http://www.hotelweb.fr

•Mercure Montmartre Hotel   308 Rooms   Map B, Dot 179
3, rue Caulaincourt POST CODE: F-75018 PHONE: 1-44-69-70-70 TELEX: 285605 F FAX: 1-44-69-70-71
Superior Tourist Class Contemporary 9-story Hotel (1982) with distinctive modular facade, situated adjacent to shopping center - Located near Moulin Rouge & the Butte Montmartre - 2 km from train station & 15 km from Charles de Gaulle Airport - Pleasant air-conditioned rooms with bath, phone, minibar & color TV - Rooms for nonsmokers - Wheelchair access - Bar - Meetings to 150 - Renovations in 1996
RATES: EP SWB FRF 780-990/1130 ($133-169/193) DWB 850-1060/1220 (145-181/208) EAP 65 (11) - Max rates Jun 10-Jul 12 - SC & Tax incl COMM: R-10 CREDIT CARDS: AE DC EC MC VISA TD: 50%
RESERVATIONS: REPS: UI RSN Toll-Free: In US (800)221-4542 CRS: Amadeus, Apollo, Axess, Galileo, Sabre, SystemOne, Worldspan Internet: http://www.hotelweb.fr

•Mercure Porte d'Orleans   192 Rooms   Map B, Dot 180
13, rue Francois Ory, Montrouge POST CODE: F-92120 PHONE: 1-46-57-11-26 TELEX: 632978 F FAX: 1-47-35-47-61
Superior Tourist Class Modern 8-story Hotel (1977) located in southern Paris, $3^1/_2$ miles from city center or Montparnasse train station - 15 km from Orly Int'l Airport - Air-conditioned rooms with bath, phone, radio, color TV & minibar - 6 Suites - Rooms for nonsmokers - Wheelchair access - Room Service - Restaurant & Bar - Meetings to 140 - Parking (charge) - Renovated 1990
RATES: EP SWB FRF 610-1120 ($104-191) DWB 710-1240 (121-212) Ste 1000-2000 (171-341) EAP 150 (26) - SC & Tax incl COMM: R-08 CREDIT CARDS: ACC AE DC EC JCB MC VISA
RESERVATIONS: REPS: UI RSN Toll-Free: In US (800)221-4542 CRS: Amadeus, Axess, Galileo, Sabre, Sita/Sahara, SystemOne, Worldspan Internet: http://www.hotelweb.fr

•Mercure Royal Madeleine   68 Rooms   Map A, Dot 181
29 rue de l'Arcade POST CODE: F-75008 PHONE: 1-42-66-13-81 TELEX: 283458 F FAX: 1-42-66-02-27
Moderate First Class Traditional 5-story Hotel (1977) in building dating from 1870 - Located 500 meters from St Lazare train station & 15 km from Orly Int'l Airport - Rooms with bath or shower, phone, radio, remote-control color satellite TV & minibar - Elevator - Breakfast Room - Bar - Restaurants nearby - Renovations in 1994
RATES: EP SWB FRF 580-910 ($99-155) D/TWB 870-1050 (148-179) - SC incl COMM: R-08 CREDIT CARDS: ACC AE DC EC JCB MC VISA TD: 50% TA
RESERVATIONS: REPS: RSN Toll-Free: In US (800)221-4542 CRS: Abacus, Amadeus, Apollo, Fantasia, Galileo, Sabre, Sita/Sahara, Worldspan Internet: http://www.hotelweb.fr

•Mercure Vincent Auriol-Place s'Italie   70 Rooms   Map B, Dot 182
178 blvd Vincent Auriol POST CODE: F-75013 PHONE: 1-44-24-01-01 FAX: 1-44-24-07-07
Tourist Class Business-oriented 7-story Hotel (1990) located downtown, near audiovisual complex & exhibition halls - 15 km from Orly Int'l Airport - Comfortable rooms with bath, hair dryer, minibar, alarm clock, phone & color TV with cable channel - Rooms for nonsmokers - Wheelchair access - Coffee Shop - Meeting Room to 100 - Parking (charge) - Convenient to transportation to EuroDisney - Renovations in 1997
RATES: BB SWB FRF 580-680 ($99-116) D/TWB 560-785 (99-134) EAP 100-120 (17-20) - SC & Tax incl COMM: R-08 CREDIT CARDS: AE DC EC MC VISA TD: 50%
RESERVATIONS: REPS: RSN Toll-Free: In US (800)221-4542 CRS: Amadeus, Apollo, Galileo, Sabre, Worldspan Internet: http://www.hotelweb.fr

•le Meridien Montparnasse Paris   953 Rooms   Map A, Dot 183
19, rue du Commandant Mouchotte POST CODE: F-75014 PHONE: 1-44-36-44-36 TELEX: 200135 F FAX: 1-44-36-49-00
Superior First Class Huge Convention-oriented Hotel (1974) in 25-story tower located near St Germain des Pres - 15 km from Orly Airport & 32 km from Charles de Gaulle Airport (shuttle bus/charge) - Soundproof, air-conditioned rooms with bath, hair dryer, phone, radio, minibar & remote-control color cable TV - 37 Suites - Rooms for nonsmokers - Wheelchair access - Restaurant - Coffee Shop - Piano Lounge - Lobby Bar - Convention Facilities to 2000 - Business Center - Guest Laundry - Babysitting Service - Shopping Mall - Parking (charge) - Renovations in 1998
RATES: EP S/D/TWB FRF 1300-2075 ($222-354) Ste 3500-4500 (597-768) EAP 400 (68) - SC incl COMM: R-08 CREDIT CARDS: AE DC EC ENR JCB MC VISA
RESERVATIONS: REPS: UI FTE MER Toll-Free: In US (800)543-4300 CRS: Abacus, Amadeus, Apollo, Axess, Galileo, Gemini, Sabre, Sita/Sahara Internet: http://www.lmeridien-paris.com

CTG Business Travel Planner

TUCSON   🏨 THE OFFICIAL LODGING DIRECTORY OF THE AMERICAN HOTEL & MOTEL ASSOCIATION

Tucson City Hotels (cont'd from p. 673)

Red Roof Inn Tucson North • 4940 W Ina Rd • 85743 ....520 744-8199
$38-71 • 🅴 • RES: RRI ■

🅰 Residence Inn by Marriott • 6477 E Speedway Blvd • 85710 ....520 721-0991
🛏🛏 $69-175 c • 🅲🅴 • STE: 128 • MTG: 2 • RES: MAR, RIM ■   FAX: 290-8323

Rodeway Inn • 1365 W Grant Rd • 85745 • *On Highway* 520 622-7791
🛏🛏 $40-65 • 🅲🅴 • RMS: 147 • MTG: 5 • Rest. • Rm. Svc. • RES: CCQ ■   FAX: 629-0201

Rodeway Inn Benson Highway • 810 E Benson Hwy • 85713 • *On Highway* 520 884-5800
$42-123 • 🅲🅴 • RMS: 99 • RES: CCQ ■   FAX: 624-2681

🅰 Sheraton El Conquistador Resort • 10000 N Oracle Rd • 85737 ....520 544-5000
🛏🛏🛏🛏 $100-310 • 🅲🅴 • RMS: 471 • MTG: 25 • Exec. flr. • Rest. • RES: SHC ■   FAX: 544-1228

🅰 Sheraton Tucson Hotel & Suites • 5151 E Grant Rd • 85712 • *Nr. Attr.* 520 323-6262
🛏🛏🛏 $70-165DWB b • 🅲🅴 • RMS: 216 • MTG: 19 • Rest. • RES: SHC ■   FAX: 325-2989

Shoney's Inn • 1550 W Grant Rd • *Near Convention Center* 520 620-6500
NP $75-95 • 🅲 • RMS: 67 • RES: SHO ■   FAX: 903-0225

🅰 Smuggler's Inn • 6350 E Speedway • 85710 • *In Suburban Area* 520 296-3292
🛏🛏 $62-89 c • 🅲🅴 • RMS: 150 • MTG: 4 • Rest. • Rm. Svc. ■   FAX: 722-3713

Starr Pass Golf Suites • 3645 W Starr Pass Blvd • 85745 • *On Golf Course* 520 670-0500
🛏🛏 $79-169 • 🅲🅴 • RMS: 182 • MTG: 2 • Rest. ■   FAX: 670-0427

🅰 Sumner Suites • 6885 S Tucson Blvd • 85706 • *Near Airport* 520 295-0405
NP $79-89 c • 🅲 • STE: 122 • MTG: 4 • RES: SHO ■   FAX: 295-9140

SunCatcher • 105 N Ave Javalina • 85748 • *At Mountains* 520 885-0883
RMS: 4 • MTG: 1 ■   FAX: 885-0883

Super 8 Motel • 1000 S Fwy • 85745 • *In City Center* 520 622-8089
🛏 $29-109 • 🅴 • Rest. • RES: SUP ■   FAX: 798-3940

Super 8 Motel • 1010 S Fwy • 85745 ....520 622-8080
🅴 • RES: SUP ■

🅰 Tanque Verde Ranch • 14301 E Speedway Blvd • 85748 • *On Hist. Dist.* 520 296-6275
🛏🛏🛏 $265-430 a • RMS: 74 • MTG: 4 • Rest. • RES: ATS ■   FAX: 721-9426

Travelodge • 1300 N Stone Ave • 85705 • *Near University* 520 770-1910
🛏🛏 $30-125 c • 🅲🅴 • RMS: 79 • MTG: 6 • Rest. • Rm. Svc. • RES: TVL ■   FAX: 770-0750

Travelodge Suites • 401 W Lavery Lane • 85704 • *Near City Center* 520 797-1710
$45-94 c • 🅲🅴 • RMS: 51 • RES: TVL ■   FAX: 797-1766

🅰 Varsity Clubs of America Suites Hotel • 3855 E Speedway Blvd • 85716 ..520 318-3777
NP $115up DWB • 🅲🅴 • STE: 60 • MTG: 2 • Rest. • Rm. Svc. • RES: ERS ■

🅰 Villa Serenas • 8111 E Broadway Blvd • 85710 • *In Residential Area* 520 886-5537
🅴 ■   FAX: 886-2123

🅰 Viscount Suite Hotel • 4855 E Broadway • 85711 • *Near Attractions* 520 745-6500
🛏🛏 $89-155 b • 🅲🅴 • STE: 216 • MTG: 6 • Exec. flr. • Rest. • Rm. Svc. • RES: UI ■

Vista Del Sol Motel • 1458 W Miracle Mile • 85705 ....520 293-9270
RMS: 26

🅰 Wayward Winds Lodge • 707 W Miracle Mile • 85705 • *In Subr. Area* 520 791-7526
🛏🛏 $46-99 c • RMS: 41 • MTG: 1 ■   FAX: 791-9502

🅰 The Westin La Paloma • 3800 E Sunrise Dr • 85718 • *In Resort Area* 520 742-6000
🛏🛏 🅲 • RMS: 487 • MTG: 30 • Exec. flr. • Rest. • Rm. Svc. • RES: WIH ■   FAX: 577-5878

🅰 Westward Look Resort • 245 E Ina Rd • 85704 • *Near Mountains* 520 297-1151
🛏🛏🛏 $89-219 • 🅲🅴 • RMS: 236 • MTG: 13 • Rest. • Rm. Svc. • RES: UI ■   FAX: 297-9023

🅰 White Stallion Ranch • 9251 W Twin Peaks Rd • 85743 • *Open Sep-May* 520 297-0252
🛏🛏🛏 $130-244 a • RMS: 32 • MTG: 1 • Rest. ■   FAX: 744-2786

🅰 Windmill Inn at St Philip's Plaza • 4250 No Campbell Ave • 85718 ....520 577-0007
🛏🛏 🅴 • STE: 122 • MTG: 4 • RES: UI ■   FAX: 577-0045

AIRPORT AREA HOTELS

🅰 Baymont Inn & Suites Tucson Airport • 2548 E Medina Rd at Tucson Blvd 520 889-6600
🛏🛏🛏 $55-65 c • 🅲🅴 • RMS: 100 • MTG: 1 • RES: BII ■   FAX: 889-6168

Baymont Inn Tucson North • 1560 W Grant Rd • 85745 • *In City Center* 520 624-3200
🛏🛏 $90-120 c • 🅴 • RMS: 57 • Rest. • RES: BII ■   FAX: 622-3212

🅰 Best Western Inn at the Airport • 7060 S Tucson Blvd • 85706 ....520 746-0271
🛏🛏 $79-99 c • 🅲 • RMS: 149 • MTG: 7 • Rest. • Rm. Svc. • RES: BW ■   FAX: 889-7391

Clarion Hotel Airport • 6801 S Tucson Blvd • 85706 • *At Airport* 520 746-3932
🛏🛏🛏 $55-159 c • 🅲🅴 • RMS: 189 • MTG: 6 • Exec. flr. • Rest. • RES: CCQ ■   FAX: 889-9934

Courtyard by Marriott Tucson Airport • 2505 E Executive Dr • 85706 ....520 573-0000
🛏🛏🛏 🅲🅴 • RMS: 149 • MTG: 2 • Rest. • Rm. Svc. • RES: CBM, MAR ■   FAX: 573-0470

🅰 Embassy Suites • 7051 S Tucson Blvd • 85706 • *Near Airport* 520 573-0700
🛏🛏🛏 $104-114 b • 🅲 • STE: 204 • MTG: 14 • Rest. • Rm. Svc. • RES: ESH ■   FAX: 741-9645

Hampton Inn Airport • 6971 S Tucson Blvd • 85706 • *At Airport* 520 889-5789
🛏🛏 $89-109 c • 🅴 • RMS: 126 • MTG: 1 • RES: HAM, HRW ■   FAX: 889-4002

Holiday Inn Express • 2803 E Valencia Rd • 85706 • *At Airport* 520 294-2500
🛏🛏 $89-109 c • 🅴 • RMS: 97 • MTG: 1 • RES: HOL ■   FAX: 741-0851

Holiday Inn Palo Verde • 4550 S Palo Verde Blvd • 85714 • *At Airport* 520 746-1161
🛏🛏 $77-137 • 🅲🅴 • RMS: 300 • MTG: 12 • Rest. • Rm. Svc. • RES: HOL ■   FAX: 741-1170

🅰 RAMADA INN PALO VERDE • 5251 S Julian Dr • 85706 • *At Airport* 520 294-5250
🛏🛏 $79-109 c • 🅲🅴 • RMS: 173 • MTG: 2 • Exec. flr. • Rest. • RES: RAI ■   FAX: 295-1058
See advertisement p. 673 and map p. 673 • Reservations: 800 2-RAMADA

SUBURBAN HOTELS

Catalina   Tucson area

🅰 Miraval Life in Balance Resort & Spa • 5000 E Via Estancia Miraval 520 825-4000
🛏🛏🛏 $330-550 • RMS: 106 • MTG: 7 • Rest. • Rm. Svc. • RES: STG ■   FAX: 825-5199

Green Valley   Tucson area

Best Western Green Valley • 111 S La Canada • 85614 • *On Highway* 520 625-2250
🛏🛏 $59-89 b • 🅲 • RMS: 108 • MTG: 1 • Rest. • Rm. Svc. • RES: BW ■   FAX: 625-0215

Holiday Inn Express • 19200 South I-19 Frontage Rd • 85614 • *In Country* 520 625-0900
🛏🛏 $69-109 c • 🅲🅴 • RMS: 60 • MTG: 2 • Rm. Svc. • RES: HOL ■   FAX: 393-0522

Tucumcari, NM   ☎ 505   Mountain Time
✈ CVN (Clovis) 83m SE   ✈ ABQ (Albuquerque) 175m W

Aruba Motel • 1700 E Tucumcari Blvd • 88401 • *Near Downtown Area* 505 461-3335
🅲🅴 • RMS: 37 • Exec. flr. • Rest. • Rm. Svc. ■

🅰 Best Western Discovery Motor Inn • 200 E Estrella Ave • 88401 ....505 461-4884
🛏🛏 🅲🅴 • RMS: 107 • MTG: 1 • Rest. • Rm. Svc. • RES: BW ■   FAX: 461-2463

🅰 Best Western Pow Wow Inn • 801 W Tucumcari Blvd • 88401 • *On Hwy.* 505 461-0500
🛏🛏 $36-65 • 🅲🅴 • RMS: 96 • MTG: 1 • Rest. • Rm. Svc. • RES: BW ■   FAX: 461-0135

Comfort Inn • 2800 E Tucumcari Blvd • 88401 • *Near City Center* 505 461-4094
🅲🅴 • RMS: 59 • RES: CCQ ■   FAX: 461-4099

Economy Inn • 901 E Tucumcari Blvd • 88401 • *On Hwy 66* 505 461-1340
RMS: 45   FAX: 461-1345

🅰 Holiday Inn • 3716 E Tucumcari Blvd • 88401 • *On Interstate* 505 461-3780
🛏🛏 $56-62 b • 🅲 • RMS: 100 • MTG: 3 • Rest. • Rm. Svc. • RES: HOL ■   FAX: 461-3931

Howard Johnson Lodge • 3604 E Tucumcari Blvd • 88401 ....505 461-2747
🛏🛏 RMS: 32 • RES: HOW ■   FAX: 461-2259

Rodeway Inn • 1023 E Tucumcari Blvd • 88401 • *In Suburban Area* 505 461-0360
🛏🛏 $24-66 • 🅲🅴 • RMS: 46 • RES: CCQ ■   FAX: 461-0360

Rodeway Inn West • 1302 W Tucumcari Blvd • 88401 • *On Highway* 505 461-3140
🛏 $31-55 • 🅲 • RMS: 61 • MTG: 2 ■   FAX: 461-3140

Royal Palacio Motel • 1620 E Tucumcari Blvd • 88401 • *I-40 Exit 333* 505 461-1212
$20-30 • 🅲🅴 • RMS: 23 • Rm. Svc.

Safari Motel • 722 E Tucumcari Blvd • 88401 • *Near Interstate* 505 461-3642
$23-38 • 🅴 • RMS: 23 ■

Super 8 Motel • 4001 E Tucumcari Blvd • 88401 • *32 mi from Conchos Lake* 505 461-4444
🛏 • RMS: 63 • RES: SUP ■   FAX: 461-4320

Travelodge • 1214 E Tucumcari Blvd • 88401 • *In Downtown Area* 505 461-1401
🛏🛏 $30-32 c • 🅲🅴 • RMS: 38 • RES: TVL ■   FAX: 461-3741

Tujunga, CA   ☎ 818   Pacific Time
✈ BUR (Burbank, Los Angeles County) 9m SW   ✈ LAX (Los Angeles) 34m SW

Tukwila, WA   ☎ 206/425   Pacific Time
✈ SEA (Seattle) 6m SW
Hotels: ....See Seattle (Airport Area - Seattle/Tacoma Intl) ..p. 626

Tulare, CA   ☎ 559   Pacific Time
✈ VIS (Visalia) 7m N   ✈ FAT (Fresno) 50m NW

Best Western Town & Country Lodge • 1051 N Blackstone Ave • 93274 ....559 688-7537
🛏🛏 $60-66 c • 🅲🅴 • RMS: 93 • MTG: 3 • RES: BW ■   FAX: 688-2163

🅰 Howard Johnson Express • 1050 E Rankin Ave • 93274 • *On Highway* 559 688-6671
🛏🛏 RMS: 59 • RES: ERS, HOW ■

Inns of America • 1183 N Blackstone St • 93274 • *Near Business District* 559 686-0985
🛏 $40-60 • 🅲🅴 • RMS: 90 • RES: ECY ■   FAX: 688-6814

Tularosa, NM   ☎ 505   Mountain Time
✈ ALM (Alamogordo) 20m S   ✈ ELP (El Paso, TX) 95m S

Tulia, TX   ☎ 806   Central Time
✈ AMA (Amarillo) 60m NE

🅰 Select Inn • Route 1 Box 60 • 79088 • *On Interstate* 806 995-3248
🛏 $50-60 c • 🅲🅴 • RMS: 37 • RES: BW ■   FAX: 995-3106

Tullahoma, TN   ☎ 931   Central Time
✈ BNA (Nashville) 69m NW

Steeplechase Inn • 1410 N Jackson • 37388 • *At Hwy 41A* 931 455-4501
🅲 • RMS: 94 • Rm. Svc.   FAX: 455-3013

🅰 Veranda House • 100 W Lincoln St • 37388 • *In City Center* 931 455-7033
RP 🅲🅴 • RMS: 22 ■   FAX: 454-9335

🅰 Wingo Inn (Military Only) • 100 Kindel Dr, Ste C-321 • 37389 ....931 454-3099
  FAX: 454-4004

Tullytown, PA   ☎ 215/267   Eastern Time
✈ PHL (Philadelphia) 28m SW

Tulsa, OK   ☎ 918   Central Time
CITY: 37 HOTELS ....Avg. min. rates: 🛏🛏 $65 🛏🛏🛏 $99 🛏🛏🛏🛏🛏 N/A

Maps: City p. 675

TULSA AIRPORTS
✈ TUL (Tulsa Intl) 9m NE

AIRLINES
Air France • American • Austrian • Continental • Delta • Northwest • Sabena • Southwest • Swissair • TWA • United

AIRPORT CAR RENTALS
Tulsa Intl .... Avis • Budget • Dollar • Enterprise • National • Sears • Thrifty

AIR CHARTER
Allied Helicopter Svc 918 425-7558
Corp. America Aviation **800 521-8585**

TULSA CLIMATE

		Jan	Feb	Mar	Apr	May	Jun	Jul	Aug	Sep	Oct	Nov	Dec
Average	(F)	25°	30°	38°	50°	59°	68°	72°	70°	63°	50°	38°	29°
Low	(C)	-4°	-1°	3°	10°	15°	20°	22°	21°	17°	10°	3°	-2°
High	(F)	46°	52°	61°	72°	80°	88°	94°	93°	85°	75°	60°	50°
	(C)	8°	11°	16°	22°	27°	31°	34°	34°	29°	24°	16°	10°
Rainfall	(in)	1.4	1.7	3.1	4.2	5.1	4.6	3.5	3.0	4.4	3.4	2.6	1.8
	(mm)	36	43	79	107	129	117	89	76	112	86	66	46

Star Service

marble combination baths furnish hair dryers and robes. Room service delivers the goods 24 hours a day, and the hotel operates from Easter to mid-Nov. The rooms are more modern and comfortable than those at other Lido hotels, but guests looking for Old World elegance should book at *Hotel des Bains*. 195 rooms. $257-$289 single, $302-$364 double. Leone Jannuzzi, mgr. (C-10) LC, Utell. Phone 041-526-0201. Fax 041-526-7276. ★★★★

(LA) FENICE ET DES ARTISTES, San Marco, 1936, SAN MARCO, in Campiello Marinoni de la Fenice, a small piazza by the burnt-out northern wall of the opera house, does little agency business, preferring to rely on a clientele that has no complaint with its world-weary staff, clashing fabrics, and disheveled appearance. Said clientele continues to frequent the place even though La Fenice's once regal productions have moved to a tent on Tronchetto. The two four-story buildings here enclose a garden and flank famed *Taverna la Fenice* restaurant, which is separate from this hotel. Dated public areas in desultory style show tuck-and-roll club chairs and other 1960s-style appointments, yet there is enough marble, leaded glass, and wrought iron to conjure up a traditional look. One attraction is a collection of oil paintings depicting the recent fire. The lone elevator makes for long walks to some guest rooms. These come in a mix of styles, all with period pieces, TVs, and modern dressers and side chairs. Thin carpeting and aging chenille detract from the nicely padded walls and art reproductions. Some rooms feature air conditioning, colorful Venetian armoires and baroque bedsteads, gilt mirrors, chandeliers, and spacious old baths, while others are done in strong, discordant colors. The intelligent staff speaks good English. The management shows blithe indifference and is not particularly focused on housekeeping. Some guests slip into it as if it were an old shoe, but for most, the shoe will not fit. Try the *Flora* and *Saturnia* instead. 69 rooms. $91-$108 single CP, $126-$194 double CP. Dante Apollonio, mgr. (C-10) Phone 041-523-2333. Fax 041-520-3721. ★★★

(HOTEL) FLORA, San Marco, 2283/A, SAN MARCO, hidden from the street in an excellent location off Calle Larga XXII Marzo, midway between Piazza San Marco and Ponte dell'Accademia, is an intimate gem for visitors who can live without minibars and food service after breakfast. The charm here derives from the two 19th-century houses built around the vine-covered patio and planted terrace that provide the view from many of the accommodations. A mosaic portrait of Titian and two concrete lions guard the entrance to the sedate reception area, which adjoins the appealingly antique breakfast room. It, in turn, opens to a similar lounge. The secluded patio, fresh with a fountain and wrought-iron furniture, is cloaked in flowers and foliage. Though only breakfast is served, restaurants galore line nearby streets. The air-conditioned guest rooms have plain fabrics, but hand-painted Venetian furnishings dress attractive, albeit often compact, environs. High ceilings help to compensate for limited floor space. The small baths offer little to loiter over. Only half have small tubs. The largest rooms overlook the garden, and rear corner rooms are the grandest of all, with gorgeous antiques, card tables, and divided baths. Two rooms accommodate disabled visitors. Under veteran management, this family-run hotel has one of the best staffs in Italy, which explains why the *Flora* is the beloved of many knowledgeable Americans, who consider it their own, private garden hideaway. 44 rooms. $137 single CP, $183 double CP. Ruggero Romanelli, mgr. (C-8) Phone 041-520-5844. Fax 041-522-8217. ★★

(HOTEL) GABRIELLI SANDWIRTH, Riva degli Schiavoni, 4110, CASTELLO, on the waterfront promenade, a 10-minute walk E of Piazza San Marco, resides in a 17th-century palazzo handsomely cut with Moorish arches and topped with dormers. Unlike most Venetian hotels, which have dilapidated exteriors and stunning interiors, this property looks best from the outside. Inside, the lobby is decidedly commercial, with little warmth, and besides hand-painted beams, little is in keeping with the history of the building. Dull velour armchairs look forlorn on the veined marble floors. A lovely terrace enlivens the dark upper-level restaurant, while the big group dining room is devoid of character except for gigantic chandeliers. The breakfast room is monotony in peach tones. Tipplers take to the chrome-finished American bar for a jigger or two. The best feature is the hotel's rooftop garden, which offers guests superb views of this watery city. Exposed radiators dot narrow, naked hallways to period-style accommodations with duvets and rich fabrics. The odd antique stands in stark contrast to TVs plopped atop minibars. Wash basins and glass-paned doors to gray marble baths are standard, and most have tubs. Heated towel racks are a nice touch, but there is scarcely enough counter space for a hairbrush. Request rooms ending in *-35, -36,* and *-37,* which are larger and have windows framing views of the lagoon. This hotel is open from Feb. until the end of Nov. Both the *Londra Palace* and *Metropole* offer considerably more panache as well as friendlier personnel at similar rates in the same neighborhood. 120

rooms. $134-$326 single CP, $211-$337 double CP. Perkhofer Family, props. (C-10) Utell. Phone 041-523-1580. Fax 041-520-9455. ★★★

(HOTEL) GARDENA, Santa Croce, 239, SANTA CROCE, in a traditional Venetian house facing the Rio Nuovo canal, across the Grand Canal from the railway station, is an excellent budget hotel for those in search of lodging away from Venice's commercial frenzy. Marble floors, quality fabrics, and *trompe l'oeil* murals sparkle throughout. The modest reception area adjoins a small lounge and TV room, both comfortably furnished with sofas and armchairs. Guests have breakfast in a simple room with bench seating and mediocre views of a courtyard. The small bar sits under open beams. Painted halls lead to midsize guest rooms in Venetian style, many with ghostly *trompe l'oeil* designs dimly haunting the walls. All have Italian-only TVs, minibars, and tiled shower-only baths with hair dryers. Request rooms facing the water, and note that corner rooms and *22* and *25* offer more space. The reception staff speaks English well. Those unable to book a waterside room here or who wish to be closer to the action might try the similarly priced *American*. 22 rooms. $120 single BB, $194 double BB. Mr. Martini, mgr. (C-10) Phone 041-523-5549. Fax 041-522-0782. ★★

GRAND HOTEL PRINCIPE, Lista di Spagna, 147, CANNAREGIO, between the *Amadeus* and *Bellini,* one block E of the railway station, comprises a multicolor jumble of six traditional buildings strung along a waterside terrace by a gondola landing. This is the quintessential budget-group hotel, and though it boasts Grand Canal frontage, individuals should look elsewhere. The big lobby is usually crowded with milling groups, and the worn seating lacks character and a few upholstered buttons. Both the large restaurant and evening piano bar open to the hotel's best feature, its long terrace, where guests can linger in the sun and watch ever-changing canal traffic. Accommodations are on the small side and come in a mix of styles from routine modern with out-of-the-catalog furnishings to older Venetian with gilt-framed mirrors and hand-painted dressers and nightstands. The only standardization guests can expect are TVs, minibars, and safes. Baths have showers, tubs, or both, and a few repel with peeling, water-stained ceilings. This is the Venetian equivalent of an airport hotel — convenient, commercial, cost-effective, devoid of character. Those who need rooms near the station should walk across the bridge and around the corner to the sibling *Gardena* or even slicker *Sofitel*. 151 rooms. $114-$177 single BB, $171-$240 double BB. Fabio Semigaglia, mgr. (C-10) Phone 041-220-4000. Fax 041-719061. ★★★

(HOTEL) GRITTI PALACE, Campo Santa Maria del Giglio, 2467, SAN MARCO, on the Grand Canal, near Piazza San Marco and the Santa Maria del Giglio landing, is the perennial rival to the *Cipriani* for honors as Venice's top hotel. Once the home of the Gritti doge, this four-story hotel in a 15th-century palazzo is smaller and more intimate than its competition, and it retains many ornate original furnishings. Another of the hotel's treasures is its staff, which is dignified — even reserved — yet goes at length to satisfy even the most demanding client. Guests can best soak up the history of this august place while lounging in the carpeted lobby. Gritti escutcheons emblazon much of the antique seating. The lovely restaurant serves fine meals beneath its beams, and a pianist entertains thrice weekly. In summer, guests migrate to the terrace for the chicest dining on the Grand Canal. Prices for meals and drinks are egregiously high. A free hourly launch runs to the sports facilities and beaches at Starwood's two Lido hotels, and this greatly enhances the value here in summer. The two conference rooms can seat 100 persons. Accommodations are unique, with superb antique furnishings, minibars, TVs, thermostats, and baths finished in red Verona marble and stocked with hair dryers, phones, and robes. The cramped seating arrangements in some rooms, the minimal counter space and tight showers in some baths, and the creaking of the old floors may irk some. The most spacious rooms face the *campo,* and the large corner doubles on the first and second floors have balconies surveying the canal. The few groups that book here do so off season. This is an outstandingly elegant hotel. Travelers seeking a lively atmosphere will probably prefer the *Danieli,* and those looking for opulence with a modicum of seclusion should set a course for the *Cipriani*. 93 rooms. $314 single, $519 double, $1194-$2389 in suites. Massimo Feriani, mgr. (C-10) LC, Utell. Phone 041-794611. Fax 041-520-0942. ★★★★★

(HOTEL) KETTE, San Marco, 2053, SAN MARCO, on the Rio delle Veste, just one tiny bridge from La Fenice, midway between Ponte dell'Accademia and Piazza San Marco, is one of the more polished hotels in its price range. Public rooms are of boutique scale, and there is no restaurant here besides the small breakfast nook, but the impression the hotel conveys is one of chilly sophistication. Much of this is due to a reception staff and concierge who behave as if this were the *Cipriani*. Motorists staying here get a 20 percent discount at a garage on Tronchetto on prior arrangement.

Choice Hotels International

FLORIDA 131

Pensacola
SLEEP INN
2591 Wilde Lake Blvd - 32526
(850) 941-0908 ● 1-800-SLEEP-INN (US&CN)
FL012
Features: 77 RMS. Seasonal outdoor pool. TAX 10.5%/XP 5.00
Points of interest: Arpt. 7 Mi. Bus & train 10 Mi. 5 restaurants 1/4 Mi. Five Flags Spdwy. 1 1/2 Mi. Golf 5 Mi. Civic ctr., Bayfront Auditorium, Saenger Theater, Wentworth Musm., Seville Qtr. & hist. dist. 10 Mi. Naval Air Station & Naval Aviation Musm. 12 Mi. Pensacola Beach 15 Mi.

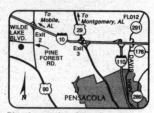

Directions: I-10 ex. 2 then S. 1 blk.

SEASONS	ONE PERSON	TWO PERSONS
11/01/99-05/15/00	55.00-119.00	55.00-119.00
05/16/00-10/01/00	55.00-129.00	55.00-129.00
10/02/00-10/31/00	55.00-119.00	55.00-119.00

Pensacola/
Pensacola Beach
CLARION SUITES
FL517   **Resort & Convention Center**
20 Via DeLuna, Pensacola Beach - 32561
(850) 932-4300 ● 1-800-CLARION (US&CN)
Features: 86 STES. Ktchnt., 2 remote ctrl. T.V's in-rm. Cribs. Pool. Mtng. rm. TAX 13.26%/XP 10.00
♦♦♦
AAA   Points of interest: Arpt. 11 Mi. Train 8 Mi. Bus 16 Mi. Golf, tennis, hist. trs. 1-5 Mi. Water sports 1/2 Mi. Naval mus., IMAX Theater 15 Mi.

Directions: Located on the gulf. I-10 ex. I-110 S.to beach, over toll bridge lt. to htl on rt.

SEASONS	ONE PERSON	TWO PERSONS
11/01/99-12/31/99	72.00-102.00	72.00-102.00
01/01/00-02/29/00	77.00-107.00	77.00-107.00
03/01/00-04/30/00	85.00-126.00	85.00-126.00
05/01/00-10/31/00	93.00-171.00	93.00-171.00

Pensacola/
Pensacola Beach
COMFORT INN
FL855   **40 Ft. Pickens Rd., Pensacola Beach - 32561**
(850) 934-5400 ● 1-800-228-5150 (US&CN)
Features: 99 RMS. Refrig/micro, coffee-maker in rm. TAX 14.5%/XP 10.00
Points of interest: Arpt. 14 Mi. Train 8 Mi. Naval Aviation Museum 15 Mi. Historic downtown 10 Mi. Gulf beach across st. Waterfront on Bay.

Directions: I-10 ex. 4 to I-110, follow sign to beaches.

SEASONS	ONE PERSON	TWO PERSONS
11/01/99-02/12/00	69.00-79.00	69.00-79.00
02/13/00-05/21/00	99.00-109.00	99.00-109.00
05/22/00-09/05/00	114.00-124.00	114.00-124.00
09/06/00-10/31/00	99.00-109.00	99.00-109.00

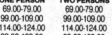
Pensacola Beach (see Pensacola)

Plant City
COMFORT INN
2003 South Frontage Rd - 33566
(813) 707-6000 ● 1-800-228-5150 (US&CN)
FL103
Features: 61 RMS. Free lcl. calls. VCR. micro/frig avail. Hairdryers, in-rm. movies. coffeemkrs. TAX 11.75%/XP 6.00
Points of interest: Arpt. 10 Mi. Tampa Bay Arpt. 25 Mi. Orlando Arpt. 45 Mi. Train, bus 2 Mi. Adventure Island 20 Mi. Busch Gardens 25 Mi. Disney World, Universal Studios, Sea World 45 Mi.

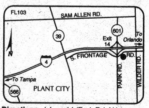

Directions: I-4 ex. 14 (Park Rd. N.) to South Frontage Rd.

SEASONS	ONE PERSON	TWO PERSONS
11/01/99-10/31/00	59.00-125.00	59.00-125.00

Port Charlotte
QUALITY INN
3400 Tamiami Trail - 33952
(941) 625-4181 ● 1-800-228-5151 (US&CN)
FL516
Features: 105 RMS. Microwave, refrig. in some rms. Coffee makers in all rms. TAX 10%/XP 6.00
Points of interest: Arpt. 35 Mi. Bus 1/4 Mi. Peace River Harbor 2 Mi. Fishermans Village (shops & rest.) 3 Mi. Texas Ranger Std. 4 Mi. Boca Granda
♦♦♦
AAA   Historic Area & beaches 17 Mi. Golf & fishing nrby. Warm Mineral Springs 10 Mi.

Directions: I-75 S. ex. 30 W. to US 41 N. 2 Mi. to hotel.

SEASONS	ONE PERSON	TWO PERSONS
11/01/99-10/31/00	50.00-130.00	50.00-130.00

Car/Hotel Voucher

A combined car/hotel voucher can be used for both accommodation and car rental, since sometimes the two services are sold together as a package (see below).

ASTOR TRAVEL SERVICES

1240 Bay Street, Suite 302
Toronto, Ontario M5R 2A7 CANADA

CONFIRMATION NO. _____

DATE CONFIRMED _____

BOOKED THROUGH _____

PLEASE PROVIDE _____   PARTY OF _____

WITH _____

FROM_____   TO _____   NTS/DAYS _____   MEALS_____

RATE $ _____   DEPOSIT _____

REMARKS_____

TO _____   _____

ADDRESS_____   TELEPHONE _____

_____   CDW/LDW _____   ALI _____

_____   PAI _____   PEP _____

☐ Unlimited Mileage   ☐ KM / MLS Free   Each Additional @ _____   TAX _____

☐ Hotel has been GUARANTEED for late arrival. Please cancel by _____to avoid penalties.

Reprinted courtesy of Astor Travel Services

Hotel Vouchers

ASTOR TRAVEL SERVICES	DATE	CONFIRMED BY	
1240 Bay Street, Suite 302			
Toronto, Ontario M5R 2A7 CANADA			

PLEASE PROVIDE OUR CLIENT(S)	PARTY OF	WITH THE FOLLOWING SERVICES	

COMMENCING	TERMINATING	NO. NIGHTS	EXP ARRIV TIME	VIA	SPECIAL REMARKS

TO

RATE	PLAN	DEPOSIT PAID AMOUNT	DATE DEPOSIT PAID	
	EP MAP AP			BY _____
	☐ ☐ ☐			

1. CLIENT INTRODUCTION   YOUR UTMOST COOPERATION IS REQUESTED TO SATISFY OUR CLIENTS.
CLIENTS WILL SETTLE IN FULL FOR SERVICES RENDERED AT TIME OF DEPARTURE.

ASTOR TRAVEL SERVICES	DATE	CONFIRMED BY	
1240 Bay Street, Suite 302			
Toronto, Ontario M5R 2A7 CANADA			

PLEASE PROVIDE OUR CLIENT(S)	PARTY OF	WITH THE FOLLOWING SERVICES	

COMMENCING	TERMINATING	NO. NIGHTS	EXP ARRIV TIME	VIA	SPECIAL REMARKS

TO

RATE	PLAN	DEPOSIT PAID AMOUNT	DATE DEPOSIT PAID	
	EP MAP AP			BY _____
	☐ ☐ ☐			

1. CLIENT INTRODUCTION   YOUR UTMOST COOPERATION IS REQUESTED TO SATISFY OUR CLIENTS.
CLIENTS WILL SETTLE IN FULL FOR SERVICES RENDERED AT TIME OF DEPARTURE.

Vouchers reprinted courtesy of Astor Travel Services

5

Car Rentals

It is particularly important to offer a rental car with all corporate reservations and with most leisure sales. Otherwise the client will often book a car upon arrival in the destination, resulting in lost commissions for the agency.

CAR RENTAL COMPANIES

Worldwide

- Hertz (the largest international car rental company, generally located in the best airport in-terminal locations)
- Avis ("We try harder")
- Budget

Canada

- Tilden is based in Canada and is the Canadian affiliate of the National Car Rental system
- E-Cars Rent-A-Car
- Discount Car and Truck Rentals
- HOJ Car and Truck Rentals
- Rent-a-Wreck
- Rite-A-Way Car and Truck Rentals

In addition, many U.S. and international car rental companies have Canadian locations.

United States

- National Car Rental
- Dollar Car Rental
- Alamo Car Rental
- Thrifty Car Rental
- Value Rent-A-Car
- Sears Car Rental
- Enterprise Rent-A-Car
- Payless Car Rental

Europe

- Europcar
- Kemwell
- Wood—United Kingdom

In addition, there are brokers representing a number of car rental companies (for example, Auto Europe). For long-term leasing, you can also contact a car dealer.

Many of the car rental companies are also set up on the agency's computer reservation system (SABRE, for example).

CHOOSING A VEHICLE

Price is always a significant factor when selecting a vehicle, but it is also important to know the client's needs when offering car rental alternatives. For example, renting the cheapest car in Europe means a standard (manual) transmission vehicle, not the best choice for someone who has always driven an automatic. Or a package deal may include a car, but if the family has three husky teenage boys travelling with their parents, getting the small, package-included car may not be a good idea.

You will need to determine the following details, before recommending a specific type of rental vehicle:

1. How many people will be riding in the car?

2. Are any of the people tall or extra large (ask delicately!), and if so, how many?

3. How much time will be spent in the vehicle?

4. How far will your clients be travelling?

5. How much luggage will be stored in the vehicle?

6. What extra features are required (air conditioning, convertible roof, etc.)?

7. Do your clients prefer standard or automatic transmission?

8. What level of luxury and comfort do they desire?

In the following table, add examples of the types of cars listed.

Types of Cars

Code	Types (smallest to largest)	Examples
ECAR	Economy or subcompact	_____
CCAR	Compact	_____
ICAR	Intermediate or midsize	_____
SCAR	Full size, 2-door	_____
FCAR	Full size, 4-door	_____
LCAR	Luxury	_____

In addition, station wagons, sports cars, vans, RVs (recreational vehicles), campers, and trucks are available for rent. An RV is a good alternative to car rental in some situations, since it not only provides transportation, but also accommodation, bedding, cooking/eating utensils, a stove, and a refrigerator. All are included in the price.

Sales Tips

Commission is paid on the amount of a sale, so the smallest car with the fewest options will be the cheapest rental yielding the least amount of commission. Remember too that the smallest/cheapest car will not always suit your client's needs. Therefore, always ask clients if they want to upgrade the vehicle category.

TYPES OF CAR RENTALS

There are various types of rental methods, and each one calculates the rate on a different basis, either by time or mileage, or by using a combination of the two.

Unlimited mileage. The rate is solely based on the number of days or weeks of the rental, with no additional charge for miles or kilometres driven. There may be a charge for gas (sometimes the car must be returned with a full tank or else the client is charged an equivalent amount; other times a charge will be based on how much gas was in the car when it was rented).

Time and mileage. The rate is based on the number of days or weeks of rental time, plus a further charge per mile/kilometre driven (there are no free miles).

Time and limited mileage. The rate is based on the number of days or weeks of rental time, plus a further charge per mile or kilometre driven beyond a set number of free miles/kilometres; for example, the weekly rate may allow 1,000 free kilometres per week.

Lease. This is a long-term rental arrangement, where the charges are based both on time and mileage, often with a number of free miles/kilometres included. It may be structured like a purchase, sometimes with a guaranteed buy-back at the end of the lease period by the leasing company. This method is commonly used in Europe where a client wishes to use the car for local transportation and then ship it back to North America afterwards.

Insurance, taxes, and fuel are not included in any of these arrangements unless specifically provided by the rental agency agreement. Time rentals will impose an additional charge for late returns (late charges may be calculated by the minute, hour, or day). Be especially careful of additional day charges in the event of late return, since this can add substantially to the final cost.

DROP-OFF CHARGES AND OTHER RESTRICTIONS

With rentals, it is assumed that the basic charge will refer to cars that are picked up at and returned to the same location. Rentals may also be arranged one way (usually at an extra charge), referred to as a *one-way rental*. A *drop-off charge* may be incurred when the vehicle is not returned to the same location where it was picked up. Some rental companies will not impose a drop-off charge if the vehicle is returned to another location within the same city or state. Also, it may be possible to avoid drop-off charges when travelling a popular route, but this is entirely at the discretion of the particular supplier.

It is also common for restrictions to be imposed regarding where a car may be driven. Often an international border cannot be crossed, and sometimes there may be restrictions against crossing a province or state boundary.

It goes without saying that each driver must possess a valid driving licence. Usually a Canadian or U.S. licence will suffice; however, when travelling in any other country, a driver should investigate obtaining an International Driver's Licence (available from the Canadian or American Automobile Associations). Also, there may be minimum age restrictions for each driver. Finally, for insurance purposes, each driver should be a co-renter on the rental contract.

RATES

Rates for the car are calculated either daily or by the week. Some car rental companies have weekend specials or three-day rates. If a client requires a long-term rental (more than seventeen days in Europe), leasing is the least expensive method.

Car rental rates are normally calculated on a 24-hour basis so a car picked up on March 1 at 10:00 a.m., for example, and returned on March 8 at 10:00 a.m. is considered to be a seven-day rental; however, if the car is returned at 12:00 noon, it is considered an eight-day rental.

Additional amounts may be charged for ski racks, baby seats, or other special features. And taxes and insurance are added to the basic rental rates. Note in particular that the cost of collision damage waiver insurance significantly increases the cost of a car rental.

INSURANCE

Each client should first check with his or her own auto insurer to determine what coverage already exists under the person's own automobile insurance policy. Many policies will cover injury sustained while driving a rental car. And some policies may also cover other aspects (for example, liability). Also, note that some credit card companies will provide coverage for damage to a rental car, when the car is driven by the credit card holder and provided the card is used to pay for the rental.

The charges for insurance can quickly mount and may equal or exceed the base rental charges. It is therefore important to know what coverage is needed and what are the various types of insurance. Following are the types of coverage:

Collision damage waiver (CDW). This coverage will compensate for accident damages to the rental car, and may or may not include a deductible amount (an amount not covered by the CDW).

Loss damage waiver (LDW). This coverage will cover not only accident damages but also losses due to theft or vandalism.

Personal accident insurance (PAI). This insurance (also called *personal injury protection*, or *PIP*) covers personal injury and provides basic protection.

Additional liability insurance (ALI). This insurance (also called *supplemental liability insurance*, or *SLI*) provides additional personal injury protection, above the basic PAI.

Personal effects protection (PEP). This insurance covers personal possessions such as clothing and luggage. Note that this may already be covered under a client's homeowner insurance. However, collectables or valuable items (jewellery or expensive cameras) may be inadequately protected under either the client's own policy or under a PEP policy, in which case the client should add the necessary coverage before travelling.

Cancellation insurance. This provides coverage for rental charges incurred notwithstanding cancellation (for example, charges for a prepaid car rental), but reimbursement is generally limited to cancellation arising from death, illness, or bereavement situations.

INFORMATION REQUIRED TO RESERVE A CAR

1. Name(s), address, and phone number for client;

2. Size of car needed;

3. Number of passengers who will be travelling together;

4. Whether automatic or standard transmission is required;

5. Date vehicle is needed;

6. Price range preferred;

7. Confirmation of who will be driving;

8. Credit card information from client;

9. Whether the trip will be one way or round trip;

10. Whether the rate is based on time, on mileage, or on a combination of the two;

11. Where the car will be picked up;

12. Insurance/collision damage waiver options;

13. Special requests (air conditioning, convertible or sunroof, disabled passengers, etc.).

WAYS TO RESERVE RENTAL CARS

1. Telephone reservation with the rental company's local office;

2. In person at the rental company office;

3. By calling the rental company's toll-free number;

4. Via a computer reservation system terminal.

Car Rental Terms

BOOT	The trunk of a car, used to store luggage, etc. (U.K. term).
EQUIPMENT	Features that are provided with a car, such as automatic transmission or power brakes.
OPTIONS	Extra features, not part of the standard equipment; will be made available at an increased cost (for example, child seats, roof rack).
PETROL	Gasoline (U.K. term).
ONE-WAY RENTAL	A car rental for a trip from an origin to a destination, with no return.
FLY/DRIVE	A package priced to include flight and a rental car.
RENTAL LOCATION	The site from which the car will be rented and picked up.
IN TERMINAL	A car rental agency with a rental counter located inside the airport terminal.
OFF AIRPORT	A car rental agency with a rental office located outside the airport terminal.
COURTESY PICK-UP	Passenger pick-up, by van, from the airport to the off-airport car rental office, provided at no extra charge.
EXPRESS SERVICE	Service offered by a car rental company (often prepaid) and in particular used for business clientele, to avoid waiting in line for service when picking up or returning a car.
RATES	Basic charges for car rental, may be charged for daily, weekly, or special rentals; usually does

	not include gas, taxes, or insurance, and may or may not include mileage.
CORPORATE RATES	Special rates offered to business clientele.
WEEKEND RATES	Special rental rate available only for weekend rentals (each company with weekend rates defines the qualifying days and times).
DEDUCTIBLE	The portion of the insured value that is not recoverable (always deducted before any insurance proceeds are paid); the client pays this amount in the event of a claim.
INCLUSIONS	The features included in the car rental price.
EXCLUSIONS	The features excluded from the car rental price.
TERMS AND CONDITIONS	The contract by which the car is rented, detailing the car to be provided, the various charges, the restrictions on use, and the liability of the renter.
GEOGRAPHIC RESTRICTIONS	Restrictions limiting the use of a car to specified areas or prohibiting use in specified areas (often there are restrictions against driving the car across an international border).
LIABILITY	Legal responsibility (in insurance, refers to coverage against injury to third parties).

Avis Worldwide Directory

AVIS Latin America

HONDURAS

The information in this section is provided as a guideline. Full details are available from the:

RESERVATION OFFICE

Telephone: 504-322510 .... Telex: 311-1473 AMA HQ

CAR NAME
GRP MODEL (or similar)   DESCRIPTION

A . . Suzuki Sedan. . . . . 2DR, 4S, MAN, R, AC
B . . Suzuko Jeep . . . . 2DR, 4S, R/C, AC, 4WD
C . . Toyota Tercel. . . . . 4DR, 5S, MAN, R/C, AC
D . . Nissan Vanetta Microbus . . . . 4DR, 5S, MAN, R/C, AC
E . . . Toyota Landcruiser. . . . . 2DR, 5S, R/C, AC, 4WD
F . . . Toyota Pickup Double Cab. . . . . . . 4DR, 5S, R/C, AC, 4WD
G . . Nissan Sunny . . . . 4DR, 5S, MAN, R, AC

The following information provides additions or exceptions to the general information section contained at the front of this directory.
Age: Minimum age is 25 with Avis-honoured charge card, travel vouchers or cash. Maximum none.
Tax: 5%
Special Services: Chauffeur drive and delivery/collection service available.

LOCATIONS

• **TEGUCIGALPA**
Address: Boulevard Suyapa HO4/3331
Frente Canal 5 TV Edif Agencia Marinakys
Telephone: 504-322510
Telex: 311-1473 AMA HO
Hours: 0700-1900 Mo-Su

Address: Hotel Honduras Maya HO7/3355
P.O. Box 1208
Telephone: 504-323191
Telex: 311-1473 AMA HO
Hours: 0700-1900 Mo-Su

HEADQUARTERS OFFICE

Address: Boulevard Suyapa Frente Canal 5 TV
Edif Agencia Marinakys
Telephone: 504-322510   **Telex:** 311-1473 AMA HO

MEXICO

The information in this section is provided as a guideline. Full details are available from the:

RESERVATION OFFICE

Telephone: (5) 5-88-88-88 . . . . **Telex:** 1762483

CAR NAME
GRP MODEL (or similar)   DESCRIPTION

A . . . VW Beetle . . . . 2DR, 5S, MAN
        Nissan Sentra . . . . 3DR, 5S, MAN
C . . Nissan Sentra . . . . 2DR, 5S, MAN
        VW Golf . . . . 4DR, 5S, R, MAN
D . . Ford Tempo . . . . 5DR., 5S, R, MAN
        VW Jetta . . . . 4DR, 5S, R, MAN
        Plymouth Shadow . . . . 4DR, 5S, R, MAN
E . . Nissan Sentra. . . . . 4DR, 5S, R, MAN
        VW Golf. . . . . 4DR, 5S, R, AC, MAN
F . . Ford Tempo . . . . 5DR, 5S, R, AC, MAN
        VW Jetta . . . . 4DR, 5S, R, AC, MAN
        Plymouth Shadow . . . . 4DR, 5S, R, AC, MAN
G . . Nissan Sentra . . . . 4DR, 5S, R, AC, MAN
        VW Golf. 4DR, 5S, R, AC, A
H . . Ford Tempo . . . . 5DR, 5S, R, AC, A
        VW Jetta . . . . 4DR, 5S, R, AC, A
        . . . . 4DR, 5S, R, AC, A
        Plymouth Shadow . . . . 4DR, 5S, R, AC, A
I . . VW Topless . . . . 2DR, 5S, MAN
J . . VW Quantum . . . . 4DR, 5S, R, AC, A
K . . Oldsmobile Cutlass . . . . 4DR, 6S, R, AC, A
L . . Buick Century . . . . 4DR, 6S, R, AC, A
        Ford Taurus . . . . 4DR, 6S, R, AC, A
M . . VW Minibus . . . . 4DR, 6S, R, AC, A
N . . Chevy Suburban . . . . 5DR, 9S, R, MAN
O . . Nissan Jeep . . . . 4DR, 4S, MAN
P . . . VW Sunroof . . . . 2DR, 5S, MAN

The following information provides additions or exceptions to the general information section contained at the front of this directory
Age: Minimum age is 21 with Avis or Avis-honoured charge card, ACTO, Avis or Avis-honoured travel voucher or MCO supported by major charge card; 25 with Avis or Avis-honoured travelvoucher or MCO not supported by major charge card. Maximum 70.
Tax: 15%. Except 6% in Chetumal, Ciudad Juarez, La Pax, Matamoros, Mexicali, Nuevo Laredo, Piedras Negras, Reynosa, San Jose del Cabo, Tijuana.
Credit Identification: No cash rentals in Mexico.
All rentals require charge card number and expiration date and require 48 hours advance notice for cancellation. If renter is 12 or more hours late for a rental a $50.00 'no-show' charge is applied to the charge card.
Special Services: Chauffeur drive (only in Mexico City) and delivery/collection service.
One-Way: a) One-way rentals into Central and South America not allowed. b) One-way rentals not available to or from Coxumel Island. c) Cars allowed to terminate in certain USA cities only on request. d) For rentals outside Mexico territory - additional Public Liability Coverage must be taken. Available at time of rental. e) Cars left in Los Angeles or San Diego may only be returned to the airport location.

LOCATIONS

• **ACAPULCO** ACA/4739
Address: International Airport
Telephone: (748) 4-16-33
Telex: 16845
Hours: 0700-2200 Mo-Su
Address: Monaco Hotel Lobby CP39670 . . . . T5R/4298
Telephone: (748) 5-64-15 / 5-64-67
Hours: 0900-1700 Mo-Su
• **AGUASCALIENTES**
Address: Airport AGU/4742
Hours: 0800-1000, 1600-1930 Mo-Su
Address: Jose Ma. Chavex 1110 . . . . AQT/6142
CP20270
Telephone: (491) 6-04-08
Hours: 0900-1400, 1600-1900 Mo-Fr; 0900-1400 Sa
• **CABO SAN LUCAS**
Refer to San Jose Del Cabo.
• **CANCUN**
Address: International Airport CP31000 . . . . . CUN/4743
Telephone: (988) 4-23-28 / 4-21-47
Telex: 753878
Hours: 0700-2100 Mo-Su
Address: Hotel Cancun Viva CP77500 . . . . CU1/4744
Telephone: (988) 3-08-28
Telex: 753878
Hours: 0700-2100 Mo-Su
Address: Mayfair Shopping Centre MU9/4617
Telephone: (988) 3-08-03 / 3-00-04
Telex: 753878
Hours: 0800-1300, 1600-1900 Mo-Su
• **CHETUMAL** AFK/1234
Address: Del Prado Hotel Lobby
Av Heroes & Chapultepec
(services Chetumal Airport). . . . .
Telephone: (983) 2-05-44
Telex: 753878
Hours: 0800-1300, 1600-1900 Mo-Su
• **CHIHUAHUA**
Address: Chihuahua Airport CUU/4746
Hours: 0830-2100 Mo-Su
Address: Av Universidad 1703 CP 31240 . . . . . CU3/4747
Telephone: (14) 4-19-99
Telex: 349786
Hours: 0830-1900 Mo-Fr; 0830-0830-1300 Sa
• **CIUDAD JUAREZ**
Address: International Airport CP 32690 . . . . . CJS/4750
Hours: 0845-2030 Mo-Su
Address: 16 de Septiembre Av CJS/4750
999 Ote Cp32000
Telephone: (16) 14-00-19
Telex: 33337
Hours: 0830-1300,1500-1900 Mo-Fr; 0830-1400 Sa; closed Su
• **CIUDAD OBREGON**
Address: International Airport CEN/3855
Hours: meets all commercial flights
Address: Hidalgo 802 B CP85000 . . . . CE6/3853
Telephone: (641) 4-81-44
Hours: 0800-1300, 1500-1900 Mo-Su
• **COATZACOALCOS / MINATITLAN**
Address: Airport MTT/4751
Hours: 0800-1300,1500-1800 Mo-Sa; 0800-0900,2000-2100 Su

Address: l. De La Llave 314. CP 96400 . . . . . . CZA/4752
Telephone: (921) 2-34-99 / 2-90-20
Hours: 0800-1300, 1500-1800 Mo-Sa; 0800-1400 Su
• **COLIMA**
Address: Plaza Del Rey Lcl. G5 CP 28000
Telephone: (331) 2-91-96 / 2-58-88
Hours: 0900-2000 Mo-Fr; 0900-1400 Sa; closed Su
• **COZUMEL**
Address: International Airport CZM/4753
Telephone: (987) 2-00-99
Telex: 753878
Hours: 0800-1900 Mo-Su
Address: El Presidente Hotel Lobby CP 77600 . . CZZ/4754
Telephone: (987) 2-02-19 / 2-03-22
Hours: 0800-1300, 1600-1900 Mo-Su
Address: Cruiseship Pier GN8/1711
Telephone: (987) 2-02-19
Telex: 665874
Hours: meets all ship arrivals/departures between 0800-1300, 1600-1900 Mo-Su.
• **CULIACAN**
Address: Airport CP 80130 . . . . CUL/4755
Telephone: (671) 4-40-87
Telex: 665874
Hours: 0800-1800 Mo-Su
Address: Blvd Madero 343 Poniente CP80000 CCY/4756
Telephone: (671) 2-23-56 / 5-02-22
Telex: 665874
Hours: 0800-1800 Mo-Sa; 0800-1400, 1600-1900 Su
• **GUADALAJARA**
Address: International Airport CP 45659 . . . . . GDL/4575
Telephone: (36) 89-02-21 / 89-05-89
Telex: 682725
Hours: 0600-0030 Mo-Su
Address: Fiesta Americana Hotel GD3/4759
Vallarta Av. & Mazamitla St. CP44100
Telephone: (36) 15-48-25 / 30-15-70
Telex: 68-2725
Hours: 0900-1400, 1600-1900 Mo-Sa; closed Su
Address: Ave ninos Heroes. GD2/4763
942 CP44100
Telephone: (36) 13-90-11
Hours: 682725
• **HERMOSILLO**
Address: International Airport HMO/4760
Hours: 0900-1930 Mo-Su
Address: Blvd. Kino Y5 De Febrero HMS/4761
Plaza Pitic 21-A CP83150
Telephone: (621) 5-14-55 / 4-66-46
Hours: 0900-1300, 1600-1900 Mo-Su
• **HUATULCO** PIH/3784
Address: International Airport
Telephone: 18857
Hours: meets all commercial flights
• **IXTAPA / ZIHUATANEJO**
Address: International Airport LAP/4764
Telephone: (743) 4-29-32 / 4-22-48
Hours: 0700-2200 Mo-Su
• **LA PAZ**
Address: International Airport LAP/4764
Telephone: (682)2-18-13 / 2-23-45
Telex: 52234
Hours: 0700-1730 Mo-Su
Address: Manuel Pineda 201 CP23000
Telephone: (682) 2-26-51 / 2-95-13
Telex: 52234
Hours: 0800-1900 Mo-Sa; closed Su
• **MANZANILLO**
Address: International Airport ZLO/4767
Telephone: (333) 3-15-90
Hours: 0700-0900, 1400-2100 Mo-Su
Address: KM 9 Carr. A. Santiago CP28200 . . . . ZL1/4768
Telephone: (333) 3-01-90 / 3-02-38 / 3-01-94
Telex: 62543
Hours: 0900-1400, 1600-1900 Mo-Sa; 0900-1300 Su
Address: Club Las Hadas Hotel P4D/6130
Av. Audiencia Y Tesoro S/N CP28200
Telephone: (333) 3-08-88 ext. 2285
Telex: 62543
Hours: 0900-1400, 1600-1900 Mo-Su
• **MATAMOROS**
Address: International Airport MAM/4769
Hours: 1130-1230, 1700-1830 Mo-Sa; 1100-1300, 1700-1800 Su

EXERCISES

A client is interested in renting a car during her visit to Chihuahua, Mexico, and needs some advice from you. Please refer to the extract from the Avis Worldwide Directory on the previous page to provide the client with the following information:

1. Give the location of the Avis office where the client could pick up the car in Chihuahua.

   _____

2. Find a phone number that could be used to call from Canada to reserve the car in Mexico.

   _____

REPLICATED EXAMPLES OF CAR RENTAL RATE SHEETS

Car-Go Rental Cars: Renting a Car in Canada

Terms and Conditions

- Car groups O–E offer 1,400 free kilometres per week or 200 free km per additional day
- Car group 1 (minivan) offers 700 free km per week or 100 free km per additional day
- Cost for each additional km varies by car group
- Minimum length of rental is three days
- Rates are prediscounted
- Rates do not include loss damage (LDW), air conditioning, personal accident insurance (PAI), refuelling service charges, gasoline, or applicable taxes
- Seasonal surcharge of $7.00 per day may be in effect in July and August, in certain cities
- One-way rentals are subject to availability and applicable one-way service fee
- 24-hour advance reservation is required. Confirmation is based on availability
- Rates are valid at participating locations
- Renter must meet our minimum age, driver, and renter qualifications

Low season: April 1 to June 30

Car Group	3–7 days	8–13 days	14–20 days	21+ days	Extra Kilometres
O (Economy)	$212.00	$29.00	$28.00	$27.00	$0.15
A (Compact 2-dr.)	222.00	31.00	30.00	29.00	0.15
B (Compact 4-dr.)	232.00	33.00	32.00	31.00	0.15
C (Intermediate)	242.00	34.00	33.00	32.00	0.15
D (Full size 2-dr.)	252.00	35.00	34.00	33.00	0.17
E (Full size 4-dr.)	262.00	37.00	36.00	35.00	0.17
1 (Minivan)	299.00	42.00	41.00	40.00	0.20

Per Day Rate applies to columns 3–7 days, 8–13 days, 14–20 days, 21+ days.

High Season: July 1 to September 15

Car Group	Per Day Rate				
	3–7 days	8–13 days	14–20 days	21+ days	Extra Kilometres
O (Economy)	$239.00	$34.00	$33.00	$32.00	$0.15
A (Compact 2-dr.)	259.00	36.00	35.00	34.00	0.15
B (Compact 4-dr.)	269.00	38.00	37.00	36.00	0.15
C (Intermediate)	289.00	41.00	40.00	39.00	0.15
D (Full size 2-dr.)	299.00	42.00	41.00	40.00	0.17
E (Full size 4-dr.)	309.00	44.00	43.00	42.00	0.17
1 (Minivan)	379.00	54.00	53.00	52.00	0.20

Off Season: September 16 to March 31

Car Group	Per Day Rate				
	3–7 days	8–13 days	14–20 days	21+ days	Extra Kilometres
O (Economy)	$219.00	$31.00	$30.00	$29.00	$0.15
A (Compact 2-dr.)	229.00	32.00	31.00	30.00	0.15
B (Compact 4-dr.)	249.00	35.00	34.00	33.00	0.15
C (Intermediate)	259.00	36.00	35.00	34.00	0.15
D (Full size 2-dr.)	269.00	38.00	37.00	36.00	0.17
E (Full size 4-dr.)	279.00	39.00	38.00	37.00	0.17
1 (Minivan)	299.00	42.00	41.00	40.00	0.20

EXERCISES—Car-Go Rental Cars

Make the following car rental cost calculations based on the Car-Go Rental Cars rates listed on the previous pages.

1. Car Group B rented in Halifax for 18 days in February (3,524 km travelled).

   *Time:*_____ *Mileage:*_____

   Total: _____

2. Compact 4-door rented in Toronto for 14 days in early September (2,956 km travelled).

   *Time:*_____ *Mileage:*_____

   Total: _____

3. Car Group O rented in Saskatoon for 5 days in March (1,392 km travelled).

   *Time:*_____ *Mileage:*_____

   Total: _____

4. Economy car rented in Montreal for 25 days in March (3,024 km travelled).

   *Time:*_____ *Mileage:*_____

   Total: _____

5. How far in advance does the passenger have to book these rates?

   _____

6. Identify some additional charges the passenger may have to pay.

   _____

   _____

Auto-Europe Car Rental
(Exclusive of CDW and tax)

AUTO EUROPE   RATE SHEETS
(EXCLUSIVE OF CDW AND TAX)

AUSTRIA

RATES IN AUS   TAX 21.2% (33.3% FOR RENTALS OF 21 + DAYS)

Group	Example of Car Type	4-7 Days	8-13 Days (per day)	14 Days (per day)
A	OPEL CORSA 1.4i	2247	321	302
B	OPEL ASTRA 1.4i	2786	398	374
C	OPEL VECTRA 1.6I	3948	564	530
D	OPEL KADETT 1.6i (A)	3948	564	530
E	OPEL OMEGA 2.0i	12299	1757	1652
F	MERCEDES 190E	13643	1949	1832

BELGIUM

RATES IN BFR   TAX 25%

Group	Example of Car Type	4-7 Days	8-13 Days (per day)	14 Days (per day)
A	OPEL CORSA 1.0	4487	641	603
B	OPEL KADETT 1.4i	6055	865	813
C	OPEL VECTRA 1.6i	7896	1128	1060
D	CITROEN BX 1.6 (A)	9471	1353	1272
E	VW PASSAT	15267	2181	2050
F	CITROEN EX 1.9 (SW)	12894	1842	1731

DENMARK

RATES IN DKR   TAX 25%

Group	Example of Car Type	4-7 Days	8-13 Days (per day)	14 Days (per day)
A	FORD FIESTA 1.0	1435	205	193
B	OPEL KADETT 1.4DX	1785	255	240
C	OPEL VECTRA 1.6i	2471	353	332
D	OPEL OMEGA 2.0DL	3563	509	478
E	BMW 320i	3962	566	532
F	BMW 520i	4305	615	578

FRANCE

RATES IN FFR   TAX 22%

Group	Example of Car Type	4-7 Days	8-13 Days (per day)	14 Days (per day)
A	OPEL CORSA VIVA 1.0	1001	143	134
B	OPEL KADETT LS 1.4	1477	211	198
C	OPEL VECTRA GL 1.6	2170	310	291
D	RENAULT CLIO 1.4RT (A)	2037	291	274
E	OPEL OMEGA 2.0 GL	2996	428	402
F	RENAULT 25 GTS 2.0 (A)	4340	620	583

CONDITIONS

Normal one-way policy applies. Reservation Required 48 hours in advance, minimum rental period as shown above.

Price Includes—Unlimited Free Mileage Only.
Price Excludes—Local Taxes, CDW, PAI, TP.
Rates are subject to change without notice.
Car "groups" only can be reserved.

GERMANY

RATES IN DMK   TAX 14%

Group	Example of Car Type	4-7 Days	8-13 Days (per day)	14+ Days (per day)
O	OPEL CORSA	217	31	29
A	VW POLO	252	36	34
B	VW GOLF	280	40	38
C	AUDI 80	392	56	53
D	VW GOLF (A)	462	66	62
E	AUDI 100	574	82	77

GREECE

RATES IN USD   TAX 18%

Group	Example of Car Type	4-7 Days	8-13 Days (per day)	14+ Days (per day)
A	SUBARU M 70DL	210	30	29
B	NISSAN CHERRY 1.0	238	34	33
C	NISSAN SUNNY 1.3	287	41	40
D	NISSAN SUNNY 1.5(AC)	357	51	50
F	NISSAN SUNNY 1.3(A)(AC)	350	50	49

Groups D and F available in Athens and Thessaloniki only

HOLLAND

RATES IN DFL   TAX 18.5%

Group	Example of Car Type	4-7 Days	8-13 Days (per day)	14+ Days (per day)
A	CITROEN AX 11	287	41	39
B	FORD FIESTA 1.1 CHEERS	343	49	47
C	FORD ESCORT 1.4CLI	434	62	59
D	FORD ORION 1.4CLI	574	82	78
E	OPEL VECTRA 1.6i GL	658	94	89
F	OPEL VECTRA 2.0i GLS	959	137	130

IRELAND

RATES IN IRL   TAX 10%

Group	Example of Car Type	4-7 Days	8-13 Days (per day)	14+ Days (per day)
A	FORD FIESTA	161	23	22
B	OPEL KADETT 1.3	203	29	27
C	OPEL VECTRA 1.6 GL	266	38	36
D	NISSAN MICRA 1.0 (A)	301	43	40
E	OPEL KADETT 1.3 (SW)	329	47	44
F	TOYOTA CARINA 1.6 (A)	441	63	59

ISRAEL

RATES IN USD   TAX 0%

Group	Example of Car Type	4-7 Days	8-13 Days (per day)	14+ Days (per day)
P	AUTOBIANCHI Y10	259	37	35
A	FIAT UNO STING	273	39	37
B	FIAT UNO (AC)	350	50	47
C	PEUGEOT 309 1.4 (AC)	441	63	59
D	SUBARU 1.6 (AC)	483	69	65
E	SUBARU 1.6 (A) (AC)	574	82	77

● Auto-Europe Car Rental
(Exclusive of CDW and tax)

AUTO EUROPE
(EXCLUSIVE OF CDW and TAX)

ITALY
RATES IN LIT · TAX 19%

Group	Example of Car Type	4-7 Days	8-13 Days (per day)	14 Days (per day)
A	FIAT PANDA 750 CL	294000	42000	39500
B	OPEL CORSA 1.0	349300	49900	46900
C	RENAULT CLIO	415100	59300	55700
D	OPEL VECTRA 1.4 GL	511700	73100	68700
E	LANCIA DEDRA 1.6	604800	86400	81200
F	OPLE OMEGA 1.8 (AC)	618100	88300	83000

SPAIN   MAINLAND & BALERICS
RATES IN PTS · TAX 13%

Group	Example of Car Type	4-7 Days	8-13 Days (per day)	14+ Days (per day)
A	FIAT UNO 45	24850	3550	3340
B	RENAULT CLIO 1.2	28910	4130	3880
C	OPEL ASTRA GL 1.4	35280	5040	4740
D	RENAULT CHAMADE 1.4 (AC)	36890	5270	4950
E	RENAULT19CHAMADE1.7 (A)	40110	5730	5390
F	RENAULT10CHAMADE 1.7(AC)	41720	5960	5600

NORWAY
RATES IN NKR · TAX 20%

Group	Example of Car Type	4-7 Days	8-13 Days (per day)	14 Days (per day)
A	FORD FIESTA	1953	279	262
B	FORD ESCORT 1.6i	2303	329	309
C	FORD SIERRA 2.0L	2709	387	364
D	VOLVO 440	3206	458	431
E	FORD SIERRA 2.0 (A)	4249	607	571
F	FORD SIERRA (SW)	6818	974	916

SWEDEN
RATES IN SKR · TAX 25%

Group	Example of Car Type	4-7 Days	8-13 Days (per day)	14+ Days (per day)
A	FORD FIESTA	1897	271	255
B	VW GOLF	2226	318	299
C	FORD SIERRA	2877	411	386
D	VOLVO 740	4865	695	653
E	VOLVO 745 (SW)	5145	735	691
F	SAAB 9000 CDi (AC)	6307	901	847

POLAND
RATES IN DMK · TAX 0%

Group	Example of Car Type	4-7 Days	8-13 Days (per day)	14 Days (per day)
A	VW POLO 1.3 CL	588	84	79
B	OPEL KADETT 1.4i LS	777	111	104
C	FORD SIERRA 2.0i	868	124	117
D	AUDI 80 1.8 S	1043	149	140

SWITZERLAND
RATES IN SFR · TAX 0%

Group	Example of Car Type	4-7 Days	8-13 Days (per day)	14+ Days (per day)
I	FIAT PANDA 1.0	210	30	28
A	OPEL CORSA 1.4	280	40	38
B	OPEL ASTRA 1.4	322	46	43
C	OPEL VECTRA 2.0	378	54	50
D	OPEL VECTRA 2.0 (A)	406	58	54
E	OPEL OMEGA 2.4 (A)	679	97	91

PORTUGAL
RATES IN ESP · TAX 17%

Group	Example of Car Type	4-7 Days	8-13 Days (per day)	14 Days (per day)
A	OPEL CORSA 1.0	20860	2980	2800
B	FIAT UNO 45	26390	3770	3540
C	OPEL CORSA 1.2 TR GL	30730	4390	4130
D	VW GOLF 1.3	35140	5020	4720
E	OPEL KADETT 1.4	41720	5960	5600
F	OPEL VECTRA 1.4 GL	82390	11770	11060

UNITED KINGDOM
RATES IN UKL · TAX 17.5%

Group	Example of Car Type	4-7 Days	8-13 Days (per day)	14+ Days (per day)
A	VAUXHALL NOVA 1.2L	84	12	11
B	VAUXHALL ASTRA 1.4L	154	22	21
C	VAUXHALL CAVALIER 1.6L	168	24	23
D	VAUXHALL ASTRA 1.6 (A)	161	23	22
E	FORD SIERRA 1.8L (SW)	350	50	47
F	FORD GRANADA 2.0I GHIA (A)	329	47	44

Some of the additional countries offering our special rates are: Czechoslovakia, Finland, Gibraltar, Hungary, Jordan, Luxembourg, Malta, Mauritius, Morocco, Tunisia, Turkey, Yugoslavia.

Price Includes—Unlimited Free Mileage Only
Price Excludes—Local Taxes, CDW, PAI, TP
Rates are subject to change without notice.
Car "groups" only can be reserved.

Auto-Europe Car Rental
(Inclusive of CDW and tax)

AUTO EUROPE
(INCLUSIVE OF CDW and TAX)

AUSTRIA

RATES IN AUS   TAX 21.2% (33.3% FOR RENTALS OF 21 + DAYS)

Group	Example of Car Type	4-7 Days	8-13 Days (per day)	14 Days (per day)
A	OPEL CORSA 1.4i	4879	697	655
B	OPEL ASTRA 1.4i	5852	836	786
C	OPEL VECTRA 1.6i	7371	1053	990
56	OPEL KADETT 1.6i (A)	8344	1192	1120
E	OPEL OMEGA 2.0i	17661	2523	2372
F	MERCEDES 190E	19614	2802	2634

BELGIUM

RATES IN BFR   TAX 25%

Group	Example of Car Type	4-7 Days	8-13 Days (per day)	14 Days (per day)
A	OPEL CORSA 1.0	8421	1203	1131
B	OPEL KADETT 1.4i	12635	1805	1697
C	OPEL VECTRA 1.6i	15267	2181	2050
D	CITROEN BX 1.6 (A)	15792	2256	2121
E	VW PASSAT	20265	2895	2721
F	CITROEN BX 1.9 (SW)	17367	2481	2332

DENMARK

RATES IN DKR   TAX 25%

Group	Example of Car Type	4-7 Days	8-13 Days (per day)	14 Days (per day)
A	FORD FIESTA 1.0	2324	332	312
B	OPEL KADETT 1.4DX	2723	389	366
C	OPEL VECTRA 1.6i	3913	559	525
D	OPEL OMEGA 2.0DL	4550	650	611
E	BMW 320i	5096	728	684
F	BMW 520i	5495	785	738

FRANCE

RATES IN FFR   TAX 22%

Group	Example of Car Type	4-7 Days	8-13 Days (per day)	14 Days (per day)
A	OPEL CORSA VIVA 1.0	1778	254	239
B	OPEL KADETT LS 1.4	2296	328	308
C	OPEL VECTRA GL 1.6	3213	459	431
D	RENAULT CLIO 1.6 RT (A)	2471	353	332
E	OPEL OMEGA 2.0 GL	3773	539	507
F	RENAULT 25 GTS 2.0 (A)	5334	762	716

CONDITIONS

Normal one-way policy applies. Reservation Required 48 hours in advance, minimum rental period as shown above.

Price Includes—Unlimited Free Mileage, CDW, Tax
Price Excludes—TP, PAI.
Rates are subject to change without notice.
Car "groups" only can be reserved.

GERMANY

RATES IN DMK   TAX 14%

Group	Example of Car Type	4-7 Days	8-13 Days (per day)	14+ Days (per day)
O	OPEL CORSA	371	53	50
A	VW POLO	399	57	54
B	VW GOLF	420	60	56
C	AUDI 80	602	86	81
D	VW GOLF (A)	609	87	82
E	AUDI 100	763	109	102

GREECE

RATES IN USD   TAX 18%

Group	Example of Car Type	4-7 Days	8-13 Days (per day)	14+ Days (per day)
A	SUBARU M 70DL	322	46	45
B	NISSAN CHERRY 1.0	357	51	50
C	NISSAN SUNNY 1.3	413	59	58
D	NISSAN SUNNY 1.5 (AC)	511	73	72
F	NISSAN SUNNY 1.3 (A) (AC)	497	71	70

Groups D and F available in Athens and Thessaloniki only

HOLLAND

RATES IN DFL   TAX 18.5%

Group	Example of Car Type	4-7 Days	8-13 Days (per day)	14+ Days (per day)
A	CITROEN AX 11	504	72	68
B	FORD FIESTA 1.1 CHEERS	588	84	79
C	FORD ESCORT 1.4 CLI	707	101	95
D	FORD ORION 1.4 CLI	861	123	116
E	OPEL VECTRA 1.6i GL	980	140	132
F	OPEL VECTRA 2.0i GLS	1337	191	180

IRELAND

RATES IN IRL   TAX 10%

Group	Example of Car Type	4-7 Days	8-13 Days (per day)	14+ Days (per day)
A	FORD FIESTA	252	36	34
B	OPEL KADETT 1.3	294	42	39
C	TOYOTA CARINA 1.6	392	56	53
D	NISSAN MICRA 1.0 (A)	427	61	57
E	TOYOTA CARINA 1.6(SW)	455	65	61
F	TOYOTA CARINA 1.6 (A)	602	86	81

ISRAEL

RATES IN USD   TAX 0%

Group	Example of Car Type	4-7 Days	8-13 Days (per day)	14+ Days (per day)
P	AUTOBIANCHI Y10	329	47	44
A	FIAT UNO STING	343	49	46
B	FIAT UNO (AC)	427	61	57
C	SUBARU 1.6 (AC)	532	76	71
D	SUBARU 1.6 (A) (AC)	574	82	77
E	SUBARU 1.6 (A) (AC)	672	96	90

Auto-Europe Car Rental
(Inclusive of CDW and tax)

AUTO EUROPE
(INCLUSIVE OF CDW and TAX)

ITALY
RATES IN LIT   TAX 19%

Group	Example of Car Type	4-7 Days	8-13 Days (per day)	14 Days (per day)
A	FIAT PANDA 750 CL	420700	60100	57100
B	OPEL CORSA 1.0	490700	70100	66500
C	RENAULT CLIO	571200	81600	77300
D	OPEL VECTRA 1.4 GL	690200	98600	93400
E	LANCIA DEDRA 1.6	802900	114700	108500
F	OPLE OMEGA 1.8i (AC)	819000	117000	110700

NORWAY
RATES IN NKR   TAX 20%

Group	Example of Car Type	4-7 Days	8-13 Days (per day)	14 Days (per day)
A	FORD FIESTA	2807	401	377
B	FORD ESCORT 1.6	3360	480	451
C	FORD SIERRA 2.0L	3661	523	492
D	VOLVO 440	4613	659	619
E	FORD SIERRA 2.0 (A)	5348	764	718
F	FORD SIERRA (SW)	8218	1174	1104

POLAND
RATES IN DMK   TAX 0%

Group	Example of Car Type	4-7 Days	8-13 Days (per day)	14 Days (per day)
A	VW POLO 1.3 CL	637	91	86
B	OPEL KADETT 1.4i LS	826	118	111
C	FORD SIERRA 2.0i	931	133	125
D	AUDI 80 1.8 S	1099	157	148

PORTUGAL
RATES IN ESP   TAX 22%

Group	Example of Car Type	4-7 Days	8-13 Days (per day)	14 Days (per day)
A	OPEL CORSA 1.0	31850	4550	4280
B	FIAT UNO 45	37380	5340	5020
C	OPEL CORSA 1.2 TR GL	41720	5960	5600
D	VW GOLF 1.3	50540	7220	6790
E	OPEL KADETT 1.4	59290	8470	7950
F	OPEL VECTRA 1.4 GL	108780	15540	14610

SPAIN MAINLAND & BALEARICS
RATES IN PTS   TAX 13%

Group	Example of Car Type	4-7 Days	8-13 Days (per day)	14+ Days (per day)
A	FIAT UNO 45	33040	4720	4440
B	RENAULT CLIO 1.2	38430	5490	5160
C	OPEL ASTRA GL 1.4	46410	6630	6230
D	RENAULT CHAMADE 1.4 (AC)	49000	7000	6580
E	RENAULT19CHAMADE1.7 (A)	53410	7630	7170
F	RENAULT10CHAMADE 1.7(AC)	56070	8010	7530

SWEDEN
RATES IN SKR   TAX 25%

Group	Example of Car Type	4-7 Days	8-13 Days (per day)	14+ Days (per day)
A	FORD FIESTA	2737	391	368
B	VW GOLF	3108	444	417
C	FORD SIERRA	3892	556	523
D	VOLVO 740	5936	848	797
E	VOLVO 745 (SW)	6209	887	834
F	SAAB 9000 CDi (AC)	7602	1086	1021

SWITZERLAND
RATES IN SFR   TAX 0%

Group	Example of Car Type	4-7 Days	8-13 Days (per day)	14+ Days (per day)
I	FIAT PANDA 1.0	308	44	41
A	OPEL CORSA 1.4	371	53	51
B	OPEL ASTRA 1.4	420	60	57
C	OPEL VECTRA 2.0	483	69	64
D	OPEL VECTRA 2.0 (A)	546	78	73
E	OPEL OMEGA 2.4 (A)	819	117	112

UNITED KINGDOM
RATES IN IRL   TAX 10%

Group	Example of Car Type	4-7 Days	8-13 Days (per day)	14+ Days (per day)
A	VAUXHALL NOVA 1.2L	161	23	22
B	VAUXHALL ASTRA 1.4L	245	35	33
C	VAUXHALL CAVALIER 1.6L	273	39	37
D	VAUXHALL ASTRA 1.6(A)	259	37	35
E	FORD SIERRA 1.8L (SW)	406	58	55
F	FORD GRANADA 2.0i GHIA (A)	392	56	53

CONDITIONS
Some of the additional countries offering our special rates are:
Czechoslovakia, Finland, Gibraltar, Hungary, Jordan, Luxembourg,
Malta, Mauritius, Morocco, Tunisia, Turkey, Yugoslavia.

Price Includes—Unlimited Free Mileage, CDW, TAX
Price Excludes— PAI, TP

Rates are subject to change without notice.
Car "groups" only can be reserved.

Sample Money Rates for Travellers

Country/Unit	Per CAD*	CAD* Equiv.
Australia/dollar	1.10	0.9084
Austria/schilling	8.62	0.1159
Bahamas/dollar	0.78	1.2768
Barbados/dollar	1.15	0.6595
Belgium/franc	25.31	0.0395
Brazil/real	1,111	.00009
Britain/pound	0.52	1.892
Denmark/krone	4.70	0.2124
Dom.Repub./peso	8.56	0.1167
E. Caribbean/dollar	1.85	0.5382
Egypt/pound	2.09	0.4765
Finland/markka	4.43	0.2254
France/franc	4.19	0.2385
Germany/mark	1.24	0.8060
Greece/drachma	163.93	0.0061
Holland/guilder	1.39	0.7175
Hong Kong/dollar	5.76	0.1734
Hungary/forint	57.80	0.0173
Ireland/pound	0.51	1.9430
Israel/shekel	1.80	0.5531
Italy/lira	1,145.2	.00087
Jamaica/dollar	16.63	0.0601
Japan/yen	91.17	.01096
Mexico/peso	2,288	.00043
New Zealand/dollar	1.43	0.6945
Norway/krone	5.23	0.1910
Portugal/escudo	109.55	.00912
Romania/leu	171.85	.00581
S. Africa/rand	2.23	0.4477
Spain/peseta	87.71	0.0114
Sweden/krona	5.55	0.1799
Switzerland/franc	1.14	0.8723
Tahiti/franc	71.42	0.0140
Trinidad/dollar	3.20	0.3122
U.S.A./dollar	0.77	1.2830
Venezuela/bolivar	57.47	.0174

* CAD is Canadian dollars

● EXERCISES—Auto-Europe Car Rental

Using the Auto-Europe Car Rental rate charts, calculate the costs for the following journeys. Where needed, add any appropriate taxes, and convert local funds into Canadian currency using the money rates table on the previous page.

1. Group C car in Amsterdam. Exclusive rate for 18 days.

2. Fiat Uno 45 in Barcelona. Exclusive rate for 7 days.

3. Opel Vectra in Milan. Inclusive rate for 15 days.

4. Vauxhall Astra 1.6 in Glasgow. Inclusive rate for 12 days.

5. Vauxhall Astra 1.6 in Glasgow. Exclusive rate for 12 days.

6. Group F car in Brussels. Exclusive rate for 5 days.

_____

_____

_____

_____

_____

7. Opel Kadett in Nice. Exclusive rate for 22 days.

_____

_____

_____

_____

CAR/HOTEL VOUCHER

In Chapter 4, an example of a car/hotel voucher was included. Another copy appears below. A travel agency will issue a similar voucher for car and/or hotel reservations so that the client may provide confirmation of the bookings to the supplier at check-in.

ASTOR TRAVEL SERVICES

1240 Bay Street, Suite 302
Toronto, Ontario M5R 2A7 CANADA

CONFIRMATION NO. _____

DATE CONFIRMED_____

BOOKED THROUGH _____

PLEASE PROVIDE_____   PARTY OF_____

WITH _____

FROM_____ TO _____ NTS/DAYS _____ MEALS_____

RATE $ _____   DEPOSIT_____

REMARKS_____

TO _____   _____

ADDRESS_____   TELEPHONE _____

_____   CDW/LDW_____   ALI _____

_____   PAI _____   PEP _____

☐ Unlimited Mileage   ☐ KM / MLS Free   Each Additional @ _____   TAX _____

☐ Hotel has been GUARANTEED for late arrival. Please cancel by _____to avoid penalties.

Reprinted courtesy of Astor Travel Services

6

Rail Transportation

WHY TAKE THE TRAIN?

Listed below are some advantages of travelling by train. At the bottom of this list fill in any other reasons you can think of.

1. Taking the train allows the passenger to sit back, relax, and enjoy the passing scenery, while providing a relatively convenient means of intercity travel.

2. In North America, rail transportation is associated with an earlier era and will appeal to those who look at train travel with nostalgia.

3. Train travel is an environmentally friendly mode of transportation.

4. _____

5. _____

6. _____

DISADVANTAGES OF RAIL TRAVEL

There are also some problems inherent to train travel:

1. In North America, the frequency of service has deteriorated due to cutbacks.

2. Many North American cities and towns are no longer served by Amtrak or Via Rail.

3. Train travel can be slow (except for some newer high-speed trains like the TGV in Europe or Japan's bullet trains).

4. _____

5. _____

6. _____

THE TRAIN SYSTEM IN NORTH AMERICA

The "iron horse" was the prime method of east-west transportation in the development of North America, and westward expansion was indeed made possible because of the railroads. The railroads have therefore historically been important to both Canada and the U.S.A. Within Canada, passenger rail service is now operated by Via Rail, which is a Crown corporation that was incorporated by the federal government in 1978.

Major Rail Systems Booked by Canadian Agents

Canada	Via Rail
U.S.A.	Amtrak
Europe	• BritRail (United Kingdom) • SNCF—French National Railways (France) • DB—German Railway (Germany) • RENFE—Spanish National Railways (Spain) • CFF/SBB—Swiss Federal Railways (Switzerland) • FS—Italian State Railways (Italy)
Australia	• Great Southern Railway • Bluebird Railtours • Queensland Railways (Traveltrain) • Countrylink • Sunstate • V/Line • TT-Line • West Coast Railway • Hoys Roadlines • Westrail • City Rail

CANADA

Within Canada, Via Rail contracts with two independent railroad companies, Canadian National and Canadian Pacific, for the use of their lines and their employees. The *LRC* (*Light, Rapid, and Comfortable*) trains have been specifically designed for the Canadian climate and track conditions and are used for short- and medium-length journeys. Via Rail also operates transcontinental service and fly/rail, bus/rail, and other tours. However, the rail system in Canada has steadily decreased in size, and the railroad is no longer the transportation system of choice. Nonetheless, the railroad continues to play a role in transportation of goods and people.

Levels of Service on Via Rail

Traditionally, trains have offered more than one class of service, and most train systems will have both first- and second-class service. Via Rail is no exception, and the following distinguishing features are found:

First- and Second-Class Service

	First Class	Second Class
Seating	More leg room, wider, fewer seats, more comfortable	Traditional coach-style seating
Reservations	Usually required	Advance booking not always required
Meals	Usually included in the price	Generally not included (snacks available for purchase)
Bar service	Complimentary beverages may be included	Not included (may be available for purchase)

Rail Terms

BERTH	A bed on a train; usually attached to a wall.
CARRIAGE	On a train, a car without sleeping accommodation; identified with a particular class of service.
COACH	A lounge car on a train; serves alcoholic beverages.
CORRIDOR	In the case of Via Rail, train travel between Quebec City, Montreal, Toronto, and Windsor.
COUCHETTE	A sleeping berth (in second class); found on trains in Europe.
DOME CAR	A rail car containing a glass dome for sightseeing on scenic routes (for example, through the Rocky Mountains).
DRAWING ROOM	A room with sleeping accommodation and washroom facilities; holds three people.
EUROCITY	European trains connecting various major European cities.
FIRST CLASS	Most expensive cars on a train, with compartments containing six seats (in Europe); may include meals.
LRC	"Light, Rapid, Comfortable": A type of train used by Via Rail in Canada.
NARROW GAUGE	The type of track on which certain trains operate.
OBSERVATION CAR	A specially designed car (with large windows and often a domed glass roof) used on scenic routes.

RAILINER	A self-propelled rail car, diesel operated, used by Via Rail on Vancouver Island and between Sudbury and White River, Ontario, and used by B.C. Rail in the interior of British Columbia.
SECOND CLASS	Less expensive cars on a train, usually consisting of rows of seats with a centre aisle; no meals included.
SECTION	An upper and lower berth.
SLEEPER/SLEEPERETTE	Sleeping accommodation with bed; found on trains in Europe.
TGV	High-speed deluxe trains operating in France, also known as "Trains Grand Vitesse"; they reach speeds of 168 mph (270 kph).
TOURIST	A class of service (usually second class).
WAGON LITS	A rail car on a European train.

Booking Information

Before booking a train reservation, you will need to obtain the following information from your client:

1. Number of passengers, their names, and (if children or seniors) their ages;

2. Smoking preference or any other special request;

3. Class of service needed;

4. Whether sleeping accommodation is needed and, if so, the type;

5. Departure and return dates;

6. Exact departure and destination points, and specific train station if there is a choice.

The following information must be obtained from the railway:

1. PNR or locator number (the number used to identify the booking);

2. Ticketing deadline date;

3. Train numbers, car numbers, and exact departure and arrival times.

To issue a Via Rail ticket, your agency must be IATA approved and Via Rail appointed. The Via Rail plate number is 830. This plate must be obtained from Via Rail and used with a ticket imprinter (similar to a credit card imprinter) to validate tickets.

How to Read the Via Rail Timetable

Examples from the timetable are included on pages 96 to 98. When reading the Via Rail timetable, first check the index for the destination city, then turn to the appropriate numbered page in the timetable. The various symbols used are explained at the back of the timetable. Also note the information regarding fares and taxes shown at the bottom of the timetable page.

When reading the timetable, follow the direction of the arrows at the top. For example, on page 96, train number 1 starts in Toronto. The downward arrow indicates that this train proceeds to Washago, then Parry Sound, and so on until its final destination of Winnipeg. Train number 2, on the other hand, operates in the reverse direction, starting from Winnipeg (page 97). Stops are only possible where times are indicated. Connections are shown in the timetable by different coloured print. (Note that all timetables and fare examples are subject to change and are not to be considered as current examples of timetables or fares now in effect.)

The following table describes the characteristics of different passenger types.

Via Rail Passenger Types

Type	Description
Adult (A)	• 25–59 years old inclusive • basic fares
Child (C)	• 2–11 years inclusive • 50% of applicable adult fare in economy class • 25% reduction on VIA1 Class only
a. Unaccompanied child	• can travel alone and qualify for 50% of adult fare if between the ages of 8 and 11; no overnight travel; no transfers en route; authorization form signed by parent or guardian, plus information on who will pick up child. Must wear "unaccompanied minor" bracelet; $10.00 surcharge each way
b. Accompanied child	• pays 50% of adult fare • children under 8 must be accompanied
Infant (I)	• under 2 years old • free in economy class if does not occupy a seat; pays child fare if seat is required; in Via 1, must occupy a seat and pay child fare • one free infant per adult
Senior (S)	• 60 years+ • minimum 10% reduction • ID required
Youth and mature student (T)	• youth 12–17 years old, no ID required • student 18–24 years old, ID required (e.g., International Student Card) • 40% reduction (economy); 10% other classes
Aboriginal (Y)	• 33% reduction if travel in economy class • territory: — New Brunswick/Nova Scotia — east of Levis and Megantic — west of Laforest including Vancouver Island

Fare Levels*

Peak (full fare). Applies to "Corridor" (Quebec City–Montreal–Toronto–Windsor) and Intercity East travel; no advance booking; applies to travel on Fridays and Sundays (except for youths under 25) and other dates as designated.

Off-peak. Applies to travel on Monday, Tuesday, Wednesday, Thursday, and Saturday; no advance booking; subject to availability.

Super saver. Applies to travel on Monday, Tuesday, Wednesday, Thursday, and Saturday; requires 5-day advance booking; subject to availability; limited seating.

Transcontinental East. Applies to travel between Montreal and Gaspe; check for dates for peak/off-peak periods (no advance booking required) and super saver dates (advance booking of 7 days required).

Transcontinental West. Applies to travel between Toronto and Vancouver; check dates for peak/off-peak periods (no advance booking required) and super saver dates (advanced booking of 7 days required).

Canrail pass. Allows 12 days of travel for a maximum of 30 days; good anywhere in Canada; pricing differs depending on peak or off-peak times; reduced costs for youths and seniors.

* For discounts see page 87. Note that discounts and advance booking requirements are subject to change.

Via Rail Ticketing

If the agency is IATA approved, and has an appointment as a ticket agency from Via Rail, the agency can itself issue the rail ticket (each sale is included in the agency's regular weekly Bank Settlement Plan [BSP] report). Before issuing the ticket, you will need the PNR (passenger name record) or locator number (a tracing number used by Via Rail to find the booking information); the complete itinerary (including train and car numbers, and all arrival and departure times); and the ticketing deadline.

When completing a Via Rail ticket, the following coding information is necessary:

Taxes	XG	=	GST
	XQ	=	Quebec provincial tax
Passenger codes	A	=	Adult
	C	=	Child
	I	=	Infant
	S	=	Senior
	E	=	Escort
	T	=	Student
Ticketing codes	UR	=	Unreserved
	GN	=	Coach nonsmoking
	CN	=	Via 1 (first class) nonsmoking
	DS	=	Daynighter smoking
	DN	=	Daynighter nonsmoking
	SX	=	Section

The Plate Number for Via Rail, as approved by IATA, is 830.

Via Rail Ticket Format

1.	Passenger name	Name of passenger in standard IATA ticketing format: SMITH/W MR
2.	Origin/destination	Via Rail city codes of origin and destination.
3.	Booking reference no.	Passenger name record (the PNR locator number).
4.	Date of issue	The date that the control number is issued by Reservia.
5.	Place of issue agency	Travel agency name, city, country, and IATA number.
6.	Passenger number and type	Number of passengers, followed by the type: Adult (A), Senior (S), Student (T), Child (C), Infant (I), Escort (E); placed in the right-hand side of the passenger name box.
7.	Stopovers/Connections	0 = Stopover X = No stopover
8.	From/to	Full city names and province codes.
9.	Carrier	Carrier code for Via Rail is 2R; Amtrak is A3.
10.	Flight	Via Rail train number.
11.	Class of service	C for Coach and J for first-class or sleeping accommodation.
12.	Date	Departure date of each part of the itinerary.
13.	Time	Departure time for each part of the itinerary; use 24-hour clock (for example, 1900 not 0700 for 7:00 p.m.).
14.	Status	Leave blank.
15.	Fare basis	Train number and car number; also the seat number for first class, or the accommodation type and number for sleeping car accommodation (for example, GN).
16.	Allowance	Leave blank.

17.	Fare calculation	Since this is not air, print "Not valid for air travel."
18.	Carrier identification plate	Name of railway, imprinted from Via Rail/Amtrak plate, using a ticket imprinter.
19.	Fare	Fare paid in CAD.
20.	Tax box no. 2	GST at 7%. (Note: Draw a line through the first tax box.) The code for GST is "XG." In New Brunswick, Nova Scotia, Prince Edward Island, and Newfoundland a Harmonized Sales Tax, or HST, equal to 15%, applies to all domestic journeys wholly within Canada with travel commencing in one of the referenced provinces regardless of where the ticket was issued.
21.	Tax box no. 3	If the origin of the ticket is Quebec then charge the QST (Quebec Provincial Tax) of 4% on the total which already includes GST. The code for the QST is "XQ."
22.	Total	Total of all taxes plus fare.
23.	Commission	Via Rail commission is 11%.
24.	Destination	Canada = 9 (U.S.A. = 0); business = 1, or pleasure = 2.
25.	Form of payment	Cash, cheque, or CC (credit card) plus credit card code and number.
26.	Tour code	Control numbers given by Via Rail. All control numbers must be shown on the ticket. List the full 9 digits of the first control number and the final 3 digits of all subsequent numbers.
27.	Endorsements	Any special requests (SSR), discount fare plans, or other restrictions. Cross-reference ticket numbers if necessary.
28.	Conjunction tickets	As per BSP instructions, when more than one ticket is required for a journey, tickets must be used sequentially (for example, 8306850663102/03.)
29.	Issued in exchange	Original ticket numbers (used for exchanges only).
30.	Validity boxes	Restrictions on days of travel, if any (otherwise leave blank).
31.	Original issue	Original ticket number if ticket is exchanged (used for exchanges only; otherwise leave blank).
32.	"PRI" or "CONJ"	One of these codes is required in this box if a conjunction ticket is used (otherwise leave blank).

Sample Train Ticket

FROM/TO DE A			ENDORSEMENTS/RESTRICTIONS (CARBON) ENDOS/RESTRICTIONS (CARBON)				AGENT COUPON AGENCE	ORIGIN / ORIGINE / DESTINATION MTRL MTRL		6971630406
	CARR. TRANSF.	FARE CALC CALCUL DU PRIX	OFF PEAK/HORS POINTE/VIA SSR VEG MEAL/REPAS VEG					BOOKING REF / REF. RES XA1234 TJ		PLACE OF ISSUE - AGENCY LIEU D'EMISSION - AGENCE ABC TRAVEL
			NAME OF PASSENGER / NOM DU PASSAGER THOMAS/P 1A			NOT TRANSFERABLE / INCESSIBLE		DATE OF ISSUE / DATE D'EMISSION 20 AUG 99	ISSUED IN EXCHANGE FOR / EMIS EN ECHANGE DE		ANYTOWN CANADA
			CONJUNCTION TICKETS BILLET(S) COMPLEMENTAIRES (S)					ORIGINAL ISSUE AIRLINE/CIE ...		GL-19999-2
NOT VALID FOR AIR TRAVEL								PREMIERE EMISSION		

X9	NOT GOOD FOR PASSAGE NON VALABLE POUR TRANSPORT		CARRIER TRANSF.	FLIGHT / CLASS VOL / CLASSE	DATE	TIME HEURE	STATUS RESERV	FARE BASIS BASE TARIFAIRE				
NON VALABLE POUR LE TRANSPORT AERIEN	O	FROM DE MONTREAL PQ	2R	16T C	20 Aug	16.00		XN				
	O	TO A TORONTO ON	2R	66 J	28 Aug	14.00		6601 JF13				
	O	TO A MONTREAL PQ	—	VOID —				NUL				
		TO A VOID/NUL	TOUR CODE / CODE I.T.									

	FORM OF PAYMENT / MODE DE PAIEMENT						PASSENGER TICKET AND BAGGAGE CHECK ISSUED BY... VIA RAIL CANADA INC.		
TOTAL FARE CALC CALC DER COUTES TOTALS	CC VS 4510123456789101								
FARE / PRIX 141.00	EQUIV.FARE PD CONTRE-VALEUR VERSEE	TAX / TAXE	TAX / TAXE 9.87 XG	TAX / TAXE 6.03 XQ		CPN / COUPON	AIRLINE/CIE AER.	FORM	SERIAL NUMBER / No DU BILLET CK / CONTROLE
TOTAL 156.90	COMMISSION % 11			DEST. 9 2		O 830	6871630406 O		

DO NOT MARK OR WRITE IN THE WHITE AREA ABOVE

Via Rail Routes

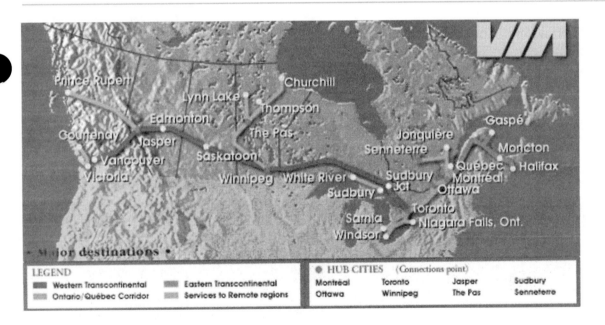

LEGEND
- Western Transcontinental
- Ontario/Québec Corridor
- Eastern Transcontinental
- Services to Remote regions

HUB CITIES (Connections point)
| Montréal | Toronto | Jasper | Sudbury |
| Ottawa | Winnipeg | The Pas | Senneterre |

Via Rail Routes continued

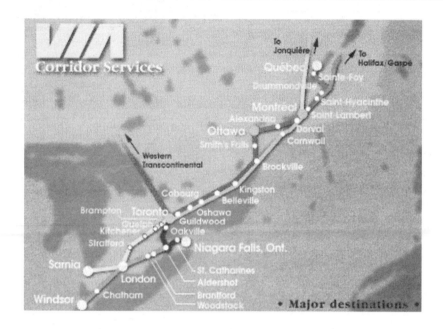

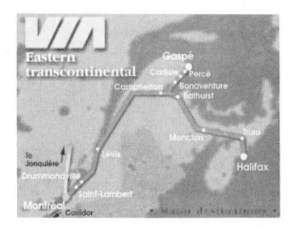

Smoking is *not* permitted on any train in the Québec City-Windsor corridor.

Il est *interdit* de fumer à bord des trains du corridor Québec-Windsor.

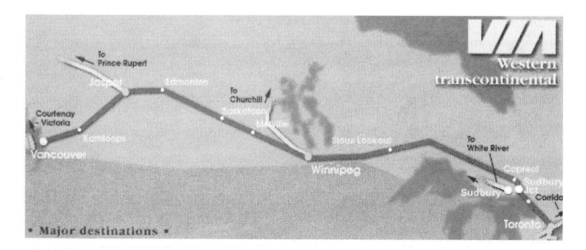

Via Summary of Fares

VIA+ VIA Rail Canada

2000 Summary of VIA Rail Canada Fares for Major Origins/Destinations
Résumé des tarifs 2000 de VIA Rail Canada par villes d'importance

Canada $CAD

ORIGIN/ORIGINE DESTINATION	ECONOMY CLASS CLASSE ECONOMIQUE			VIA1 1 WAY	SLEEPING CLASS / CLASSE VOITURE-LITS TOTAL FARE PER PERSON / TARIF TOTAL PAR PERSONNE								
					PEAK / POINTE			OFF PEAK / HORS POINTE			SUPER SAVER / SUPER ESCOMPTE		
	FF/PT	One-way	Return	Al Stmp	S	W	F/P	S	W	F/P	S	W	F/P
BETWEEN / ENTRE HALIFAX, NS &													
SYDNEY, NS	$210		$316	←	Service Bras d'Or Service								
TRURO, NS	$18	$13	$24										
AMHERST, NS	$34	$25	$42										
SACKVILLE, NS	$37	$27	$46										
MONCTON, NB	$44	$33	$56										
MIRAMICHI, NB	$60	$45	$76										
SAINT-JOHN, NB	$66	$50	$84										
BATHURST, NB	$71	$53	$90										
CHARLO, NB	$80	$60	$102										
CAMPBELLTON, NB	$82	$62	$104										
QUÉBEC (CHARNY), QC	$139	$104	$176		$170	$212	$236				$112	$131	$146
MONTRÉAL, QC	$166	$125	$210		$204	$240	$267				$126	$149	$166
OTTAWA, ON	$185	$139	$234		$216	$252	$279				$138	$161	$178
TORONTO, ON	$226	$170	$284		$233	$269	$296				$155	$178	$195
BETWEEN / ENTRE MONCTON, NB &													
TRURO, NS	$29	$22	$36										
AMHERST, NB	$14	$12	$24										
SACKVILLE, NS	$12	$12	$24										
MIRAMICHI, NB	$22	$16	$28										
BATHURST, NB	$33	$25	$42										
CHARLO, NB	$44	$33	$56										
CAMPBELLTON, NB	$46	$34	$58										
QUÉBEC (CHARNY), QC	$108	$81	$136		$149	$175	$195				$92	$109	$121
DRUMMONDVILLE, QC	$116	$87	$146		$155	$183	$207				$96	$113	$129
MONTRÉAL, QC	$137	$103	$172		$182	$214	$238				$113	$133	$148
OTTAWA, ON	$160	$120	$202		$194	$226	$250				$125	$145	$160
TORONTO, ON	$199	$149	$250		$211	$243	$267				$139	$162	$177
BETWEEN / ENTRE QUÉBEC (CHARNY) &													
BATHURST, NB	$81	$60	$102		$108	$127	$142				$67	$79	$88
CAMPBELLTON, NB	$66	$49	$82		$86	$101	$114				$53	$63	$70
GASPÉ, QC	$97	$73	$122		$133	$157	$176				$83	$97	$109
DRUMMONDVILLE, QC	$29	$22	$38	$52									
ST-HYACINTHE, QC	$39	$29	$50	$69									
MONTRÉAL, QC	$50	$38	$66	$88									
OTTAWA, ON	$75	$56	$98	$122									
KINGSTON, ON	$88	$66	$126	$137									
TORONTO, ON	$126	$95	$164	$201									
LONDON, ON	$149	$112	$194	$163									
BETWEEN / ENTRE MONTRÉAL, QC &													
TRURO, NS	$154	$116	$194		$187	$220	$245				$116	$137	$152
SACKVILLE, NS	$141	$105	$178		$177	$208	$232				$110	$129	$144
NEWCASTLE, NB	$112	$84	$142		$150	$176	$199				$93	$109	$124
SAINT-JOHN, NB	$137	$103	$172		$182	$214	$238				$113	$133	$148
BATHURST, NB	$107	$80	$134		$143	$168	$190				$88	$104	$118
CAMPBELLTON, NB	$96	$72	$120		$129	$151	$172				$80	$94	$107
GASPE, QC	$133	$100	$168		$179	$210	$234				$111	$130	$145
CHANDLER, QC	$127	$95	$160		$168	$198	$221				$107	$126	$142
NEW CARLISLE, QC	$115	$87	$146		$158	$186	$208				$98	$115	$129
RIMOUSKI, QC	$88	$66	$110		$124	$145	$161				$74	$90	$100
RIVIERE-DU-LOUP, QC	$76	$57	$96										
JONQUIERE, QC	$65	$49	$82										
SENNETERRE, QC	$98	$74	$124										
OTTAWA, ON	$40	$30	$52	$75									
KINGSTON, ON	$56	$42	$72	$99	$99	$117	$146						
TORONTO, ON	$95	$71	$124	$143	$133	$156	$195						
NIAGARA FALLS, ON	$105	$79	$136	$167									
LONDON, ON	$115	$86	$150	$192									
SARNIA, ON	$130	$98	$170	$209									
WINDSOR, ON	$139	$104	$180	$218									
WINNIPEG, MB	$360	$222	$394		$655	$754	$912	$515	$589	$708	$419	$480	$578
SASKATOON, SK	$394	$276	$488		$712	$821	$990	$558	$640	$766	$454	$521	$626
EDMONTON, AB	$435	$314	$556		$779	$900	$1,089	$608	$699	$841	$496	$570	$687
JASPER, AB	$501	$351	$622		$853	$987	$1,196	$664	$764	$921	$566	$648	$778
VANCOUVER, BC	$599	$419	$742		$1,108	$1,287	$1,567	$855	$989	$1,199	$700	$810	$984

Via Summary of Fares continued

VIA   VIA Rail Canada

2000 Summary of VIA Rail Canada Fares for Major Origins/Destinations
Résumé des tarifs 2000 de VIA Rail Canada par villes d'importance

Canada $CAD

ORIGIN/ ORIGINE DESTINATION	ECONOMY CLASS / CLASSE ECONOMIQUE			VIA1	TOTEM CLASS / CLASSE TOTEM — TOTAL FARE PER PERSON / TARIF TOTAL PAR PERSONNE					
	1WAY / AL SIMP			1 WAY	PEAK / POINTE					
	FF/PT	One-way	Return	Al Simp	J					
BETWEEN / ENTRE										
JASPER, AB &										
KAMLOOPS NORTH, BC	$98	$69	$122							
PRINCE GEORGE, BC	$68	$51	$86		$197					
SMITHERS, BC	$109	$81	$136		$347					
TERRACE, BC	$122	$91	$154		$347					
PRINCE RUPERT, BC	$139	$104	$176		$347					
BETWEEN / ENTRE										
KAMLOOPS N, BC &										
PRINCE GEORGE, BC	$130	$120	$208		$295					
PRINCE RUPERT, BC	$184	$173	$298		$445					
BETWEEN / ENTRE										
PRINCE GEO., BC &		One-way	Return							
PRINCE RUPERT, BC	$87	$65	$110		$197					
BETWEEN / ENTRE										
VICTORIA, BC &										
NANAIMO, BC	$19	$14	$24							
COURTENAY, BC	$37	$28	$46							

Effective/en vigueur 11-JAN-00

Accommodation Definitions / *Définitions des places*:

VIA 1 (J):	VIA1 Class/ Classe VIA1
S :	Upper Berth / Couchette du haut
W :	Lower Berth / Couchette du bas
F/P:	Single or Double Bedroom(per person) / Chambre simple ou double (par personne)
R:	Triples also available (about 5% less per person) / Triples aussi disponibles (environ 5% de moins par personne)
A:	Double Berth i.e. Upper +Lower Berth / Couchette Double i.e. couchettes du haut et du bas
J:	Totem Class (Skeena) and Bras d'Or Class (Bras d'Or) / Classe Totem (Skeena) et Classe Bras d'Or (Bras d'Or)

Other Fare Plans available / *Autres tarifs disponibles*:

Seniors aged 60 and over receive a 10% additional discount throughout VIA system on any fare plan.
Les aînés de 60 ans et plus bénéficient d'un rabais additionnel de 10% sur tous les tarifs.
Youths 12 to 17 and students with ISIC cards are guaranteed a 40 % discount in Economy class; 50% off on "6-Paks"
Les jeunes de 12 à 17 et les étudiants avec la carte ISIC bénéficient d'un rabais de 40% en classe économique en tout temps; 50% sur "6-packs"
CANRAILPASS: 1JUN00-15OCT00->Adult.:$616,60+/2-24yrs/Student(Etudiant):$545 Else(Sinon)-> Adult.:$390, 60+/2-24yrs/Student(Etudiant):$355
up to 3 extra days may be purchased / jusqu'à 3 jours peuvent être achetés @ $52,$46; - / $33, $30 respectively / jours supplémentaires:
NORTH AMERICA RAIL PASS: 30 days 1JUN00-15OCT00->Adult:$965, 60+/2-24yrs/Student(Etudiant):$858
                                    Off-peak->Adult: $675, 60+/2-24yrs/Student(Etudiant):$608
PASSE AMÉRIQUE DU NORD: 30 jours 1JUN00-15OCT00->Adulte $965, 60+/2-24yrs/Etudiant:$858: Hors-pointe->Adulte $675, 60+/2-24yrs/Etudiant:$608

Windsor-Quebec City Corridor / *Corridor Québec-Windsor*:
  Local travel in the Maritimes / *Voyages locaux dans les Maritimes*:
The one-way and return discount fares require 5 day advance purchase (limited seats) /
Les tarifs à sens unique ou aller-retour de rabais doit être acheté 5 jours d'avance (places limitées)

Toronto-Vancouver -> The CANADIAN / *Le CANADIEN*:
Peak Period (Full Fare) / *Période de pointe (plein tarif)* : 1JUNE00 - 21OCT00/ *1JUIN00 - 21OCT00*
Super Saver /Super escompte: 01JAN00-31MAY00 AND 22OCT00-31MAY01 / *01JAN00-31MAI00 ET 22OCT00-31MAI01*
(fare requires 7 day advance purchase (limited seats) /** *doit être acheté 7 jours d'avance (places limitées)*
MEALS INCLUDED FOR ALL SLEEPER CLASS / *REPAS INCLUS POUR LA CLASSE VOITURE-LITS.*

Montreal-Halifax/Gaspe -> The Ocean & Chaleur / *L'Ocean et le Chaleur*:
Peak Period / *Période de pointe*: 25JUN00 - 04SEP00 AND 16DEC00 - 02JAN01 / *25JUN00 - 04SEP00 ET 16DEC00 - 02JAN01*
Super Saver / Super escompte: 04JAN00 - 24JUN00 AND 05SEP00 - 15DEC00 / *24JAN00 - 24JUN00 ET 05SEP00 - 15DEC00*
Any discount fare requires 7 day advance purchase (limited seats)/ *Tous les tarifs réduits doivent être achetés 7 jours d'avance (places limitées)*

Malahat, Hudson Bay & other Mandatory Services / *Les liaisons essentielles*:
Peak Period / *Période de pointe*: Economy class: None;   Sleeper class: 01JUL00 - 30JUL00 AND 16SEP00 - 15NOV00
                             Classe économique: aucune;   classe voiture-lits: 01JUL00 - 30JUL00 ET 16SEP00 - 15NOV00
Super Saver/Super escompte: Economy class: Valid year round; Sleeper class: 01JAN00 - 30JUN00, 01AUG00 - 15SEP00, 16NOV00 - 30JUN01 /
               classe économique: valable à l'année;   classe voiture-lits: 01JAN00 - 30JUN00, 01AUG00 - 15SEP00, 16NOV00 - 30JUN01
Super Saver fare requires 7 day advance purchase (limited seats) /*Le tarif super escompte doit être acheté 7 jours d'avance (places limitées)*

Skeena:
Totem Class / *Classe Totem:* 14MAY00 - 15OCT00 / *14MAI00 - 15OCT00*
Super Saver / Super escompte: Economy class: **Valid year round**;   *Classe economie: valable à l'année*

Bras d'Or:
Bras d'Or Class / *Classe Bras d'Or:* 09MAY00 - 18OCT00 / *09MAI00 - 18OCT00*

Via Rail Fare Plans

2000 VIA RAIL FARE PLANS – January 20, 2000

	JAN	FEB	MAR	APR	MAY	JUN	JUL	AUG	SEP	OCT	NOV	DEC

EASTERN TRANSCONTINENTALS : THE OCEAN AND THE CHALEUR

SUPERSAVER year-round – 7days, AP, "Q" or "B"(*); O/W 25%, R/T 37%; SC $15

ÉCONOMY CLASS

SLEEPER CLASS
- SUPERSAVER – 7days AP; 38%; SC $15 — Jan 4 – June 25
- PEAK — June 26 – Sept 7
- SUPERSAVER – 7days AP: 38%; SC $15 — Sept 8 – Dec 15
- PEAK — Dec 16-Jan 3

THE CANADIEN

ÉCONOMY CLASS
- SUPERSAVER - 7days AP,"Q",O/W 25%, R/T 38%, SC $15. BASIC FARE: -25% in "Y", no condition Jan 1 – May 31
- PEAK — June 1 - October 21
- 7days AP "Q"; O/W 25%, R/T 38%, SC $15; or -25% in "Y" no cond. Oct 22 – Dec 31

SLEEPER CLASS
- SUPERSAVER - 7days, AP, 38%, SC $50. BASIC FARE: -25% in "Y" no condition Jan 1 – May 31
- PEAK — June 1 - October 21
- SUPERSAVER - 7days AP, 38%, SC $50; or -25% in "Y" no cond. Oct 22 – Dec 31

THE HUDSON BAY

SUPERSAVER year-round – 7days, AP,"Q". O/W 25%, R/T 38%, SC $15.

ÉCONOMY CLASS

SLEEPER CLASS
- SUPERSAVER – 7days, AP, 40%, SC $15. — Jan 1 – June 30
- PEAK — July 1 -31
- SUP.SAVER – 7days, AP, 40%, SC $15 — Aug 1 - Sep 15
- PEAK — Sep 16 - Nov 15
- SUP.SAVER – 7days, AP, 40%, SC $15 — Nov 16 - Dec 31

NORTHERN SERVICES AND THE MALAHAT

(Victoria-Courtenay, Jasper-Prince Rupert, The Pas-Lynn Lake, Sudbury-White River, Montreal-Jonquiere, Montreal-Senneterre)

SUPERESAVER year-round – 7days AP,"Q"; O/W 25%, R/T 38%, SC $15

ÉCONOMY

TOTEM CLASS
- TOTEM CLASS (SKEENA): May 15 - Oct 16

CORRIDOR

DISCOUNTED ECONOMY : O/W 25%, R/T 35% - 5 days, AP,"Q" or "B"(*); SC $10

ÉCONOMY

Full fare 7 days a week.

INTERCITY EAST

(Local travel between and including - Halifax, Gaspé and Rivière-du-Loup)

DISCOUNTED ECONOMY: - 5 days, AP,O/W 25%, R/T 37% "Q", SC $10

ÉCONOMY

VIA 1

HALIFAX – SYDNEY

BRAS D'OR : May 09 - October 18

AP = advance purchase requirement **O/W** = one-way **R/T** = round trip. (Q or B * seats required both ways.)

"Q" = Discounted economy, quantity limited. **(*)"B"** = same as Q, but used only for East-Corridor connections.

SC = maximun service charge per one-way trip (plus taxes) for exchanges or refunds. **References** : under "Fare Policies", see : "Services Charges" and "Re-qualification ..."

DISCOUNTS BASED ON AGE, i.e. SEN (-10%), CHD(-50%) et STU(*), apply on the best applicable fare.

(*)STU = unrestricted 40% discount Économy (-50% off with 6Pak); 10% discount in VIA 1 and sleeper. **References** : "Fares Policies", see "Students"; "Products & services" see "6 Pak".

CANRAILPASS = peak fare June 1 to October 15. **Restriction**: In Silver & Blue during peak season; upgrades allowed only 21 days or less prior to departure. **Reference** : see "Products & services".

NORTH AMERICA RAIL PASS = Peak fare June 1 to Oct. 15. **Restr.** :In Silver & Blue class, during peak: upgrades allowed only 21 days or less prior to dep. **Reference** : see "Products & services".

NORTH EASTERN NORTH AMERICA RAIL PASS: = Peak fare July 1 to August 31. **Reference** : see "Products & services".

Via Rail Fare Plans continued

CLASSES OF SERVICE
CORRIDOR

VIA 1 First Class - Active bookings	
Assigned seating	J
Assigned seating (discounted)	D

Coach Class - Active bookings	
Coach seat	Y
Coach seat (discounted)	Q

TRANSCONTINENTALS & SERVICES TO
REMOTE REGIONS

Sleeper Classes - Passive bookings		
Drawing room	*3 Pax	R
Standard bedroom	*2 Pax	P
Roomette	*1 Pax	F
Upper berth (section)	*1 Pax	S
Lower berth (section)	*1 Pax	W

*Recommended passenger limits per unit.

Coach class - Passive bookings	
Coach seat	Y
Coach seat (discounted)	Q

VIA Rail Canada

Également disponible en français.
Appelez Envoi et Imprimerie Automatique au (514) 761-5577; télécopieur (514) 762-0451.

® Registered trademark of VIA Rail Canada Inc.
Printed in Canada   VIA-119- 4E-G2

FARE PLANS
CORRIDOR

CHILD (2-11 years)	Fare Basis Codes	Discounts
VIA 1 First Class	JCHILD	25% off adult fare
Coach Class	YCHILD	50% off adult fare
Coach (Discounted)	Q5X57CH Child except Fri & Sun 5 day advance purchase	50% off discounted adult fare

Notes: (Infants - Less than 2 years old)
1. Infants are permitted in VIA 1 First Class (J Class), but they <u>must</u> <u>occupy a confirmed seat</u> and hence must be booked, priced and ticketed as a child.
2. In coach (Y or Q Class) infants may travel free if they do not occupy a seat. Show as "and infant" in standard name field format. If a seat is desired, the infant should be booked, priced and ticketed as a child.

YOUTH (12-24 years)		
VIA 1 First Class	JYOUTH	10% off adult fare
Coach Class	YYOUTH	10% off adult fare
Coach (discounted)	Q5YOUTH	50% off adult fare

ADULT (25-59 years)		
VIA 1 First Class	J	--------
Coach Class	Y	--------
Coach (discounted)	Q5X57	40% off adult fare

SENIOR (60 years +)		
VIA 1 First Class	JSENIOR	10% off adult fare
Coach Class	YSENIOR	10% off adult fare
Coach (discounted)	Q5X57SEN	50% off adult fare
No senior companion discount permitted	------	-----

For fare plans on the Transcontinentals and services to remote areas, please contact VIA.

Via Rail Car Diagrams

Car Diagrams      **Schémas de voitures**

The following diagrams show typical interiors in VIA Corridor trains.   Les schémas ci-dessous constituent des exemples d'aménagement intérieur des trains de VIA dans le Corridor.

Corridor Coach / Voiture-coach du corridor

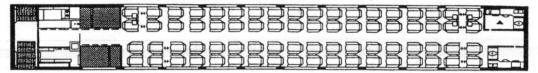

Overhead bins are reserved for carry-on baggage.
Des casiers suspendus au-dessus des sièges servent à ranger les bagages à main.
Seat arrangements may vary / *La disposition des sièges peut varier*

▲ **Accessible washroom / *Toilette accessible***

LRC Car Diagram – VIA 1 Seat Selection
Schéma de la voiture LRC – Sélection des sièges VIA 1

◀ ◀ ◀ ◀ **DIRECTION OF TRAVEL / *SENS DE LA MARCHE*** ◀ ◀ ◀

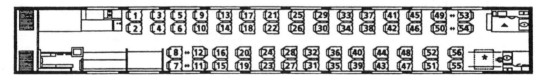

▶ ▶ ▶ **DIRECTION OF TRAVEL / *SENS DE LA MARCHE*** ▶ ▶ ▶

▲ **Accessible washroom / *Toilette accessible***
⊕ ***Power outlets are located between each seat / Prise de courant disponible entre chaque siège***
* Wheelchair tie-down device / Dispositif d'immobilisation de fauteuil roulant

Car diagrams

Schémas de voitures

The following diagrams show typical interiors in VIA transcontinental trains.

Les schémas ci-dessous constituent des exemples d'aménagement intérieur des trains transcontinentaux de VIA.

Transcontinental Coach / *Voiture-coach du Transcontinental*

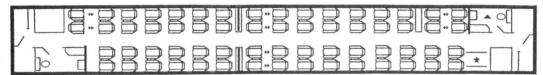

Seat arrangements may vary / *La disposition des sièges peut varier*
* Wheelchair tie-down device / *Dispositif d'immobilisation de fauteuil roulant*   ▲ Accessible washroom / Toilette accessible

"Manor" Sleeper / *Voiture-lits «Manor»*

Limited space is available for carry-on baggage in sleeper class / *Dans la classe voiture-lits, un espace limité est réservé aux bagages à main*
Baggage may be checked on trains where baggage service is available. / *Les bagages peuvent être enregistrés à bord des trains où ce service est offert.*

"Chateau" Sleeper / *Voiture-lits «Chateau»*

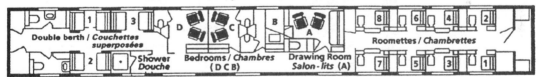

Limited space is available for carry-on baggage in sleeper class / *Dans la classe voiture-lits, un espace limité est réservé aux bagages à main*
Baggage may be checked on trains where baggage service is available. / *Les bagages peuvent être enregistrés à bord des trains où ce service est offert.*

"Park" Car / *Voiture «Parc»*

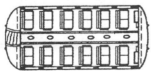

Dome / *Salon panoramique*

LEGEND	LÉGENDE
Roomette (single bedroom)	Chambrette (chambre occupation simple)
Bedroom (double bedroom)	Chambre (chambre occupation double)
Drawing Room (triple bedroom)	Salon-lits (chambre occupation triple)

Via Rail Station Codes

VIA STATION CODES
(CRS CITY CODES AND INTERLINE POINTS)

LEGEND

◉ **CRS Hub cities (VIA)**
● **Interline connections (VIA)**
▲ **Interline bus service**
■ **Interline train service**

CITY	CRS	VIA	CITY	CRS	VIA	CITY	CRS	VIA
Acton Vale, QC		ACTV	▲Bishop Falls, NF		BSHF	Chambord, QC		CHBD
Ahuntsic, QC		AHUN	Blue River, BC		BLUE	Chandler, QC		CHND
■Albany, NY		ALBY	Bolger, QC		BGQU	Chapleau, ON	YLD	CHAP
Aldershot, ON		ALDR	Bolkow, ON		BOLK	Charette, QC		CHRT
Alexandria, ON		ALEX	Bonaventure, QC	YBV	BVNT	Charlebois, MB		CHLB
Aleza Lake, BC		ALZL	▲Borden, PEI		BRDN	Charles, MB		CHLS
Allanwater Bridge, ON		ALWB	Boston Bar, BC		BBAR	Charlo, NB	YCL	CHLO
Amery, MB		AMRY	Bourmont, QC		BRMT	▲Charlottetown, PEI		CLTT
Amesdale, ON		AMDL	Boyd, MB		BOYD	Charny, QC		CHNY
Amherst, NS		AMHS	Brampton, ON		BRMP	Chatham, ON	XCM	CHAT
Amos, QC	YEY	AMOS	Brandon North, MB	YBR	BRNN	Chelmsford, ON		CHEL
Amqui, QC		AMQU	Brantford, ON		BRTF	Chemainus, BC		CNUS
■Amsterdam, NY		AMST	Brereton Lake, MB		BRTL	Cherokee, QC		CHER
▲Annapolis Royal, NS		ANNR	Bridgar, MB		BRGR	Chesnaye, MB		CHES
▲Antigonish, NS		ANTI	▲Bridgetown, NS		BRGT	■Chicago, IL		CHIG
Armstrong, ON	YYW	ARMG	Brockville, ON	XBR	BRKV	Chilliwack, BC	YCB	CHIL
▲Arnolds Cove, NF		ARNC	Brooks, QC		BRQU	Churchill, MB	YYQ	CHUR
Arnot, MB		ARNO	Brower, ON		BRWR	▲Clarenville, NF		CLRV
Ashcroft, BC	YZA	ASHN	Brownville Jct., ME		BRNJ	Clearwater, BC		CLWT
Atik, MB		ATIK	Buckley Bay, BC		BUCB	Clercs-St-Viateur, QC		CLSV
Atikameg Lake, MB		ATKL	Budd, MB		BUDD	Cliffside, BC		CLFS
Auden, ON		AUDN	■Buffalo (Depew), NY		BUFF	Clova, QC		CLOV
▲Auld Cove, NF		AULD	■Buffalo (Exchange) NY		BUFX	Club Beaudin Inc, QC		BDNC
Azilda, ON		AZIL	Burns Lake, BC	YPZ	BRNL	Club Bélanger, QC		BLGC
Back, MB		BACK	Button, MB		BUTT	Club Grégoire, QC		GRGC
▲Baddeck, NS		BADD	Bylot, MB		BYLO	Club Iroquois, QC		IRQC
▲Badger, NF		BADZ	Campbellton, NB		CBTN	Club Nicol, QC		NCLC
▲Baie Verte, NF		BVER	Cann, QC		CANN	Club Rita Inc, QC		RTAC
Barachois, QC		BARA	Canora, SK		CANO	Club Summit, QC		SMMC
Barraute, QC		BRTE	Canyon, ON		CNYK	Club Triton, QC		TRTC
Barrie, ON		BRRI	▲Cape Tormentine, PEI		CTOR	Club Vermillion, QC		VMLC
Bathurst, NB	ZBF	BTRS	Caplan, QC		CAPL	Club Wigwam, QC		WGWC
■Battle Creek, MI		BATT	Capreol, ON		CAPR	■Cobalt, ON		COBA
Belcher, MB		BLCH	Caramat, ON		CARA	Cobble Hill, BC		COBH
Belleville, ON		BLVL	Caribou, QC		CARI	Cobourg, ON		CBRG
Bend, BC		BEND	Carleton, QC		CARL	●■Cochrane, ON	YCN	COCH
Benny, ON		BENN	Cartier, QC		CART	Collins, ON		COLL
▲Berwick, NS		BERW	Casey, QC		CASY	▲Come By Chance, NF		CBCX
Bi-Ma, QC		BIMA	Casselman, ON		CSLM	Consolidated Bathurst, QC		CBAT
Biggar, SK		BIGG	Cassidy, BC		CASY	Copeland's Landing, ON		COPE
Bird, MB		BIRD	Causapscal, QC		CAUS	Coquar, QC		COQU
Biscotasing, ON		BISC	Cedarvale, BC		CEDA	Cormorant, MB		CORM

CITY	CRS	VIA	CITY	CRS	VIA	CITY	CRS	VIA
▲Corner Brook, NF		CRBK	Felix, ON		FELX	Herriot, MB		HERR
Cornwall, ON	YCC	CWLL	Ferguson, QC		FERG	Hervey, QC		HERV
▲Cornwallis, NS		CWLS	Ferland, ON		FERL	Hibbard, QC		HIBB
Coteau, QC		COTO	Finger, MB		FING	Hillbank, BC		HLBK
Courtenay, BC	YCA	COUR	Fitzpatrick, QC		FITZ	Hillsport, ON		HLSP
Cowichan, BC		COWI	▲Flat Bay Jct., NF		FBAY	Hinton, AB		HINT
Cranberry Portage, MB		CRNP	Flindt Landing, ON		FLTL	Hirondelle, QC		HRDL
Cressman, QC		CRSM	■Flint, MI		FLIN	Hockin, MB		HOCK
Cromarty, MB		CROM	Foleyet, ON		FOLE	▲Holyrood Jct., NF		HOLZ
■Croton Harmon, NY		CROT	Forsythe, QC		FORS	Hope, BC	YHE	HOPE
Dalton, ON		DALT	Fort Fraser, BC		FFRA	Hornepayne, ON	YHN	HNPN
Danforth, ME		DANF	Franz, ON		FRNZ	▲Howley Jct., NF		HOWL
Dauphin, MB	YDN	DAUP	Fredericton, NB	YFC	FRDN	Houston, BC	ZHO	HOUS
Da-Rou-Lac-Lodge, QC		DRLL	Fredericton Jct., NB		FRDJ	Hudson, ON		HDSN
Deep Bay, ON		DPBA	Gagnon, QC		GAGN	Hudson Bay, SK	YHB	HBAY
▲Deer Lake, NF		DRLZ	▲Gambo, NF		GAMB	▲Hunter River, NS		HNTR
Dering, MB		DERI	Gananoque, ON		GANA	■Huntsville, ON		HNTV
Dessane, QC		DESS	▲Gander, NF	YQX	GAND	Hutton, BC		HUTT
Devon, ON		DEVN	Garneau, QC		GARN	Ilford, MB	ILF	ILFO
▲Digby, NS		DIGB	Gaspé, QC	YGP	GASP	Ingersoll, ON		INGR
Digges, MB		DIGG	Georgetown, ON		GEOR	Iroquois Falls, ON		IRQF
Dix, QC		DIXX	Gilbert Plains, MB		GLBP	Jackman, ME		JACK
Dome Creek, BC		DOMC	Gillam, MB	YGX	GILL	Jacques Cartier Club, QC		JACC
Dorreen, BC		DORR	Girdwood, ON		GIRD	Jacquet River, NB		JACR
Dorval, QC	YUL	DORV	Gladstone, MB		GSTO	◉Jasper, AB	YJA	JASP
▲Doyles, NF		DOYL	Glencoe, ON		GLNC	Jetait, AB		JETA
Drummondville, QC		DRMV	Glenella, MB		GLNA	Joliette, QC		JOLI
Drybrough, MB		DRYB	▲Glenwood Jct., NF		GLNW	Jonquière, QC		JONQ
Duncan, BC	DUQ	DUNC	▲Glovertown Jct., NF		GLOV	■Kalamazoo, MI		KALA
Dundas, ON		DNDS	Goat River, BC		GOAT	Kamloops North, BC	YKA	KAMN
Dunlop, MB		DUNL	Gogama, ON		GOGA	Kamsack, SK		KAMS
Dunsmuir, BC		DNSM	▲Goobies Jct., NF		GOOB	Kapitachuan Club, QC		KPTC
Dunster, BC		DNST	Grande-Rivière, QC		GDRV	■Kapuskasing, ON	YYU	KAPU
Duplessis, QC		DUPL	▲Grand Falls, NF		GFNZ	Kellett, MB		KLTT
■Durand, MI		DURA	Grand'mère, QC		GMRE	▲Kensington, PEI		KENS
Dyce, MB		DYCE	Grandview, MB		GVIE	▲Kentville, NS		KNTV
Eades, ON		EADS	■Gravenhurst, ON		GRVH	Kettle Rapids, MB		KETR
Earchman, MB		EARC	Greening, QC		GRNG	▲Kingston, NS		KGNS
■East Lansing, MI		EASL	Greenville, ME		GRNV	Kingston, ON	YGK	KGON
▲Eastport Jct., NF		EASJ	Grimsby, ON		GRIM	Kinogama, ON		KINO
Edmonton, AB	YXD	EDMO	Guelph, ON		GUEL	Kiskisink, QC		KISK
Edson, AB	YET	EDSN	Guildwood, ON		GUIL	Kitchener, ON	YFK	KITC
Elma, MB		ELMA	Halcrow, MB		HALC	Kitwanga, BC		KITW
Elsas, ON		ELSA	Halifax, NS	YHZ	HLFX	Kondiaronk, QC		KOND
Endako, BC		ENDA	■Hammond Whiting, IN		HAMM	Kormak, ON		KORM
Endeavour, SK		ENDV	▲Hampden Jct., NF		HDEN			
■Englehart, ON		ENGL	Harvey, BC		HRVY			
Esher, ON		ESHR	Hayward, BC		HAYW			
Esquimalt, BC	YPF	ESQU	■Hearst, ON	YHF	HRST			
Evansburg, AB		EVAN	Hébertville/Alma, QC	YTF	HEBV			
Fairie, QC		FAIR	Heming Lake, MB		HMGL			
Farlane, ON		FARL	Herchmer, MB		HERC			

VIA Rail Canada

CITY	CRS	VIA	CITY	CRS	VIA	CITY	CRS	VIA
Kwinitsa, BC		KWIN	McKee's Camp, ON		MCKC	O'Day, MB		ODAY
Lac-Bouchette, QC		LBOU	McTavis Club, QC		MCTC	Odhill, MB		ODHI
Lac Darey, QC		LDAR	McVeigh, MB		MCVE	Ophir, MB		OPHR
Lac des Roches, QC		LDES	Medard, MB		MEDA	Optic Lake, MB		OPTL
Lac-Édouard, QC		LEDW	Mégantic, QC		MEGA	Orillia, ON		ORIL
Lac Malouin, QC		LMAL	Megiscane, QC		MEGI	Orok, MB		OROK
Ladysmith, BC		LADY	Melville, SK		MELV	Oshawa, ON	YOO	OSHA
Laforest, ON		LAFO	Metagama, ON		MTGM	Oskelaneo Lodge, QC		OSKL
Lamprey, MB		LAMP	▲Meteghan, NS		METE	Oskelaneo River, QC		OSKR
Langford, BC		LNGF	▲Middleton, NS		MIDD	◉Ottawa, ON	YOW	OTTW
Langlade, QC		LNGL	Mikado, SK		MIKA	Ottermere, ON		OTTM
■Lapeer, MI		LAPE	Minaki, ON	YMI	MNKI	Pacific, BC		PACI
La Perouse, MB		LPRS	Miquick, QC		MIQK	Palmer, BC		PALM
La Pocatière, QC		LPOC	Missanabie, ON		MSBI	Parent, QC		PARE
Larchwood, ON		LARC	▲Monastery, NS		MONA	Parksville, BC		PRKV
La Reine, QC		LREI	●■Moncton, NB	YQM	MCTN	●■Parry Sound, ON	YPD	PARS
La Sarre, QC	SSQ	LSAR	Monet, QC		MNET	▲Pasadena, NF		PASA
L'Assomption, QC		LASS	Montjobagues, QC		MJBG	Paterson, MB		PATE
La Tuque, QC	YLQ	LTUQ	Mont-Joli, QC	YYY	MJLI	Pawistik, MB		PAWI
Laurier, MB		LRIE	Montmagny, QC		MMGY	Pearl Lake, QC		PRLL
Lawledge, MB		LAWL	■◉●Montréal, QC	YMY	MTRL	Penny, BC		PENN
Le Gardeur, QC		LGAR	Moosonee, ON	YMO	MSNE	Percé, QC		PERC
Levack, ON		LEVA	Mud River, ON		MUDR	Petit Rocher, NB		PROC
Leven, MB		LEVN	Munk, MB		MUNK	Pikwitonei, MB	PIW	PIKW
Lévis, QC		LEVI	Musk, ON		MUSK	Pipun, MB		PIPN
Lizotte Club, QC		LIZO	Nakina, ON	YQN	NAKI	Pit Siding, MB		PITS
Lochalsh, ON		LOCH	●■Nanaimo, BC	YCD	NANA	Plumas, MB		PLUM
London, ON	YXU	LNDN	Nanoose Bay, BC		NANB	Pogamasing, ON		POGA
Longlac, ON		LLAC	Napanee, ON		NAPN	Pointe-aux-Trembles, QC		PATX
Longworth, BC		LWTH	Nemegos, ON		NEME	Pont-Beaudet, QC		PBDT
Loos, BC		LOOS	New Carlisle, QC		NCAR	Ponton, MB		PNTN
Lowbush River, ON		LBSR	Newcastle, NB		NCAS	■Porquis, ON		PORQ
Luke, MB		LUKE	▲New Glascow, NS		NGLA	Portage-la-Prairie, MB	YPG	PLPX
Lyddal, MB		LYDD	New Hazelton, BC		NHAZ	▲Port aux Basques, NF		PABX
Lynn Lake, MB	YYL	LYNN	■New Liskeard, ON		NLIS	▲Port Blandford, NF		PBLN
Macamic, QC		MACA	Newmarket, ON		NMKT	Port Coquitlam, BC	YBD	PCQN
Mace, ON		MACE	New Richmond, QC		NRCH	Port Daniel, QC		PDAN
Malachi, ON		MLCH	■New York, NY		NEWY	▲Port Hawkesbury, NS		PHAW
Malahat, BC		MLHT	■Niagara Falls, NY		NFNY	Port Hope, ON		PHOP
Maniwawa Club, QC		MWWC	●Niagara Falls, ON		NIAG	■Port Huron, MI		PHUR
Matago, MB		MTGO	Nicholson, ON		NICH	■Poughkeepsie, NY		POUG
Matapédia, QC		MTPD	■Niles, MI		NILE	Prescott, ON		PRSC
■Matheson, ON		MATH	Nonsuch, MB		NONS	Press, QC		PRSS
Matsqui, BC		MTSQ	Norembega, ON		NORE	Prince George, BC	YXS	PGEO
Mattawamkeag, ME		MTWK	■North Bay, ON	YYB	NBAY	Prince Rupert, BC	YPR	PRUP
Maxville, ON		MAXV	▲North Sydney, NS		NSYD	Prospector, MB		PROS
McAdam, NB		MCAD	▲Notre Dame Jct., NF		NRDJ	Pukatawagan, MB	XPK	PUKA
McBride, BC		MCBR	Nouvelle, QC		NOUV	Qualicum Beach, BC	YQU	QLCB
McCarthy, QC		MCCA	Oakville, ON		OAKV	Québec, QC	YQB	QBEC
M'Clintock, MB		MCLI	Oba, ON		OBAX	Ramsey, ON		RAMS
McCreary, MB		MCCR	O'Brien, ON		OBRI	Rapide-Blanc, QC		RAPB
McGregor, BC		MCGR	Ochre River, MB		OCHR	Rawebb, MB		RAWE

CITY	CRS	VIA	CITY	CRS	VIA	CITY	CRS	VIA
Reddit, ON		RDDT	Sinclair Mills, BC		SINM	Union Bay, BC		UNNB
Red Lake Road, ON	YRL	RLRX	Sioux Lookout, ON	YXL	SLKT	Unity, SK		UNIT
Reserve, SK		RSRV	Sipiwesk, MB		SIPI	Upper Fraser, BC		UFRZ
■Rhinecliffe, NY		RHIN	Sisco Club, QC		SSCC	Usk, BC		USKX
Rice Lake, ON		RCLK	Smithers, BC	YYD	SMTR	■Utica, NY		UTIC
Richmond, QC		RCQU	Smiths Falls, ON	YSH	SMTF	Valemount, BC		VLMT
Rimouski, QC	YXK	RMSK	Smooth Rock, ON		SMOO	Van Bruyssels, QC		VBRU
Rivers, MB	YYI	RVRS	▲South Branch Jct., NF		SBRA	Vanceboro, ME		VBRO
Rivière-à-Pierre, QC		RAPX	▲Southbrook Jct., NF		SBRK	●■Vancouver, BC	YVR	VCVR
Rivière-du-Loup, QC	YRI	RDLX	■South River, ON		SRVR	Vanderhoof, BC		VDRH
▲Roaches Line, NF		RCLN	South Wellington, BC		SWLT	Vandry, QC		VDRY
Roberts, ON		RBRT	▲Springdale Jct., NF		SPRD	Veregin, SK		VERE
▲Robertson Jct., NF		ROBI	Springhill Jct., NS		SPRJ	●■Victoria, BC	YYJ	VICT
Roblin, MB		RBLN	Stadacona, QC		STAD	Viking, AB		VKNG
■Rochester, NY		ROCH	Starks, BC		STRK	Wabowden, MB		WBDN
Rogersville, NB		RGRV	▲Stephenville, NF		STVA	Wainwright, AB		WAIN
■Rome, NY		ROME	▲Stephenville Crsng, NF		STVX	Wanless, MB		WANL
Root Lake, MB		RTLK	Stimson, ON		STIM	●■Washago, ON		WSHG
Rousseau, QC		ROUS	Strachan, QC		STRN	Watford, ON		WATF
Ruddock, MB		RUDD	Stralak, ON		STRL	Watrous, SK		WATR
Ruel, ON		RUEL	Stratford, ON		STRF	Weir River, MB		WEIR
St.Catharines, ON	YCM	SCAT	Strathcona Lodge, BC		SCNL	Wekusko, MB		WEKU
▲St.Fintans Jct., NF		SFIN	Strathroy, ON		STRR	Wellington, BC		WLGT
Sainte-Foy, QC		SFOY	Sturgis, SK		STGS	Westree, ON		WSTR
▲Saint-Georges, NF		SGEO	⊙Sudbury, ON	YSB	SUDB	Weymont, QC		WYMT
Saint-Hilaire, Portneuf, QC		SHPN	Sudbury Junction, ON		SUDJ	▲Weymouth, NS		WYMH
Saint-Hyacinthe, QC		SHYA	Sultan, ON		SULT	▲Whitbourne Jct., NF		WHTZ
▲St.John's, NF		SJNF	▲Summerside, PEI		SMSD	White River, ON	YWR	WHTR
Saint John, NB	YSJ	SJNB	Summit, QC		SMQU	▲Whycocomagn, NS		WHYC
Saint-Justin, QC		SJUS	Sussex, NB		SUSX	Wilde, MB		WILD
Saint-Lambert, QC		SLAM	■Swastika, ON		SWAS	Willow River, BC		WILR
St.Marys, ON		SMYS	Sydney, NS		SYDN	Windigo, QC		WNDG
Saint-Maurice riv. Boom, QC		SMRB	■Syracuse, NY		SYRA	▲Windsor, NS		WDNS
Saint-Tite, QC		STIT	Taschereau, QC		TASC	●■Windsor, ON	YQG	WDON
Sackville, NB		SACK	Telkwa, BC		TELK	⊙Winnipeg, MB	YWG	WNPG
Sanford, QC		SANF	■Temagami, ON		TEMA	Winnitoba, MB		WNTB
Sanmaur, QC		SANM	Terrace, BC	YXT	TRRC	Wivenhoe, MB		WVHO
●■Sarnia, ON	YZR	SARN	The Pas, MB	YQD	TPAS	▲Wolfville, NS		WOLF
Saskatoon, SK	YXE	SASK	Thibaudeau, MB		THIB	Woman River, ON		WOMR
Savant Lake, ON		SAVL	Thompson, MB	YTH	THOM	Woodstock, ON		WDST
Sayabec, QC		SAYA	Thicket Portage, MB	YTD	THKP	Wyoming, ON		WYOM
■Schenectady, NY		SCHE	Tidal, MB		TIDL	Yarmouth, NS		YARM
■Seattle, WA		SEAT	Timbrell, QC		TIMB	■Yonkers, NY		YONK
Senneterre, QC		SENN	■Timmins, ON	YTS	TIMM			
Shawinigan, QC		SHWN	Togo, SK		TOGO			
Sahwinigan, BC		SHNG	⊙●■Toronto, ON	YBZ	TRTO			
Sheaban, ON		SHEA	Transcona, MB		TRAN			
Sherbrooke, QC	YSC	SHRB	Tremaudan, MB		TREM			
Sherridon, MB		SHRD	Trenton Jct., ON	YTR	TRNJ			
Signai, QC		SIGN	Trois-Pistoles, QC		TPIS			
Silcox, MB		SILC	●■Truro, NS		TRUR			
Simonhouse, MB		SIMG	Turnbull, MB		TURN			

VIA Rail Canada

® Registered trademark of VIA Rail Canada Inc.
Printed in Canada   VIA-119-4E-G3.2

Également disponible en français.
Appelez Envoi et Imprimerie Automatique au (514) 761-5577; télécopieur (514) 762-0451.

Via Rail Timetables

Western Canada

Train			51
Connections Correspondances	DAYS/JOURS		x6
	Montréal, QC		2330
	Kingston, ON		0550
	Toronto, ON		0820

VIA

TORONTO • WINNIPEG •

	TRAIN	KM	1
	NAME NOM		Canadian Canadien
	DAYS/JOURS		2,4,6
DP	**Toronto, ON** ET/HE	0	0845
	Washago	147	1115
	Parry Sound	245	1249
	Sudbury Jct. **	426	1534
AR	Capreol	448	1630
DP			1655
	Laforest	496	1750
	McKee's Camp ★	506	1758
	Felix ★	524	1814
	Ruel ★	532	1825
	Westree	553	1839
	Gogama	588	1910
	Foleyet	688	2043
	Elsas	744	2131
	Oba	863	2257
AR	Hornepayne	926	0020
DP			0055
	Hillsport	994	0151
	Caramat ★	1050	0237
	Longlac	1088	0304
	Nakina	1137	0340
	Auden ★	1227	0440
	Ferland ★	1269	0514
	Mud River ★	1277	0523
	Armstrong ET/HE	1317	0645
	Collins CT/HC	1351	0615
	Allanwater Bridge ★	1405	0655
	Flindt Landing ★	1425	0710
	Savant Lake	1444	0724
AR	Sioux Lookout	1541	0852
DP			0917
	Amesdale ★	1623	1025
	Red Lake Road	1656	1055
	Canyon ★	1687	1121
	Farlane ★	1724	1156
	Redditt	1740	1213
	Minaki	1763	1235
	Ottermere ★	1784	1253
	Malachi ★	1788	1258
	Copeland's Landing ★	1790	1301
	Rice Lake, ON ★	1800	1311
	Winnitoba, MB ★	1805	1317
	Ophir ★	1809	1322
	Brereton Lake ★	1830	1338
	Elma ★	1858	1400
	Transcona 73	1933	1451
AR	**Winnipeg, MB** CT/HC	1946	1540

(2,4,6 bracket; 3,5,7 bracket)

Ouest du Canada

VANCOUVER

	TRAIN	KM	1
	NAME NOM		Canadian Canadien
	DAYS/JOURS		3,5,7
DP	**Winnipeg, MB** CT/HC	1946	1640
	Portage la Prairie	2036	1747
	Brandon North	2154	1856
	Rivers, MB	2178	1916
	Melville, SK	2398	2230
	Watrous	2606	0040
AR	**Saskatoon**	2706	0155
DP			0220
	Biggar	2796	0348
	Unity, SK CT/HC	2889	0446
	Wainwright, AB MT/HR	3021	0504
	Viking	3092	0551
AR	**Edmonton**	3226	0755
DP			0840
	Evansburg	3329	1002
	Edson	3429	1108
	Hinton	3517	1214
AR	**Jasper, AB** MT/HR	3599	1400
DP			1530
	Valemount, BC PT/HP ★	3720	1627
	Blue River	3812	1802
	Clearwater ★	3921	1956
AR	**Kamloops North**	4037	2220
DP			2255
	Ashcroft (CN Stn./Gare) ★	4116	0024
	Boston Bar	4238	0244
	Hope ★	4303	0400
	Chilliwack	4354	0444
	Matsqui (Mission)	4379	0507
AR	**Vancouver, BC** PT/HP	4451	0751
	(Pacific Central Stn./Gare Centrale du Pacifique)		

(3,5,7 bracket; 4,6,1 bracket; 5,7,2 bracket)

** Sudbury Jct., ON 10 km from Sudbury, ON (no shuttle service).

Sudbury Jct. (ON) à 10 km de Sudbury (ON) (aucun service de navette).

★ Stops on request.

Arrête sur demande.

73 Stops on request to detrain customers.

Arrête sur demande pour laisser descendre les clients.

Note: As the Province of Saskatchewan does not observe Daylight Saving Time, schedules are shown one hour later.

Nota: Comme l'heure avancée n'est pas en vigueur en Saskatchewan l'horaire indique une heure plus tard.

Western Canada

VIA | **VANCOUVER • WINNIPEG •**

	TRAIN	KM	2
	NAME / NOM		Canadian / Canadien
	DAYS/JOURS		2,5,7
DP	**Vancouver, BC** PT/HP	0	1730
	(Pacific Central Stn./Gare Centrale du Pacifique)		
	Matsqui (Mission)	72	1912
	Chilliwack	97	1936
	Hope ★	148	2021
	Boston Bar	213	2137
	Ashcroft ★	335	2357
	(CN Stn./Gare)		
AR DP	**Kamloops North**	414	0157 / 0232
	Clearwater ★	530	0419
	Blue River	639	0616
	Valemount, BC PT/HP ★	731	0752
AR DP	**Jasper, AB** MT/HR	852	1115 / 1225
	Hinton	934	1337
	Edson	1022	1440
	Evansburg	1122	1543
AR DP	**Edmonton**	1225	1745 / 1830
	Viking	1359	2008
	Wainwright, AB MT/HR	1430	2056
	Unity, SK CT/HC	1562	2314
	Biggar	1655	0045
AR DP	**Saskatoon**	1745	0200 / 0225
	Watrous	1845	0330
	Melville, SK	2053	0602
	Rivers, MB	2273	0826
	Brandon North	2297	0843
	Portage la Prairie	2415	0952
AR	**Winnipeg, MB** CT/HC	2505	1110

(column brackets annotations: 2,5,7 ; 3,6,1 ; 4,7,2)

** **Sudbury Jct., ON** 10 km from Sudbury, ON (no shuttle service).

Sudbury Jct. (ON) à 10 km de Sudbury (ON) (aucun service de navette).

★ Stops on request.

Arrête sur demande.

Note: As the Province of Saskatchewan does not observe Daylight Saving Time, schedules are shown one hour later.

Nota: Comme l'heure avancée n'est pas en vigueur en Saskatchewan, l'horaire indique une heure plus tard.

Ouest du Canada

TORONTO

	TRAIN	KM	2
	NAME / NOM		Canadian / Canadien
	DAYS/JOURS		4,7,2
DP	**Winnipeg, MB** CT/HC	2505	1210
	Transcona	2518	1224
	Elma ★	2593	1314
	Brereton Lake ★	2621	1334
	Ophir ★	2642	1350
	Winnitoba, MB ★	2646	1355
	Rice Lake, ON ★	2651	1401
	Copeland's Landing ★	2661	1411
	Malachi ★	2663	1414
	Ottermere ★	2667	1419
	Minaki	2688	1438
	Redditt	2711	1500
	Farlane ★	2727	1517
	Canyon ★	2764	1551
	Red Lake Road	2795	1623
	Amesdale ★	2828	1650
AR DP	**Sioux Lookout**	2910	1830 / 1855
	Savant Lake	3007	2016
	Flindt Landing ★	3026	2030
	Allanwater Bridge ★	3046	2044
	Collins CT/HC ★	3100	2126
	Armstrong ET/HE	3134	2305
	Mud River	3174	2338
	Ferland ★	3182	2345
	Auden ★	3224	0019
	Nakina	3314	0120
	Longlac	3363	0155
	Caramat ★	3401	0221
	Hillsport	3457	0307
AR DP	**Hornepayne**	3525	0430 / 0505
	Oba	3588	0553
	Elsas	3707	0719
	Foleyet	3763	0814
	Gogama	3863	0940
	Westree	3898	1011
	Ruel ★	3919	1036
	Felix ★	3927	1040
	McKee's Camp ★	3945	1046
	Laforest	3955	1100
AR DP	**Capreol**	4003	1225 / 1250
	Sudbury Jct. **	4025	1310
	Parry Sound	4206	1557
	Washago	4304	1732
AR	**Toronto, ON** ET/HE	4451	2000

(column brackets annotations: 4,7,2 ; 5,1,3)

Train *Connections* *Correspondances*

TRAIN	50
DAYS/JOURS	x6
Toronto, ON	2330
Kingston, ON	0235
Montréal, QC	0800

How to use the timetable

The **NATIONAL, QUICK FINDS** section is an easy way to look up schedules between main cities.

In all sections, schedules are linear and read down. In general, the schedule for each route indicates the departure time only. Stations at which the train stops are listed on the left. Locations (in bold) indicates a possible connection to various points.

Specific symbols are explained at each table. Please consult the REFERENCE section, for further information on our services, reservations, carry-on or checked personal baggage and the features of our discount fare plans.

Comment utiliser l'horaire

La section **CONSULTATION RAPIDE - RÉSEAU NATIONAL** est une façon simple de consulter les horaires entre les principales villes.

Les horaires de chaque section sont linéaires et se lisent vers le bas. En général, l'horaire de chaque liaison n'indique que l'heure de départ. Le nom des localités desservies est inscrit à la gauche. Les localités (en gras) indiquent une possibilité de correspondance.

Les symboles spécifiques sont expliqués à chaque tableau. Pour des renseignements sur nos services, les réservations, les bagages personnels à main ou enregistrés et les tarifs réduits, veuillez consulter la section RÉFÉRENCE

Train
Connections
Correspondances

TRAIN		21		23	23	25	25
DAYS/JOURS		x6,7					
Québec, QC		0620		0820	0820	1310	1310
Montréal, QC		0906		1114	1114	1604	1604

MONTRÉAL · ALEXANDRIA   OTTAWA

TRAIN		KM	31	631	33	635	35	37	39
DAYS/JOURS			x6,7	6		6,7	x6	x6,7	
DP **Montréal, QC** ET/HE (Central Stn./Gare Centrale)		0	0645	0730	1000	1255	1510	1625	1800
Dorval	✈	19	0702	0747	1017	1313	1527	1642	1824
Coteau, QC		63							1849
Alexandria, ON	★	100	0755	0832	1103	1359	1621	1729	1920
Maxville	★	117			1115				
Casselman	★	140	0818	0902	1126[7]				
AR **Ottawa, ON** ET/HE		187	0849	0934	1156	1458	1720	1835	2012

*The above schedule is only an example. / *L'horaire ci-dessus n'est qu'un exemple.

★ Stops on request.
Arrête sur demande.

7 Stops on request Sundays.
Arrête sur demande le dimanche.

✈ AirConnect
A complimentary shuttle service for VIA's customers runs between Dorval Station and the Dorval Airport.

Un service de navette, gratuit pour les clients de VIA, est assuré entre la gare de Dorval et l'aéroport de Dorval.

Time zone

NT	Newfoundland Time
AT	Atlantic Time
ET	Eastern Time
CT	Central Time
MT	Mountain Time
PT	Pacific Time

Fuseaux horaires

HTN	Heure de Terre-Neuve
HA	Heure de l'Atlantique
HE	Heure de l'Est
HC	Heure du Centre
HR	Heure des Rocheuses
HP	Heure du Pacifique

Days of operation   Jours où le train est en service

Monday	1	Lundi
Tuesday	2	Mardi
Wednesday	3	Mercredi
Thursday	4	Jeudi
Friday	5	Vendredi
Saturday	6	Samedi
Sunday	7	Dimanche
Except	x	Sauf
Except Saturday and Sunday	x6,7	Sauf les samedi et dimanche
Daily	Blank / Aucun symbole	Quotidien

VIA RAIL CODE: 2R

APOLLO/GALILEO CANADA: S* VIA/

SABRE: Y/RAL/VRR

WORLDSPAN: GWTS VIA RAIL

EXERCISES—Via Rail

1. a. What days of the week does The Canadian depart Toronto for Vancouver?

   _____

   b. What days does this train return from Vancouver?

   _____

2. What time does the train depart Sioux Lookout for Vancouver?

   _____

3. How many days does it take to travel from Toronto to Vancouver?

   _____

4. What time does the train depart Jasper to travel through the Rockies to Vancouver?

   _____

5. a. What is the fare from Quebec City to Toronto one way? _____

   b. What is the child fare? _____

   c. If you booked one week in advance what would the fare be for a return trip?

   _____

UNITED STATES

The United States, like Canada, has experienced a gradual decline in passenger rail service. As the private railroads cut back on their service, the government established Amtrak in 1970 (similar to its counterpart, Via Rail, in Canada), and it has been gradually expanded through a number of major rail company mergers. The actual operation of the railways is left to the individual railroads. Equipment, baggage arrangements, types and standards of service, and key sales features are quite similar to those available in Canada. Certain bus services are operated by or for Amtrak, thereby expanding its service, and it also offers a variety of hotel and tour packages.

The route system operated by Amtrak is rather limited, and primarily offers commuter travel between certain cities in the Washington, D.C., to Boston, Massachusetts, corridor or along the California coast. One popular train operated by Amtrak, the Auto Train, permits passengers to take their vehicles on board with them when travelling from the north (Lorton, Virginia) to Florida (Sanford is the end of the line).

Reservations can be made at an Amtrak office, a travel agency, or by calling toll free 1-800-USA-RAIL (872-7245). Some services require advance reservations (club car, custom class, or sleeping cars, and sometimes coach seats).

Each fare-paying passenger is entitled to the following luggage allowance: up to three bags checked (maximum 50 pounds/23 kilograms each, 150 pounds/68 kilograms total) and two pieces of carry-on luggage. There are additional charges for special items (such as bicycles).

Children under 8 years old must be accompanied; between ages 8 and 11 they may travel unaccompanied under certain conditions and with prior permission from Amtrak (unaccompanied children pay full fare).

Classes of Service on Amtrak

COACH	Sometimes reservations are needed; offers reclining seats and overhead luggage racks.
CLUB CAR	Must be reserved; offers more luxurious seating and personalized service (for example, beverage service); surcharge for personal services.
SLUMBERCOACH	Must be reserved; offers a basic room with single bed and wash facilities (no toilet).
DOUBLE SLUMBERCOACH	Must be reserved; offers a basic room with two beds and wash facilities (no toilet).
ROOMETTE	Must be reserved; offers a larger room with single bed and toilet facilities.
BEDROOM	Must be reserved; offers a larger room with two beds plus two foldaway beds, washroom facilities, and closet space.

Where to Find Information

You can find information about Amtrak's service, fares, and ticketing procedures by checking the following sources:

- *Official Railway Guide*
- *Amtrak Sales Guide*
- Amtrak system train timetables

See the following pages for examples, and p. 112 for the Exercises.

Amtrak

GENERAL INFORMATION

These policies and procedures apply only to trains operating outside the Northeast Corridor and which are contained in this timetable. For the policies and procedures for trains which operate within the Northeast Corridor, see the Amtrak Northeast Timetable.

ADVANCE PAYMENT OPTIONS

You can pay for your Amtrak® tickets with a major credit card at the same time you make your reservations by phone when you call 1-800-USA-RAIL, then pick up tickets any time prior to travel. No additional charge for advance payment by phone.

Amtrak also accepts prepayment of tickets and cash advances at any Amtrak ticket office and at most Amtrak travel agencies, for pickup by another person at any other Amtrak ticket office. A non-refundable service charge applies to prepaid ticket sales.

ALCOHOL

Passengers are not permitted to consume their private stock of alcoholic beverages in a public area. Only Sleeping Car accommodations for which a passenger has a valid ticket are considered non-public areas.

AMTRAK EXPRESS®

Amtrak Express Shipping Services: Amtrak offers small package and less-than-truckload (LTL) shipping services to more than 160 downtown cities. Fixed, predictable, frequent schedules, in addition to low rates make Amtrak Express Shipping more economical than air transportation, yet faster than less-than-truckload shipping. Pickup and delivery service is available in selected cities to qualified customers.

Small Package Shipments: Each item must not exceed 75 lbs. (34 kg) and 3' x 3' x 3' (90 x 90 x 90 cm) in size, with a limit of 500 lbs. (227 kg) per shipment.

Heavy and Commercial Shipments: Major stations handle packages up to 100 lbs. (45 kg) and 4' x 4' x 4' (120 x 120 x 120 cm) in size, with a limit of 1,000 lbs. (454 kg) per shipment, and can handle pallets up to 2,000 lbs. (908 kg), with a limit of 8,000 lbs. (3632 kg) per shipment.

Human Remains: Amtrak Express offers station-to-station shipment of remains to all express cities. At smaller stations, funeral directors must load and unload the shipment onto and off the train.

Information: Call toll-free 1-800-368-TRAK (8725) and consult with Agent for rates, schedules, prohibited articles, and pickup and delivery stations. (This number does not provide passenger information.)

AMTRAK® VACATIONS

Rail inclusive vacation packages are available by calling 1-800-321-8684.

ANIMALS/PETS

Trained service animals accompanying passengers with disabilities are the only animals permitted on Amtrak trains. Trained service animals must be kept under the control of their owners at all times.

BAGGAGE

Checked Baggage Service: Amtrak offers checked baggage service at many stations and on many trains and Amtrak Thruway buses throughout the country. Trains and stations that handle baggage are indicated in this timetable. Each ticketed passenger may check three pieces, not to exceed 50 lbs. (23 kg.) per piece, at no charge. A maximum of three additional pieces, and overweight items up through 75 lbs. (34 kg.), will be accepted upon payment of a surcharge. Oversize items checked to destinations served by connecting Thruway motorcoaches offering checked baggage are subject to delay; tandem bicycles are not handled on these services.

Checking Baggage: Baggage checked less than 30 minutes prior to departure (one hour for bicycles that need to be boxed at the station) may be delayed. Pack your baggage using sturdy luggage or containers, able to withstand normal handling, and attach your name and address to each item; free identification tags are available. Bicycle boxes, shipping boxes, and ski bags are available for purchase at stations that accept checked baggage.

Claiming Baggage: Checked baggage will be available for claiming within 30 minutes of arrival. Always identify your baggage by the claim check numbers. Amtrak will collect your claim checks when you receive your checked baggage. Storage charges apply to baggage not claimed within two days of arrival.

Special Items and Bicycles: Amtrak accepts a number of special items such as baby strollers, bicycles, golf bags, musical instruments, skis (one per bag), etc. In most cases there is a handling charge. Bicycles must normally be in containers provided by the passenger or Amtrak; certain trains, identified in this timetable, can handle bicycles not in containers; a reservation for this space is usually required for which a nominal charge is made.

Prohibited Items: Dangerous, fragile, and valuable items, as well as animals, household goods, and overweight and oversize items, are prohibited in checked baggage service.

Liability: Amtrak accepts liability for checked baggage to a maximum of $500.00 per ticketed passenger. You may declare additional valuation, up through $2500.00, upon payment of the applicable charge. Amtrak disclaims liability under certain circumstances and for certain items. Claims must be submitted within 30 days of travel.

Carry-On Baggage: Amtrak trains have limited room for carry-on baggage. Passengers are encouraged to use checked baggage service whenever it is available. For the safety and comfort of everyone on board, we encourage passengers to bring no more than two pieces per person. Sleeping car passengers may bring additional pieces but only two or three average-sized suitcases will fit in the largest of rooms. Only carry-on baggage of reasonable quantity, size, and weight (50 lbs./23 kg. maximum per piece) is permitted. Amtrak disclaims liability for carry-on baggage, including bicycles carried on trains by passengers. Dangerous or illegal items, **including all firearms and weapons of any type,** are prohibited on board trains.

Baggage to/from Canada: Checked baggage to or from Canada will only be accepted on the same train as the passenger. Customs regulations prevent unaccompanied baggage being handled across the border. All baggage must be locked for Customs inspection and bear an identification tag with passenger's name and address.

Assistance with Baggage: Baggage assistance is provided free of charge by Red Caps at many major stations. All baggage handled by Red Caps is protected by a claim check. Amtrak recommends that you accept assistance only from a uniformed Amtrak Red Cap and that you ask for claim checks for each piece. Items handled by Red Caps are *not* checked baggage, and you are responsible for them once loaded onto trains. Maximum liability is $50.00 per bag. In addition to Red Cap service, many stations have self-service luggage carts available free or at a nominal charge.

For more information: Amtrak's brochure, "Checked Baggage Service," contains complete details about Amtrak's baggage services, including lists of special and prohibited items, charges, and conditions under which Amtrak disclaims liability. This brochure is available at all stations or can be sent to you by mail.

BOARDING TIMES

Passengers should be at their boarding stations at least 30 minutes prior to departure (Auto Train passengers should arrive at the station at least 2 hours prior to departure). Extra time is recommended if you need extensive ticketing or baggage services. If a train should arrive late, every effort is made to depart as soon as possible. In such cases, the amount of time the train remains in the station may be less than what is shown in this timetable. Since schedules are subject to change, passengers should reconfirm departure times one day before travel, particularly if tickets have been purchased in advance.

COMMENTS ON SERVICE

We encourage you to give us the benefit of any comments, compliments, or suggestions you may have regarding Amtrak service. Amtrak customer relations representatives may be reached at 1-800-USA-RAIL; ask for customer relations. Correspondence may also be sent to Office of Customer Relations, Amtrak, 60 Massachusetts Avenue, NE, Washington, DC 20002-4285 (include your original ticket receipt), or through our web site (www.amtrak.com).

CONNECTING TRAINS

Amtrak does not normally guarantee connections of less than 60 minutes (90 minutes between arriving long-distance trains and local trains in the Northeast Corridor). Consult Amtrak or your travel agent if your planned itinerary includes a shorter connection. A guaranteed connection *does not* ensure that such a connection will always be made. In the case of a missed guaranteed connection, Amtrak will provide alternate transportation on Amtrak, another carrier, or overnight hotel accommodations, at Amtrak's discretion.

CREDIT AND DEBIT CARDS

Amtrak accepts American Express, Carte Blanche, Diners Club, Discover, Japan Credit Bureau (JCB), MasterCard, Visa and Air Travel Card (ATC), at all ticket offices. These cards (except JCB) are also accepted on board for the sale of tickets. These cards (except ATC and JCB) are also accepted on board for dining car meals. Debit (ATM) cards are accepted at all ticket offices. Cards that are not signed on the back with the signature of the person whose name is embossed on the card are not accepted.

CROSSING U.S. BORDERS

Customs and Immigration Information

Amtrak trains crossing international borders are subject to Customs and Immigration inspections en route. Although time is allotted in Amtrak schedules for these inspections, Customs and Immigration officials may delay trains if necessary for the performance of their duties. Customs regulations prevent unaccompanied baggage being handled across the border.

Entry into Canada/U.S.: U.S. or Canadian citizens crossing the U.S./Canadian border are required to have a passport (preferred), or an original or certified birth certificate, citizenship certificate, or naturalization certificate plus current government-issued photo identification. **(Note: a driver's license is not sufficient.)** Non-U.S. citizens permanently or temporarily residing in the United States must have an Alien Registration Card (I-551, or I-688 bearing the proper endorsement on the reverse). All citizens of countries other than the United States or Canada not bearing an Alien Registration Card must have a passport, and citizens of many countries must also have a visa. U.S. Employment Authorization Card showing 210 as a section of law, or Canadian Form IMM 1000. Passengers not having proper documentation are prohibited from entering the U.S. or Canada, and will be detrained prior to reaching the U.S./Canadian border. Persons under 18 years old who are not accompanied by an adult must bring a letter from a parent or guardian giving them permission to enter into Canada. Passengers planning international travel should contact one of the following for most current information and restrictions and for further information: Immigration and Naturalization Service, United States Department of Justice, 425 I St.,

Amtrak continued

GENERAL INFORMATION

NW, Washington, DC 20536, or Embassy of Canada, Consular & Visa Section, 501 Pennsylvania Avenue, NW, Washington, DC 20001.

EN ROUTE UPGRADING OF ACCOMMODATIONS

Sleeping Car, Metroliner First Class and Business Class accommodations may be purchased on board trains if unsold space is still available. Guests wanting to purchase an upgrade of accommodations should consult the Conductor or Chief of On Board Services.

FALL AND SPRING TIME CHANGES

Amtrak® operates according to the prevailing local time—either daylight saving or standard time. On the last Sunday of October, when most communities set clocks back one hour at 2 AM, Amtrak trains, where necessary, will hold back for one hour to be "on time"—not early—according to local time at subsequent stations. On the first Sunday of April, when most communities set clocks ahead one hour, Amtrak trains will become one hour late at the time change, and we will attempt to make up this time at subsequent stations. Note: Arizona and parts of Indiana do not observe daylight saving time. Please read footnotes on trains in these two states to accurately determine your departure or arrival time.

FARES

Amtrak offers a variety of fares. On reserved trains, a range of fares may apply; lower fares are more widely available at certain times of the year. Amtrak will quote and price your travel **at the lowest fare available at the time you make your reservation.** On unreserved trains, the lowest fares may be restricted during peak travel periods. Changes to your itinerary may affect the fare, and a fee may apply when tickets are reissued. Some discount fares may be non-refundable once paid for.

GIFT CERTIFICATES

Gift Certificates good for Amtrak travel are available in amounts from $25 to $1,000 at Amtrak ticket offices, travel centers and travel agencies.

LIABILITY

The schedules, services and accessibility information shown in this timetable are not guaranteed, are subject to change without notice, and form no part of the contract between Amtrak and a passenger. Amtrak reserves the right to change its policies without notice. Amtrak disclaims liability for inconvenience, expense, or damage resulting from errors in this timetable, shortages of equipment, or delayed trains, except that when such a delay causes a passenger to miss a guaranteed connection, Amtrak will provide alternate transportation on Amtrak, another carrier, or overnight hotel accommodations at Amtrak's discretion. Also see page 7 for Thruway service information.

LOST ARTICLES

Please report lost or misplaced articles left on trains or in stations to a station baggage agent as soon as possible. Every effort will be made to recover the item promptly. Amtrak disclaims liability for lost or misplaced articles.

LOST, STOLEN OR DESTROYED TICKETS

Your tickets have value. Please safeguard them as you would cash. Amtrak disclaims liability for lost, stolen, misplaced or destroyed tickets. In order to travel, you will need to repurchase the tickets.

MEDICATION

Passengers requiring medication en route must carry it with them. Do not put medication in checked baggage or leave it in your car on Auto Train.

OVERNIGHT TRAVEL

On overnight trains, sleeping car passengers are provided with all necessary bedding for the journey. Coach passengers may want to bring a blanket and pillow for added comfort.

PERSONAL CHECKS/MONEY ORDERS

Amtrak does not accept personal checks in California, except from customers age 62 or older. In all other states, Amtrak accepts personal checks of $25.00 or more from customers who provide a valid photo identification and one of the credit cards noted on the preceding page. Checks must be for the amount of purchase only, and contain a current address (P.O. Box addresses and mailing service addresses not acceptable) and preprinted name. To obtain a refund at a station on tickets purchased by check, please provide a copy of both sides of the cancelled check. Tickets purchased with money orders will not be refunded until 21 days from the date purchased. Consult Amtrak for details about acceptable money orders.

RADIOS AND TAPE PLAYERS

To maintain a pleasant environment for all passengers, Amtrak requires that earphones be used when listening to radios, tape players, etc., and that the volume be kept low.

REFUND POLICY

Rail Fare: Most tickets are refundable before travel begins; a refund fee applies in most cases. **Some discount tickets may be non-refundable once issued.** In most cases,

partially-used tickets purchased at **regular one-way fares** may be returned for partial refund without a fee. Advance-paid or prepaid reservations are subject to the refund policies of the fare plan used, even if tickets have not yet been issued.

Time Limit: Tickets become non-refundable twelve months after the date of original issue.

Sleeping Car Accommodation Charge: Refundable if sleeping car reservations are cancelled at least **24 hours** prior to departure. If cancelled less than 24 hours prior to departure (but before actual departure), the accommodation charge is not refundable, but may be applied to future sleeping car accommodation charges. If not cancelled before actual departure ("no show"), the accommodation charge is neither refundable nor may it be applied to future travel.

Metroliner® First Class Accommodation Charges: Refundable if reservations are cancelled at least **one hour** prior to departure. If not cancelled in time, the amount of the First Class accommodation charge will not be refunded, but may be applied to other First Class travel on the same date only.

Total Charges: Please note that the total charge for Sleeping Car or Metroliner First Class travel is the sum of the rail fare plus the accommodation charge. The underlying rail fare may have a refund fee even if the accommodation is cancelled in time.

Late Train Exception: The accommodation charge penalty will not be assessed if the passenger chooses to cancel travel on account of the train being late two hours or more (sleeping car) or one hour or more (Metroliner First Class) at the boarding station.

On-Board Refunds: Passengers who downgrade accommodations or reduce the number of their party on board trains must obtain a Refund Authorization Form from the conductor; actual refundability, if any, will be determined by the rules that apply to the ticket purchased.

Must Return Original Tickets: Cancellation or change of reservations does not generate a refund (except for unticketed advance-paid reservations); the actual original unused or partially used ticket (not a photocopy) must be submitted.

Where to Obtain Refunds: Most refunds can be processed at Amtrak ticket offices, depending on the type of ticket and the form of payment. Exceptions do exist; please ask for details. Tickets purchased at a travel agency must normally be returned to that agency; however, Amtrak will process travel agency ticket refunds caused by a downgrade or a service disruption.

Mail Refunds: Amtrak can process your unused ticket refund by mail. Send original tickets via certified mail with return receipt requested to: Amtrak Customer Refunds, Box 70, 30th St. Station, 30th & Market Sts., Philadelphia, PA 19104-2898.

RESERVATIONS

Amtrak toll-free reservation and information numbers listed on page 66 are accessible 24 hours a day. Special teletypewriter service for hearing impaired persons is available from 5:00 AM to 11:00 AM (in all time zones).

Reservations are required for all First Class, Business Class, Sleeping Car and accessible accommodations. The "Services" information for each train in this timetable will indicate whether reservations are required for coach travel. Reservations are subject to cancellation if tickets are not purchased by the date assigned when reservations are made, or if unticketed passengers board at locations other than those from which reserved. **Seating in trains with unreserved coach service is not guaranteed.**

If your travel plans change, please contact your travel agency or Amtrak at 1-800-USA-RAIL. Penalties may apply for non-cancellation; fees may apply for reticketing, or if an advance-paid reservation is changed.

SMOKING

Smoking is prohibited entirely in all areas of all non-overnight trains, as well as on the Coast Starlight and the Twilight Shoreliner. On other long-distance overnight trains, cigarette smoking (only) is permitted at designated times either in lounge areas or in a specially designated area only—not in coaches, sleepers, dining cars or any other area. The crew on each train will announce the designated lounge area smoking times. See the "Services" section of each train for more information. Cigarettes are not sold on board trains that do not permit smoking.

SPECIAL ASSISTANCE

Passengers with disabilities, elderly and other passengers needing special seating or special assistance, such as a wheelchair, special food service (24 hours advance notice needed) or baggage assistance, must call Amtrak at 1-800-USA-RAIL as much in advance of travel as possible. This applies to unreserved as well as reserved trains. Advance notice may be required for accessible Thruway bus service, where available. Call 1-800-USA-RAIL for more information.

TICKETS BOUGHT ON TRAINS

A substantial penalty per person, with limited exceptions, is assessed for tickets bought on trains when a ticket office is open at time of departure. A receipt is issued for all fares paid on board trains.

UNACCOMPANIED CHILDREN

Children under 8 years old may not travel unaccompanied. Children ages 8 through 11 years may travel unaccompanied on Amtrak trains (not on connecting Thruway services) during daylight hours if no transfer is required, both boarding and detraining stations are staffed, and with prior written permission from the person in charge at the boarding station. (Such children are not considered "Accompanied" unless they are travelling with a guardian aged 18 or over.) Full adult fares are charged. Please call 1-800-USA-RAIL for details.

HOW TO USE THE TIMETABLE

STEP-BY-STEP TRAVEL PLANNING

1. Locate your destination on the alphabetical list of stations on pages 8-20.

2. Turn to the page indicated to find your schedule.

3. Locate your starting point in the column of cities. **NOTE:** If the schedule does not list your starting point, turn to the map on the inside back cover. Find your starting point on the map and trace the route(s) to your destination. The number blocks along the route(s) indicate the page(s) where the schedule can be found.

4. Read across to determine which trains arrive and/or depart from your station at which times.

5. Some schedules list trains going in one direction only. Others list trains going in both directions. Simply check the arrows at the top of the column to determine whether to read *up or down,* and you can easily determine what time the train you have chosen arrives at your destination and where it stops along the way.

(EXAMPLE ONLY)

Ⓐ Normal days of operation—during holiday periods, days of operation may vary—be sure to check "Will Also Operate" and "Will Not Operate" areas to determine holiday schedules.

Ⓑ On-board service symbols—services applicable to each train are noted by symbols across the top of each train schedule. See the Glossary of Amtrak Services and Amenities on pages 6 and 7 for explanation of symbols.

Ⓒ Italic type indicates connecting services. A blue background indicates a connecting Amtrak or VIA Rail train. Motorcoach, ferry or other rail services appear on a grey background.

Ⓓ Nearby cities and points of interest are listed in parentheses. ✹ Amtrak Vacations available at these destinations.

Ⓔ Station service symbols—see the Glossary of Amtrak Services and Amenities on pages 6 and 7 for explanations.

Ⓕ 🛄 Amtrak® Express Shipping and Checked Baggage Service—this baggage symbol indicates stations and trains offering both Express Shipping and Checked Baggage Service. The baggage symbol without a box 🛄 indicates stations and trains offering Checked Baggage Service only. These will be displayed in either the symbol column or in the train time column.

Other Reference Marks are explained on the same page as the schedule, or on the facing page.

1-800-USA-RAIL

(Boston) • New York • Philadelphia • Washington • Richmond • Raleigh • Charleston • Savannah • Jacksonville

Silver Star	Silver Meteor	◄ Train Name ►				Silver Meteor	Silver Star
91	97	◄ Train Number ►				98	92
Daily	Daily	Ⓐ ◄ Days of Operation ►				Daily	Daily
Ⓡⲷ✕ 🖬✹	Ⓡⲷ✕ 🖬✹	Ⓑ ◄ On Board Service ►				Ⓡⲷ✕ 🖬✹	Ⓡⲷ✕ 🖬✹
Read Down		▼	Mile	Symbol	▲	**Read Up**	
Ⓡ95/191(ExSu)	163 (ExSa)	*Connecting Train No.*		Ⓔ		Ⓡ 64/164	176
6 20A	*12 22P* Dp	*Boston, MA–South Sta.* ✹ (ET)	0	♿	Ar	*5 55P*	*11 59P*
10 50A Ⓒ	*5 10P* Ar	*New York, NY–Penn Sta.*	231	♿	Dp	*12 30P*	*6 35P*
2 35P	*8 52P* Ar	*Washington, DC* ✹	457	♿	Dp	*8 40A*	*2 40P*
🖬11 30A	🖬 7 05P Dp	New York, NY–Penn Sta. ✹ (ET)	0	♿	Ar	🖬 9 40A	🖬 4 10P
🖬Ⓡ11 48A	🖬Ⓡ 7 23P	Newark, NJ–Penn Sta. Ⓓ	10	♿		🖬D 9 18A	🖬D 3 44P
		Metropark, NJ	25	♿			
Ⓡ12 40P	Ⓡ 8 01P	Trenton, NJ	58	♿		D 8 41A	D 2 51P
🖬Ⓡ 1 55P	🖬Ⓡ 8 37P	Philadelphia, PA–30th St. Sta. ✹	91	♿		🖬D 8 00A	🖬D 1 35P
🖬Ⓡ 2 23P	🖬Ⓡ 9 01P	Wilmington, DE	116	♿		🖬D 7 35A	🖬D 1 08P
🖬Ⓡ 3 32P	🖬Ⓡ 9 53P	Baltimore, MD–Penn Sta. ✹	185	♿		🖬D 6 44A	🖬D12 11P
		BWI Rail Station, MD	196	♿		Ⓕ	
		New Carrollton, MD	216	♿			
🖬Ⓡ 4 15P	🖬Ⓡ10 30P Ar	Washington, DC ✹	225	♿	Dp	D 6 10A	D11 33A
🖬Ⓡ 4 35P	🖬Ⓡ10 59P Dp				Ar	🖬D 5 45A	🖬D11 21A
4 54P		Alexandria, VA	233	♿			10 59A
		Franconia/Springfield, VA	240	●			
		Quantico, VA	260	●			
		Fredericksburg, VA	280	●			

SERVICES ON ATLANTIC COAST ROUTE TRAINS

Coaches: Reservations required on all trains.
Sleeping Cars:
● First Class Viewliner® Service on Trains 89, 90, 91, 92, 97 and 98.
● First Class Superliner® Service on Trains 1 and 2.
● Amtrak's Metropolitan Lounge® available in New York, Philadelphia and Washington, and private waiting area available in Miami, for First Class Service passengers.
Carolina Business Class Service: On Trains 79 and 80. Complimentary beverages, newspaper and audio and visual entertainment offered between Washington and Charlotte.

GLOSSARY OF AMTRAK SERVICES AND AMENITIES

Amtrak® trains and connecting Thruway Service routes connect over 500 destinations with a variety of amenities tailored to each route. These two pages give you a summary of the services available on our trains and at our stations, and explain the service symbols that appear throughout this timetable.

COACH CLASS

Coach Class is available on all trains. Amtrak coaches feature big, comfortable seats with fold down trays and individual reading lights (may not be available on some short-distance trains). Reservations are required for coach travel on all trains which operate overnight service (for both daytime and overnight travel) and on many shorter-distance routes as well. On certain short-distance routes, coach seating is unreserved. Unreserved seats are available to boarding passengers on a first-come, first-served basis; while every effort is made to provide seats for every passenger on unreserved trains, seating is not guaranteed.

BUSINESS CLASS

Ⓑ Amtrak **Business Class** offers reserved, deluxe seating and complimentary non-alcoholic beverage service on many short- to medium-distance trips. Check the Services listings in this timetable for trains which feature Business Class. The Carolinian between New York and Charlotte offers an enhanced Business Class experience featuring at-seat audio and video. On the San Diegans between Southern California points, Pacific Business Class includes light snack service, pillows and blankets.

FIRST CLASS

🛏 On long-distance trains, **First Class** on Amtrak means a private room in a sleeping car, with all necessary bedding for a comfortable overnight trip. First Class service includes complimentary meals, a bedtime sweet, wake-up service with a newspaper, and coffee, tea and orange juice in the morning (6:30 AM to 9:30 AM). And, a First Class ticket includes access to Amtrak's Metropolitan Lounges . . . see page 7 for details.

A variety of sleeping car accommodations is available:

Superliner® cars are bi-level cars offering First Class service in Superliner Standard Bedrooms, Family, Deluxe and Accessible Bedrooms. Deluxe and Accessible Bedrooms include two berths (upper and lower), with sink and toilet. In **Deluxe Bedrooms,** on the upper level, the restroom facilities are enclosed and include a shower. **Accessible Bedrooms,** on the lower level, are designed for passengers with mobility impairments, providing ample space for a wheelchair. In Superliner Accessible Bedrooms, sink and toilet are separated from the room by a curtain. **Superliner Standard Bedrooms,** on both levels, include an upper and lower berth. **Family Bedrooms,** on the lower level, include two adult-size berths plus two smaller berths designed for young children. In Superliner Standard and Family Bedrooms, restroom facilities are not located within the room but are available nearby, as is a public shower, which is not wheelchair accessible.

Viewliner® Cars are state-of-the-art single-level cars with upper windows providing more light by day, and upper berth passengers their own windows by night. Accommodations available in Viewliners include **Viewliner® Standard Bedrooms** and **Deluxe Bedrooms.** All room types include two berths (upper and lower), with sink and toilet. The Deluxe Bedrooms in Viewliners are similar to those in Superliners described above; in addition, each Viewliner sleeping car includes one Deluxe Bedroom that is fully **accessible** to passengers with mobility impairments, including accessible sink, toilet and shower. Viewliner accommodations also feature a video display with movies and music. A public shower is available.

On the Three Rivers between New York and Chicago, single-level **Heritage** cars offer **Roomettes** with a single berth, and **Bedrooms** with an upper and lower berth. Accessible Roomettes are available. All Heritage rooms include a sink and toilet (enclosed in Bedrooms). Meals are not included with this service.

DINING CAR

✕ **Dining Cars** offer complete sit-down meals in a restaurant setting. Choose from a selection of freshly-prepared entrees and desserts, with a full range of beverages available to complement your meal.

Dining Cars will be open 6:30 AM-10:30 AM for breakfast, 11:30 AM-2:30 PM for lunch, and 4:30 PM-9:00 PM for dinner. Meals in dining cars are generally available to passengers boarding the train by 10:00 AM for breakfast, 2:00 PM for lunch, and 8:45 PM for dinner. Consult Amtrak for exceptions.

LOUNGE AND CAFE CARS

☕ Carry-out style food service featuring soup and salad, pizza, sandwiches and other snacks and beverages is available on most trains in **Lounge, Dinette** or **Cafe** cars.

⌧ Ready-to-go tray meals are available in **Dinette** or **Diner/Lounge** service on certain trains.

Lounge cars, and Dinette cars outside of meal periods, offer comfortable, casual seating for sightseeing and socializing and tables for writing or playing cards and other games. The Lounge Car is the place for on-board entertainment on certain trains—see the Services listings in this timetable for details. In most cases, lounge/cafe cars will be open from 6:00 AM until midnight while long-distance trains are en route.

For additional Amtrak information, call toll-free: 1-800-USA-RAIL or your travel agent.

GLOSSARY OF AMTRAK SERVICES AND AMENITIES

AMTRAK'S METROPOLITAN LOUNGE®

For First Class passengers, your ticket entitles you to the use of **Amtrak's Metropolitan Lounges** in Boston, Chicago, New York, Philadelphia, Washington and Portland. These quiet havens feature such amenities as complimentary beverages, television, conference rooms and telephones. Private, comfortable waiting rooms for First Class sleeping car passengers are also available in New Orleans and Miami.

RAILFONE®

☎ On-board public telephone service is available on selected short- to medium-distance routes. **Railfone®** allows you to make private calls at your convenience.

STATION TICKETING SERVICES

You can obtain your tickets from Amtrak agents at many of our stations; unless otherwise noted on the schedule tables in this timetable, an agent is on duty at least 30 minutes prior to the departure of each train or Thruway bus shown in the particular table. Note that where a ticket agent is on duty, a penalty in addition to the rail fare will be collected from each passenger who boards without a ticket and pays his or her fare on board (see the General Information section on the rear fold out pages for more information).

Exceptions are noted in the schedule tables as follows:
● Tickets cannot be purchased at this location.
⊘ Ticket office available, but not open for all departure times.

In addition: Quik-Trak self-serve ticketing machines are available at many stations. Purchase must be by a major credit card or debit (ATM) card. Customers may purchase coach tickets to any city listed on the machine. Purchase of tickets for previously-made reservations requires entering the reservation number.

BAGGAGE AND EXPRESS SERVICES

On many Amtrak trains, you may check baggage to or from major stations along the route. Amtrak's nationwide parcel and pallet shipping service, *Amtrak Express®*, is offered at most of these locations. Specific trains and stations offering these services are noted in the train schedules in this timetable:

🛅 indicates that both Checked Baggage Service and Amtrak Express are available.
🛅 indicates that Checked Baggage Service is available, but not Amtrak Express.

See the General Information section on pages 64 and 65 of this timetable for more information on checked baggage, carry-on baggage, and baggage assistance.

THRUWAY SERVICE

Thruway Service is the easy, convenient way to reach many cities where Amtrak trains do not stop. Thruway connections provide coordinated train/motorcoach service with guaranteed connections at the Amtrak station (in most cases), as well as through fares (on most services) and ticketing. Passengers traveling on Thruway connecting services must be ticketed before boarding the coach in order to obtain through fares. Tickets may be purchased at Amtrak stations, travel agencies or via ticket-by-mail. Except where identified as "Amtrak Thruway," Amtrak acts as selling agent only for connecting carriers and disclaims liability for travel performed over other carrier lines. Such other carriers may provide vehicles which are not accessible to passengers who use wheelchairs; consult Amtrak for details. Connecting service to other carriers cannot be guaranteed. Thruway services are identified by grey shading in the schedule tables.

The 🚌 symbol next to a city name in a schedule table indicates that either connecting Thruway or other carrier's service is available to this destination, and information about this connecting service appears on the same or an adjoining page.

CONNECTING LOCAL SERVICES

This timetable describes selected connecting services provided by carriers other than Amtrak to additional destinations not served by Amtrak or by connecting Thruway service. Service may operate from a different terminal than Amtrak. Individual carrier's fares and policies apply. Contact an Amtrak agent or the individual carrier listed for more information.

SPECIAL ASSISTANCE AND STATION ACCESSIBILITY

Amtrak is committed to making travel accessible for passengers with disabilities, senior citizens and others requiring assistance such as a wheelchair, special food service or baggage assistance. Please call 1-800-USA-RAIL as far in advance of travel as possible. TDD/TTY service is available at 1-800-523-6590.

For specific information regarding our accessible services, ask for our *Access Amtrak* brochure, or call 1-877-268-7252 (9 AM-5 PM Eastern Time) or consult our web site at www.amtrak.com.

Amtrak cannot provide assistance with personal hygiene such as assistance in feeding, restrooms or administering medication. If this assistance is needed, a traveling companion is required.

Schedules in this timetable provide information on the accessibility of station facilities to individuals with mobility impairments:

♿ indicates all available station facilities are fully accessible to persons using wheelchairs, and there are no barriers to access between the station and any of the trains shown in this particular table.

♿ indicates barrier-free access between street or parking lot, station platform, and all trains in this particular table; however, not all facilities within the station are fully accessible.

If neither of the above symbols appears in a given table, there may be barriers to access between the street/parking lot and the station building or the trains. Call 1-800-USA-RAIL for more information.

For additional Amtrak information, call toll-free: 1-800-USA-RAIL or your travel agent.

NORTHEAST

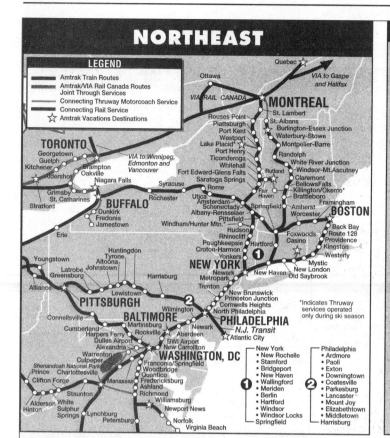

LEGEND
- Amtrak Train Routes
- Amtrak/VIA Rail Canada Routes Joint Through Services
- Connecting Thruway Motorcoach Service
- Connecting Rail Service
- ☆ Amtrak Vacations Destinations

1 New York	Philadelphia
• New Rochelle	• Ardmore
• Stamford	• Paoli
• Bridgeport	• Exton
• New Haven	• Downingtown
• Wallingford	• Coatesville
• Meriden	• Parkesburg
• Berlin	• Lancaster
• Hartford	• Mount Joy
• Windsor	• Elizabethtown
• Windsor Locks	• Middletown
Springfield	Harrisburg

*Indicates Thruway services operated only during ski season

CONNECTING LOCAL SERVICES

Grand Central Terminal–New York
Amtrak offers through ticketing between Grand Central and Empire Service cities via Metro-North Hudson Line trains. Consult Amtrak agent for details.

Metro-North trains also provide frequent service between Grand Central, New Rochelle, Stamford, Bridgeport and New Haven. Purchase ticket from Metro-North: (800) 638-7646 or (212) 532-4900.

Newark Airport
Frequent Airlink bus service operates between Amtrak's Newark Station and Newark Airport. (973) 762-5100. Purchase ticket from bus driver.

Philadelphia Center City
SEPTA operates frequent rail service between Philadelphia 30th Street Station and Center City (Penn Center/Suburban Station and Market East Station). Amtrak tickets to or from Philadelphia are honored between 30th Street and Center City.

Philadelphia International Airport
SEPTA operates commuter rail service every 30 minutes between the upper level of 30th Street Station and Terminals A, B, C, D, E at Philadelphia Airport. Purchase tickets at SEPTA ticket office or vending machine. SEPTA (215) 580-7800.

Philadelphia–Atlantic City
New Jersey Transit operates connecting commuter rail service between Philadelphia's 30th Street Station and Cherry Hill, Lindenwold and Atlantic City, NJ. Through Amtrak ticketing and fares are available to/from all Northeastern cities. In New Jersey: (800) AC-TRAIN; other areas: (215) 569-3752.

Philadelphia–New Jersey Seashore
NJ Transit operates service between Philadelphia and New Jersey Seashore communities, including Cape May, the Wildwoods and Ocean City. NJ Transit buses depart from the Greyhound Terminal at 10th and Filbert Streets, a short cab, commuter rail or subway ride from Amtrak's 30th Street Station. Purchase tickets locally from NJ Transit. (215) 569-3752.

See page 7 for connecting service information.

NORTHEAST CORRIDOR SERVICE

Amtrak provides frequent service between Boston, Springfield, New York, Philadelphia, Washington, Richmond and Newport News, with connecting Thruway services to Foxwoods Casino, Atlantic City, downtown Richmond locations, Norfolk and Virginia Beach. For complete schedules, see the Amtrak Northeast Timetable.

COMMUTER RAIL AND RAPID TRANSIT CONNECTIONS

Montréal—
Montréal Urban Community Transit commuter rail, subway & bus: (514) 288-6287

Boston—
Massachusetts Bay Transportation Authority (commuter rail, subway, light rail & bus): (617) 222-3200 or (800) 392-6100

New Haven—
Shore Line East (commuter rail): in Conn. (800) ALL-RIDE; outside Conn. (203) 777-RIDE
Connecticut Transit (bus service): (203) 624-0151

New York—
Metro-North Railroad: (800) 638-7646 or (212) 532-4900
Long Island Rail Road (LIRR) (commuter rail): (718) 217-LIRR
New Jersey Transit (commuter rail & bus): in New Jersey: (800) 772-2222; outside New Jersey: (973) 762-5100
New York City Transit Authority (subway & bus): (718) 330-1234

Newark—
New Jersey Transit (commuter rail, subway & bus): in Northern New Jersey: (800) 772-2222; in Southern New Jersey: (800) 582-5946; outside New Jersey: (973) 762-5100
Port Authority Trans-Hudson Corporation (PATH) (subway): (800) 234-PATH

Philadelphia—
Southeastern Pennsylvania Transportation Authority (SEPTA) (commuter rail, light rail, subway & bus): (215) 580-7800

Baltimore—
MARC (commuter rail): (800) 325-RAIL
Mass Transit Administration (MTA) (bus, light rail & subway): in the Baltimore/Washington metropolitan area: (800) 543-9809; other areas: (410) 539-5000

Washington—
MARC (commuter rail): (800) 325-RAIL
Virginia Railway Express (commuter rail): (800) RIDE-VRE
Metrorail & Metrobus (subway & bus): (202) 637-7000

Buffalo—
Metro (light rail & bus): (716) 855-7211

Toronto—
GO Transit (commuter rail): (416) 869-3200
Toronto Transit Commission (subway, streetcar & bus): (416) 393-4636

CAPITOL LIMITED

Chicago • (Detroit) • Toledo • Cleveland • Pittsburgh • Washington • (New York)

30			◄Train Number►		Symbol		29
Daily			◄Days of Operation►				Daily
ReadDown	Mile	▼			Symbol	▲	Read Up
7 45P	0	Dp	Chicago, IL–Union Sta. ✳ (CT)		🅿 ♿	Ar	9 35A
			🚌 Madison—see page 42				
[19] 8 45P	16		Hammond-Whiting, IN (CT)		🅿 ♿		[19] 8 12A
[69] 10 48P	84		South Bend, IN (ET)		🅿 ♿		[69] 8 08A
[69] 11 10P	101		Elkhart, IN		⊘ ♿		[69] 7 41A
[69] 12 03A	156		Waterloo, IN (Ft. Wayne)		● ♿		[69] 6 51A
1 24A	234	Ar	Toledo, OH		🅿 ♿	Dp	5 37A
1 49A		Dp	🚌 E. Lansing, Detroit—see below			Ar	5 02A
3 08A	316		Elyria, OH		● ♿		3 19A
3 47A	341		Cleveland, OH ✳		🅿 ♿		2 49A
			🚌 Columbus, Cincinnati—see below				
4 58A	397		Alliance, OH (Canton)		● ♿		1 38A
6 51A	480	Ar	Pittsburgh, PA ✳		🅿 ♿	Dp	►11 59P
40			Connecting Train at Pittsburgh				41
8 43A	480	Dp	Pittsburgh, PA ✳		♿	Ar	10 50P
D 4 53P	833	Ar	Philadelphia, PA–30th St. Sta. ✳		♿		R 3 00P
7 25P	924	Ar	New York, NY–Penn Sta. ✳		♿	Dp	12 45P
► 7 11A	480	Dp	Pittsburgh, PA ✳		🅿 ♿	Ar	└ 11 34P
8 47A	540		Connellsville, PA		●		9 39P
11 19A	628		Cumberland, MD		● ♿		7 19P
12 48P	702		Martinsburg, WV		●		5 41P
1 13P	720		Harpers Ferry, WV		●		5 14P
1 58P	758		Rockville, MD		● ♿		4 29P
2 40P	775	Ar	Washington, DC ✳		🅿 ♿	Dp	4 05P
			🚌 Charlottesville—see below				
148			Connecting Train at Washington, DC				195/195/191
4 05P	0	Dp	Washington, DC ✳		♿	Ar	2 35P
4 50P	40	Ar	Baltimore, MD–Penn Sta. ✳		♿		1 49P
6 00P	135		Philadelphia, PA–30th St. Sta. ✳		♿		12 35P
7 57P	225		New York, NY–Penn Sta. ✳		♿	Dp	11 10A
97			Connecting Train at Washington, DC				92
10 59P	0	Dp	Washington, DC ✳		🅿 ♿	Ar	11 21A
9 49A	604	Ar	Savannah, GA ✳		🅿 ♿		10 25P
12 08P	751		Jacksonville, FL ✳		🅿 ♿		8 11P
3 56P	898		Orlando, FL (Walt Disney World*) ✳		🅿 ♿		4 29P
D 7 49P	1099		West Palm Beach, FL		🅿 ♿		R12 35P
9 46P	1163	Ar	Miami, FL ✳ (ET)		🅿 ♿	Dp	11 05A

LAKE SHORE LIMITED

Chicago • (Detroit) • Toledo • Cleveland • Buffalo • Albany • Boston/New York

48			◄Train Number►		Symbol		49
Daily			◄Days of Operation►				Daily
ReadDown	Mile	▼			Symbol	▲	Read Up
7 00P	0	Dp	Chicago, IL–Union Sta. ✳ (CT)		🅿 ♿	Ar	11 15A
			🚌 Madison—see page 42				
[19] 7 50P	16		Hammond-Whiting, IN (CT)				[19] 10 06A
[69] 9 56P	84		South Bend, IN (ET)				[69] 10 01A
[69] 10 21P	101		Elkhart, IN		⊘ ♿		[69] 9 34A
[69] 11 13P	155		Waterloo, IN (Ft. Wayne)		● ♿		[69] 8 44A
11 38P	180		Bryan, OH		● ♿		8 16A
12 33A	234	Ar	Toledo, OH		🅿 ♿	Dp	7 24A
12 50A		Dp	🚌 Ann Arbor, Detroit—see below			Ar	7 04A
1 40A	281		Sandusky, OH		● ♿		6 09A
2 16A	316		Elyria, OH (Lorain)		● ♿		5 35A
3 08A	341		Cleveland, OH–Lakefront Sta. ✳		🅿 ♿		5 05A
			🚌 Columbus, Cincinnati—see below				
4 37A	435		Erie, PA		●		3 01A
6 06A	528	Ar	Buffalo-Depew, NY ✳		🅿 ♿	Dp	1 19A
6 16A		Dp				Ar	1 09A
7 35A	589		Rochester, NY		🅿 ♿		12 09A
8 54A	668		Syracuse, NY		🅿 ♿		10 51P
9 51A	722		Utica, NY		🅿 ♿		9 52P
11 13A	800		Schenectady, NY		🅿 ♿		8 35P
D11 55A	818	Ar	Albany-Rensselaer, NY		🅿 ♿	Dp	►R7 55P
448			Thru Cars Chicago-Boston				449
1 25P	818	Dp	Albany-Rensselaer, NY		🅿 ♿	Ar	6 45P
2 29P	867		Pittsfield, MA		●		4 59P
3 45P	919	Ar	Springfield, MA		🅿 ♿	Dp	3 26P
3 50P						Ar	3 21P
5 02P	973		Worcester, MA		🅿 ♿		2 01P
D 5 30P	996		Framingham, MA		●		R 1 31P
D 5 58P	1016		Boston, MA–Back Bay Sta. ✳		🅿 ♿		R 1 05P
6 30P	1017	Ar	Boston, MA–South Sta. ✳		🅿 ♿	Dp	1 00P
D12 15P	818	Dp	Albany-Rensselaer, NY		🅿 ♿	Ar	R 7 10P
D 2 04P	926		Croton-Harmon, NY		[9]		R 5 18P
3 00P	959	Ar	New York, NY ✳ (ET)		🅿 ♿	Dp	4 35P
286			Connecting Train at Albany-Rensselaer				291/257
2 00P	818	Dp	Albany-Rensselaer, NY		♿	Ar	6 10P
2 25P	845	Ar	Hudson, NY		♿		5 45P
2 46P	870		Rhinecliff-Kingston, NY		♿		5 22P
3 01P	886		Poughkeepsie, NY		♿	Dp	5 07P

LAKEFRONT THRUWAY CONNECTIONS

East Lansing • Detroit • Toledo

9 20P	0	Dp	East Lansing, MI (ET)	⊘	Ar	9 00A
R10 40P	55		Ann Arbor, MI	🚌		D 7 50A
R11 35P	84		Dearborn, MI ✳	🚌		D 7 05A
R11 55P	91		Detroit, MI	🚌		D 6 40A
1 15A	149	Ar	Toledo, OH (ET)	🚌	Dp	[36]

SHORTWAY THRUWAY CONNECTIONS

Ann Arbor • Toledo

9 55P	0	Dp	Ann Arbor, MI (ET)	🚌	Ar	9 55A
R10 50P	29		Dearborn, MI ✳	🚌		D 9 10A
R11 15P	36		Detroit, MI	🚌		D 8 45A
12 50A	94	Ar	Toledo, OH (ET)	🚌	Dp	7 20A

GREYHOUND LINES THRUWAY CONNECTIONS

NOTE—Greyhound schedules subject to change January 11, 2000.

Cleveland • Columbus • Cincinnati

8 35P	0	Dp	Cincinnati, OH–Greyhound Sta. (ET)	●	Ar	10 00A
11 00P	107		Columbus, OH–Greyhound Sta.	●	Ar	7 05A
1 40A	249	Ar	Cleveland, OH–Amtrak Sta. ✳		Dp	4 45A
4 45A	0	Dp	Cleveland, OH–Amtrak Sta. ✳		Ar	1 40A
7 05A	142		Columbus, OH–Greyhound Sta.	●		11 00P
10 00A	249	Ar	Cincinnati, OH–Greyhound Sta. (ET)		Dp	8 35P

Washington • Charlottesville

6 10P	0	Dp	Washington, DC–Union Sta. ✳	●	Ar	11 59A
7 05P	35	Ar	Dulles Int'l Airport, VA			11 05A
7 55P	69		Warrenton, VA			10 15A
9 30P	136	Ar	Charlottesville, VA–Amtrak Sta. ✳		Dp	8 50A

GREYHOUND LINES THRUWAY CONNECTIONS

NOTE—Greyhound schedules subject to change January 11, 2000.

Cleveland • Columbus • Cincinnati

8 35P	0	Dp	Cincinnati, OH–Greyhound Sta. (ET)	●	Ar	2 40P
11 00P	107		Columbus, OH–Greyhound Sta.	●	Ar	12 20P
1 40A	249	Ar	Cleveland, OH–Amtrak Sta. ✳		Dp	8 30A
4 45A	0	Dp	Cleveland, OH–Amtrak Sta. ✳		Ar	1 40A
7 05A	142		Columbus, OH–Greyhound Sta.	●		11 00P
10 00A	249	Ar	Cincinnati, OH–Greyhound Sta. (ET)	●	Dp	8 35P

THROUGH CAR SERVICE

Through passengers who are traveling between a point on the Capitol Limited (Trains 29 and 30) and a point on the Southwest Chief (Trains 3 and 4—see page 42) can stay aboard their car during the layover in Chicago, or leave their luggage on board and go out on the town. Ask for details when you make your reservations. Call 1-800-USA-RAIL or your Travel Agent.

Amtrak Timetable continued

SERVICES ON THE CAPITOL LIMITED

Coaches: Reservations required
Sleeping Cars: First Class Superliner® Service
● Exclusive First Class section in the dining car
● Amtrak's Metropolitan Lounge® available in Chicago and Washington for First Class Service passengers
Dining Car: Full meal service
Sightseer Lounge: Sandwiches, snacks and beverages
Entertainment: Feature movies and hospitality hour in the Sightseer Lounge
Smoking: Cigarette smoking is permitted in a designated portion of the lounge area. At certain times of the day, as announced by the train crew, the lounge area will be entirely non-smoking. No smoking in sleepers, coaches, or dining cars.

SERVICES ON THE LAKE SHORE LIMITED

Coaches: Reservations required
Sleeping Cars: First Class Viewliner® Service
● Amtrak's Metropolitan Lounge® available in Chicago and New York for First Class Service passengers
Dining Car: Full meal service on Trains 48 and 49 between Chicago and New York.
Lounge Service: Sandwiches, snacks and beverages
Smoking: Cigarette smoking is permitted in a designated portion of the lounge area. At certain times of the day, as announced by the train crew, the lounge area will be entirely non-smoking. No smoking in sleepers, coaches, or dining cars.

Note—Checked Baggage services for connecting passengers:
● Connecting checked baggage service is available to Baltimore, Wilmington, Philadelphia and Newark (also New York for Capitol Limited passengers) but baggage will be delayed
● Accompanied hand baggage only checked to Detroit, Dearborn and Ann Arbor via connecting Thruway motorcoach; passengers boarding at East Lansing may check baggage during stop at Ann Arbor

D   Stops only to discharge passengers.
R   Stops only to receive passengers.
Ⓡ   Coach reservations required on this train.
⑨   Quik-Trak ticket machine available for credit/debit card sales. No Amtrak ticket office. (Cash fares may be paid on board without penalty.)
⑲   Passengers not carried locally between this station and Chicago except when connecting at Chicago to/from other Amtrak trains.
㊱   Direct transfer between train and motorcoach at Amtrak station for connecting passengers only.
㊴   This location does not observe Daylight Saving Time. Local time will be one hour earlier from the first Sunday in April to the last Saturday in October.

POINTS OF INTEREST

CHICAGO—See page 35
NORTHERN INDIANA—
● Indiana Dunes National Lakeshore
SANDUSKY—
● Cedar Point Amusement Park
CLEVELAND—
● Rock-n-Roll Hall of Fame
UPSTATE NEW YORK—
● Adirondack and Finger Lakes recreation areas
PITTSBURGH—
● Fort Pitt/Point State Park
● Monongahela and Duquesne Inclines
HARPERS FERRY—
● National Historical Site
BOSTON/NEW YORK/PHILADELPHIA/ WASHINGTON—See page 21

SCENIC HIGHLIGHTS

Lake Shore/Capitol Limited Routes—
Lake Michigan, Indiana
Sandusky Bay, Ohio
Lake Erie, Ohio/Pennsylvania
Capitol Limited Route—
Pittsburgh skyline, Pennsylvania
Cumberland Gap, Maryland
Potomac Valley, Maryland/West Virginia

COMMUTER RAIL AND RAPID TRANSIT CONNECTIONS

The Northeast—See page 21
Chicago—See page 35
Cleveland—
Greater Cleveland Regional Transit Authority rapid transit & bus: (216) 621-9500
Buffalo—
Metro light rail & bus: (716) 855-7211
Pittsburgh—
Port Authority Transit light rail & bus: (412) 442-2000

For details on train, station and baggage services, see pages 6-7.

THREE RIVERS / PENNSYLVANIAN

New York • Philadelphia • Harrisburg • Altoona • Johnstown • Pittsburgh • Chicago

Pennsyl-vanian 43 Daily	Three Rivers 41 Daily	Mile	▼	◄ Train Name ► / ◄ Train Number ► / ◄ Days of Operation ► / ◄ On Board Service ►	Symbol	▲	Three Rivers 40 Daily	Pennsyl-vanian 44 Daily
R ☎	R ☎ ☎			On Board Service			R ☎ ☎	R ☎ ☎
Read Down		Mile	▼		Symbol	▲	**Read Up**	
67				*Connecting Train at Philadelphia*				12
1 46A	12 45P	0	Dp	New York, NY –Penn Sta. ✴ (ET)	&	Ar	7 25P	6 38A
2 10A	R 1 03P	10		Newark, NJ	&		D 6 53P	6 21A
2 25A		25		Metropark, NJ	&			
2 49A	R 1 48P	58		Trenton, NJ	⊘&		D 6 00P	5 43A
3 20A	R2 20P	91	Ar	Philadelphia, PA ✴	&	Dp	D 5 25P	5 14A
12	142			*Connecting Train at Philadelphia*			187	67
3 00A	12 05P	0	Dp	Washington, DC ✴	&	Ar	8 30P	6 20A
3 39A	12 48P	40		Baltimore, MD ✴	&		7 46P	5 33A
4 49A	1 59P	135	Ar	Philadelphia, PA ✴	&	Dp	6 30P	4 10A
6 35A	R3 00P	91	Dp	Philadelphia, PA ✴	&	Ar	D4 53P	12 52A
6 50A		99		Ardmore, PA	[9]			
7 08A	R 3 29P	110		Paoli, PA	⊘		D 4 18P	12 18A
7 25A		123		Downingtown, PA	•			12 01A
8 01A	R 4 20P	159		Lancaster, PA	&		D 3 25P	11 27P
8 20A		177		Elizabethtown, PA	•			11 04P
8 44A	R 5 05P	195	Ar	Harrisburg, PA	&	Dp	D 2 31P	10 42P
9 14A	R 5 20P		Dp	(Scranton/Reading 🚌)		Ar	D 2 21P	10 12P
10 21A	6 32P	256		Lewistown, PA	•		12 52P	8 49P
10 58A	7 12P	293		Huntingdon, PA	•		12 11P	8 11P
※11 24A		313		Tyrone, PA			※ 7 43P	
11 47A	7 58P	327		Altoona, PA	&		11 25A	7 28P
12 48P	9 02P	366		Johnstown, PA	&		10 19A	6 28P
1 27P	※ 9 42P	403		Latrobe, PA	•		※ 9 37A	5 46P
1 39P	9 54P	413		Greensburg, PA	•		9 27A	5 35P
2 32P	10 50P	444	Ar	Pittsburgh, PA ✴	&	Dp	8 43A	4 53P
2 44P	11 20P		Dp	(New Castle 🚌) / 🚌 Columbus—see below		Ar	8 28A	4 43P
4 23P		527		Alliance, OH	•&			2 27P
6 07P		583		Cleveland, OH ✴	&			1 15P
6 38P		608		Elyria, OH (Lorain)	•&			12 29P
7 11P		643		Sandusky, OH	•&			11 57A
8 30P		690		Toledo, OH (🚌 Detroit, Jackson—see at right)	&			11 10A
[69] 9 44P		768		Waterloo, IN	•&			[69] 9 49A
[69] 10 35P		823		Elkhart, IN	⊘&			[69] 8 56A
[69] 11 02P		840		South Bend, IN (ET)	•			[69] 8 30A
	1 10A	510		Youngstown, OH (ET)	•		6 03A	
	2 09A	563		Akron, OH	•		4 55A	
	4 05A	672		Fostoria, OH	•		3 10A	
	[69] 6 37A	812		Nappanee, IN (ET)	•&		[69] 12 43A	
D11 07P	D 6 55A	892		Hammond-Whiting, IN (CT)	&		[19][69] 10 19P	R 6 28A
12 26A	8 20A	908	Ar	Chicago, IL ✴ (CT) / 🚌 Madison—see page 42	&	Dp	9 25P	6 00A

GREYHOUND LINES THRUWAY CONNECTIONS

NOTE—Greyhound schedules subject to change January 11, 2000.

Pittsburgh • Columbus

6 15P	12 35A	0	Dp	Pittsburgh, PA (ET)		Ar	4 50A	2 30P
7 55P		57		Wheeling, WV	•			12 55P
9 25P		130		Zanesville, OH	•			11 10A
10 25P	3 45A	184	Ar	Columbus, OH (ET)	•	Dp	1 35A	10 10A

For Amtrak reservations, call toll-free 1-800-USA-RAIL.

GREYHOUND LINES THRUWAY CONNECTIONS

Washington • Pittsburgh

43	Mile	▼	Connecting Train No.	Symbol	▲	44
6 00A	0	Dp	Washington, DC (ET)		Ar	12 55A
7 35A	49		Frederick, MD	•	Ar	11 25P
8 25A	73		Hagerstown, MD	•	Ar	10 35P
12 15P	245	Ar	Pittsburgh, PA (ET)		Dp	7 00P

LAKEFRONT THRUWAY CONNECTIONS

Toledo • Detroit • Jackson

43	Mile	▼	Connecting Train No.	Symbol	▲	44
8 30P	0	Dp	Toledo, OH (ET)		Ar	10 30A
D 9 45P	58		Detroit, MI	•		R 9 15A
D10 15P	65		Dearborn, MI	•		R 8 45A
D11 00P	94		Ann Arbor, MI	•		R 8 00A
11 59P	132	Ar	Jackson, MI (ET)	⊘	Dp	7 00A

SCENIC HIGHLIGHTS

Philadelphia's Schuylkill River, Pennsylvania
Horseshoe Curve, Pennsylvania

CONNECTING LOCAL SERVICES

Harrisburg–Scranton–Reading
Capitol Trailways operates service between Amtrak's Harrisburg Station and Scranton and Reading, PA. Purchase ticket from Trailways agent. (800) 444-2877.

Pittsburgh–New Castle
New Castle Area Transit Authority operates service Monday through Friday between New Castle, PA and the Amtrak station in Pittsburgh. Bus departs New Castle at 5:50 AM to connect to Train 40. Returning service departs Pittsburgh 5:20 PM, arriving New Castle 6:40 PM. Pay fare to driver. (724) 654-3130.
See page 7 for connecting service information.

D Stops only to discharge passengers.
R Stops only to receive passengers.
※ Stops only on signal, or advance notice to conductor.
[9] Quik-Trak ticket machine available for credit/debit card sales. No Amtrak ticket office. (Cash fares may be paid on board without penalty.)
[19] Passengers not carried locally between this station and Chicago except when connecting at Chicago to/from other Amtrak trains.
[36] Direct transfer between train and motorcoach at Amtrak station for connecting passengers only.
[69] This location does not observe Daylight Saving Time. Local time will be one hour earlier from the first Sunday in April to the last Saturday in October.

SERVICES ON THE THREE RIVERS

Coaches: Reservations required
Sleeping Cars: Heritage Roomettes and Bedrooms
• Complimentary coffee, tea and juice. Meals are not included.
• Amtrak's Metropolitan Lounge® available in New York, Philadelphia and Chicago for sleeping car passengers
Lounge: Sandwiches, snacks and beverages
Smoking: Cigarette smoking is permitted in a designated portion of the lounge area. At certain times of the day, as announced by the train crew, the lounge area will be entirely non-smoking. No smoking in coaches or sleeping cars.

SERVICES ON THE PENNSYLVANIAN

Coaches: Reservations required (except for travel locally between Philadelphia and Harrisburg)
Dinette: Sandwiches, snacks and beverages
Railfone® public telephone service available in food service cars
Smoking: Cigarette smoking is permitted in a designated portion of the lounge area. At certain times of the day, as announced by the train crew, the lounge area will be entirely non-smoking. No smoking in coaches.

CARDINAL

Chicago • Indianapolis • Cincinnati • Charleston • Washington • (New York)

50			◄ Train Number ►				51
Dp CHI TuThSa			◄ Days of Operation ►				Ar CHI MoThSa
ReadDown	Mile	▼		Symbol		▲	Read Up
8 10P	0	Dp	Chicago, IL–Union Sta. ● (CT)	Ⓢ 🅰 ♿	Ar		9 45A
9 11P	28		Dyer, IN	●			7 51A
9 52P	73		Rensselaer, IN (CT)	● ♿			7 05A
🅢10 48P	121		Lafayette, IN (EST)	🖥 ♿		🅢	6 14A
🅢11 18P	148		Crawfordsville, IN	●		🅢	5 41A
🅢12 55A	195	Ar	Indianapolis, IN	🏧 ♿	Dp	🅢	4 35A
🅢 1 05A		Dp	(Nashville 🚌)		Ar	🅢	4 20A
🅢 2 25A	257		Connersville, IN (EST)	●		🅢	2 25A
4 30A	300	▼	Hamilton, OH (ET)	● ♿			2 30A
5 35A	327	Ar	Cincinnati, OH–Union Term.	🅰 ♿	Dp		1 40A
5 55A		Dp			Ar		1 25A
7 14A	390		Maysville, KY	● 🅰			11 49P
8 03A	441		So. Portsmouth-So. Shore, KY	● ♿			10 55P
9 11A	477		Catlettsburg, KY (Ashland, KY & Kenova, WV)	●			9 53P
9 32A	487		Huntington, WV	🅰 ♿			9 33P
10 35A	537		Charleston, WV ●	🅰 ♿			8 35P
11 06A	563		Montgomery, WV	●			7 41P
✕11 54A	605		Thurmond, WV			✕	6 52P
12 11P	616		Prince, WV (Beckley via Yellow Cab)	🅰 ♿			6 36P
12 42P	639		Hinton, WV	●			6 06P
✕ 1 12P	659		Alderson, WV	●		✕	5 33P
1 46P	684		White Sulphur Springs, WV (Greenbrier)	●			5 02P
2 38P	718	Ar	Clifton Forge, VA (Homestead)	●	Dp		4 13P
2 41P		Dp			Ar		4 10P
3 52P	775		Staunton, VA	●			3 03P
5 11P	814	▼	Charlottesville, VA ●	🅰 ♿			2 05P
🚌 Amtrak Thruway Bus Connection—Richmond, VA/Charlottesville, VA—Schedule Below							
6 15P	862	Dp	Culpeper, VA	●			12 59P
6 55P	896		Manassas, VA	●			12 24P
D 7 42P	920	▼	Alexandria, VA	🅰 ♿			11 49A
8 10P	929	Ar	Washington, DC ●	Ⓢ 🅰 ♿	Dp		11 30A
Ar WAS WeFrSu							Dp WAS SuWeFr

66/76			Connecting Train at Washington, DC				79
WeFrSu			◄ Days of Operation ►				SuWeFr
🅰10 00P	0	Dp	Washington, DC ●	Ⓢ ♿	Ar	🅰	9 50A
	9	Ar	New Carrollton, MD	Ⓢ ♿			9 32A
10 31P	30		BWI Airport, MD	⊘ ♿			9 15A
🅰10 53P	40		Baltimore, MD–Penn ●	Ⓢ 🅰		🅰	9 02A
11 48P	109		Wilmington, DE	Ⓢ 🅰		🅰	8 11A
🅰12 10A	135		Philadelphia, PA ●	Ⓢ ♿		🅰	7 48A
12 57A	167		Trenton, NJ	Ⓢ ⊘ ♿			7 12A
🅰 1 42A	215	▼	Newark, NJ–Penn Sta.	⊘ ♿		🅰R6	34A
🅰 2 00A	225	Ar	New York, NY –Penn Sta. ● (ET)	Ⓢ ⊘ ♿	Dp	🅰	6 15A

Connecting Services (See page 7 for details.)

🚌 Amtrak Thruway Bus Connection—Chicago, IL/Madison, WI—See page 35							
🚌 Amtrak Thruway Bus Connection—Charlottesville, VA/Richmond, VA							
🚌	0	Dp	Charlottesville, VA—Union Sta. ●	🏧	Ar		1 45P
6 45P	69	Ar	Richmond, VA (ET)	🏧	Dp		12 15P

SERVICES ON THE CARDINAL

Coaches: Reservations required
Sleeping Cars: First Class Superliner Service featuring tray meal service in the Sightseer Lounge
Sightseer Lounge: Sandwiches, snacks and beverages
Entertainment: Guides provide scenic commentary between Charleston, WV and White Sulphur Springs, WV eastbound on Train 50
Smoking: Cigarette smoking is permitted in a designated portion of the lounge area. At certain times of the day, as announced by the train crew, the lounge area will be entirely non-smoking. No smoking in sleepers, coaches, or dining cars.

AMTRAK THRUWAY BUS SERVICE

Chicago • Indianapolis • Louisville • Cincinnati

Daily	SuMo WeFr			◄ Days of Operation ►				Daily	SuTu WeFr
Read Down		Mile	▼		Symbol	▲		Read Up	
4 45P	7 30P	0	Dp	Chicago, IL ● (CT)	Ⓢ	Ar		11 45A	1 00P
8 55P	11 40P	195	Ar	Indianapolis, IN –Amtrak Sta. (EST)	◌	Dp		8 00A	8 10A
12 15A		306		Louisville, KY –Greyhound Sta. (ET)	●			6 35A	
	3 00A	327	Ar	Cincinnati, OH –Greyhound Sta. (ET)	●	Dp			5 30A

POINTS OF INTEREST

CHICAGO—See page 35
INDIANAPOLIS—
• *Indianapolis Motor Speedway*
• *Indianapolis Children's Museum*
CINCINNATI—
• *Athenaeum of Ohio*
• *Taft Presidential Museum*
HUNTINGTON—
• *Coal Mine Exhibit*
CHARLESTON—
• *West Virginia State Capitol*
WHITE SULPHUR SPRINGS—
• *Greenbrier Resort*
CLIFTON FORGE—
• *The Homestead*
STAUNTON—
• *Gateway to Shenandoah National Park*
CHARLOTTESVILLE—
• *Monticello*
WASHINGTON/PHILADELPHIA/NEW YORK—See page 21

SCENIC HIGHLIGHTS

New River Gorge, West Virginia
Blue Ridge Mountains, West Virginia/Virginia
Potomac River and monuments, District of Columbia

COMMUTER RAIL AND RAPID TRANSIT CONNECTIONS

Chicago—See page 35
The Northeast—See page 21

Note—Checked Baggage services for connecting passengers: Connecting checked baggage service is available to Baltimore, Wilmington, Philadelphia, Newark and New York, but baggage may be delayed

For details on train, station and baggage services, see pages 6-7.

27

AMTRAK®

International Route

Winter 2000 Effective January 16

Chicago...Kalamazoo...Battle Creek... Flint...Port Huron...Toronto

Train Name ▶				Inter-national	Lake Cities	Twilight Limited
Train Number ▶				**364**	**352**	**354**
Days of Operation ▶				Daily	Daily	Daily
Train Service ▶				Ⓡ Ⓣ ⓢ 🚭	Ⓡ Ⓡ Ⓣ ⓢ 🚭	Ⓡ Ⓡ Ⓣ ⓢ 🚭
	Mile	Symbol		Read Down		
Chicago, IL –Union Sta. ● (CT)	0	ⓢ	Dp	9 30A	ⓒ 2 10P	ⓒ 5 45P
Hammond-Whiting, IN	16	ⓢ		9 58A	ⓒ 2 39P	ⓒ 6 14P
Michigan City, IN	52	●				6 51P
Niles, MI (South Bend) (ET)	90	ⓢ		12 09P	ⓒ 4 51P	ⓒ 8 28P
Dowagiac, MI	102	●				8 41P
Kalamazoo, MI	138	ⓢ		1 01P	ⓒ 5 40P	ⓒ 9 21P
Battle Creek, MI	162	🄱	Ar	1 38P	ⓒ 6 12P	ⓒ 9 53P
			Dp		🚆 7 00P	🚆 10 40P
East Lansing, MI	208	🄱		2 38P	🚆 8 20P	🚆 11 50P
Durand, MI	233	●		3 12P		
Flint, MI	258	🄱	Ar	3 39P	🚆 9 40P	🚆 1 10A
Lapeer, MI	274	● ⓢ	Dp	4 00P		
Port Huron, MI	319	🄱 ⓢ	Ar	5 19P		
			Dp	5 35P		
Sarnia, ON	322	🄱 📠	Ar	5 57P		
			Dp	6 57P		
Strathroy, ON	361	📠	Ar	7 37P		
London, ON	381	📠		8 00P		
St. Marys, ON	401	📠		8 37P		
Stratford, ON ●	412	📠		9 01P		
Kitchener, ON	430	📠		9 30P		
Guelph, ON	452	📠		9 59P		
Georgetown, ON	471	📠		10 23P		
Brampton, ON	479	📠		10 33P		
Toronto, ON ● (ET)	501	📠	Ar	11 00P		

Services on the International Route

🄱 Business Class—Reserved coach seating in a separate section of the train. Complimentary beverages and newspaper.

Ⓡ All reserved train. Reservations required.

Ⓣ Sandwich, snack and beverage service.

ⓒ Amtrak Express® Shipping and Checked Baggage Service available at stations indicated.

🚭 Smoking is not permitted on these trains.

📠 Service is financed in part through funds made available by the Michigan Department of Transportation. State supported trains are operated at the discretion of each state and their operation is dependent upon continued state financial support.

Note—Trains 364, 365 and 367 operated jointly by Amtrak and VIA Rail Canada. Trains operating within Canada are subject to VIA Rail Canada regulations.

CROSSING THE U.S./CANADIAN BORDER
Customs and Immigration Information

Amtrak trains crossing international borders are subject to Customs and Immigrations inspections en route. Although time is allotted in Amtrak schedules for these inspections, Customs and Immigration officials may delay trains if necessary for the performance of their duties.

Entry into Canada/U.S.: U.S. or Canadian citizens crossing the U.S./Canadian border are required to have a passport (preferred), or an original or certified birth certificate, citizenship certificate, or naturalization certificate plus current government-issued photo identification. **(Note: a driver's license is not sufficient.)** Non-U.S. citizens permanently or temporarily residing in the United States must have an Alien Registration Card (I-551, or I-688 bearing the proper endorsement on the reverse.) All citizens of countries other than the United States or Canada not bearing an Alien Registration Card must have a passport, and citizens of many countries must also have a visa, U.S. Employment Authorization Card showing 210 as a section of law, or Canadian Form IMM 1000. Passengers not having proper documentation are prohibited from entering the U.S. or Canada, and will be detained prior to reaching the U.S./Canadian border. Persons under 18 years old who are not accompanied by an adult must bring a letter from a parent or guardian giving them permission to enter into Canada. For the most current information and requirements, passengers planning international travel should write for customs information to: Immigration and Naturalization Service, United States Department of Justice, 425 I St., NW, Washington, DC 20536, or Embassy of Canada, Consular & Visa Section, 501 Pennsylvania Avenue, NW, Washington, DC 20001.

EXERCISES — Amtrak

Using the excerpts from the Amtrak timetable for travel between New York and Chicago, complete the following exercises:

A passenger and the passenger's 101-year-old mother are interested in travelling from New York to Chicago on Wednesday, November 15 and returning on Wednesday, November 22.

1. If there is a choice of trains, they would like the latest departure on each date. Select the most appropriate trains for your clients. For both outward and return journeys, provide the departure and arrival times and give train names and numbers where possible. Also note the exact days of arrival, if you pick an overnight service.

    _____

    _____

    _____

2. Write the names of the stations at New York and Chicago that your clients will be using

    _____

3. What type of accommodation would you advise the passengers to reserve on their outward train?

    _____

4. Considering the mother's age, what other service might you offer upon arrival at Chicago Station?

    _____

EUROPE

While the railroads have declined in relative importance in Canada and the U.S., they are still extremely important in Europe, where the network of trains is very extensive. The following are the major advantages and disadvantages of travelling by train in Europe:

Advantages of Train Travel in Europe

1. **Convenience.** The extensive network of trains serves almost every city and town, and train stations are generally located centrally.
2. **Frequency of service.** There are many trains on most routes; usually daily.
3. **Dependability.** European trains have acquired a reputation for departing on time, no matter what the weather.
4. **Comfort.** European trains are among the most modern and luxurious (especially the TEE or Trans Europe Express, which has deluxe service and facilities).

5. **Speed.** European intercity trains tend to be much faster than their North American counterparts, (particularly the TGV [Train Grand Vitesse] in France); also, since distances are shorter than in North America, intercity travel in Europe by train may well be faster than flying.

6. **Scenery.** Train travel allows clients to enjoy the spectacular vistas of Europe without worrying about car breakdowns, reading maps and road signs, or the high cost of gas.

7. **Meeting Europeans.** Train travel provides travellers with an easy way of meeting Europeans.

Disadvantages of Train Travel in Europe

1. Cities often have more than one station, and several trains may share the same track. This can be confusing if you aren't familiar with the system.

2. Language may present a problem when information is needed. There are many different languages spoken within a relatively small area.

3. Rail passes often must be pre-booked before arrival in Europe.

4. There are many different rail passes, and not all passes can be used in all countries.

5. First-class travel is much more costly than second-class travel; and second-class travel is far less luxurious and tends to be crowded.

6. Because of the popularity of train travel in Europe, more common routes may sell out early for prime travel dates.

While each country in Europe operates its own national railroad system, there is a large degree of cooperation, and it is possible for North Americans to purchase passes (for example, the Eurailpass) that allow travel on more than one country's system at a flat price. The U.K., however, maintains a separate train network (BritRail) that has its own passes and is not part of the European rail system.

Types of Service

TGV (Train Grand Vitesse). A very fast train (speeds of up to 165 mph/265 kmp) operating only in France; advance reservations are required.

TEE (Trans Europe Express). First-class service, requiring advance reservations and a supplement to the fare; provides rapid intercity trains with comfortable accommodations.

IC (Intercity). First- and second-class service; same speed and comfort as the TEE but with more frequent service.

EC (Eurocity). Mostly first class; this service has replaced most TEEs and ICs.

In addition to these services, there are many local trains plus a few private railroads operating in Europe.

Reference Material

Note that European timetables show all times using a 24-hour clock.

Thomas Cook Timetable—Schedule for Paris to Basel

FRANCE

PARIS · BASEL — 380

km		1641	EC 113 D	1753 †	1743	1745 G	1643	1847 ©	1747	1945	1645 L	EC 115 E	1947 H	1647 ©	11647	11849 ©	117 E	1749 F		1849	1649	469	1949 ⊙
0	Paris Est.....d.	...	0703	0730	0800	0841	1140	1238	1328	1335	1607	1631	1659	1802	1802	1805	1805	1845	1845		1850	2008	2238	2326
110	Nogent sur Seine...d.	...	0803		0903		1337			1740				1908	1913	1924					1956	2124		
129	Romilly sur Seine...d.	...	0815		0916		1350			1755				1922	1928	1939					2010	2138		0041
166	Troyes.....d.	0658	0835		0937	1014	1411	1454		1737	1833		1931	1945	1951	2001	2014	2014			2032	2205	0019	0106
221	Bar sur Aube.....d.	0737	0907		1010		1439			1909											2100	2238	0054	0139
262	Chaumont 378.....d.	0809	0824	0942		1033	1103	1502	1543		1828	1936		2022							2125	2303	0123	0206
296	Langres 378.....d.		0844	1003		1053		1522									2105				2146	2325	0147	0230
307	Culmont Chalindrey 378.d.		0855	1015		1104	1133	1534													2157	2336	0200	0244
380	Vesoul.....a.			1036			1214	1449		1646	1652	1935		2008	2127			2206	2212			0248	0326
442	Belfort.....a.			1111			1258	1530		1728	1728	2014		2042	2211			2245	2257			0335	0415
442	Belfort §.....d.			1113			1307	1539		1731	1731	2016		2044	2214			2247	2259			0341	0431
491	Mulhouse §.....a.			1141			1336	1606		1759	1759	2045		2113	2242			2315	2327	2346			0414	0505
525	Basel §.....a.			1211			1405	1633		1836	1836			2140						0019				0458

		468 B	11640 Ⓐ	11642 ⚒	1640 ⚒	112 Ⓑ	1642 ⚒		1940 Ⓑ	1942 ⚒	114 L	11644 Ⓐ	1644 Ⓑ	1844 G	1742 Ⓐ	1744 †	11646 Ⓝ	1746 Ⓓ⊙	1948 Ⓔ	11748 Ⓐ	1846 R	1646 †	EC 118 Ⓓ⊙	1757	118	1748
	Basel §.....d.	0028					0536				0823													1648		1830
	Mulhouse §.....d.	0109			0510		0608	0630	0632	0848			1143	1329			1525					1714		1804	1906
	Belfort §.....d.	0141			0540		0659	0703	0916			1210	1402			1602					1739		1832	1940
	Belfort.....d.	0152			0542		0701	0705	0918			1219	1405			1604					1748		1834	1942
	Vesoul.....d.	0236			0617		0735	0745	0953			1259	1446			1644					1823		1908	2021
	Culmont Chalindrey 378..d.	0329		0619				0829			1044	1116			1632	1725		1748	1801		1909		2103
	Langres 378.....d.	0341		0630				0840			1054	1126			1644			1759	1812		1920		
	Chaumont 378.....d.	0403		0652		0802		0901			1115	1147		1553	1705	1753		1821	1833		1940	2011	2132
	Bar sur Aube.....d.	0428		0713		0824		0924			1136	1209			1728			1843	1855		2003		
	Troyes.....d.	0501	0556	0640	0743		0857		0959	1142	1200	1208	1242		1642	1756	1758	1845	1914	1916	1927	2036	2055	2220
	Romilly sur Seine.....d.		0619	0704			0918		1021		1221		1302			1818	1820		1936	1942	1948	2058		
	Nogent sur Seine.....d.		0633	0719			0932		1034		1233	1239	1315			1831	1833		1950	1954	2001		
	Paris Est.....a.	0646	0748	0803	0914	0929	1035		1043	1142	1313	1343	1343	1411	1612	1814	1943	1943	2019	2110	2110	2110	2136	2219	2224	2349

B – 🚲 1,2 cl., 🛏 2 cl. and 🔲 Paris - Basel - Chur and v.v.; 🔲 Paris - Basel and v.v.
D – LE CORBUSIER – ①-⑥ (not July 14, Aug. 16); 🔲 and ⚒ Paris - Basel.
E – ⑤ (also ⑦ to June 29 and from Aug. 31); also Aug. 14; not Aug. 15.
F – Daily except dates in note E.
G – ⑤⑥ (daily July 6 - Aug. 30).
H – ①-④ (not July 14, Aug. 14).
L – L'ARBALETE – 🔲 and ✗ Paris - Basel - Zürich and v.v.
R – LE CORBUSIER – daily except ⑥ (not July 13, Aug. 15); 🔲 and ⚒ Basel - Paris.

e – Also July 14; not July 13.
f – Also Aug. 14; not Aug. 15.
n – Also June 26, July 31, Aug. 14; not Aug. 15.
t – Also July 13, Aug. 15.

✓ – Supplement payable.
§ – For other trains Belfort - Mulhouse and Mulhouse - Basel see Table 385.

NANCY · ÉPINAL · BELFORT — 381

km		✗	✗	✗ J 2		Ⓐ	✗	Ⓐ		✗	✗ J 2		✗	Ⓓ J 2	✗		Ⓐ		Ⓑ	Ⓑ	⑥t	E	F	G
0	Paris Est 390.....d.	...																						
0	Nancy.....d.	0608	0608	0634	0741	0850	0944	...	1044	1137	1216	1240	1349	1618	1639	1651	1737	...	1811	1850	1944	1944	1945	2039	2153	2240
74	Épinal.....d.	0717	0722	0732	0837	0949	1036	1119b	1140	1234	1318	1348	1449	1713	1735	1800	1832	1840	1912	2006	2033	2036	2037	2144	2248	2345
	Remiremont.....d.	...	0752		0901			1204n			1512n	1740	1805			1904					2102	2102		2317f	...
182	Belfort.....a.	0840				1237		1353t							1948r										

		Ⓐ	⑤	Ⓐ	✗	Ⓐ J	✗	P	P	⑦	✗ J		✗		Ⓐ J	✗ J	✗ J	B	✗	M	✗	Ⓓ	L		C	†
	Belfort.....d.					0600							1127					1328					1914			
	Remiremont.....d.			0603	0641		0715	...	0734		0925v	1111x							1702						
	Épinal.....d.	0503	0524	0543	0631	0709	0717	0742	0742	0758	0806	0948	1139	1217	1245	1256	1356	1408h	1537	1605t	1655a		1808	1915	...
	Nancy.....a.	0558	0628	0648	0725	0801		0834	0834	0853	0900	1050	1231	1324		1353	1451		1540	1700	1731	1818		1928	2032	2131	2321
	Paris Est 390.....a.							1137																...	...

B – ⑥ (✗ July 7 - Aug. 30).
C – ⑤⑥ (also July 14, Aug. 14).
E – Ⓐ to July 4 and from Sept. 1; ⑤ July 12 - Aug. 30.
F – ① (daily to July 10 and from Sept. 6).
G – ⑤⑦ (daily July 7 - Aug. 31).
J – Runs to July 5 and from Sept. 1.
L – ①②③④⑤ (not July 14, Aug. 14).
M – † (⑦ to July 6 and from Sept. 1).
P – ①-⑥ (not July 14).
s – Ⓐ only.

b – Depart 1047 on Ⓐ July 7 - Aug. 29 (by 🚌 to Aillevillers).
f – ⑤ (not Aug. 15).
h – ⑤ July 12 - Aug. 30.
k – Also July 13, Aug. 14.
n – Not Ⓐ July 7 - Aug. 29.
r – Arrive 1953 on ⑤ (also Aug. 14; not Aug. 15).
t – ⑥ only.
v – ⑥ (daily to July 4 and from Sept. 1).
z – ⑥ (✗ to July 5 and from Sept. 1).

ÉPINAL · ST DIÉ · STRASBOURG — 382

km		Ⓐ	ⓒ	✗	E	✗	†	⑥	Ⓐ	⑥			Ⓐ	✗	⑥	†		G	Ⓐ	⑤	⑥	⑥
0	Épinal.....d.	0740r	1100	...	1238	...	1544	...	1644	1704b	1748	1821	1907	Strasbourg.....d.	...	0538	0646	0830	1040	...	1210	1240	...	...	1740
60	St Dié.....d.	0840	1158	1218	1345	1544	1635	1748	1810	1849	1919	2010	St Dié.....d.	0618	0739	0833	1011	1231	1242	1415	1415	1647	1814	1909
147	Strasbourg.....a.	0958	...	1355	...	1730	1809	...	1955	...	2130	Épinal.....a.	0721	0841	...	1344	...	1515	1746	1923	2008c

E – ⑥ (✗ to July 5 and from Sept. 1).
G – ⑥ (daily to July 6 and from Sept. 1).
b – † only.
c – ⑥ only.
r – ✗ only.

STRASBOURG · SAARBRÜCKEN — 383

km		✗	†	⑥	Ⓐ	2	⑥	✗	A		⑥					✗	Ⓐ		†	✗	✗	†		Ⓓ2 †	✗
0	Strasbourg.....d.	0800	1005	1100	1231	...	1302	1639	...	1838	Saarbrücken.....d.	0632	...	0710	...	1132	...	...	1710	1732	...
71	Diemeringen.....d.	0903	1107	1202	1334	...	1405	1742	...	1938	Forbach.....d.		0721		...		...			...	1753
97	Sarreguemines.....a.	0924	1133	1223	1358	...	1430	1806	...	2003	Sarreguemines.....a.	0656	...	0754	...	1156	...	...	1728	1756	1829
97	Sarreguemines.....d.	0927	1227	...	1403	1502	...	1811	...	2008	Sarreguemines.....d.		0705	0756	1010		1211	1606	1735	...	1832
	Forbach.....d.										Diemeringen.....d.		0729	0819	1034		1245	1628	1800	...	1857
139	Saarbrücken.....a.	0946	1246	...	1428	1525	...	1830	...	2028	Strasbourg.....a.		0828	0916	1134		1351	1728	1900	...	2000

A – ①-⑥ (not Aug. 15).

NANCY and METZ · LONGWY — 384

km		Ⓐ		B	✗	✗		✗	⑦s			P	✗2	✗		R	Ⓓ⊙	✗	⑥		†
0	Nancy.....d.	0610		1236	1346	...	1714	...	1834	2224	...	Longwy.....d.	0519	0610	0652	...	1213	1620	1839	1843	...	1930
28	Pont-à-Mousson.....d.	...		1256	1407	...	1737	...	2243	...	Longuyon.....d.	0533	0624	0707	0946	1226	1633	1854	1856	1937	1944
71	Conflans-Jarny.....d.	0657		1333	1439	...	1819	...	1920	2317	...	Metz.....a.		0723		1037	...	...	...	...	...	2032	...
	Metz.....d.		0755			1714		1843		...	Conflans-Jarny.....d.	0602		0742	...	1255	1703	1925	1924	...	2013
112	Longuyon.....d.	0726	0851	1402	1507	1818	1854	1934	1949	2348	Pont-à-Mousson.....d.	0633		0815	...	1326	1730	1958		...	2043
128	Longwy.....a.	0738	...	1414	1518	1830	1906	...	2008	0001	Nancy.....a.	0652		0834	...	1345	1748	2017	2010	...	2100

B – ⑤ (also ⑥ to July 5 and from Sept. 6).
P – ①-⑤ (not July 14, Aug. 15).
R – ⑦ to June 29 and from Sept. 7.
s – Also July 14; not July 13.
🚌 Metz - Longwy (journey 55 minutes, rail tickets valid):
From Metz: 0840, 1755✗, 2010Ⓓ.
From Longwy: 0632†, 0737⑥, 0947✗, 1905Ⓓ.

© the Thomas Cook Group 1997. This table taken from the Thomas Cook European Timetable which is published monthly and available from Forsyth Travel Library at (816) 942-9050 or email forsyth@gvi.net

Cook Overseas Timetable—published monthly; contains schedules for all European countries including the Commonwealth of Independent States (Russia, Ukraine, etc.) and for Morocco. Also lists ferry/steamship services, maps of all railroad terminals, baggage and customs information, etc. An extract from the *Thomas Cook Timetable* has been included for your reference. While the *Cook Timetable* is published monthly, you should at least obtain the October and June issues each year.

Eurail Timetable—published monthly; lists schedules for major European cities and tourist locations.

Individual railway timetables.

Classes of Service

European trains offer first-class and second-class service. The car windows are marked "1" or "2" to differentiate the cars.

First-class cars provide reclining seats in compartments of six seats (three on each side of the compartment).

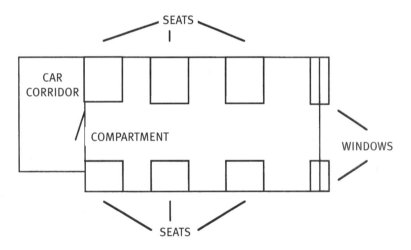

Second-class cars do not have compartments but simply offer rows of seats divided by a centre aisle (similar to airplane seating).

Accommodation on European Trains

Reservations are advisable for most long distance express trains and some intermediate trains. If there is overnight travel involved, it is also necessary to reserve sleeping accommodation if required.

Types of Accommodation

Couchettes. These are located in second class; the seats convert into six bunks, each with a mattress, pillow, blanket, and sheet, but with no privacy, and a flat fee charged as a supplement.

Sleepers. Allow for privacy, and may be single (one bed, first class), double (two beds, first class), or tourist (two or three beds, second class), and the charge depends on distance and type.

ACCOMMODATION ON EUROPEAN TRAINS

Couchette coach with compartments of 4 and 6 berths.   Voiture-couchettes ave compartiments à 4 et à 6 couchettes.

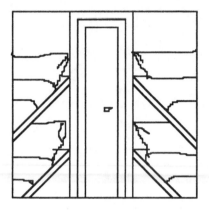

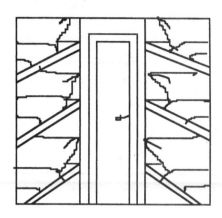

1st class ticket + couchette supplement
billet 1re classe + supplément couchette

2nd class ticket + couchette supplement
billet 2e classe + supplément couchette

MULTI CAR TRAINS

Sleeping car with small compartments with power plug and wash basin. Voiture-lits à petits compartiments avec prise de courant électrique et lavabo.

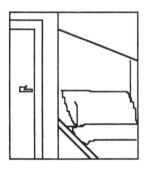

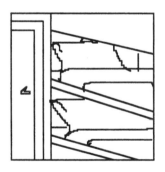

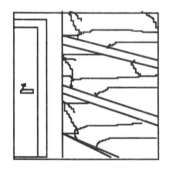

1st class ticket + **Special** supplement

2nd class ticket + **Double** supplement

2nd class ticket + **Tourist** supplement

Sleeping car with big compartments with power plug and wash basin. Voiture-lits à grands compartiments avec prise de courtant électrique et lavabo.

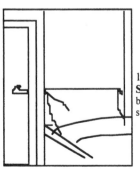

1st class ticket +
Single supplement
billet 1re classe +
supplément Single

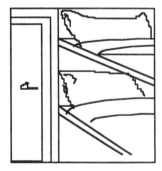

1st class ticket +
Double supplement
billet 1re classe +
supplément Double

Railway Tickets

Railway tickets may be sold separately for point-to-point travel (for one trip) or by rail pass (multi-trip). However the Eurail pass and the BritRail passes must be purchased before arrival in Europe.

How to Make a Reservation

There are various ways of booking European trains. The following is a list of the more common methods used by travel agents:

Britain	• BritRail • Tickets can also be issued on your airline computer system on regular IATA ticket stock.
Europe	• Rail Europe (a division of French Rail) • DER Travel (associated with German Rail) • CIT Travel (associated with Italian Rail) • Major tour operators also include some rail passes in their brochures.
Japan	• Japan Travel Bureau (represented in Canada).
Australia	• Goway Travel (represented in Canada).

The above railway representatives sometimes package the railway tickets. For example, a three-day French Rail pass plus a three-day car rental and perhaps hotel reservations might be offered by Rail Europe.

There may be an added service charge when making reservations with the above companies.

Passes

As mentioned before, it is possible to purchase a pass for travel across more than one country (they must be purchased in North America before travelling to Europe). The best known passes are the *Eurail passes*, and they are available in the following varieties:

Adult Eurail pass. First-class unlimited travel for blocks of 15 or 21 days or for 1, 2, or 3 months. Note that children under 4 years old can travel free; children between ages 4 and 11 travel at a 50% discount.

Youth Eurail pass. Second-class unlimited travel for blocks of 15 days or for 1 or 2 months; available only for persons under 26 years old.

Adult Eurail flexipass. First-class travel for a limited number of days in a maximum amount of time (you can purchase either 10 or 15 days of travel in a 2-month period).

Youth Eurail flexipass. Second-class travel for a limited number of days in a maximum amount of time (10 or 15 days of travel in a 2-month period), available only for persons under 26 years old.

Eurail saverpass. First-class travel for a block of 15 days, 21 days, or one month; designed for several people wishing to travel together (2 or more adults in low season and 3 or more adults in high season, which is between April 1 and September 30).

Europass. A first-class flexipass or a second-class youth pass, available for travel through three or more of the following countries: France, Germany, Italy, Spain, and Switzerland; and provided the countries selected border each other. Greece, Portugal, Austria, Belgium, and Luxembourg can be added at an additional charge. The first-class Europass is valid for 5, 6, or 7 days of travel; a passenger can add a fourth country for 8 to 10 days, and a fifth country for 11 to 15 days of travel. The youth second-class Europass is valid for 5 to 10 days (four bordering countries); a passenger can add a fifth country for 11 to 15 days of travel.

In addition passes are available for particular countries (for example, the Swiss pass) or for regions (the Scanrail pass in Scandinavia).

List the factors you would consider when determining which pass your client should purchase?

_____

_____

_____

_____

_____

Passes may also include discounts on ferries and buses, and other features.

Eurostar

Since its inception in November 1994, Eurostar has travelled via the Chunnel (a tunnel under the English Channel) between London Waterloo Station and either Paris Gare du Nord Station or Brussels at speeds of up to 186 mph (300 kph). Reservations are necessary, and seating is available in either first class or standard class.

BritRail Passes

BritRail passes are available for travel within the United Kingdom only (England, Scotland, and Wales). The various Eurail passes cannot be used in the U.K. As with Eurail, there are a number of passes offered:

- **BritRail classic pass.** Either first class or standard for adults, or standard for youths (16 to 25 years old); valid for 8 days, 15 days, 22 days, or 1 month.

- **BritRail flexipass.** Either first class or standard for adults, or standard for youths (16 to 25 years old); valid for any 4 days, 8 days, or 15 days in a 2-month period.

- **BritRail senior pass.** First class only for seniors (60 years and over); provides a 20% discount off the adult classic pass or the adult flexipass.

- **BritRail kid's pass.** One child (5 to 15 years old) is entitled to a free pass where an adult pass or senior pass is purchased for accompanied travel. Additional child passes can be purchased at 50% off the price of a regular adult pass. Children under 5 travel free.

- **BritRail pass + Eurostar.** Includes a standard-class Eurostar round-trip ticket from London to Paris or Brussels, and a BritRail flexipass for either first-class or standard service for any 4 days or any 8 days in a 3-month period. There is no reduction for children.

- **BritRail pass + Ireland.** Includes round-trip ship or catamaran ticket between London and Ireland, and a BritRail flexipass for either first-class or standard service for any 5 days or any 10 days in a 1-month period. BritRail kid's pass is available, and children under 5 travel free.

- **Freedom of Scotland Travelpass.** Includes unlimited standard-class travel throughout Scotland for any 4 days in an 8-day period, any 8 days in a 15-day period, or any 12 days in a 20-day period.

- **BritRail pass + car.** Includes a 3-day BritRail flexipass plus 3-day car rental within 1 month, or a 6-day BritRail flexipass plus 7-day car rental within 1 month. Rail travel is either first class or standard, and rates are adult or senior (60+ years old). A BritRail kid's pass is also available, and children under 5 travel free. Rental cars are either manual transmission (economy size, compact, or intermediate) or automatic transmission (intermediate size, full size, or premium). A rail supplement (either standard or first-class service) is charged for each additional adult, and children (5 to 15 years old) pay 50% of the supplement. Mileage is unlimited for the rental cars, and pick-up/drop-off is permitted at any participating Hertz location. Additional car rental days are available.

- **BritRail Weekender.** A 4-day pass (first class or standard), which must include a Saturday night.

- **BritRail SouthEast Pass.** Covers the southeast of England (first class or standard) for any 3 or 4 days in an 8-day period, or any 7 days in a 15-day period.

- **Great British Heritage Pass.** Includes a pass for 7 days, 15 days or 1 month, and entry to over 500 historic properties.

Sealink tickets for the hovercraft and ferry services are also sold through BritRail, as are regular point-to-point train tickets.

Australian Rail Passes

- Austrail pass/Austrail flexipass

- Sunshine pass

- Victoria pass

- New South Wales discovery passs

- East Coast discovery pass

- Southern discovery pass

Europe Point-to-Point Fares

Point-to-Point Fares

For single rail journeys from one destination in Europe to another along a specific route. Access our web site for more point-to-point fares and schedules at **www.raileurope.com**.

The listing below shows average journey times and fares to/from some of the major cities. The information is listed under the city name that is first in alphabetical order, whether it is your departure or destination city. For example, whether you are traveling from Amsterdam to Paris, or Paris to Amsterdam, the information will be listed under the Amsterdam heading.

Price Range for Sleeper Supplements

	1st Class Single	1st Class Double	2nd Class Double/Triple
Price Range	$102 to $292	$60 to $151	$38 to $148

Couchette Supplement

2nd Class	$43

All prices per person. Prices in CAN dollars. Subject to change.

Sleeping Accommodations on the Train

Sleepers

1st class ticket plus single supplement

1st class or 2nd class ticket plus double supplement

2nd class ticket plus triple supplement

Couchette

6 berth 2nd class ticket plus couchette supplement

Group Discounts

Group Discounts are available for all tickets: groups of 6 or more receive a 30% discount. Call our EuroGroups division at 1-800-462-2577.

City Pairs		One Way Fares* 1st Class	2nd Class	Average Travel Time
Amsterdam to	Berlin	$263	$179	6h 30m
	Brussels	Thalys from	$ 49	2h 48m
	Cologne	$104	$ 70	3h
	Frankfurt	$206	$137	5h 30m
	Munich	$353	$236	8h 30m
	Paris	Thalys from	$110	4h 13m
Athens to	Vienna	$339	$235	30h 30m
Avignon to	Barcelona	$111	$ 76	6h 30m
	Nice	$ 92	$ 64	4h
	Paris	$162	$127	3h 30m
Barcelona to	Madrid	$121	$ 86	7h
	Paris	Talgo night from	$241	11h 30m
	Valencia	$ 66	$ 48	3h
Basel to	Frankfurt	$168	$114	3h
	Paris	$131	$ 93	5h
	Zurich	$ 73	$ 48	1h
Bath to	London	$122	$ 83	1h 11m
Berlin to	Frankfurt	$216	$148	6h
	Hamburg	$137	$ 95	3h
	Munich	$263	$180	7h
	Prague	$127	$ 89	6h 30m
	Warsaw	$ 76	$ 54	6h
Bordeaux to	Paris	$146	$113	3h
Bratislava to	Prague	$ 84	$ 58	5h
Brig to	Disentis	$ 86	$ 54	5h
	Zermatt	$ 75	$ 48	1h 30m
Brindisi to	Patras	$254	$218	17h 30m
Brugge to	Paris	Thalys from	$ 92	2h 28m
Brussels to	Cologne	Thalys from	$ 49	2h 37m
	London	Eurostar from	$181	2h 45m
	Paris	Thalys from	$ 86	1h 25m
Budapest to	Prague	$136	$ 96	9h 30m
	Vienna	$ 81	$ 58	2h 30m
Cannes to	Nice	$ 22	$ 17	30m
	Paris	$194	$146	6h
Cologne to	Frankfurt	$108	$ 75	2h 30m
	Hamburg	$178	$124	4h
	Munich	$266	$180	6h
	Paris	Thalys from	$105	4h
Copenhagen to	Hamburg	$165	$113	4h 30m
	Oslo	$265	$174	10h 30m
	Paris	$505	$352	15h
	Stockholm	$239	$142	7h
Dijon to	Paris	$105	$ 76	2h
Edinburgh to	Glasgow	$ 32	$ 23	50m
	London	$274	$195	4h
Florence to	Milan	$ 70	$ 48	2h 30m
	Paris	$327	$203	13h 30m
	Rome	$ 70	$ 48	1h 30m
	Venice	$ 63	$ 43	3h
	Zurich	$201	$127	7h
Frankfurt to	Munich	$206	$139	3h 30m
	Paris	$206	$145	6h 15m
	Zurich	$233	$154	5h
Geneva to	Lyon	$ 67	$ 51	2h
	Milan	$160	$ 99	6h
	Paris	$187	$136	3h 30m
	Zurich	$154	$ 96	3h
Helsinki to	Stockholm	$ 93	$ 93	14h

City Pairs		One Way Fares* 1st Class	2nd Class	Average Travel Time
Innsbruck to	Munich	$ 75	$ 54	4h
	Vienna	$134	$ 93	8h
	Zurich	$131	$ 86	5h
Lausanne to	Milan	$134	$ 84	4h 30m
	Paris	$175	$124	3h 45m
Lisbon to	Madrid	$114	$ 80	9h 30m
London to	Manchester	$171	$133	2h 30m
	Paris	Eurostar from	$181	3h
	York	$222	$143	1h 57m
Lourdes to	Paris	$177	$139	6h 30m
Lucerne to	Paris	$186	$125	7h 30m
	Zurich	$ 54	$ 35	1h
Lugano to	Milan	$ 43	$ 29	1h 30m
	Zurich	$122	$ 76	3h 30m
Lyon to	Paris	$152	$114	2h
Madrid to	Malaga	Talgo 200 from	$ 87	4h 25m
	Sevilla	AVE from	$104	2h 30m
Marseille to	Nice	$ 69	$ 51	2h 30m
	Paris	$171	$127	4h 15m
Milan to	Paris (day)	Artesia from	$140	6h 40m
	Rome	$114	$ 75	4h
	Venice	$ 63	$ 43	2h 30m
	Zurich	$148	$ 93	3h 30m
Monte Carlo to	Nice	$ 16	$ 13	15m
Montpellier to	Paris	$171	$127	4h 15m
Munich to	Paris	$274	$195	8h 30m
	Prague	$140	$ 96	6h
	Rome	$212	$140	13h
	Salzburg	$ 66	$ 48	2h
	Vienna	$145	$102	6h
	Zurich	$162	$107	5h
Nantes to	Paris	$140	$ 99	2h
Naples to	Rome	$ 55	$ 38	2h
Nice to	Paris	$203	$152	6h 30m
	Rome	$134	$ 87	10h
Oslo to	Stockholm	$192	$133	6h 30m
Paris to	Rome	$327	$203	14h 30m
	Strasbourg	$128	$ 89	4h
	Toulouse	$174	$136	5h
	Tours	$107	$ 84	1h
	Venice	$327	$203	12h 15m
	Vienna	$411	$289	13h 30m
	Zurich	$197	$133	6h
Pisa to	Rome	$ 73	$ 49	4h
Prague to	Vienna	$101	$ 70	5h
Rome to	Venice	$108	$ 70	4h 30m
	Zurich	$242	$152	8h 30m
Salzburg to	Vienna	$ 87	$ 63	4h
St. Moritz to	Zermatt	$250	$152	7h 30m
	Zurich	$130	$ 81	4h
Venice to	Vienna	$154	$104	8h
	Zurich	$190	$121	8h
Vienna to	Warsaw	$111	$ 78	9h
	Zurich	$228	$152	12h
Zermatt to	Zurich	$216	$133	6h

*Prices include $8 service fee and are subject to change without notice. Children 4–11 (5–15 in UK) half fare. Fares shown are one way. Round trip fares are double the amount shown, except in the United Kingdom. Fares and times may vary according to routings. Prices in CAN dollars. Subject to change.

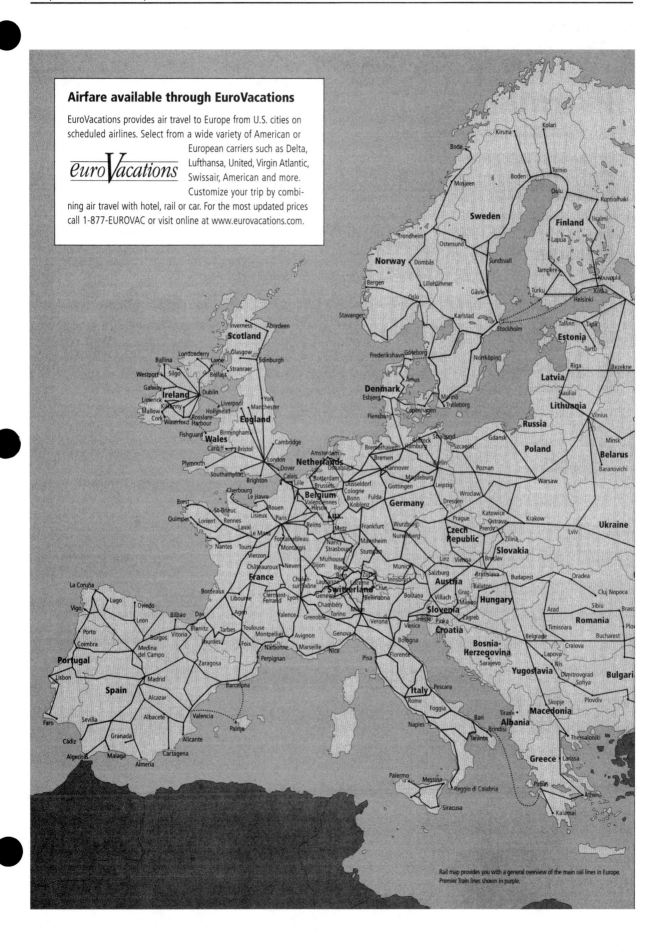

Rail map provides you with a general overview of the main rail lines in Europe. Premier Train lines shown in purple.

Passes At A Glance

Eurailpass (see page 12)

Austria, Belgium, Denmark, Finland, France, Germany, Greece, Hungary, Ireland (Republic of), Italy, Luxembourg, Netherlands, Norway, Portugal, Spain, Sweden and Switzerland. (England, Scotland, Wales and Northern Ireland are not included.)

	Adult 1st Class	Youth** 2nd Class
15 consecutive days	$ 843	$ 590
21 consecutive days	$1092	$ 759
1 month	$1353	$ 947
2 months	$1916	$1341
3 months	$2369	$1656

Eurail Flexipass (see page 12)

	Adult 1st Class	Youth** 2nd Class
Any 10 days in 2 months	$ 995	$697
Any 15 days in 2 months	$1311	$911

Eurail Saverpass (see page 12)

	1st Class*
15 consecutive days	$ 715
21 consecutive days	$ 928
1 month	$1150
2 months	$1630
3 months	$2013

Eurail Saver Flexipass (see page 13)

	1st Class*
Any 10 days in 2 months	$ 846
Any 15 days in 2 months	$1113

EurailDrive Pass (see page 34)

Any 6 days (4 rail & 2 car) within 2 months + 5 additional rail + additional car days

Car Categories	2 Adults* 1st Class	1 Adult 1st Class	Add'l Car Day
Economy	$590	$679	$89

Europass (see page 14)

France, Germany, Italy, Spain and Switzerland

	Adult 1st Class	Youth** 2nd Class
Any 5 days in 2 months	$529	$355
Any 8 days in 2 months	$681	$476

Europass Saverpass (see page 14)

France, Germany, Italy, Spain and Switzerland

	1st Class*
Any 5 days in 2 months	$450
Any 8 days in 2 months	$581

Europass Drive (see page 34)

Any 5 days (3 rail & 2 car) within 2 months + 7 additional rail + additional car days

Car Categories	2 Adults* 1st Class	1 Adult 1st Class	Add'l Car Day
Economy	$460	$545	$89

BritRail Classic Pass (see page 16)

	Adult 1st Class	Stnd	Senior*** 1st Class	Youth** Stnd
8 consecutive days	$553	$369	$470	$295

BritRail Flexipass (see page 17)

	Adult 1st Class	Stnd	Senior*** 1st Class	Youth** Stnd
Any 4 days in 2 months	$485	$323	$412	$259

BritRail Pass 'n Drive (see page 35)

Any 5 days (3 rail & 2 car) within 2 months + additional car days

Car Categories	2 Adults* 1st Class	1 Adult 1st Class	Add'l Car Day
Mini	$460	$545	$89

BritRail SouthEast Pass (see page 18)

	Adult 1st Class	Standard
Any 3 days in 8	$146	$106

BritRail Pass + Ireland (see page 19)

	Adult 1st Class	Standard
Any 5 days in 1 month	$743	$562

Freedom of Scotland Travelpass (see page 19)

	Standard
Any 4 days in 8	$200

Great British Heritage Pass (see page 18)

7 days	$78

London Visitor Travelcard (see page 23)

	All Zone	Central Zone
3 consecutive days	$45	$31

Austrian Railpass (see page 32)

	1st Class	2nd Class
Any 3 days in 15	$235	$159

Balkan Flexipass (see page 32)

Bulgaria, Greece, Macedonia, Romania, Turkey and Yugoslavia

	Adult 1st Class	Youth** 1st Class
Any 5 days in 1 month	$232	$137

Benelux Tourrail Pass (see page 32)

Belgium, Netherlands and Luxembourg

	2 Adults* 1st Class	2nd Class	1 Adult 1st Class	2nd Class	Junior** 2nd Class
Any 5 days in 1 month	$248	$178	$330	$236	$159

Bulgarian Flexipass

	1st Class
Any 3 days in 1 month	$107

Czech Flexipass (see page 32)

	1st Class
Any 5 days in 15	$105

European East Pass (see page 26)

Austria, Czech Republic, Hungary, Poland, Slovakia

	1st Class
Any 5 days in 1 month	$312

Finnrail Pass (see page 33)

	1st Class	2nd Class
Any 3 days in 1 month	$283	$189

France Railpass (see page 24)

	1 Adult 1st Class	2nd Class
Any 3 days in 1 month	$320	$274
Additional rail day (6 max.)	$ 46	$ 46

France Saverpass (see page 24)

	1st Class*	2nd Class*
Any 3 days in 1 month	$260	$222
Additional rail day (6 max.)	$ 46	$ 46

France Youthpass (see page 24)

	2nd Class
Any 4 days in 2 months	$250
Additional rail day (6 max.)	$ 31

France Rail 'n Drive Pass (see page 35)

Any 5 days (3 rail & 2 car) within 1 month + 6 additional rail + additional car days

Car Category	2 Adults* 1st Class	2nd Class	1 Adult 1st Class	2nd Class	Add'l Car Day
Economy	$305	$270	$425	$379	$72

Greek Flexipass Rail 'n Fly (see page 33)

	Adult 1st Class	Junior** 1st Class
Any 3 days rail + 2 air journey in 1 month	$308	$283

Holland Railpass (see page 33)

	2 Adults* 1st Class	Senior*** 1st Class	Junior** 2nd Class
Any 3 days in 1 month	$112	$119	$80

Hungarian Flexipass (see page 33)

	1st Class
Any 5 days in 15	$98

Iberic Railpass (see page 26)

	1st Class
Any 3 days in 2 months	**$312**

Italy Rail Card (see page 27)

	1st Class	2nd Class
8 days	**$455**	**$303**
15 days	**$567**	**$379**
21 days	**$659**	**$440**

Italy Flexi Rail Card (see page 27)

	1st Class	2nd Class
4 days in 1 month	**$364**	**$242**
8 days in 1 month	**$508**	**$339**

Italy Rail 'n Drive Pass (see page 35)

Any 5 days (3 rail & 2 car) within 1 month + additional car days

Car Categories	2 Adults* 1st Class	2nd Class	Add'l Car Day
Economy	**$399**	**$285**	**$69**

Norway Railpass (see page 33)

	1st Class	2nd Class
Any 3 days in 1 month	**$276**	**$212**

Paris Visite (see page 25)

2 consecutive days	**$61**

Portuguese Railpass (see page 33)

	1st Class
Any 4 days in 15	**$160**

Romanian Pass

	1st Class
Any 3 days in 15	**$92**

Scanrail Pass (see page 28)

Denmark, Finland, Norway and Sweden

	Adult 1st Class	2nd Class	Youth** 1st Class	2nd Class
Any 5 days in 2 months	**$411**	**$304**	**$309**	**$228**

Scanrail Senior Pass (see page 28)

	1st Class***	2nd Class***
Any 5 days in 2 months	**$367**	**$271**

Scanrail Rail 'n Drive (see page 36)

Any 7 days (5 rail & 2 car) within 2 months + additional car days

Car Category	2 Adults* 1st Class	2nd Class	1 Adult 1st Class	2nd Class	Add'l Car Day
Economy	**$495**	**$390**	**$579**	**$475**	**$89**

Spain Flexipass (see page 29)

	1st Class	2nd Class
Any 3 days in 2 months	**$304**	**$236**

Spain Rail 'n Drive (see page 36)

Any 5 days (3 rail & 2 car) within 2 months + additional rail + additional car days

Car Categories	2 Adults* 1st Class	1 Adult 1st Class	Add'l Car Day
Economy	**$395**	**$465**	**$79**

Sweden Railpass (see page 33)

	1st Class	2nd Class
Any 3 days in 1 month	**$321**	**$238**

Swiss Pass (see page 30)

	Saverpass* 1st Class	2nd Class	1 Adult 1st Class	2nd Class
4 consecutive days	**$317**	**$207**	**$373**	**$244**
8 consecutive days	**$428**	**$285**	**$502**	**$335**

Swiss Flexipass (see page 30)

	Saverpass* 1st Class	2nd Class	1 Adult 1st Class	2nd Class
Any 3 days in 1 month	**$301**	**$201**	**$356**	**$238**
Any 5 days in 1 month	**$411**	**$274**	**$484**	**$323**
Any 7 days in 1 month	**$507**	**$338**	**$596**	**$397**

*2 Adults: Prices per person based on two people traveling together at all times; Saverpass: Prices per person based on two or more people traveling together.
**Junior and youth fares available only for passengers under 26 years of age on their first date of travel.
***Senior fare available to adults 60 years and older.
Prices in CAN dollars. Subject to change.

Eurail Passes

From $715 —

The famous pass that offers unlimited and economical travel in 17 European countries: Austria, Belgium, Denmark, Finland, France, Germany, Greece, Hungary, Ireland (Republic of), Italy, Luxembourg, Netherlands, Norway, Portugal, Spain, Sweden and Switzerland. (England, Scotland, Wales and Northern Ireland are not included.)

PREMIER Trains

On at least part of your journey, consider taking a Premier Train. With our Eurail Passes special fares are available.

Bonus

- Special fare on high-speed Premier Trains such as Eurostar, AVE, Thalys and Artesia.
- Free or discounted travel on selected ferries, lake steamers, boats and buses.
- A complete list of bonuses is included on the complimentary Eurail map you will receive with your pass.
- Free timetable.

Note to Flexipass holders: travel bonuses may constitute usage of a travel day.

If you'd like to rent a car with your Eurailpass, it's easy. See pages 34–37. And finding hotels to suit your specific needs is also a snap (pages 38–42) just as transatlantic airfare is from the U.S.

Eurailpass

For travel on any or all days, this pass gives you plenty of time to explore the wonders of Europe.

INCLUDES:
- Choice of five consecutive-day pass durations:
  - –15 days unlimited travel or,
  - –21 days unlimited travel or,
  - –1 month unlimited travel or,
  - –2 months unlimited travel or,
  - –3 months unlimited travel.
- 1st class train travel.
- Special travel bonuses (see Bonus).

	1st Class
15 consecutive days	$ 843
21 consecutive days	$1092
1 month	$1353
2 months	$1916
3 months	$2369

Children 4–11: half adult fare. Under 4: free. Prices in CAN dollars. Subject to change.

Eurail Flexipass

Individual days of train travel allow you to discover Europe at your own pace.

INCLUDES:
- Choice of two pass durations:
  - –any 10 days unlimited train travel in a 2 month period or,
  - –any 15 days unlimited train travel in a 2 month period.
- 1st class train travel.
- Special travel bonuses (see Bonus).

	1st Class
Any 10 days in 2 months	$ 995
Any 15 days in 2 months	$1311

Children 4–11: half adult fare. Under 4: free. Prices in CAN dollars. Subject to change.

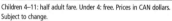

Belgium Train

The TGV Premier Train

Eurail Saverpass

Specially designed for groups of 2 or more, this features consecutive travel days.

INCLUDES:
- Choice of five consecutive-day pass durations:
  - –15 days unlimited travel or,
  - –21 days unlimited travel or,
  - –1 month unlimited travel or,
  - –2 months unlimited travel or,
  - –3 months unlimited travel.
- lst class train travel.
- Special travel bonuses (see Bonus).

	1st Class
15 consecutive days	$ 715
21 consecutive days	$ 928
1 month	$1150
2 months	$1630
3 months	$2013

Price per person based on 2 or more people traveling together. Children 4–11: half adult fare. Under 4: free. Prices in CAN dollars. Subject to change.

A pack on your back, a Eurailpass Youthpass in hand and you're all set

Eurail Saver Flexipass

For groups of 2 or more, you select the exact days you'd like to travel.

INCLUDES:
- Choice of two pass durations:
  - any 10 days unlimited train travel in a 2 month period or,
  - any 15 days unlimited train travel in a 2 month period.
- 1st class train travel.
- Special travel bonuses (see Bonus).

	1st Class
Any 10 days in 2 months	$ 846
Any 15 days in 2 months	$1113

Price per person based on 2 or more people traveling together. Children 4–11: half adult fare. Under 4: free. Prices in CAN dollars. Subject to change.

Heppenheim, Germany

Eurail Youthpass

A special pass for those under age 26, travel any or all days consecutively.

INCLUDES:
- Choice of five consecutive-day pass durations:
  - 15 days unlimited travel or,
  - 21 days unlimited travel or,
  - 1 month unlimited travel or,
  - 2 months unlimited travel or,
  - 3 months unlimited travel.
- 2nd class train travel.
- Special travel bonuses (see Bonus).

	2nd Class
15 consecutive days	$ 590
21 consecutive days	$ 759
1 month	$ 947
2 months	$1341
3 months	$1656

Available only if passenger is under 26 years of age on their first date of travel. Prices in CAN dollars. Subject to change.

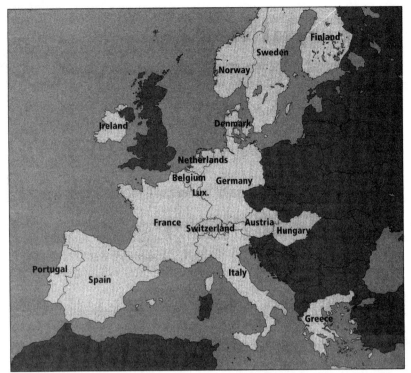

Eurail Youth Flexipass

For those under age 26, travel the days you want without losing any time on your pass.

INCLUDES:
- Choice of two pass durations:
  - any 10 days unlimited train travel in a 2 month period or,
  - any 15 days unlimited train travel in a 2 month period.
- 2nd class train travel.
- Special travel bonuses (see Bonus).

	2nd Class
Any 10 days in 2 months	$697
Any 15 days in 2 months	$911

Available only if passenger is under 26 years of age on their first date of travel. Prices in CAN dollars. Subject to change.

Special for Youth

50% off a BritRail Youth Pass when you purchase any Eurail Youthpass or Europass Youth.

EurailDrive Pass

Extend your travel options throughout these countries by including a car. See page 34 for more.

Sample Itinerary

To give you just one idea of all you can see and do, here's an itinerary you may wish to consider using the 15 day in 2 month Eurail Flexipass. And note the cost savings: if you were to do the same with individual tickets in first class, it would cost $2,527 instead of just $1,311. That's a savings of $1,216.

Itinerary includes stops in the following cities: Amsterdam, Cologne, Hamburg, Copenhagen, Oslo, Stockholm, Malmo, Berlin, Munich, Vienna, Venice, Rome, Nice, Barcelona, Madrid, Paris.

Europasses

From $450 —

Europass gives you the flexibility of unlimited travel in France, Germany, Italy, Spain and Switzerland with the option of visiting Associate Countries as well. Associate Countries include Austria/Hungary, Benelux, Portugal and Greece.

PREMIER Trains

Experience a variety of Premier Trains with this pass. Special fares are available.

Save with the Saverpass

Europass Saverpass is ideal for a group of 2 or more. You get the same benefits as Europass but at a discounted rate. So call your friends and pack your bags!

Bonus

- Special fare on high-speed Premier Trains such as Eurostar, AVE, Thalys and Artesia.
- Free or discounted travel on selected ferries, lake steamers, boats and buses.
- A complete list of bonuses is included on the complimentary map you will receive with your pass.
- Free timetable.

Travel bonuses may constitute usage of a travel day.

Europass

When you want the flexibility of a Eurail Flexipass but plan to travel only in these 5 European countries (or the Associate Countries), this is the pass for you.

INCLUDES:
- Choice of five pass durations: –any 5, 6, 8, 10 or 15 days in a 2 month period.
- 1st class train travel.
- Special travel bonuses (see Bonus).

OPTIONS:
- Add Associate Countries to extend the geographic coverage of the pass.

	1st Class
Any 5 days in 2 months	$ 529
Any 6 days in 2 months	$ 560
Any 8 days in 2 months	$ 681
Any 10 days in 2 months	$ 803
Any 15 days in 2 months	$1107

Children 4–11: half adult fare. Under 4: free. Prices in CAN dollars. Subject to change.

Enjoy outstanding views while traveling by train

The kids love the Thalys Premier Train

Europass Saverpass

Groups of 2 or more traveling together can receive this special rate. Includes the same benefits as Europass, including bonuses and 1st class train travel.

	1st Class
Any 5 days in 2 months	$450
Any 6 days in 2 months	$478
Any 8 days in 2 months	$581
Any 10 days in 2 months	$684
Any 15 days in 2 months	$943

Price per person based on 2 or more people traveling together. Children 4–11: half adult fare. Under 4: free. Prices in CAN dollars. Subject to change.

Sample Itinerary

You can make your way from Rome to Zurich using the 5 day in 2 month Europass. And note the savings: if you were to do the same with individual tickets in first class, it would cost $1,013 instead of just $529. That's a savings of $484.

Europass Youth

A special pass for those under 26 years of age, this is the same as the Europass including travel bonuses, but in 2nd class.

	2nd Class
Any 5 days in 2 months	**$355**
Any 6 days in 2 months	**$385**
Any 8 days in 2 months	**$476**
Any 10 days in 2 months	**$552**
Any 15 days in 2 months	**$780**

Available only if passenger is under 26 years of age on their first day of travel. Prices in CAN dollars. Subject to change.

Just your everyday home in Chaumont, France

Associate Countries

Extend the geographic reach of the pass even further by adding up to two of the following countries:
- Austria/Hungary.
- Benelux (Belgium, Netherlands & Luxembourg).
- Greece (includes ferry crossing).
- Portugal.

Associate Countries can be visited on any or all of the travel days. Associate Countries extend the geographical scope of your pass; they do not extend the passes' length in days.

	1 Adult 1st Class	Saverpass* 1st Class	Youth** 2nd Class
1 associate country	**$ 92**	**$ 80**	**$ 69**
2 associate countries	**$152**	**$131**	**$119**

*Price per person based on 2 or more people traveling together.
**Available only if passenger is under 26 years of age on their first day of travel.
Children 4–11: half adult fare. Under 4: free. Prices in CAN dollars. Subject to change.

Note: Travel within an Associate Country is only covered when issued in conjunction with a Europass. Certain trains may transit through a country not covered by the pass. In that case an additional ticket must be purchased. Refer to the Europass map and general conditions included with your pass.

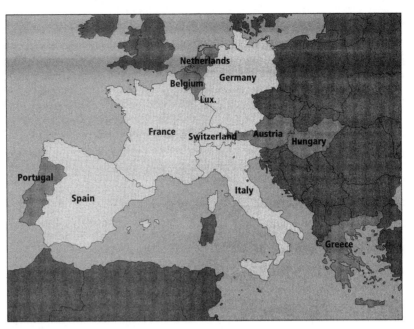

Europass Drive

Combining the train with your own rental car is the ultimate in flexibility. See pages 36–39 for the Europass Drive and other rail and car options.

Even the dolls know how to dress in Hungary

Switzerland's Glacier Express near Zermatt

Special for Youth

50% off a BritRail Youth Pass when you purchase any Eurail Youthpass or Europass Youth.

Need a hotel while traveling on your Europass? We've got a wide variety to suit your needs. See pages 38–42. We can also provide you with car rentals (see pages 34–37) and trans-atlantic airfare from the U.S.

BritRail

From $323 —
The BritRail Pass puts England, Scotland and Wales at your fingertips making exploration of these delightful countries a treat not to be missed. Visit famous cities like London, Chester and Edinburgh, arriving right in the city center. There is no better way to enjoy Britain.

Bonus

- Special fare on Eurostar.
- Includes travel on Gatwick and Heathrow Express.

BritRail Classic Pass

Ideal for consecutive day travel, this pass even features special rates for seniors and youths.

INCLUDES:
- Choice of four consecutive-day pass durations:
  –8 days unlimited travel or,
  –15 days unlimited travel or,
  –22 days unlimited travel or,
  –1 month unlimited travel.
- Choice of 1st or standard class train travel.
- Special travel bonuses (see Bonus).

OPTIONS:
- A discounted standard class pass available to passengers under 26 years of age.
- A free BritRail Family Pass lets one child (ages 5–15) travel free with each adult or senior pass you purchase.
- Special 50% discount for parties of three or four traveling together in 1st class (ask for the BritRail Party Pass).

BritRail Senior Pass

For those over 60 years of age, you can enjoy a BritRail Flexipass, BritRail Classic Pass or the BritRail Pass 'n Drive in 1st class at an attractively reduced rate.

The houses are nestled together like stepping stones in Dorset Shaftsbury

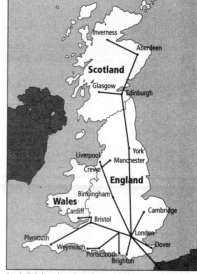

Premier Train lines shown in purple.

Adult	1st Class	Standard
8 consecutive days	$ 553	$369
15 consecutive days	$ 830	$553
22 consecutive days	$1051	$701
1 month	$1244	$830

Senior*	1st Class
8 consecutive days	$ 470
15 consecutive days	$ 705
22 consecutive days	$ 893
1 month	$1058

Youth**	Standard
8 consecutive days	$295
15 consecutive days	$387
22 consecutive days	$490
1 month	$581

Many local trains in England, Scotland and Wales have Standard accommodations only. This has been allowed for in the 1st Class pass price.
*Senior: Available for passengers 60 and over.
**Youth: Available only for passengers under 26 on their first date of travel.
One child (5–15) can travel free with each adult or senior pass by requesting the BritRail Family Pass. Children from 5–15: half adult fare. Children under 5: free. Prices in CAN dollars. Subject to change.

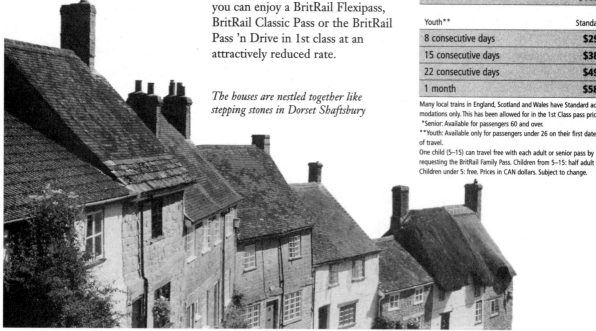

GNER trains connect London, Edinburgh and Glasgow

BritRail Flexipass

Named for its flexibility, this allows you to pick your specific days of travel.

INCLUDES:

- Choice of three pass durations:
  - any 4 days unlimited train travel or,
  - any 8 days unlimited train travel or,
  - any 15 days unlimited train travel.
- 2 months to complete your travel.
- Choice of 1st or standard class train travel.
- Special travel bonuses (see Bonus).

OPTIONS:

- Same options as the BritRail Classic Pass.

Adult	1st Class	Standard
Any 4 days in 2 months	$ 485	$323
Any 8 days in 2 months	$ 704	$469
Any 15 days in 2 months	$1067	$712

Senior*	1st Class
Any 4 days in 2 months	$412
Any 8 days in 2 months	$598
Any 15 days in 2 months	$907

Youth**	Standard
Any 4 days in 2 months	$259
Any 8 days in 2 months	$328
Any 15 days in 2 months	$498

Many local trains in England, Scotland and Wales have Standard accommodations only. This has been allowed for in the 1st Class pass price.
*Senior: Available for passengers 60 and over.
**Youth: Available only for passengers under 26 on their first date of travel.
One child (5–15) can travel free with each adult or senior pass by requesting the BritRail Family Pass. Children from 5–15: half adult fare. Children under 5: free. Prices in CAN dollars. Subject to change.

Talk to us about favorable transatlantic air fares from the U.S. And if you're looking for a hotel or car, see pages 34–42.

BritRail Weekender

Even if you are only going to Britain for the weekend, you can explore more than London by getting this 4 day pass. Stay must include a Saturday night.

	1st Class	Standard
4 consecutive days	$190	$152

Valid for travel 1/1/00 – 3/31/00 and 10/01/00 – 12/31/00.
Travel must be either for Friday through Monday or any 4 days which include a Saturday night. Prices in CAN dollars. Subject to change.

Victoria Station

Free BritRail Family Pass

Buy one adult or senior pass, and one accompanying child (ages 5–15) gets a pass of the same type and duration free. Additional children purchase the appropriate pass at half the price of an adult. Children under 5 travel free. Please request the BritRail Family Pass when booking. Applicable with a BritRail Classic Pass, BritRail Flexipass, BritRail Senior Pass, BritRail Pass 'n Drive or BritRail Pass + Ireland.

BritRail Pass 'n Drive

Combining rail and your own rental car throughout these three countries lets you explore areas that you may otherwise not be able to enjoy. See page 35 for details.

A leisurely stroll through town offers hidden treasures

Sample Itinerary

Using the 8 day BritRail Classic Pass, we hit all the spots in Scotland, England and Wales, and saved a bundle. To do the same with individual tickets in first class, it would cost $1,261 instead of just $553!

Leave London and be in the heart of the Lake District in just over 3 hours

BritRail SouthEast Pass

From $106 —

Ideal for day trips out of London, this gives you access to an extensive rail network throughout the south-east of England. Consider the rolling South Downs, Oxford, Salisbury, Cambridge, Exeter and Brighton.

Stonehenge is just a short distance from Salisbury

BritRail SouthEast Pass

A terrific pass centering on a large area around London (see map).

INCLUDES:
- Choice of three pass durations:
  - any 3 days train travel in a 8 day period or,
  - any 4 days train travel in a 8 day period or,
  - any 7 days train travel in a 15 day period.
- Choice of 1st or standard (2nd) class train travel.

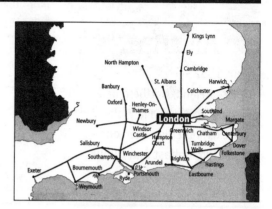

	1st Class	Standard
Any 3 days in 8	$146	$106
Any 4 days in 8	$199	$146
Any 7 days in 15	$265	$199

Many trains in the rail pass area have standard class accommodations only. This has been allowed for in the 1st class pass price. Railpass not valid to Bath or on other services via Reading for example, to Exeter. Not valid on Great Western trains. Please refer to the map of SouthEast Pass validity. Children from 5–15 years old $42 1st class, $29 Standard class. Children under 5: free. Prices in CAN dollars. Subject to change.

Great British Heritage Pass

From $78 —

This is truly your passport to the heritage and treasures of Britain. Wherever you go, you are within striking distance of fairy-tale castles, breathtaking stately homes and gardens, and medieval manor houses. The pass allows you entry to over 500 public and privately-owned historic properties.

Great British Heritage Pass

INCLUDES:
- Choice of three pass durations:
  - 7 consecutive days or,
  - 15 consecutive days or,
  - 1 month.
- Entry to over 500 of Britain's historic properties.
- The Great British Heritage Pass Gazetteer, a free full color planning guide listing the properties.

7 days	$ 78
15 days	$110
1 month	$145

Non-refundable. No discount for children. Not valid for entrance to Buckingham Palace. 50% off entrance to Tower of London. Not all properties open during off season; refer to Great British Heritage Pass Gazeteer. Prices in CAN dollars. Subject to change.

Edinburgh Castle, Scotland

Here are just some of the historic properties you can visit with this pass:

Greater London: Hampton Court Palace, HM Tower of London*, Kensington Palace State Apartments and Royal Ceremonial Dress Collection.

Scotland: Edinburgh Castle, Glamis Castle, Palace of Holyroodhouse, St. Andrews Cathedral, Stirling Castle, Urquhart Castle.

England's North Country: Castle Howard, Fountains Abbey.

Central England: Anne Hathaway's Cottage, Shakespeare's Birthplace, Shugborough Hall, Warwick Castle.

South of England: Blenheim Palace, Sissinghurst Garden, Roman Baths and Pump Room, Stonehenge, Windsor Castle.

*50% discount.

BritRail Pass + Ireland

From $562 —

Explore Ireland, Northern Ireland, England, Scotland and Wales and visit exciting cities like London, Edinburgh, Belfast and Dublin. Or, choose less traveled routes, including Irish attractions like Cork and The Mountains of Mourne. Included is a round trip sea crossing between Britain and Ireland, and the flexibility to enter through one port and exit by another.

BritRail Pass + Ireland

INCLUDES:
- Choice of two pass durations:
  - any 5 days unlimited train travel or,
  - any 10 days unlimited train travel.
- 1 month to complete your travel.
- Round trip Stena Line service between Britain and Ireland.*
- Choice of 1st or standard class rail travel.

*Sea Crossings to Ireland via ship, HSS or Stena Lynx Catamaran between Holyhead and Dún Laoghaire; Fishguard and Rosslare; Stranraer and Belfast.

	1st Class	Standard
Any 5 days in 1 month	$ 743	$562
Any 10 days in 1 month	$1058	$798

Includes round trip Stena Line service between Holyhead and Dun Laoghaire or Dublin, Fishguard and Rosslare or Stranraer and Belfast via ship, HSS or Stena Lynx Catamaran. One child (5–15) can travel free with each adult pass by requesting the BritRail Family Pass. Additional children from 5–15: half adult fare. Children under 5: free. Prices in CAN dollars. Subject to change. Reservations for sea crossing are not required with this pass.

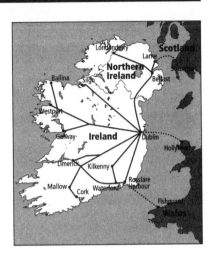

You can get a free BritRail Family Pass with your BritRail + Ireland pass. See page 17 for details.

Freedom of Scotland Travelpass

From $200 —

When you want to concentrate your travel in Scotland, we give you unlimited travel on the national rail network plus special ferries to the islands.

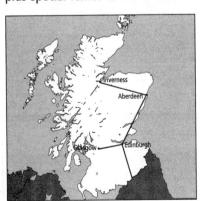

Freedom of Scotland Travelpass

Unlimited train travel throughout Scotland.

INCLUDES:
- Choice of three pass durations:
  - any 4 days train travel in a 8 day period or,
  - any 8 days train travel in a 15 day period or,
  - any 12 days train travel in a 20 day period.
- Standard class train travel.
- Transportation on all Caledonian and MacBrayne ferries to the islands.
- Discount on some P&O ferry routes.

The bagpiper ends the day in Scotland with a traditional tune

- Complimentary pack of timetables upon validation of your pass in Britain.
- Travel on the Glasgow Underground.

	Standard
Any 4 days in 8	$200
Any 8 days in 15	$276
Any 12 days in 20	$301

Children under 5: free. Children 5–15: half adult fare. Prices in CAN dollars. Subject to change.

EXERCISES—European Rail

Using the material provided on European rail travel, answer the following questions:

1. List the approximate travelling times for rail travel between the following European cities:

    a. Vienna to Budapest _____

    b. Rome to Naples _____

    c. Madrid to Seville _____

    d. Paris to Copenhagen _____

2. For the following three passengers, calculate whether it is cheaper to buy separate tickets for their journeys or to buy a rail pass.

    a. A 23-years-old is interested in travelling (second class) for 3 weeks.

        Itinerary: Paris–Frankfurt–Munich–Paris

        Separate ticket = $ _____

        Rail pass   = $ _____

        The passenger should purchase _____

    b. A passenger is interested in travelling (second class) for 2 weeks.

        Itinerary: Copenhagen–Oslo–Stockholm–Helsinki

        Separate ticket = $ _____

        Rail pass   = $ _____

        The passenger should purchase _____

    c. A passenger is travelling (second class) for 14 days.

        Itinerary: Amsterdam–Berlin–Frankfurt–Paris–Rome

        Separate ticket = $ _____

        Rail pass   = $ _____

        The passenger should purchase _____

3. In your own words, give a brief outline of the difference between a BritRail classic pass and a BritRail flexipass.

    _____

    _____

    _____

    _____

    _____

SCENIC TRAINS OF THE WORLD

Rail travel can be much more than a method of travelling from point A to point B. Across the world there are many famed rail journeys, known for their thrills and spectacular scenery. They have been long travelled by tourists who are looking for a different type of vacation. Some are short day trips while others are longer and require sleeping accommodation.

The following are some examples:

Canada

- White Pass & Yukon Route (between Fraser or Whitehorse and Skagway, Alaska)
- The Canadian (Transcontinental service)
- Cariboo Prospector (Vancouver, B.C., to Prince George, B.C.)
- Rocky Mountaineer (Vancouver–Jasper–Banff–Calgary)
- Royal Hudson (Vancouver, B.C., to Squamish, B.C.)
- Via Rail's Skeena (Jasper, Alberta, to Prince Rupert, B.C.)
- Via Rail's Malahat (Victoria, B.C., to Courtenay, B.C.)
- Whistler Explorer (Whistler, B.C., to Kelly Lake, B.C.)
- B.C. Rail's Pacific Starlight Dinner Train (North Vancouver, B.C., to Porteau Cove, B.C.)
- Algoma Central Railway (Sault Ste. Marie, Ontario, to Agawa Canyon, Ontario)
- Ontario Northland Railway's Polar Bear Express (Cochrane, Ontario, to Moosonee, Ontario)
- Port Stanley Terminal Rail (Port Stanley, Ontario, to St. Thomas, Ontario)
- York-Durham Heritage Railway (Stouffville, Ontario, to Uxbridge, Ontario)
- South Simcoe Railway (Tottenham, Ontario, to Beeton, Ontario)
- Via Rail's Chaleur (Montreal, Quebec, to Gaspe, Quebec)
- Hull-Wakefield Steam Train (Gatineau Hills, Quebec)
- Via Rail's Hudson Bay (Winnipeg, Manitoba, to Churchill, Manitoba)
- Salem & Hillsborough Railroad (New Brunswick)

U.S.A.

- Sierre Madre Express (Tuscon, Arizona, to Mexico's Copper Canyon)
- American Orient Express (various U.S. and Canadian locations)
- Grand Canyon Railway (Arizona)
- Hocking Valley Scenic Railway (Ohio)
- Central Scenic Railway (Ohio)
- Cuyahoga Valley Scenic Railway (Ohio)
- Chattanooga Choo Choo (Tennessee; now a part of a Holiday Inn hotel)
- Spirit of Washington (Washington State)
- Coast Starlight (Los Angeles, California, to Seattle, Washington)
- Cumbres & Toltec Scenic Railroad (New Mexico and Colorado)
- Napa Valley Wine Train (California)
- Durango & Silverton Narrow Gauge Railroad (Colorado)

Mexico

- Copper Canyon Trip (Chihuahua to Los Mochis)

South America

- Train from Cuzco to Machu Picchu (Peru)
- Train from Puno to Cuzco (Peru)

Europe

- Venice Simplon Orient Express
- Trans Siberian (Russia)
- TGV (between Paris, France, and Geneva, Switzerland)
- Nice–Digne Line (France)
- Flam Line (Norway)
- Oslo–Bergen Route (Norway)
- The Raumaline (Norway)
- Flying Scotsman, formerly known as the Royal Scotsman (London to Edinburgh)
- Bernina Express (Switzerland)
- Jungfraubahn (Switzerland)
- Centovalli Railway (Switzerland)
- William Tell Express (Switzerland)
- Golden Pass (Switzerland)
- Eurostar (France, U.K.)
- Glacier Express (Switzerland)

Africa

- Blue Train (Pretoria–Johannesburg–Cape Town, South Africa)
- Rovos Rail Steam Train (South Africa, Zimbabwe, Zambia, and Tanzania)
- Nile Valley Express (Egypt)

Asia

- Bullet Trains (Tokyo to Takayama, Japan)
- Eastern Orient Express
- Darjeeling Himalayan Railway (India)
- Palace on Wheels (India)
- Toy Train (India)

Australia

- Indian Pacific (between Sydney and Perth)
- Trans Australia (between Adelaide and Perth)
- Queenslander and Sunlander (between Brisbane and Cairns)
- Great Southern Express (between Sydney and Cairns; Australia's version of the Orient Express)
- The Ghan (Sydney–Melbourne–Adelaide–Alice Springs)

7

Motorcoach and Escorted Tours

Travellers frequently use motorcoaches for part or all of their journey. Modern motorcoaches bear no resemblance to school buses or local transit buses. They are in every sense of the word a coach and not a bus. They normally seat forty-two to forty-seven passengers.

Features may include a washroom, footrests, video monitors, reclining seats, air conditioning, overhead bins for hand luggage, and even a bar.

There are also executive coaches available for up to twenty-five people, with lounge chair seating and other features.

TYPES OF MOTORCOACH TRAVEL

Airport Transfers

This refers to travel back and forth between the airport and the hotel. Most ITC packages (inclusive tour charters) include airport transfers (some include a car instead). FIT packages (foreign independent tours) offer transfers as an option at an extra charge.

Day Trips

Included in this group are local sightseeing tours and affordable getaways from major cities for all age groups. For example, one-day tours are used by visitors to see places such as Niagara Falls (near Toronto), Oxford (near London, England), Versailles (near Paris, France), Taxco (near Mexico City, Mexico), and Whistler (near Vancouver).

The following major organizations in North America offer day trips:

- Gray Line
- American Sightseeing

In addition, day trips are offered by various tour operators and may be considered for FIT tours. Frames of London, England, is a well known local organizer of day trips, for example. Citirama is a similar operation based in Paris, France.

Independent Point-to-Point Travel

Independent travel by bus is not often sold by travel agents because commissions are rarely offered and the value of the sale is low. However, bus passes are popular and may be purchased through various tour operators to complement an FIT tour.

Following are some examples of bus passes sold by travel agents:

- Europabus in continental Europe
- National Express in Britain
- London Visitor travel pass
- Bus passes in Costa Rica
- Greyhound in U.S.A.

Some of these passes allow travel on selected routes, while others permit travel over an entire network.

Charters

With charters, a bus is reserved for any group of passengers with a common interest (for example, school groups and seniors groups).

Some, but not all, travel agents will charter buses for groups and add a markup to the cost of renting the bus to make a profit.

Escorted Tours

As the title suggests, this is a motorcoach tour with a guide, although not all escorted tours include buses.

The following items may be included in an escorted bus tour. List below any other possible inclusions you can think of.

- Motorcoach transportation
- A guide/escort to give sightseeing details
- Photo opportunities and rest stops
- Museum or gallery entrance charges
- Meal or snack

- _____

- _____

- _____

The following items are usually not included in the price. Add any other items below.

- Tips
- Beverages, meals, and snacks above those included in the price
- Entry fees, above those included in the price

- _____

- _____
- _____

Listed below are several advantages of taking an escorted bus tour vs. travelling independently. Add any other reasons you can think of.

- Transportation and guide are provided for a fixed price
- May eliminate standing in line at popular attractions
- Convenient
- Good way to meet other people with similar interests
- Can be less expensive than reserving individual components of the tour separately
- Eases some concerns of a traveller visiting a country (especially if it is a first-time visit)

- _____
- _____
- _____

Examine several examples of motorcoach brochures from North America and Europe. Then describe any differences you see between North American and European coach tours.

_____
_____
_____
_____
_____
_____

Note that some escorted tours cater to particular age groups (Contiki is an example of an escorted tour geared to young singles; others cater to adults or retired singles). It is important to match the client with an appropriate tour, where fellow travellers will be similar in age and where activities will be appropriate to that group.

MAJOR COACH OPERATORS

Canada

Point-to-point travel
- Voyageur Colonial Ltd.
- Gray Coach Lines Ltd.
- Canada Coach Lines
- Eastern Canadian Greyhound Line Ltd.
- Greyhound Canada
- PCL (Pacific Coach Line)
- Charter Bus Lines
- City Link Bus Lines
- Quick Shuttle

| Day tours | • Gray Line Company |
| | • Perimeter Transportation Ltd. (day trips to Whistler) |

| Airport transfers | • Pacific Western (Toronto/Vancouver) |

Escorted Tours	• Gray Coach Travel
	• Voyageur Tours
	• Trentway Wagar Tours
	• Travelways Tours
	• Denure Tours
	• Contiki Tours (passengers up to age 35)
	• Horizon Holidays
	• Pathway Tours
	• Brewster Tours
	• Cosmos Tours
	• Trafalgar Tours
	• Globus Gateway Tours
	• Maverick Coach Lines
	• Cardinal Tours
	• International Stage Lines
	• Gray Line Company

U.S.A.

| Point-to-point travel | • Greyhound |
| | • National Travelways |

| Day tours | • Gray Line Company |
| | • American Sightseeing |

| Airport transfers | • New York Airport Service (New York City) |

Escorted tours	• Trafalgar Tours
	• Globus Gateway Tours
	• Contiki Tours (passengers up to age 35)
	• Horizon Holidays
	• Pathway Tours
	• Cosmos Tours
	• Tauck Tours
	• Mayflower Tours
	• Maupintours
	• Domenico Tours
	• American Express Vacations

Europe

| Point-to-point travel | • Europabus |

Day tours	• Frames Tours (U.K.)
	• Ricketts Tours (U.K.)
	• Britrail "Britainshrinkers" (U.K.) rail/bus
	• Citirama (France)
	• Paris Vision (France)
	• C.I.T. (Italy)

Escorted tours	• Trafalgar Tours
	• Globus Gateway Tours
	• Contiki Tours (passengers up to age 35)
	• Kompas Tours
	• Horizon Holidays
	• Cosmos Tours
	• Kuoni Tours
	• Olson-Travelworld Tours
	• Unitours, Inc.
	• Maupintours
	• Jetset Tours
	• Brendan Tours
	• American Express Vacations

Asia

Escorted tours	• American Express Vacations
	• Globus Gateway Tours
	• J & O (Japan and Orient) Pacific Tours
	• Jetset Tours
	• Olson-Travelworld
	• Pacific Bestours, Inc.
	• Unitours, Inc.

BASIC STEPS IN SELLING A MOTORCOACH OR ESCORTED TOUR

1. Once the client decides to investigate taking a tour, provide three or four brochures after obtaining basic information (number of people; their ages; dates of travel; preferred destinations; specific interests; budget considerations).

2. Encourage early booking; if there is sufficient time before departure, suggest checking for availability and making a tentative booking, especially if travel will be at peak periods such as Christmas or spring break. If a tentative booking is made, make a note to follow up for final confirmation before the booking deadline.

3. Finalize the reservations by the tour operator's deadline. Obtain payment from the client and forward it to the operator (often a deposit is necessary). A UCCCF (universal credit card charge form), or an MCO (miscellaneous charges order) is issued for the deposit.

4. When reservations have been confirmed, cover all of the details of the trip with the client (scheduling information, payment deadlines, cancellation penalties, insurance options, etc.) and highlight key information from the brochures.

5. Open a client file (to contain copies of forms, receipts, letters, etc.), and note any important dates on your office calendar (and on the computer, if the reservation was made through a computer reservation system).

6. Arrange for final payment by any deadline imposed by the tour operator.

7. Obtain tickets/vouchers from the tour operator, and deliver them to the client with an itinerary before departure (along with ticket jackets, travel bags, baggage tags, etc.). A tour order form may have to be issued.

8. Follow up with client after his or her return, to inquire about the trip (this is useful for dealing with the same client's needs or concerns in the future, and this will also assist you in anticipating potential problems with a particular tour operator).

Motorcoach Terms

MOTORCOACH	A specially designed bus used for touring purposes.
MINIBUS	A small bus, used primarily for airport transfers to and from the hotel or rental car, or for shuttles from hotel to beach, shopping, etc.
DOUBLE DECKER	A bus with two levels, used for public transit in the U.K. and now used for sightseeing by many companies around the world.
CHARTER	A bus reserved for use by a group.
SIGHTSEEING	Refers to the use of motorcoach travel to gain an overview of a city or area, its buildings, monuments, and attractions.

REFERENCE MATERIAL

Russell's Official National Motor Coach Guide—published monthly

Russell's Official Canada Bus Guide—published monthly.

The Gray Line Official Worldwide Services Directory

American Sightseeing International Worldwide Tours Planning Tariff

Specialty Travel Index

Official Tour Directory

Worldwide Brochures Directory

Official Recreation Guide

Europabus timetable and tour information

Individual bus line/tour operator timetables and brochures

Escorted tour operator brochures

Trade magazines and guide books

8

Sea Transportation

Ships have long been used as a means of transatlantic travel, and the first quarter of the twentieth century was the zenith of steamship travel as a means of point-to-point transportation. At the time, ship travel was directed to the wealthy traveller and to the immigrant. But seagoing passenger travel declined with the rise of transatlantic jet flights in the 1950s and 1960s. However, a resurgence of ocean travel has come about with the rise of the modern era cruise industry primarily geared to the vacation traveller. It is now possible to find a cruise ship for most passenger interests and within most price ranges.

Use the space below to write your thoughts about the future of cruise vacations.

_____

_____

_____

_____

THE IMPORTANCE OF CRUISES TO TRAVEL AGENTS

It is important to recognize that, although the cruise industry is quite young, it has been growing by leaps and bounds, and there is a huge market potential. Past clients have rated cruises very highly in performance and satisfaction when compared with other travel industry alternatives.

Commissions from cruises can be substantial, and there are sometimes increased commissions available to agencies belonging to a consortium, chain, franchise group, or some other allied grouping, or based on high sales volume with a particular cruise line.

Although there are many reasons for taking a cruise, cruises are not for everyone. Recognize the advantages and disadvantages.

ADVANTAGES OF A CRUISE VACATION

1. Almost all costs are included.

2. The client only needs to unpack once while on vacation.

3. Entertainment, shows, and a variety of other activities are included in the price.

4. Cruises provide a variety of ports (and countries) to experience.

5. They provide gourmet food in unlimited quantities.

6. A cruise allows the client to really relax, without hassles of independent travel arrangements.

7. Cruising provides an opportunity to enjoy the fresh air and the at-sea experience.

8. It offers safety.

9. There is an element of glamour and prestige.

10. Gambling is readily available.

DISADVANTAGES OF A CRUISE

1. Other types of vacations could be less expensive (although there is a wide range of pricing available).

2. Cabin space can be limited and is certainly smaller than most luxury hotel spaces.

3. Port stays can be quite short, particularly if the client wants anything more than a basic introduction to that destination.

4. There is a risk of seasickness (this has become less of a problem with medical advances, preventative medicines, and better-designed ships).

5. It is difficult to control one's diet, especially for the client with weight problems.

6. Alternatives are more limited than for land-based holidays, especially in the event of bad weather.

7. Some people may feel that there are too many people in a relatively confined space—a cruise may not be the answer for someone who is looking for seclusion.

8. Advance reservations, dinner reservations, and other reservations may be required.

Typical Client Objections to a Cruise

Below are some client objections to a suggestion of a cruise vacation. Add any of your own ideas to this list.

1. Fear of seasickness;

2. Fear of high cost;

3. Not enough to do on a ship;

4. Preference for more active vacation;

5. Desire to get away from it all;

6. _____

7. _____

LENGTH OF VOYAGE

Following are descriptions of short, medium, and long cruises.

Short cruise. Includes 1-day cruises, and otherwise is usually from 3 days to 14 days in length; typically directed at a person with limited time and funds or at first-time cruise passengers.

Intermediate cruise. 15 days to 24 days; typically directed at persons who have previously taken at least one cruise; may be oriented to all different budgets.

Long cruise. 25 days and up; typically directed at experienced cruise passengers, usually quite well-to-do and with substantial time available (such as those who are retired); includes round-the-world cruises.

Types of Cruises

CONVENTIONAL CRUISES	a.	Mass market: Cruises with few frills; oriented to low-budget passengers.
	b.	Premium or upscale: Oriented to experienced passengers with more money to spend; offers first-class service and more exotic itineraries.
	c.	Deluxe or luxury: Elegant cruise experience, ultra modern ships and amenities, unique itineraries; caters to the wealthy.
AIR-CRUISE		The cruise line offers an air allowance or a special add-on airfare as part of a package.
SPECIALTY CRUISE		Special-interest cruise (for example, whale watching or exploration).
BOAT/YACHT CHARTER		Yachts and other boats can be chartered for groups, and this is arranged through brokers.
POINT-TO-POINT MARKET (TRANSATLANTIC)		Travel from one point to another as a means of transportation; includes repositioning transatlantic cruises (certain ships change locations according to the seasons; for example, a move to the Caribbean in winter and to the Mediterranean or Alaska in summer).
RIVER CRUISES		In Canada, on the St. Lawrence and Saguenay Rivers; in the U.S.A., on the Mississippi and Ohio rivers; in Europe, on the Rhine and Moselle

	rivers in Germany, Danube River cruises in Austria, and barge cruises in France, England, Belgium, and Holland; the Nile in Egypt; the Amazon in South America; Yangtze River cruises in China; and Volga River cruises in Russia.
FERRIES	There are many ferry services available in North America and elsewhere; ferries are available for port-to-port service within a country or for travel between countries. A list of some ferries is found in Appendix C.
FREIGHTERS	Ships carrying cargo from port to port may also carry passengers (some may be luxury combination cruise/freighter ships, but most are not). A list of some freighter companies is found in Appendix C.

SOME CRUISE VACATIONS

Listed below are some popular areas for cruise vacations. List any others you can think of in the space below.

- Caribbean
- Alaska
- West Coast of Mexico (Pacific)
- Mediterranean
- Orient
- _____
- _____
- _____
- _____
- _____

Cruise Lines

There are an incredible number of companies involved in operating cruises. A list of the better-known cruise lines is located in Appendix C of this book.

Cruise Tour Operators

Some tour operators arrange cruise packages. Examples of Canadian tour operators who package cruises are Regent Holidays, Sunquest, and Conquest Tours.

Ferry Services, Freighters, and Major Cruise Ports

Turn to Appendix C of this book for a list of some of the more popular ferry services utilized by travellers. Also included are freighters and major cruise ports.

WHAT DOES THE PRICE OF A CRUISE VACATION INCLUDE?

- Private cabin accommodation (varying prices depending on size and location)
- Gourmet food served at various locations (poolside barbeque, restaurants, formal dining room, buffets, etc.)
- Activities/entertainment (sports, movies, nightclub, disco, library, game rooms, etc.)
- Transportation
- Religious services
- Deck chairs/pool
- Medical facilities
- Room service
- Business centre
- Health and fitness centre
- Captain's party/dinner

Items Not Included (Optional Expenses)

- Alcoholic beverages
- Tips and taxes (bedroom steward and dining room waiters typically get $1.50 to $2.00 tip per person, per day, paid at the end of the cruise; bar waiters and the maitre d' usually get a 15% tip paid at the time of service)
- Gambling
- Beauty salon/barbershop
- Shore excursions
- Baggage and health insurance
- Baby-sitting
- Laundry service
- Massage service
- Phone/fax ship-to-shore communication
- Emergency medical service
- Gifts and sundry items

DECIDING WHICH CRUISE TO RECOMMEND

There are a number of factors to consider in determining quality of a ship:

Gross registered tonnage (GRT). The amount of enclosed cubic space on board ship including all public areas.

Space ratio. Ratio of the size of the ship to the number of passengers (divide GRT by passenger capacity).

Passenger/crew ratio. Ratio of the number of crew to the number of passengers.

Itineraries. Where the ship visits and the length of the cruise.

Accomodation. Types of cabins and what they contain.

Activities. The types of entertainment, sports, casinos, shows, etc. offered.

Climate. Caribbean, Mexico, and South American cruises are best taken during November to April; Alaska, Mediterranean, and Aegean Sea cruises are best taken during May to September; and Orient cruises are best taken during September to November or during March to May.

INFORMATION REQUIRED TO BOOK A CRUISE

Below is a list of information needed to book a cruise vacation. Add any other items below.

1. Names, addresses, ages, and phone numbers of passengers;

2. Length of time available;

3. Preferred departure dates;

4. Purpose (to relax, sightsee, special interest);

5. Preferred itinerary;

6. Price/level of product preferred;

7. Type of accommodation needed;

8. _____

9. _____

10. _____

The price of cabin accommodation aboard a ship depends on the following:

Location. An inside cabin is normally cheaper than an outside cabin, and price also depends on the deck on which it is located.

Number of persons. Prices are usually "per person," and a cabin that accommodates more people is cheaper on a per-person basis.

When comparing the cost of a cruise vacation vs. a land-based vacation, remember that a cruise already incorporates most of the expenses in the cost. To get a truer idea you need to do a side-by-side cost comparison for a client and you may want to use a chart like the one below.

Land-Based Vacations vs. Cruise Vacations

Cost Components	Land	Cruise
Base fare		
Airfare		
Transfers		
Accommodation		
Meals and snacks		
Activities		
Entertainment		
Night clubs		
Drinks		
Gratuities		
Taxes and service charges		
Total		

Other Pricing Considerations

Below are some factors to consider when calculating the cost of a cruise:

Cabin rate	• Category (outside/inside cabins) • Location on ship (what deck is it on and where on the deck?) • Is there a balcony? • Is the cabin a suite of rooms? • Bed types and number of beds.
Air/sea supplement or cruise only	• Where does the client live? From which city is the cruise departing? • Cost of air charter
Third/fourth guest	• Cost of extra people sharing a cabin (may be cheaper per person) • Type of beds (can they be moved?)
Children	• Do child rates apply?
Single guest	• Guaranteed share (will client agree to share to save a supplementary charge?) • Single cabin—how much is the single supplement?
Early booking discount	• How soon must the client book to qualify?
Upgrades	• Cabin categories may be upgraded; at what cost?

Port charges/airport taxes	• These are additional per person charges
Pre- or post-tour	• Extra days of hotel space may be needed before or after cruises
Cruise protection	• Insurance is an extra cost
Currency	• U.S. or Canadian funds? (may need to add exchange costs, if cruise is to be paid in another currency)
Departure Date	• Is the cruise in peak season for the area covered?

Pricing—Cruise Only

When pricing "cruise-only" vacations (no air transportation involved), the cost is generally calculated by the following method:

Basic cabin rate* (x 2)
Plus single supplement (if applicable)
Plus additional 3rd person rate (if applicable)
Plus additional 4th person rate (if applicable)
Minus deduction for air transportation[†]

Equals total cabin rate

Plus port charges[‡] (per person)
Plus any additional taxes/charges/supplements

Equals total cruise cost

* Basic cabin rates will vary based on deck selected and location on the deck. Basic rates are quoted per person based on double occupancy.
[†]Where basic rates include air transportation, there is usually a specified "cruise only" deduction applicable to a single passenger or to the first two passengers. There will either be a smaller deduction available or a special "cruise only" rate for third or fourth passengers in the same cabin.
[‡] Travel agency commissions are calculated as a percentage of the total cabin rate, excluding any port charges and taxes.

Also, note that specials, promotions, group rates, senior discounts, child rates, early booking discounts, or volume discounts may affect brochure prices.

Pricing—Air/Sea

When pricing an "air/sea" combination (cruise plus air transportation), round trip airfare is generally included in the basic cabin rate, per person. This will include air transportation between the passenger's point of origin and the point of departure of the ship. Hotel accommodation may also be included at the departure port city for the night before the cruise begins.

BASIC STEPS TO SELLING CRUISES

1. **Client Contact.** The process begins when the client first contacts you to seek information, either by visiting your agency or by phone.

2. **Dates/length of cruise.** The client usually begins by asking about possible dates of departure and length of cruises (if he or she has previously been on a cruise); otherwise, seek out this information.

3. **Brochures.** Client should be offered one or two choices of cruise brochures, after you have determined possible types of ship preferred, dates, budget considerations, interests, etc.

4. **Availability.** With one or two possibilities in mind, contact cruise lines to determine availability.

5. **Reservations.** The client may want to take several brochures away to consider choices (especially if departure is more than several months away), or to immediately focus on a particular brochure (based on client's information and ship availability). The client may even consider making a tentative booking (especially if departure is within six months or during a peak period or holiday).

6. **Reservation/inquiry form.** Complete a form with name(s) of client, citizenship, address, phone numbers (home/business), number of adults and children travelling, previous cruise experience, detailed information about the cruise options under consideration (including departure dates, name of cruise line, phone number, ship name, type of cabin, meal sitting, confirmation number, per-person prices, deposit information, and payment due dates), and a checklist of final ticketing procedures, etc.

7. **Business cards.** If clients are not ready to book, provide a business card and highlight pertinent information on their brochure copies for their consideration.

8. **Follow-ups.** Call back prospective clients if they haven't booked tentatively. For tentative bookings, follow up on deposit or payment requirements.

9. **Confirm reservations.** Set an appointment with clients to cover details of itinerary and payment deadlines and to offer helpful hints and general information, answer any questions, provide travel insurance information, receive payment of deposits, issue UCCCFs for credit card payments, and issue receipts.

10. **Deadlines.** The agent should write all deadlines (payment, ticketing, etc.) in a calendar and add it to the computer system used for reserved bookings.

11. **Client file.** Office copies of all forms, brochures, receipts, etc. should be placed in a client file. Client files should be tabbed by client name and departure date, and placed in a central file storage area (easily accessed) and filed either in alphabetical order (last name of client) or by departure date.

12. **Final payment.** Invoice the client and obtain final payment by the deadline; issue a receipt and UCCCFs for credit card payments.

13. **Ticketing.** Provide client with tickets, vouchers, travel documentation, travel checklist, cruise information sheet, and insurance (or obtain signed insurance waiver).

14. **Bon voyage gift.** Some agencies arrange a gift (flowers, candy, champagne, or a bottle of wine, etc.) to be delivered to the client's cabin for departure.

15. **Post-cruise.** A follow-up letter or phone call should be made by the agent a week or two after the client returns to get feedback.

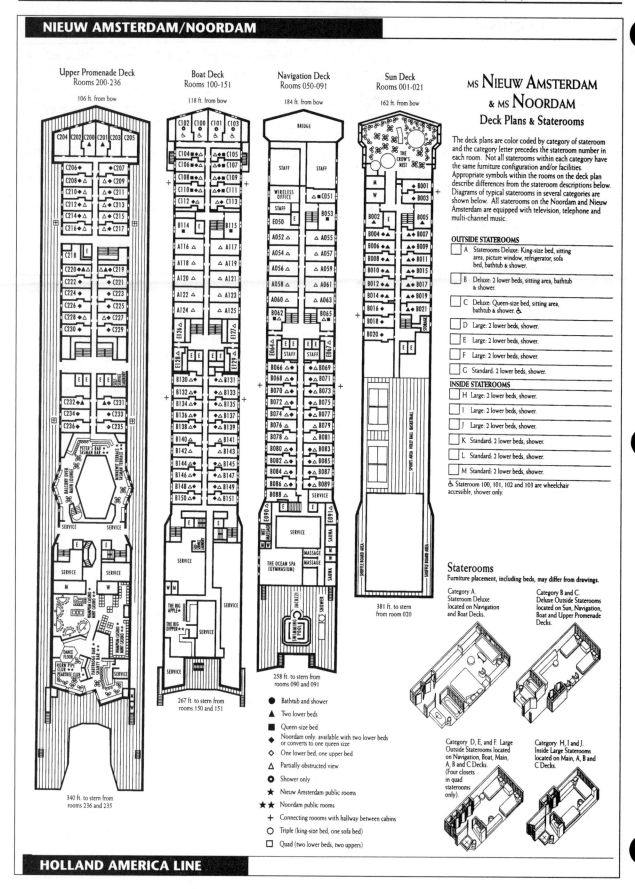

NIEUW AMSTERDAM/NOORDAM

Upper Promenade Deck
Rooms 200-236

Boat Deck
Rooms 100-151

Navigation Deck
Rooms 050-091

Sun Deck
Rooms 001-021

MS NIEUW AMSTERDAM & MS NOORDAM
Deck Plans & Staterooms

The deck plans are color coded by category of stateroom and the category letter precedes the stateroom number in each room. Not all staterooms within each category have the same furniture configuration and/or facilities. Appropriate symbols within the rooms on the deck plan describe differences from the stateroom descriptions below. Diagrams of typical staterooms in several categories are shown below. All staterooms on the Noordam and Nieuw Amsterdam are equipped with television, telephone and multi-channel music.

OUTSIDE STATEROOMS

A — Staterooms Deluxe: King-size bed, sitting area, picture window, refrigerator, sofa bed, bathtub & shower.

B — Deluxe: 2 lower beds, sitting area, bathtub & shower.

C — Deluxe: Queen-size bed, sitting area, bathtub & shower. ♿

D — Large: 2 lower beds, shower.

E — Large: 2 lower beds, shower.

F — Large: 2 lower beds, shower.

G — Standard: 2 lower beds, shower.

INSIDE STATEROOMS

H — Large: 2 lower beds, shower.

I — Large: 2 lower beds, shower.

J — Large: 2 lower beds, shower.

K — Standard: 2 lower beds, shower.

L — Standard: 2 lower beds, shower.

M — Standard: 2 lower beds, shower.

♿ Stateroom 100, 101, 102 and 103 are wheelchair accessible, shower only.

Staterooms
Furniture placement, including beds, may differ from drawings.

Category A.
Stateroom Deluxe located on Navigation and Boat Decks.

Category B and C.
Deluxe Outside Staterooms located on Sun, Navigation, Boat and Upper Promenade Decks.

Category D, E, and F. Large Outside Staterooms located on Navigation, Boat, Main, A, B and C Decks. (Four closets in quad staterooms only).

Category H, I and J. Inside Large Staterooms located on Main, A, B and C Decks.

Legend:
- ● Bathtub and shower
- ▲ Two lower beds
- ■ Queen-size bed
- ◆ Noordam only: available with two lower beds or converts to one queen size
- ◇ One lower bed, one upper bed
- △ Partially obstructed view
- ○ Shower only
- ★ Nieuw Amsterdam public rooms
- ★★ Noordam public rooms
- + Connecting rooms with hallway between cabins
- ○ Triple (king-size bed, one sofa bed)
- □ Quad (two lower beds, two uppers)

HOLLAND AMERICA LINE

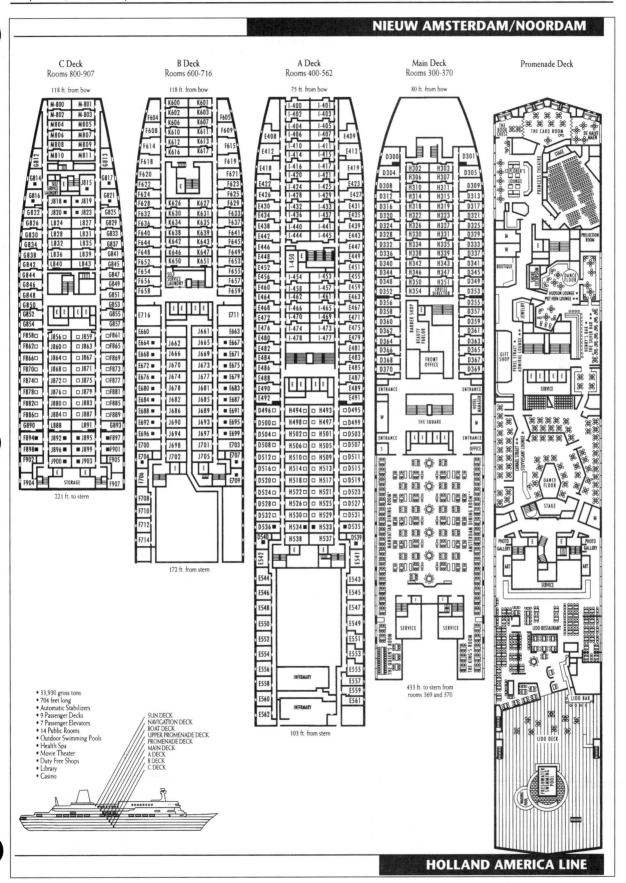

C Deck
Rooms 800-907

118 ft. from bow

221 ft. to stern

B Deck
Rooms 600-716

118 ft. from bow

172 ft. from stern

A Deck
Rooms 400-562

75 ft. from bow

103 ft. from stern

Main Deck
Rooms 300-370

80 ft. from bow

433 ft. to stern from rooms 369 and 370

Promenade Deck

- 33,930 gross tons
- 704 feet long
- Automatic Stabilizers
- 9 Passenger Decks
- 7 Passenger Elevators
- 14 Public Rooms
- Outdoor Swimming Pools
- Health Spa
- Movie Theater
- Duty Free Shops
- Library
- Casino

SUN DECK
NAVIGATION DECK
BOAT DECK
UPPER PROMENADE DECK
PROMENADE DECK
MAIN DECK
A DECK
B DECK
C DECK

HOLLAND AMERICA LINE

READING CRUISE BROCHURES

Each travel agent who sells cruises must fully familiarize himself or herself with the brochures and to keep current copies on hand. Reference copies should be kept on file, with specific information highlighted for future easy reference (booking procedures, payment deadlines, etc.).

Information on booking, deadlines, cancellations, etc. is often found in the section at the back of the brochures. This information is particularly important to highlight since it is this information that clients will expect you to advise them about and explain. Of course, you will also want to review with the client all other relevant information in the rest of the brochure that is applicable to the cruise selected (ship amenities, ports of call, etc.).

It is important to know how to read a deck plan to be able to identify the general location of the cabin in relation to the other areas of the ship (see examples on pp. 150–151). However, not all cabin information can be determined from a deck plan. You will need to check elsewhere in the brochure or directly with the cruise line to determine cabin size and shape, bed types, extent of noise (if the cabin is located near an elevator or disco, for example), whether there is a window that opens or a sealed porthole (if an outside cabin), and if the views are obstructed.

It is also important to recognize that brochures change frequently. Be certain that you are using the most current brochure.

CRUISE PROMOTIONS

The following are the more common methods used by travel agencies to promote cruises:

Advertising. Feature cruises in a newspaper ad by your agency, or approach cruise lines about adding your agency name to the list in their advertisement.

Direct mail. Send flyers or brochures, possibly including a discount coupon; add a personalized note if targeting previous clients.

Window display. Use nautically themed materials and posters in the agency's front window, if it is at street level.

Telemarketing. Telephone campaigns can be used to publicize an upcoming cruise or special discounted rates.

Cruise nights. Present slides, videos, possibly entertainment, and giveaways/door prizes; this is often done in conjunction with a cruise line's own representatives.

Specialized staff. Use special incentive bonuses for agents selling cruises; staff members get thorough training and experience with cruising.

Ticket stuffers. Insert cruise flyers or discount coupons with other travel documents or airline tickets.

Consortiums. Agencies can join a group that specializes in cruises, in order to get discounts, promotional assistance, etc.

Some agencies specialize in "cruise only" travel. They may or may not offer other travel products, and may not necessarily have approval to issue airline tickets (this would be done through an alliance with another travel agency who issues the air tickets and splits the commission).

Cruise Ship Personnel

CAPTAIN	The head of the ship, in charge of the vessel, its officers, and crew.
PURSER	Provides banking services, mail, ship-to-shore telephone service and sale of shore excursions, and handles general problems and questions.
CRUISE DIRECTOR	Arranges entertainment, activities, and lectures and offers advice and assistance.
CABIN STEWARD	Provides all cabin services, including linen supply, making beds, and cleaning.
DECK STEWARD	Provides deck services; specifically, service of food and beverages to passengers while on deck.
BARTENDERS/BAR STEWARD	Tends bar and prepares mixed drinks.
WINE STEWARD	Offers wine with meals.
BUS BOY/WAITER	Provides dining room service.
MAITRE D'	Head waiter; seats guests and oversees dining room service.
ENTERTAINMENT AND ACTIVITIES STAFF	Provides and supervises various entertainment and recreational activities.
ENGINEER	Operates the engine room.
SHIP'S DOCTOR	Provides medical services.

Nautical Terms

AFT	The back of the ship.
AMIDSHIP	The middle of the ship.
BERTH	A bed on a ship (usually attached to a wall); also, the space where a ship docks.
BOW	The front part of a ship.
BRIDGE	The location of the ship's steering apparatus, and the captain's work area.

BULKHEAD	The partition walls separating parts of a ship.
CABIN	A room on a ship used for sleeping (see also stateroom).
CLIA	Cruise Lines International Association—an association of cruise lines.
COLOURS	The flag under which the ship sails.
DEBARKATION	Getting off the ship (going ashore).
DECK	The level, or floor, of the ship (for example, lower deck or upper deck).
DECK PLAN	A diagram of a ship; shows location of the cabins and public areas.
DOCK	The place or structure used to secure a ship while it is at rest in a port of call (see also *quay*).
DRAFT	The depth of water drawn by a ship.
EMBARKATION	Getting on the ship (going aboard).
FATHOM	A nautical measure that equals six feet of depth in water.
FORWARD, PROW, OR FORE	A direction towards the bow or front of the ship.
FREE PORT	A port that has no customs duty or other customs regulations.
FUNNEL	Smokestack of a ship.
GALLEY	The ship's kitchen.
GANGWAY	The ramp for leaving and entering the ship.
GRATUITIES	Tips.
GRT (GROSS REGISTERED TON)	A measurement of the cubic content of the enclosed space of a ship.
HELM	The steering apparatus located on the bridge.
HOLD	The cargo storage area.
HULL	Outer walls of a ship.
INSIDE CABIN	A cabin located in the interior of the ship (no external water view window).

KNOT	A unit of speed (equals one nautical mile per hour or 1.15 land miles/1.85 kilometres per hour).
LEE OR LEEWARD	The direction away from the wind.
LOG	Official record of the daily progress of the ship.
MANIFEST	A list of the ship's passengers.
NAUTICAL MILE	A nautical measure of distance at sea, equal to approximately 6,080 feet/1,852 metres.
OPEN SITTING	A policy of "no table assignments" for meal seating.
OPTION	A tentative booking with a deposit deadline for confirmed status.
OPTION DATE	Date by which payment must be made or reservations will be cancelled.
OUTSIDE CABIN	A cabin located on the exterior of the ship (with water view window).
PADDLE WHEEL	A steam-operated water wheel used to propel a vessel.
PORT	The left side of the ship.
PORTHOLE	Window on a ship (usually sealed).
PORT OF CALL	The various ports visited by the ship.
PORT TAXES	A tax imposed by an individual port of call on each passenger.
QUAY	A wharf, pier, or dock, where the ship rests at port.
REGISTRY	The country in which a ship is registered and that issues the ship's certificate of registration.
REPOSITIONING	Movement of a cruise ship into a new cruise area.
RUDDER	A moveable device used to steer the ship.
RUN-OF-THE-SHIP RATE	A low fare where the cabin is assigned by the cruise line (not passenger's choice).
SITTING	The time at which a meal is served; there is usually more than one sitting (for example, first sitting or second sitting).

STABILIZER	A device used to reduce the rolling effect of ocean currents and waves.
STARBOARD	The right side of the ship.
STATEROOM	The passenger's cabin.
STERN	The aft, or back, of the ship.
TENDER	A small boat used to transport passengers from ship to shore, used where the ship itself cannot dock at port (when the water is too shallow).
TRADE WINDS	Ocean winds between 30° north latitude and 30° south latitude.
WAITLIST (OR STANDBY)	A requested booking where there is no current availability.
WAKE	Waves caused by movement of the ship.
WINDWARD	The direction facing the wind.

REFERENCE MATERIAL

OAG (Official Airline Guide) Worldwide Cruise and Shipline Guide

Official Steamship Guide International

Official Cruise Guide

CLIA Cruise Manual

Berlitz Complete Guide to Cruising

Stern's Guide to the Cruise Vacation

Ford's International Cruise Guide

ABC Shipping Guide

Fielding's Worldwide Cruises

Frommer's Cruises

Ford's Freighter Guide

Cruise magazines (*Cruise Views, Cruise Travel*)

Various cruise brochures and videos

Cruise computer software

CLIA and industry pamphlets and newsletters

9

Booking Land Arrangements with a Wholesaler

A growing trend in the travel industry is to reserve "land arrangements" with tour operators. This includes such items as car rentals, hotel rooms, local sightseeing, and theatre.

ADVANTAGES OF TOUR OPERATOR BOOKINGS

1. Prices are generally processed in local currency (Canadian dollars if in Canada, U.S. dollars if in the U.S.A.).

2. The prices are usually better than booking direct.

3. You may receive a higher commission.

4. Ease of reservation—just call the tour operator. There is no need to fax a foreign destination and wait for the reply (quoted in that country's local currency). One domestic call reserves everything.

5. The tour operator may have blocks of rooms reserved and therefore may be able to obtain a confirmation even when the hotel is "sold out."

6. The tour operator issues the vouchers and other documentation, leaving less work for the travel agent.

DISADVANTAGES OF TOUR OPERATOR BOOKINGS

1. A minimum stay may be required—normally three nights.

2. The client must fully prepay well in advance.

3. Choices and hotel locations may be limited.

Example of Land Arrangements—Waikiki Sunrise Hotel

Per Person, per night, accommodation only	Gardenview			Mountainview			Oceanview			Mountainview			Oceanview			Oceanfront Room		
	Dbl	Tpl	Quad	Dbl	Tpl	Quad	Dbl	Tpl	Quad	Dbl	Tpl	Quad	Dbl	Tpl	Quad	Dbl	Tpl	Quad
Sep 01/00 - Dec 18/00	70	59	53	76	63	55	97	77	66	173	162	156	187	170	162	200	179	169
Dec 19/00 - Dec 31/00	78	64	63	89	71	63	110	85	73	248	229	219	270	243	230	288	255	239
Jan 01/01 - Jan 19/01	69	58	58	81	66	58	98	77	67	248	229	219	270	243	230	288	255	239
Jan 20/01 - Mar 31/01	78	64	63	89	71	63	110	85	73	248	229	219	270	243	230	288	255	239
Apr 01/01 - Dec 18/01	69	58	58	81	66	58	98	77	67	239	222	214	257	235	223	276	247	233
Hotel & Service tax	10.17%			10.17%			10.17%			10.17%			10.17%			10.17%		
Children Free Under	18			18			18											
Meal Plan	EP			EP			EP			INCL			INCL			INCL		

Facilities: Pool • Jacuzzi • 6 tennis courts • Beach activities •Restaurants • Café • Poolside snack bar •Lounge • Entertainment • Golf adjacent • Fitness Centre • Hawaiian activities • Laundry • Free parking • 547 rooms.

Accommodation: Air conditioned rooms with 1 king or 2 double beds • Colour TV with pay movies • Tub/shower • Regrigerator • In room safe • Lanai • Wheelchair accessible and non-smoking rooms available.

EXERCISES—Waikiki Sunrise Hotel

1. A couple will travel to Honolulu, March 1 to 8 and wish to stay in a garden-view room at the Waikiki Sunrise Hotel. Calculate the price below and include taxes.

2. Another couple require the same hotel for three nights commencing November 1. Provide costing on an ocean-view room basis and include meals and taxes.

3. A third couple and their daughter (age 7) wish to visit the Waikiki Sunrise Hotel commencing April 12 for a one-week stay. They would like an ocean-front room with meals included. Prepare a costing for their stay.

Example of Land Arrangements—New York City "Away" Tours

New York City Accommodation

Left table

Hotel Name	Validity	Room Type	Twin	Triple	Quad	Single	Child (free)
Malibu Studios	Jan 01-Mar 31, Dec 16-31	ROH	122	144	164	100	-12
	Apr 01-Dec 15		132	156	176	111	
Americana	Jan 01-Mar 31	ROH	140	-	-	140	-12
	Apr 01-Sep 30		162	-	-	162	
	Oct 01-Dec 31		184	-	-	184	
Consulate	Jan 01-Mar 31	ROH	140	167	196	120	-16
	Apr 01-Dec 31		163	201	219	136	
Manhattan	Jan 01-Mar 31	ROH	150	174	196	150	-12
	Apr 01-Sep 30		172	195	216	172	
	Oct 01-Dec 31		214	237	256	214	
Wentworth	Jan 01-Mar 31	ROH	150	174	196	150	-12
	Apr 01-Sep 30		172	195	216	172	
	Oct 01-Dec 31		214	237	256	214	
Wolcott	Jan 01-Dec 31	ROH	154	192	220	154	-3
Milford Plaza	Jan 01-Mar 31	ROH	168	201	224	168	-2
	Apr 01-Dec 31		198	219	272	198	
Belvedere	Jan 01-Dec 31	ROH	170	192	204	170	-15
Wellington	Jan 01-Dec 31	ROH	182	216	272	172	as adult
Edison	Jan 01-Oct 27, Nov 14-Dec 13	ROH	190	210	232	182	as adult
	Oct 28-Nov 13		280	309	336	254	
Ameritania	Jan 01-Dec 14	ROH	200	240	276	200	-15
	Dec 15-31		176	213	252	176	
Pennsylvania	Jan 01-Jun,16 Sep 10-Oct 28		204	243	-	204	-12
	Oct 29-Nov 05		320	354	-	320	
	Jun 17-Sep 09, Nov 06-Dec 31		190	231	-	190	
Doral Inn	Jan 01-Mar 31, Sep 15-Dec 31	ROH	208	-	-	208	as adult
	Oct 28-Nov 13		230	-	-	230	
St. Moritz On-The-Park	Jan 01-Mar 31	Standard	210	-	-	210	-11
		Parkview	312	-	-	312	
	Apr 01-Dec 31	Standard	250	-	-	250	
		Parkview	354	-	-	354	
Mayflower	Jan 01-Mar 31	ROH	216	246	280	216	-12
		Parkview	246	279	308	246	
	Apr 01-Dec 31	ROH	242	273	304	242	
		Parkview	274	306	336	274	
Crowne Plaza Manhattan-BP	Jan 01-31	ROH	240	297	352	240	-18
	Feb 01-Mar 31		276	300	324	276	
	Apr 01-Jun 29		350	396	440	350	
	Jun 30-Aug 31		276	324	368	276	
	Sep 01-Dec 31		376	423	468	376	
Roger Smith-CP	Jan 01-Apr 15	ROH	242	273	-	242	-17
		Suite	346	346	346	346	
	Apr 16-Jun 28	ROH	274	306	-	274	
		Suite	366	366	366	366	
	Jun 29-Aug 31	ROH	262	294	-	262	
		Suite	346	346	346	346	
	Sep 01-Dec 31	ROH	294	327	-	294	
		Suite	366	366	366	366	

Right table

Hotel Name	Validity	Room Type	Twin	Triple	Quad	Single	Child (free)
Millennium Broadway	Jan 01-Mar 31	ROH	246	288	332	246	-16
	Apr 01-30 (Mon-Thurs)		330	372	416	330	
	Apr 01-30 (Fri-Sun)		288	330	372	288	
	May 01-03, 08-31, Jun 01 05-08, 12-14, 20		350	393	436	350	
	Sep 01-Oct 30, Nov 04-30 Jun 21-Aug 03, 07-10		308	351	396	308	
	Aug 14-Sep04, Dec 15-31 May 04-07, Jun 02-04, 09-11 15-19, Aug 04-06, 11-13 Oct 31, Nov 01-03, Dec 01-14		448	486	524	448	
Woodward	Jan 01-Dec 31	ROH	246	288	288	246	-18
Beverly - CP	Jan 01-Sep 14	ROH	254	327	352	254	As Adult
	Sep 15-Dec 31		267	354	380	267	
Sheraton Manhattan	Jan 01-Mar 31	ROH	284	336	–	284	-17
	Apr 01-Jun 22		350	402	–	350	
	Aug 03-Sep 02		304	357	–	304	
	Sep 03-Dec 18		396	447	–	396	
	Dec 19-31		294	345	–	294	
Sheraton New York	Jan 01-Mar 31	ROH	284	336	–	284	-17
	Apr 01-Jun 30		350	402	–	350	
	Jul 01-Sep 02		304	357	–	304	
	Sep 03-Dec 18		396	447	–	396	
	Dec 19-31		294	345	–	294	
Loews New York - BP	Jan 01-Jun 19	ROH	292	315	–	292	-12
	Jun 20-Sep 02		262	279	–	262	
	Sep 03-Dec 18		310	336	–	310	
	Dec 19-31		267	285	–	267	
The Algonquin - CP	Jan 01-Mar 31	ROH	304	354	408	304	-18
	Apr 01-Sep 01		354	405	460	354	
	Sep 02-Dec 14		396	447	500	396	
	Dec 15-31		374	426	480	374	
SoHo Grand	Jan 01-Jun 14	ROH	338	–	–	338	As Adult
	Jun 15-Sep 13, Dec 15-31		314	–	–	314	
	Sep 14-Nov 30		360	–	–	360	
	Dec 01-14		476	–	–	476	
Waldorf Astoria	Jan 01-Mar 31	ROH	399	471	–	399	-17
		Deluxe	461	534	–	461	
	Apr 01-Jun 30, Sep 08-Dec 14	ROH	430	504	–	430	
		Deluxe	482	555	–	482	
	Jul 01-Sep 07, Dec 15-31	ROH	388	462	–	388	
		Deluxe	440	513	–	440	

Rates are per room, per night, in Canadian Dollars and INCLUDE 13.25% State and City Tax, and Occupancy Tax of $3.00 CAD room night. For bookings under 2 nights a surcharge of $10 CAD per night will apply.
Note: Date of check-in determines rate for entire stay.
*BP offer valid Jan01-31 ONLY. ** Sheraton Manhattan closed for renovations Jun 23 - Aug 02

New York City Sightseeing Tours

Code	Tour	Price: Adult	Child
1LW	Lower Manhattan Walking Tour - 2 hrs	$18	Free
2UW	Harlem Walking Tour -2hr	$18	Free
CPT	Central Park Trolley Tour - 2 hrs	$25	$13
1*	Downtown Tour Loop - 2hrs	$28	$19
2*	Uptown Tour Loop - 2 hrs	$28	$19
3*	Downtown Loop plus Statue of Liberty / Ellis Island - 5 hrs	$38	$32
2W	Historic Harlem by Coach and by Foot - 5 hrs	$43	$30

Code	Tour	Price: Adult	Child
3*	Grand Tour Loop of Upper and Lower Manhattan - 4 hrs	$43	$32
1RC	Downtown Loop plus Radio City Music Hall Tour - 5 hrs	$43	$35
1CL	Downtown Loop plus Circle Line Cruise -5hrs	$46	$30
WP	West Point - US Military Academy (unescorted) - 8 hrs	$52	$29
5*	Grand Tour Loop plus Statue of Liberty / Ellis Island - 6 hrs	$53	$44

Code	Tour	Price: Adult	Child
3RC*	Grand Tour Loop plus Radio City Music Hall Tour - 5 hrs	$58	$47
6L	Manhattan Comprehensive (lunch included) - 9 hrs	$77	$67
8	Night on the Town (incl. Human Feast) - 6hrs	$80	$80
1H1*	Downtown Loop plus 7 mile Helicopter Tour - 3hrs	$93	$93
3H1*	Grand Tour Loop plus 7 mile Helicopter Tour - 5hrs.	$108	$105

*Note: Manhattan Loop Tours include hop-on, hop-off service whereby guests may get on and off as often as they wish throughout the day. Prices shown are per person in Canadian Dollars. Children under 5 years of age travel free on all Manhattan Loop Tours when not occupying a separate seat. Child rate applies to children 5-11 years when accompanied by at least one adult. All state taxes included. All Tours depart from the Gray Line Terminal : 8ᵗʰ Avenue between 53ʳᵈ and 54ᵗʰ Street. Tour durations are approximate and are based on single journeys.

New York City — Theatre Tickets

$73	Φ Born to Sing Φ Forbidden Broadway Strikes Back Φ The Fantastiks
$92	Φ Blue Man Group in Tubes Φ Cakewalk Φ Cowgirls Φ Full Gallop Φ Grace and Glorie ΦJuan Darien Φ Magic on Broadway Φ Master Class Φ Sex and Longing Φ Stomp Φ Taking Sides
$128	Φ An Ideal Husband Φ Defending the Caveman Φ Love Thy Neighbour Φ Present Laughter Φ Skylight
$146	Φ Beauty and the Beast Φ Bring in 'Da Noise / Bring in 'Da Funk Φ Candide Φ Cats Φ Chicago Φ Grease Φ Les Miserables Φ Miss Saigon Φ Phantom of the Opera Φ Rent Φ Smokey Joe's Café Φ Sunset Boulevard
$159	Φ A Funny Thing Happened… Φ Once Upon a Mattress Φ The King and I Φ Titanic Φ Victor / Victoria Φ Whistle Down the Wind

Above rates are in Canadian Dollars and include tax as well as a service fee imposed by our Theatre Ticket Agent in New York. Tickets confirmed in Top-Price Orchestra or Front Mezzanine. Shows listed may be terminated and/or replaced at any time. Theatre tickets sold on their own are subject to a $10 CAD per ticket service fee.

General Terms and Conditions

Deposit: A deposit of $50.00 per person is required at time of confirmation.

Theatre Tickets: Full payment required at time of booking.

Balance of Payment: Full payment is due 6 weeks prior to departure date.

Cancellation Policy:

Hotels: Up to 7 days prior to departure $50 per person, within 7 days prior to departure 100% non-refundable.

Theatre Tickets: 100% non-refundable.

Sightseeing Tours/Transfers: 100% non-refundable.

Change Fees: $300 per change.

Credit Card Policy: Besides payment made by cheque, we accept Master Card, Visa, American Express and Diners as forms of payment. If your payment is made by credit card, please be advised that the operator will appears as the vendor on your credit card statement, not your travel agency. Your authorization to use your credit card number for payment indicates your compliance with our booking terms and conditions, whether or not you have actually signed the appropriate forms. In other words, verbal authorization of your credit card confirms your acceptance of these terms and conditions.

Accommodations: Accommodations offered in our tours are to the best of our knowledge available at the time of publication and are accurately described. From time to time, factors beyond our control may change from the description in the brochure. If these changes effect your stay then please contact the manager of the property during your stay to see what can be done to rectify the matter.

Documentation: Visitors must possess valid identification for entry into the United States. Consult your travel agent.

Local Representatives: We do not employ local representatives at their destinations as we feel our passengers are capable of making their own arrangements for local tours through their hotel front desks. Should a passenger find that their accommodation is lacking in any way we request that you contact the hotel manager and discuss the situation. We strongly recommend your consideration of the various types of insurance coverage that are available through your travel agent to protect you in the event of trip cancellation, protection to your baggage

possessions and valuables and to cover against personal accident, sickness, injury and medical expenses.

Photographs: Although we make every effort to ensure that the information and photographs contained in this brochure are accurate, the occasional error or change in circumstances will occur. Inclusions may vary or be withdrawn with or without prior notice.

Laws and Customs: In order to familiarize yourself with relevant laws and customs and what documentation is necessary for your travel and return to Canada, we recommend you discuss these matters with your travel agent who can refer you to the relevant tourist boards and/or embassies or consulates for the countries that you will be visiting.

Pricing: Prices quoted in this brochures are in Canadian dollars and are based on fixed costs at the time of printing. These costs are dependent on full costs/rates of exchange and Suppliers Service Fees. Should these costs increase we reserve the right to increase the cost of any tour. In the event this increase is in excess of 7% (other than government tax), you are entitled to cancel the travel arrangements and receive a full refund. Every effort will be made to advise you of any price increase at least 25 days prior to your departure date.

Publishing Date: The date of publishing of this brochure is the 15th December, 1996. This brochure was printed many weeks before the validity of this brochure commences and variations may occasionally have to be made to the published dates. When such changes are necessary, they usually are of minor nature and unlikely to affect the enjoyment of your vacation.

Refunds and Complaints: Refunds for unused hotel accommodation must be made through your travel agent and by providing hotel receipts confirming the nights stayed. All refund requests will be liable to a $25 per person processing fee and must be made within 15 days of your return to Canada. Any complaints must be fully stated in writing through the booking Travel Agent and be received no later than 15 days after the passengers booked dates have expired.

Responsibility: The operator as the tour operator and/or its agents act only in the capacity of agent for the client in all matters pertaining to travel. They shall not be liable for any injury, damage or loss, occasioned by neglect or default of any company or hotel/resort proprietor or car rental organization or other persons supplying services or materials in connection with the hotel/resort accommodations. All prices are based on tariffs and exchange rates in effect at the time of publication of this folder (December 15, 1996) are subject to reconfirmation when final payment is made. The hotel/resorts indicated in this brochure are not held responsible for any act, omission or event during the time the clients are not staying at their establishments.

The operator and/or their agents are not held responsible for any act, omission or event during the time clients are travelling to and from the hotel/resort and while they are staying at the hotel/resort at which accommodation is booked.

The hotel voucher furnished by The operator for the hotels/resorts when issued shall constitute the sole contract between the hotels/resorts and the purchasers of the accommodations and/or the clients. Neither the operators (and/or their agents) nor the hotels/resorts concerned are to be held responsible for payment of any refund for unused accommodations or meals occasioned by late arrivals or non-arrivals by the clients.

Errors and Omissions: The operator shall not be liable for any loss, including loss of enjoyment or damages resulting from misdescription of accommodation, facilities and services due to printing errors or omissions in this brochrue. In the event of printing errors or omissions affecting the prices of services listed, theprices are subject to change and the purchaser will be required to pay the applicable price or will be refunded for overpayment. Should any purchaser regard payment of the additional sum as a hardship and so advise The operator within forty-eight hours of notice of the change, The operator agrees to cancel the booking and to refund all monies paid and shall have no further liability.

Acknowledgment: The passenger(s) hereby acknowledge(s) having read the within provisions relating to our responsibility.

Validity: January 01, 1997 to December 31, 1997.

Available only through your professional travel agent.

Ontario Registration No. 1234567

EXERCISES — New York City

1. a. A client needs a hotel in New York for three nights including a ticket to
        Les Miserables. She wants a three-star hotel in the Central Park area and
        you have selected the St. Moritz-on-the-Park Hotel. If she is arriving on
        May 19, what is the package cost, including tax, for a standard room?

        _____

        _____

        _____

        _____

    b. How much would the deposit be and when is the balance due?

        _____

        _____

        _____

        _____

2. a. A couple are attending a convention and want to stay at the Waldorf
        Astoria Hotel for five nights. They are arriving on July 4 and want a luxu-
        ry room, if possible. They want a night tour that will include dinner and a
        day tour to West Point. How much will it all cost?

        _____

        _____

        _____

        _____

        _____

        _____

    b. Where do their tours depart from?

        _____

        _____

        _____

        _____

    c. If they cancel either tour after arrival, is there a cancellation penalty, and if
        so, how much?

        _____

        _____

        _____

        _____

10
Inclusive Tour Charters

Some passengers prefer a "package deal" where most if not all of the elements are included. This type of travel is called an *ITC* or *inclusive tour charter*. (Independent tours—DITs and FITs—will be discussed in Chapter 11.)

Tour operators construct the elements of their tours before their sale to the public, often a year ahead of time. The arrangements are based on a large number of people travelling together, even though ITCs are intended to be sold to individuals. ITCs include both outbound tour operators and inbound tour operators. A list of common tour operators can be found in Appendix D.

Outbound tour operators are based in one country, and create and market tours offered in another country. They specialize in sending tourists to international destinations (for example, Sunquest and Regent).

Inbound tour operators are based in, and operate tours within, the same country and are also known as *destination management companies (DMCs)*. An example is Frame's Tours in the U.K.

Following are some of the advantages and disadvantages of selling inclusive tour charters. Add any of your own ideas below each section.

ADVANTAGES OF SELLING ITCs

1. Cost is reduced by bulk buying.

2. Avoids the need to separately book each element of the tour.

3. Ticketing is provided by the tour operator, not the travel agent.

4. A group of people with similar language, customs, and interests can travel together.

5. Last-minute sell-offs are possible.

6. _____

7. _____

DISADVANTAGES OF SELLING ITCs

1. It is not always possible to provide a client's exact needs and preferences with an ITC.

2. Once a booking is made, there is less flexibility to make changes.

3 _____

4. _____

MAJOR COMPONENTS IN A BASIC ITC

- Return airfare with a specified carrier (usually charter);
- Accommodation as selected, generally for 7 or 14 nights;
- Transfers to and from hotel/airport or rental car.

Items Not Included

Basic ITC packages generally do not include the following items:

- Meals and sightseeing unless specified;
- Hotel service charges and taxes (local government and airport taxes are normally added to the basic rate and prepaid by the client);
- Items of a purely personal nature (for example, laundry, bar);
- Travel insurance.

All-Inclusive ITCs

All-inclusive ITCs include the basic components as above, plus the following items:

- Meals as outlined;
- Liquor and/or cigarettes;
- Hotel service charges and taxes;
- Activities such as some water sports and theme parties.

COSTINGS/RATES

Clients who purchase a package tour instead of making their own arrangements can save as much as 20% of the cost of their vacations.

Rates are generally quoted per person, based on double occupancy. A single rate may be published or a supplement may be added to the per-person rate. Triple and quadruple reductions may be deducted from the per-person double rate.

Most hotels do not charge rates for children (usually 2 to 11 years old, but age may vary) if sharing the same room with two full-paying adults. However, airfare is extra for the children.

Costing an ITC

Following are some items that you may have to consider when pricing a tour package:

Basic price—prices are per person, for 7 or 14 nights

    Add the following charges:

- **Single supplement**—may be added when only one adult is travelling.

- **Club seat**—larger, wider seat on plane (sometimes offered).

- **Ocean-view room**—sometimes a supplement is charged for room location.

- **Surcharge for spring break or Christmas**—a supplement may be added for selected departure dates.

- **Meal plan**—most meal plans are booked in advance and paid for separately at the destination, if offered as an option. If not included, it is added to the basic rate. Discuss alternatives with the client at time of booking.

- **Car rental**—some tour operators always include cars, others offer rentals only in some destinations such as Florida. If included, the client may wish to upgrade to a larger car.

- **Travel insurance**—if purchased through the tour operator.

- **Subtotal**—the items listed above are generally commissionable.

- **Airport taxes**—may be one total amount or separated into the various international taxes. A Canadian navigational surcharge is included in the fare, and taxes are noncommissionable.

Subtract the following (where applicable):

- **Triple/quad reduction**—when there are 3 or 4 adults travelling.

- **Early booking discount**—applies with some tour operators.

CREATION OF AN ITC

When a tour operator designs an ITC, there are several key aspects to the process:
- Planning
- Brochure production
- Promotion

Planning

The Planning stage involves negotiating contracts with various suppliers of travel products that will be part of the ITC. These include the following products:
- Airlines
- Hotels
- Local tour companies

Brochure Production

Once contracts have been negotiated with service suppliers, a brochure must be prepared. The tour operator ensures that its brochures are attractive and eye catching as well as informative. Glossy photos, easily readable print size and style and upbeat positive descriptions all make the brochure the travel agent's primary sales tool. At the same time, descriptions of the tour elements must not be exaggerated and need to be truthful.

Promotion

Although the tour operator's brochure is its main method of advertising, the tour operator will seek to promote its products in as many ways as it can, since there is much competition. In addition to conventional methods of advertising (newspapers, TV, radio, magazines, etc.), many tour operators provide product launches for industry personnel (these often include food and drinks, entertainment, prizes, and free trips) and engage in a variety of other methods to promote their products.

INFORMATION REQUIRED TO RESERVE AN ITC

1. Name(s) and address of client;

2. Client's home and business phone numbers;

3. Number of people in the party, travelling together on the ITC;

4. Number of rooms required;

5. Hotel name/package name requested, from supplier's brochure;

6. Preferred location of rooms in the hotel;

7. Dates required (and alternative dates);

8. Form of payment preferred by client;

9. Optional items and special requests needed (hotel: ocean-view rooms, extra beds, meal plans, etc.; air: special meal requests, early boarding privileges, etc.);

10. Insurance requirements (compare ITC insurance to independent insurance).

HOW TO MAKE A RESERVATION

1. Complete a reservation form, with all information needed.

2. Obtain the phone number of the tour operator (see terms and conditions of supplier brochure), and make phone reservation quoting package name, commencement date, name of hotel selected, and any special requests and extras (for example, meal plans, pool-view room, extra bed).

3. Confirm whether cancellation insurance is being purchased from the tour operator.

4. Confirm package rate including any applicable discounts, surcharges, taxes, and service charges, and verify deposit and final payment amounts and deadlines.

5. Verify ITC cancellation policy (What must be done? By what date? At what penalty?).

6. Provide client's credit card details if payment is being made by credit card.

7. Obtain the name of the reservation agent and a confirmation number.

8. Open a file for the client, with a copy of the reservation form and the tour operator brochure, and note the reservation agent's name and the confirmation number received on the reservation form.

BASIC ITCs VS. ALL-INCLUSIVE HOLIDAYS

Whether one is better than the other will depend upon the particular client's needs. A client who wants to have the full cost of a holiday predetermined and prepaid would prefer an all-inclusive holiday. A client who likes to have freedom of choice (for example, to sample restaurants outside the all-inclusive resort) or who is not likely to make use of all of the facilities and activities included, might prefer a basic ITC.

TOUR OPERATORS AND GENERAL SALES AGENTS

In Appendix D, you will find a list of many of the tour operators in Canada and the U.S.A.

General Sales Agents (GSAs)

Airbridge International Inc.—Montreal, Quebec

Comprehensive Travel Industry—Vancouver, B.C.

Discover the World Marketing—Etobicoke, Ontario

Jetset Tours—Toronto, Ontario

New Concepts Canada Travel Ventures—Richmond, B.C.

North-Cott Tour Planning—Iqaluit, Northwest Territories

Repworld Inc.—Vancouver, B.C.

The RMR Group Inc.—Toronto, Ontario

Tix Travel & Ticket Agency Inc.—Nyack, New York

Trade Wind Associates Canada—Toronto, Ontario

Vacation Care Inc.—Winnipeg, Manitoba

World Access Travel Marketing—Willowdale, Ontario

REFERENCE MATERIAL

Information on tour operators, tours, and tour packages can be found from the following reference material:

Gray Line Worldwide Services Directory—provides information on both domestic and international local sightseeing tours offered by the Gray Line Company.

ASI—American Sightseeing International Worldwide Tour Planning Tariff—provides tour information on over one hundred cities worldwide.

Specialty Travel Index—a tour operator directory.

Jax Fax Travel Marketing Magazine—a monthly publication listing air tours and prices.

Travel World News—a monthly publication of air tours and prices.

Official Tour Directory

Worldwide Brochures Directory

Trade magazines—(for example, *Travel Weekly, Travel Agent, Travel Trade, Tours and Resorts, Resorts and Incentives, Canadian Travel Press*).

ACTA Travel and Tourism Directory

Various tour operator brochures.

11

Independent Tours (DITs/FITs)

Many clients prefer independent ground arrangements, preferring the flexibility and the less restrictive nature of this type of travel. This independent type of tour is referred to as a *DIT—domestic independent tour*—if within Canada and/or the U.S.A. (although this title is rarely used) or an *FIT—foreign independent tour*—if outside Canada or the U.S.A. While such travel is arranged in the same manner as any other, the result is a holiday tailor-made to the client's own specifications and wishes.

Below are some of the advantages and disadvantages of booking independent tours. Add your own ideas to the lists.

ADVANTAGES OF DITs AND FITs

1. They can be tailored to meet the client's exact interests and requirements.

2. Scheduling is at the discretion of the client, and not dependent on a tour operator's specific dates and times.

3. It is easier to make last-minute changes or cancellations.

4. _____

5. _____

DISADVANTAGES OF DITs AND FITs

1. It requires a great degree of skill to plan and book the various components.

2. They are time consuming to put together.

3. They may be more expensive (an agent can't rely on volume discounting or sell-offs by the supplier).

4. _____

5. _____

Throughout the rest of this chapter, all information supplied for FITs will also apply to DITs.

Comparing ITCs to FITs

ITCs	FITs
Easy to book since most elements are pre-packaged. A client can even book it directly with a PC.	Requires a little creativity in order to secure the sale.
Pre-packaged 7- and 14-night stays.	Minimum stay of 3 nights is required.
Does not necessarily cater to your client's needs.	You can customize your client's vacation with a 2- or 3-centre holiday.
Client must take package as-is with no deviation.	Last-minute changes are possible. This is perfect for the client who uses frequent flyer points or drives to the destination.

SUPPLIERS

Various types of travel companies supply the components for an FIT including air transportation, hotels, car companies, etc. In addition, there are companies that specialize in this type of tour.

A list of companies that specialize in air transportation for ITCs can be found in Chapter 3; find detailed lists of accommodation providers in Chapter 4 and in Appendix B; and a list of car rental companies in Chapter 5.

Since an FIT, by its very nature, is independently arranged, one FIT can differ greatly from another. There are many possible features that can be included. You may be able to add some others.

- Air transportation
- Hotel reservations
- Car rental
- Train tickets/passes
- Local sightseeing tours
- Theatre tickets
- Museum passes

- _____

- _____

- _____

COMMISSIONS

The travel agency will receive a commission from the suppliers, and the agency may also choose to add a service charge for consulting time or to cover the cost of faxes, telephone calls, and so on, since it can take considerable time and effort to put together an FIT.

COSTING THE FIT

Since numerous tour operators are likely to be used and many different features may be included in order to make up an FIT, it is important to carefully keep track of the costs involved. The first thing to do is to prepare an outline to cost the proposed itinerary. An outline of costs will ensure that no feature is missed. Creating an outline permits you to discover whether changes may be needed to the proposed itinerary before bookings are finalized.

When preparing an outline, consider the following process:

1. Start the outline with fixed dates, such as dates for a special event (for example, the Edinburgh Tattoo), or a cruise sailing date.

2. You may organize the items and costs by one of the two following methods:

   a. Group similar items together, such as long distance transportation (flights), local transportation (rail, car rental), accommodation (hotels, camper vans), and sightseeing (shows, attraction tickets); or

   b. List items chronologically in the order of use to ensure nothing is missed (for example, Day One, in the morning, Paris Vision city tour; Day Two, in the evening, Illuminations tour; Day Three, ... , etc.)

3. Set up separate columns for adult, senior, and child pricing, as applicable. All prices should be per person.

4. With each item be sure to list the tour operator/supplier, date item required, and any special notes (for example, ocean-view room, category E car).

5. Add travel insurance. When obtaining insurance for an FIT, it is preferable to obtain all of the insurance from one company (for example, Voyageur) so that only one policy will be required for the entire trip.

6. In some cases you may charge your client in Canadian dollars for some features and American dollars for other features. Keep a separate column for each currency where this applies.

7. Add any markup or service charge at the end.

8. Finally, total the adult columns (times number of adults) and child columns (times number of children).

Note: Sometimes it may also be a good idea to complete a draft itinerary in date order (especially for complicated itineraries), listing the various options to review with your client, prior to completing a more detailed costing outline.

Example of an FIT Itinerary and Costing Outline

A family of two adults and a ten-year-old child wish to visit Britain, and an FIT is to be costed.

Proposed Itinerary

July 30	Depart Toronto for London
August 1 to 7	5 nights in London including a Tube pass, rail pass to visit nearby sites, show ticket, and city tour
August 7 to 14	One week exploring Britain with a rental car, staying at B&Bs and local inns
August 14 to 16	3 nights in Edinburgh
August 17	Fly home

Costing Outline, British FIT

	Brochure Page	Adults (× 2)	Children (× 2)
Flights			
July 30, Toronto to London	8	$309.00	$269.00
August 17, Edinburgh to Toronto	11	320.00	280.00
U.K. airport tax	11	48.00	48.00
Local Transportation			
Transfer from Gatwick to London standard class	21	23.00	11.50
London visitor pass, 4 days	21	45.00	17.00
BritRail Flexipass, 4 days in one month, 2nd class	32	255.00	127.50
Vauxhall Vestra rental car with CDI/TRI 51.00 × 7 days ÷ 2	25	178.50	–
VAT 17.5%		31.24	–
Sightseeing			
Full-day London tour	78	112.00	100.80
"Starlight Express" theatre ticket, top seat, Saturday evening, August 5	78	89.00	89.00
Accommodation			
Prince Henry Hotel (August 1 to 7), $86.00 × 6 nights, continental breakfast included	41	516.00	free
B&Bs of Britain (August 7 to 11), full breakfast, VAT included, 55.00/27.00 × 4 nights	64	220.00	108.00

Costing Outline, British FIT continued

	Brochure Page	Adults (× 2)	Children (× 2)
Inns of Britain (August 11 to 14), full breakfast, VAT included, 71.00/free × 3 nights	66	213.00	free
Town Court Hotel (August 14 to 17), full breakfast included, 173.00 × 3 nights	42	519.00	free
Subtotal		2,878.74	1,050.80
Voyageur Deluxe Package tour insurance, value of nonrefundable deposits only, 137.00/77.00 + 8% PST		147.96	83.16
Total per person		3,026.70	1,133.96
		× 2	× 2
Total cost		$6,084.40	$2,298.92

12

Insurance

While there is a legal obligation to offer certain types of insurance to the travelling passenger, it is also an important source of income for the travel agency. Frequently, the commissions will reach 40% or more.

Insurance is definitely in the interest of the client. In the event of a loss or injury, the client will be able to avoid the need to go to court to get compensation, and may also avoid a huge, unanticipated expense. While each of the Canadian provinces administers a health insurance plan, coverage for medical expenses incurred outside the province is usually limited to the amount that would have been paid if the expense had been incurred at home. And it is well known that medical costs in the U.S.A. and elsewhere are far higher than in Canada, and a hospital stay there under the care of a doctor can quickly escalate into thousands of dollars. The excess medical cost not covered by the provincial medical insurance plan can be recovered by purchasing a travel insurance policy. However, as medical costs have risen, so have the costs of these policies. This has had a considerable impact on the numbers of elderly people who have been accustomed to travel to warm weather climates (for example, Florida) for lengthy vacations to avoid the Canadian winter.

It is the responsibility of the travel counsellor to advise the passenger of the various types of insurance available. A client who has not been advised about the need for insurance and ends up having to pay for a loss or emergency situation will probably not return to your agency again. But more importantly, the agency may well be legally liable for the extra costs because they did not offer the insurance to the client. Some agencies carry E & O coverage (Errors and Omissions insurance) to protect themselves from this type of claim, but the best way to avoid the problem is to remember to offer the insurance. When an informed client signs an insurance waiver, the onus is shifted to the client for failing to purchase appropriate insurance to cover an emergency.

In some jurisdictions, you must have a licence to sell insurance or at least have met certain qualifications.

MAJOR TRAVEL INSURANCE COMPANIES

- Voyageur Insurance Company
- Mutual of Omaha
- John Ingle
- Blue Cross
- Zurich
- Medi-Select Advantage (Canada Life)

In addition, companies such as Holidair offer coverage through tour operators.

TYPES OF TRAVEL INSURANCE

The following types of insurance are typically sold by travel agencies:

Trip Cancellation Insurance

This insurance is provided to compensate for expenses incurred from the cancellation of any travel component or package, typically where cancellation is the result of sickness, injury, death, or jury duty.

Airfare, unless it is a normal fare (that is, first class, business class, or economy class), is subject to a cancellation penalty, and usually the cheaper fares (for example, excursion fares) have more restrictions and higher cancellation penalties.

Other travel components (transportation, accommodation, or inclusive tour packages) will also have cancellation penalties, dependent on their individual terms and conditions (consult the terms and conditions section of the particular wholesaler's brochure). Trip cancellation insurance covers these cancellation penalties.

It is the agent's job to determine what the cancellation penalty will be and under what circumstances a penalty will arise. If this information is unclear, the agent should contact the wholesaler for details.

Trip cancellation is one of the most important types of travel insurance, and *it must be offered to each passenger*. It must also be purchased at the time of booking when the deposit is paid; it cannot be purchased after booking (even if it is still prior to departure), as with all other types of travel insurance. However, premium rates for this insurance coverage, benefits, conditions, and exclusions will vary from company to company.

Emergency Accident and Sickness Hospital Medical Expense Insurance

This supplementary insurance covers the passenger against emergency sickness or accident expenses that are not recoverable by the passenger's provincial health plan. The coverage may include a time limit (covering all expenses incurred within a certain number of months of the sickness or accident) or a benefit limit (covering up to a maximum cost amount for expenses). There may also be restrictions against compensating for certain types of expenses, or there may be maximum amounts payable for specific expenses.

Air-Flight Accident Insurance

Typically called *flight insurance*, this is available for flights operated by both scheduled and charter airlines, and provides protection against accidental injury while boarding, leaving, or riding as a passenger. This coverage may also include the passenger's time on the airport premises or on an approved airport bus or limousine service.

Worldwide Travel Accident Insurance

This type of insurance provides 24-hour coverage, worldwide, against all types of accidents, including accidental death, loss of limb or sight, or a total permanent disability, but it does not cover expenses for sickness or disease. Such policies may also include supplementary medical expenses (not paid by a government health plan) and limited disability insurance (where a monthly income is paid if there is any loss of income due to time off from work).

Baggage and Personal Effects Insurance

Also called *all risks*, this insurance protects against loss, theft, damage, or disappearance of luggage and contents. It is intended to cover the traveller for all losses that are not normally covered by homeowner insurance. It is obviously important for the client to know whether he or she is already covered and, if so, exactly what is protected under the homeowner policy.

This insurance covers items normally taken when travelling but not items used in earning an income (for example, a camera is covered unless the client is a professional photographer). Also excluded are automobiles, animals, household furniture, securities, tickets, and documents. If money is covered at all, it is usually only in the event of an armed robbery and then for a very small amount. (Traveller's cheques and replaceable credit cards are the best protection; advise the client against carrying large amounts of cash.) Remember that it is better to have too much personal effects coverage rather than not enough (people tend to underestimate the value of their possessions).

Combination Insurance

Also called a *vac-pac* or a *trav-pac*, this refers to several types of insurance packaged together at one premium. It is designed to meet the needs of the average traveller but also provides various upgrades in coverage for additional premiums.

Package Tour Insurance

This is an all-inclusive type of insurance package, available for ITCs (and sold by insurance companies in competition with a tour operator's own insurance package). Various types of insurance are offered at a reduced overall cost in these packages.

Annual Air-Flight and/or 24-Hour Accident Coverage

This insurance is intended for the frequent traveller to avoid having to purchase a new policy for each trip. It is less expensive than purchasing insurance for each trip separately. The premium will be payable once annually. Usually some accident protection and baggage and personal effects protection are included.

Group Travel Insurance

This is insurance arranged for a group of people travelling together, with coverage tailored to the needs of the group. The cost to each person is less than it would be if they obtained coverage individually.

Hospital and Medical Insurance for Visitors

This hospital and medical insurance (prepaid or purchased within 72 hours of arrival), covers a client's relatives visiting from overseas. Visitors to Canada will not qualify for coverage under the provincial health plans, and therefore some hospital/medical insurance is vital to avoid significant costs.

Rental Car Accidental Damage

Also referred to as *collision* (or *loss*) *damage waiver*, this insurance is obtained from the car rental company as protection against an accident or other damage to the vehicle. Some credit card issuers also offer this coverage to clients who pay the rental charges on that credit card. Clients should also check the insurance policy on their own vehicles since damage to rental cars may already be covered there.

Waivers

Under the Travel Industry Act, in Ontario the travel agent is legally obliged to offer travel insurance. In order to protect yourself and your agency from legal action, if a client declines the offer of insurance, obtain a signed waiver from the client. The waiver should make clear what insurance was offered and that the client was advised to purchase this insurance and yet declined with full understanding of the consequences. A sample waiver has been included at the end of this chapter.

Although the legal obligation to offer insurance may vary outside Ontario, it is wise to have waivers signed in any case to avoid being blamed for the client's failure to have adequate coverage in the event of an emergency.

GENERAL INFORMATION ABOUT TRAVEL INSURANCE

- In some provinces and states the travel agent is legally obliged to offer travel insurance.
- Trip cancellation insurance must be paid for in full at the time of booking. Other types of travel-related insurance can be sold up to (and in some cases even after) departure.
- The policy must be issued immediately when the premium is paid, in order to bind the insurance company to the insurance contract.
- The policy cannot be back-dated.
- Some companies offer "late policy issuance" where you may be permitted, within two business days of the date of initial deposit, to issue trip cancellation insurance, provided your client knows of no reason that would prevent him or her from travelling as booked.
- Pre-existing conditions (such as heart conditions) may prevent you from issuing coverage. If in doubt call the insurance company, before issuing the policy, for their decision about any pre-existing medical conditions.

- Some companies may have a maximum limit on trip cancellation insurance (usually around $10,000).

- Although travel for infants is generally free, insurance is still necessary for health-related coverage. Normally infants are added to the parent's policy for little or no cost, *but they must be separately named on the policy to be covered.*

- Trip cancellation insurance is effective at the time the policy is issued and paid for; all other types of insurance are effective at 12:01 a.m. on the date of departure and terminate at midnight on the date of return. The departure and return days must be included when calculating the number of days of insurance required. For example, for travel from July 1 to 23, coverage must be calculated for 23 days.

- If a claim becomes necessary, a client should call the supplied phone number immediately to report the claim and to avoid penalties.

- Some insurance companies advance funds directly to the billing hospital or doctor; others require the client to pay the expenses and then reimburse the client upon receiving expense receipts after he or she returns home.

- Premiums paid for insurance are nonrefundable.

- Check to see if one policy can be issued for a family travelling together. However, each person will need a separate policy if travelling at different times or for different lengths of time.

- The insurance application must be fully completed, to be effective.

- Certain types of policies must be signed by the insured person to be effective.

- Any errors in a policy should not be changed or corrected. Rather, the policy should be voided (marked "SPOILED") and returned at the end of each month to the insurer. A new policy should immediately be issued for the client.

- A monthly sales report is sent by the agency to the insurer, enclosing copies of issued and cancelled policies as well as payment of premiums owing to the insurer.

TOUR OPERATOR INSURANCE VS. PRIVATE INSURANCE

When purchasing a tour operator's insurance, that insurance is specially designed for the typical needs of an average client taking that tour operator's package; it is possibly provided at a cost that reflects the bulk purchasing power of the tour operator. On the other hand, choosing this insurance prevents you from comparison shopping. Cheaper policies may be available with coverage even more appropriate to your particular client's needs. Also, the exclusions from the tour operator's own insurance may be more restrictive than alternative insurance available.

Cancellation/Changes to Policy

After a trip cancellation insurance policy has been issued, it cannot be cancelled and refunded, since it is effective as soon as the premium is paid. Other types of insurance, however, can be cancelled and refunded as long as the cancellation occurs before the date of departure.

Changes can be made if

- The client extends their trip; or
- The client changes departure date.

When making a change, advise the insurance company prior to the previous policy expiring. The policy to be cancelled should be obtained from the client and marked "REFUND—TRIP CANCELLED," and the cancelled policy must be sent back to the insurer. The monthly sales report from the agency must reflect an adjustment for the cancellation (either by showing it as a void item, if cancelled in the same month that it was issued, or by deducting the refund from monthly total sales reported, if cancelled in a subsequent month).

COMMON OBJECTIONS TO INSURANCE

In the spaces provided below, write how you might handle each objection.

1. "Insurance is too expensive."

   _____

   _____

2. "I don't need insurance."

   _____

   _____

3. "I want to think about it."

   _____

   _____

4. "I have insurance with my company," or "I bought it at the bank."

   _____

   _____

5. "I am covered by my credit card."

   _____

   _____

6. "I don't need cancellation insurance; I am going no matter what."

   _____

   _____

7. "I am covered with a group plan."

   _____

   _____

Common Insurance Terms

POLICY	A contract whereby a client pays a premium in return for insurance against a defined risk.
COVERAGE	A description of the type and extent of risk that the insurance policy protects against.
PREMIUM	The cost of buying insurance protection for the client.
TERM	The period of time, starting with the effective (or start) date and time, and ending with the lapse (or end) date and time of the policy, during which the policy is valid.
CLAIM	A loss covered by an insurance policy for which notice has been given to the insurer for payment.
DEDUCTIBLE	That part of a loss that insurance does not cover and for which the client is personally responsible.
ESTATE	The ownership of a person's assets on death. In the event of death, the surviving heirs of the deceased are legally entitled to receive any assets (including insurance proceeds).
BENEFICIARY	The person (or persons) entitled to receive the proceeds of insurance in the event of a client's death.
INSURED	The person who is insured against a defined risk.
APPLICANT	The person who applies for the insurance and pays the premium (not necessarily the same person as the insured).

EXERCISES

1. Name two advantages for a travel agent of booking separate insurance rather than taking the insurance offered by a tour operator or supplier.

    _____

    _____

2. If insurance is declined by a client, what do you as a travel counsellor have to do, and why is this so important?

    _____

    _____

3. If a client is taking out the baggage and personal effects insurance, what important limitation is worth mentioning to the client?

    _____

    _____

4. a. What benefit is there for a vacationer taking out emergency accident and sickness hospital and medical expense insurance?

    _____

    _____

    b. What would this insurance *not* cover your clients for?

    _____

    _____

13

Special Needs Travellers

Recent figures indicate that there are 36 million disabled people in the United States who are actual or potential travel agency clientele. Significant numbers also exist in Canada. In addition, there are a large number of seniors and children travelling today who have special requirements.

The various types of special needs can be categorized as follows:

- Physical impairment that prevents the passenger from moving easily from place to place or from climbing stairs
- Visual impairment or blindness
- Hearing impairment or deafness
- Other health impairments
- Senior citizens
- Children

The Canadian Transportation Agency (CTA) has published the following two items for air travellers: *Fly Smart* contains general consumer information about flying to, from, and within Canada. *Taking Charge of the Air Travel Experience: A Guide for Persons with Disabilities* is particularly useful for disabled travellers who might need help in planning and preparing for their air travel.

PHYSICAL IMPAIRMENT

Travellers may have different degrees of physical impairment, requiring various levels of assistance. A traveller may be

- Partially immobile, requiring a wheelchair but still able to climb aircraft stairs and move about the cabin unassisted;
- Unable to climb stairs unassisted while still able to move about the cabin on his or her own; or
- Fully impaired, requiring assistance both with climbing stairs and with movement within the cabin.

When booking air travel for a passenger who requires the use of a wheelchair, you need to determine the exact details of the impairment and what limitations there are on the traveller's mobility. Then you must advise the airline of the information when making the booking.

Passengers with physical disabilities may request assistance when boarding the aircraft. Where there is no boarding ramp, a lift device may be used (usually this is done in private and is completed before other passengers board). Passengers using small mobility aids (such as canes, folding walkers, or crutches) are generally permitted to store them in the aircraft cabin. Wheelchair users may be asked to use smaller chairs provided by the carrier since the aisles of many aircraft are very narrow. In many cases, electric wheelchairs will have to be disassembled before being allowed onto an aircraft. Passengers requiring the use of a wheelchair should confirm beforehand whether there are wheelchair-accessible washroom facilities on board (the new, larger generation of aircraft offer more accessibility features). If there are no wheelchair-accessible facilities, passengers needing washroom assistance must travel with an attendant to help them. However, flight attendants will provide other additional limited assistance for disabled passengers (including cutting food or pouring liquids at mealtime, or retrieving mobility aids from storage bins).

Note that medical clearance from a physician may be required if the airline determines that the passenger may create a hazard, may be unable to care for him- or herself without some special assistance on board, or may be at risk to the overall safety of the flight. (The standard medical information form—called a *MEDIF*—and the frequent traveller's medical card—called a *FREMEC*—avoid the need for a new clearance for each trip.) Under IATA rules, the airline may also refuse to carry a passenger who is unable to sit in the seat or who is unable to occupy the seat in a fully upright position for takeoff or landing.

Many Canadian air carriers will maintain a permanent file (PNR or passenger name record) for any disabled passenger who travels frequently with that airline. The airline will then have ready access to the person's phone number and information relating to any special services needed.

The flights being booked for the physically impaired should be nonstop and direct if possible (if connecting flights are needed, allow extra time for a wheelchair passenger). The passenger needs to allow substantial amounts of extra time for checking in and security clearance. Seating should be pre-arranged, and preboarding should be requested if required.

While most ground transportation will be accessible to those with physical disabilities, it may be necessary to decide beforehand which type of transportation is most suitable, and the necessary booking arrangements should be made by the passenger before the intended travel date. For travellers using private vehicles, parking is normally provided close to terminal entrances for vehicles bearing the proper disability identification.

When booking hotels, check for wheelchair accessibility and facilities (ramps, larger doorways, etc.) and ensure that a room designed for disabled occupancy is available. Information on the hotel's facilities can be checked in the *Official Hotel Guide* (or similar), and written confirmation of the booking and special requirements should be obtained and a copy given to the client.

When booking a cruise, ensure that the cabin is suitable for the disabled and that it is near the elevator and other facilities. Refer to the ship's deck plan to avoid locating the traveller beside the narrower hallways on the ship (most walkways will be quite narrow). Verify which facilities are available to disabled passengers and confirm whether a medical certificate will be required. Also, determine what type of transfer service is provided (or available) to get a disabled passenger between the ship and the airport. Again, written confirmation of the booking and the special requirements should be obtained from the cruise line and should be given to the client before departure.

When booking rail travel, check to see if there is a manual or mechanical lifting service available to lift the wheelchair passenger on and off the train; if not, arrange for special assistance with the railway and for a station wheelchair. If an escort is needed for medical reasons, the escort may qualify for free transportation (meals are extra).

Wheelchairs can be stored in the baggage compartment (nonfolding wheelchairs) or in the overhead luggage rack (folding chairs). Book direct express trains with no stops, where possible. Choose seating that is located near the lavatories and exits. When using Via Rail, book the LRC trains if available (they have some wheelchair accessibility), and advise the railway of the passenger's special needs. Also, advise the passenger how he or she will be taken care of and by whom. Amtrak also provides special assistance for disabled passengers, and a list of their services can be found in their publication called *Access Amtrak*.

VISUAL IMPAIRMENT

When booking air travel for a person who is blind or visually impaired, pre-arrange seating with the airline. Keep in mind that the person may be accompanied by a guide dog. Each airline will have its own policy on seating regarding guide dogs. Provided the airline was advised at booking, the guide dog will generally not require an extra charge to travel in the cabin with its owner. Some airlines may insist that the guide dog be put into the baggage compartment along with pets. For foreign travel, a vaccination certificate may be needed, indicating that the dog has had all required shots, especially for rabies. Some countries may even insist on a quarantine period for animals; the embassy, consulate, or tourist board of the country should be contacted for possible quarantine information.

Aboard the aircraft, a Braille card may be available on request. This card will give the blind passenger the required safety information about the plane (including details about where the various function switches are located—for fresh air, overhead reading light, and to call a flight attendant—and how to get to the nearest exit).

A passenger may require a personal attendant (typically this will be needed for the passenger who is both blind and deaf). Some airlines will provide transportation at a reduced rate for one personal attendant for a passenger who is blind and deaf. If the passenger wishes to travel unaccompanied, be sure to obtain the consent of the airline first.

When booking a hotel for a blind passenger with a guide dog, make sure that the dog will be permitted in the room. Some hotels provide Braille lettering on elevators and on room door numbers, and Braille menus in the hotel's restaurants.

When booking a cruise, ensure that a guide dog is permitted in the passenger's cabin. Select a cabin that is near an elevator and easily accessible to and from the facilities that the passenger will most want to use.

When booking rail for a blind passenger, advise the railway if there will be a guide dog (the dog can travel free and there are no restrictions on where the dog is kept). If there is an escort, free transportation will be given only on production of a form 92B, which confirms that the blind person needs assistance. The form is obtainable from the Canadian National Institute for the Blind. (The American equivalent form is issued by the American Foundation for the Blind.) Via Rail publishes a booklet in large print and in Braille that describes in detail its services provided for the visually impaired.

HEARING IMPAIRMENT

When booking air travel for someone who has a hearing problem, advise the airline of this at the time of booking (there are usually staff available who are knowledgeable in sign language and who can provide assistance at time of check-in as well as on board the aircraft). You must also obtain a phone number of a hearing contact person (in case of schedule changes). The hearing impaired client must be given a detailed written explanation of all travel arrangements and must be instructed to inform a flight attendant when boarding (to get written information on services and safety procedures).

When booking a hotel, ensure that the hotel is advised of the hearing impairment at the time of booking so the staff are adequately prepared in the event of an emergency. Obtain a room that is close to an exit or elevator, and inquire whether there are specific safety devices for the hearing impaired (for example, fire alarms that flash light in addition to sounding an alarm).

When booking rail, the reservation staff must be made aware of the impairment at the time of booking so that they can provide the appropriate level of assistance. The client should produce written identification to the train conductor when boarding, to confirm the need for assistance.

OTHER HEALTH IMPAIRMENTS

An airline may refuse to carry a passenger who has an infection or disease that puts other passengers or the plane's crew at risk, or any passenger who, for health reasons, cannot occupy a seat or manage to place the seat in an upright position for landings and takeoffs. For certain medical conditions, you may have to obtain medical clearance from the airline. They may ask to see the passenger's medical documentation (the MEDIF or FREMEC). Special dietary meals (for example, low sodium or low fat) are generally available if pre-arranged. All planes that allow smoking on board will have separate smoking and nonsmoking areas, and seating in a nonsmoking area can be selected when booking. Many airlines have entirely prohibited smoking on board their planes and these flights should be selected, where possible, if the client has a breathing problem (for example, asthma or an allergic reaction to smoke). For diabetic passengers, insulin can usually be kept refrigerated while on board the plane.

When booking hotels, keep in mind that more and more hotels in North America (but less so elsewhere) have smoke-free rooms available (or even smoke-free floors). Be aware than many hotel properties, particularly those outside of North America, may not have air conditioning or elevators (especially older properties), and these may not suit the client with health problems.

When booking a cruise, note that some cruise lines require a medical certificate setting out the passenger's medical condition. It may be possible to request a nonsmoking cabin. While most ships have a doctor, and common drugs will be available on board the ship, ensure that the passenger carries an adequate supply of prescription drugs. Most ships have the ability to keep insulin refrigerated for the diabetic passenger. Special dietary requests may also be pre-arranged.

When booking rail, special dietary requests can be requested when booking, and separate smoking and nonsmoking areas are provided.

There are restrictions on travel during pregnancy (generally prohibited after the thirty-first week). Check details with both the airlines and the insurance companies.

SENIOR CITIZENS

Each tour operator and service supplier will set its own age requirements for who is considered a senior. While many senior citizens are healthy and active, it is an unfortunate fact of life that many people become increasingly frail and subject to illness as they age. This requires the tour operator to take additional steps to assist such passengers, such as providing wheelchairs and special dietary requests.

Many travel agencies and tour operators design tours with seniors in mind. Their itineraries will cater to the interests of seniors and will be paced at a more relaxed level than the average tour. It is understandable that agencies and operators would focus on providing these tours when you consider the following information:

- Seniors have more time available for travelling and may take longer trips or frequent short trips (for example, bus tours).
- Many seniors have paid for their homes and have the money to purchase major trips.
- The "golden age" of seniors has arrived, and it is increasingly popular for seniors to lead an active lifestyle that includes travel.
- Numerous seniors migrate south in the winter to states such as Florida and Arizona, providing an excellent opportunity to sell flights, travel insurance, and other travel products. And there are other sales opportunities available for agents who deal with senior clients. You may want to ask your senior clients travelling south if they would also be interested in a short cruise during their Florida stay.

CHILDREN

Many family vacations used to involve packing the kids in the car and driving to nearby attractions. But now, resorts and cruise lines in particular are catering to this market. Incentives may include free accommodation for children, free meals in some cases, and activity programs. Tour operators and service suppliers will set age requirements for who is considered a child.

Some examples of current tour-operator-designed family vacations include the following:

- Disney Cruise Line is a family holiday package that combines Disney World and three- or four-night cruises from Florida. Premier Cruise offers a similar program.
- Club Med offers a circus school for children at a number of its resorts.
- Boscobel Beach in Jamaica features a children's pool and an extensive program for kids of all ages. "Super nannies" offer these activities from 9:00 a.m. to 10:00 p.m. daily.

REFERENCE MATERIAL

Official Hotel Guide (formerly known as the OHRG)—this guide indicates which hotel properties have wheelchair accessibility.

Travel planners—these guides provide airport diagrams that show wheelchair ramps and where wheelchair-accessible washrooms are located.

Access Travel—also provides information on facilities in airports.

Incapacitated Passengers Air Travel Guide—an IATA publication.

The Disabled Traveller, by Cinnie Noble—has been designed to assist travel counsellors to effectively service their disabled clients. (May be purchased from the CITC in Canada).

Handi-Travel—a resource book for disabled and elderly travellers, published by the Canadian Rehabilitation Council for the Disabled in Toronto.

EXERCISES

1.   When selling travel insurance to seniors or disabled people, what are the two major questions you should ask?

   _____

   _____

2.   If a client has just booked a flight with you and appears to have difficulty walking, what are some questions you might ask?

   _____

   _____

   _____

   _____

14

Travel and the Law

The legal systems in Canada, the United States, and the United Kingdom are all based on English common law. Legal precedent is equal in importance to statute laws and, at least in the case of the United States (and to a somewhat lesser extent, Canada), to written constitutional documents.

In Ontario, you need to know in particular about the Travel Industry Act, legislation that was set up in 1975 to protect the consumer. Similar legislation has been enacted in British Columbia with the Travel Agents Act. Although most other provinces do not have specific travel industry legislation, there are many other statutes that will also impact on the travel agent's business. Therefore, travel-related law is complex and may sometimes require legal counsel. It is better to be safe than sorry. When in doubt about the legal consequences of a certain action (or inaction), consult a lawyer who is knowledgeable about the matters at hand, both for the client's benefit and for the protection of you and your agency.

Basically, you are required to provide full and accurate disclosure to the consumer, avoiding false statements, misrepresentations, and puffery (for example, avoid saying "This hotel has the best rooms in the country"). Also, the sale of travel services constitutes a contract and all of the legal requirements of any contract (too detailed to list here) must be followed if the contract is to be valid and enforceable and if damages are to be avoided. Contracts should be drafted only after receiving proper legal advice.

Note, however, that a travel agent, the travel agency, and the wholesaler may not only be liable for breach of contract but may also have a noncontractual liability for a loss that arises from some negligent misstatement even in the absence of a contract. This claim for losses may be made quite apart from whether there is a contractual basis for damages. (This is a principle of common law decided upon in the famous English House of Lords decision of Hedley Byrne & Co. Ltd. vs. Heller & Partners Ltd.—know as the Hedley Byrne decision—a case of negligent misstatement that has been consistently followed by Canadian courts and is well established law in Canada).

ONTARIO TRAVEL INDUSTRY ACT

This Act regulates the travel industry in Ontario through enactment of the following requirements:

1. It requires every travel agency and every supplier of a travel service to register with the Travel Industry Council of Ontario. A copy of the registration, when issued, will display the name and registration number of the agency, as well as its date of expiry, and it must be displayed in a public space within the agency. The licence is revocable in the event of breaches of the Act's obligations. A loss of licence would mean closure of the agency since it would no longer have the right to deal with the public.

2. It sets up a compensation fund (to which each travel agency or travel supplier who registers contributes), intended to compensate for the loss of services purchased from an agency or wholesaler who ceases operations or otherwise fails to meet its contractual obligations. The contribution required will vary, depending on the type of registrant (for example, $2,500 is the charge for a new travel agency).

   The protection offered by the fund is only available for agencies located in Ontario or for suppliers who do business within (and are therefore registered in) Ontario. Ontario residents who deal with agencies outside Ontario are not protected by this fund. When the fund falls below a certain amount, a levy may be assessed against all of the registrants to bring the fund back up to an acceptable level. In addition to reimbursement for prepaid services that are not delivered, the client may qualify for compensation for passengers stranded outside Canada (to provide alternate accommodation or return transportation home).

3. It imposes certain obligations on agents and suppliers to ensure accuracy in their advertising and business practices.

BRITISH COLUMBIA TRAVEL AGENTS ACT

In British Columbia, travel agents, wholesalers, and tour operators are registered under the provisions of the B.C. Travel Agents Act and regulations, administered by the Registrar of Travel Services, Ministry of the Attorney General. In B.C., a travel agent selling insurance products must also meet the licensing requirements of the Insurance Council of British Columbia.

Under the B.C. Travel Agents Act, a person must apply to the Registrar of Travel Services for registration as a travel agent (using the prescribed form and paying the assigned fee). A person cannot act as or represent him- or herself as an agent unless properly registered. Once registered an agent must provide travel services only in his or her registered name and at the registered address(es).

BUSINESS PRACTICE REQUIREMENTS

Your first obligation is to be fully informative and to presume that your client will not know what information is needed in advance; your second obligation is to be cautious, accurate, and truthful in the information or opinions that you might express.

You will need to provide the following information to your client:

1. Supply to the client as soon as possible a copy of any brochure or wholesaler's information; if changes are made to the details in the brochure or the wholesaler's information, communicate these changes in writing to the client immediately.

2. Fully inform the client about who is supplying the service (which airline and hotel are being used, and who is the tour operator).

3. Explain to the client the importance of the terms and conditions of the wholesaler's brochure, and point out the key portions.

4. Point out to the client any entry requirements, including the need for a valid passport, visa, inoculation, or other health requirements, and any social customs that might be relevant. For example, a traveller may be counselled as to what may be considered inappropriate clothing in certain countries; or a traveller may be warned of harsh penalties for drug use in specific areas.

5. Warn the client if their travel destination is considered to be a health risk. For example, you may advise a first-time traveller to a third-world country of the possibility of "Montezuma's revenge"; or you may inform a client that specific areas are currently known for disease or epidemics.

6. You must fully inform the client about air travel arrangements made, including exact departure date and times, airports, check-in times, pre-flight confirmation of departure requirements, and the names of all carriers. A detailed itinerary should be provided.

7. Give the client a fully detailed breakdown of all the costs to be incurred (including all taxes, service charges, other fees, and cancellation charges) as well as the deposit and final payment requirements. A detailed invoice should be provided.

8. Advise the client about the nature of the accommodation (the standard it meets, where it is located, and where the particular room will be located on the property, if known). If the property is under construction, fully inform the client, before booking, about what problems may be faced (dirt, noise, unsightliness) and which facilities will not be available.

9. When booking a cruise, inform the client about the name of the cruise line and the ship, the type of accommodation selected, what is included in the price, what country the ship is registered with, the gross tonnage, and the ports of call offered.

10. When a car is being rented, inform the client about the name of the rental company, the type and size of car chosen, whether fuel is included, and what costs are extra.

11. Advise the client about anticipated climatic conditions (for example, if the client wishes to travel during a time when there is a risk of hurricanes or during the rainy season).

12. Advise the client what currency is used when quoting fares (a U.S. tour operator, for example, will probably quote in U.S. dollars; a U.K. car rental cost will probably be quoted in English pounds or in Euros). The conversion can have a substantial impact on the final price payable; indicate the quoted currency on all receipts and invoices.

13. Advise the client of the right to cancel when there is an increase in cost of 7% or more between the time of booking and the time allowed for cancellation by the wholesaler.

14. Advise the client about the need for travel insurance, and indicate the comparative coverage and restrictions in the plans you offer the client. Obtain a signed waiver of insurance from each passenger who refuses insurance, and supply the passenger with a copy of the form.

Some Responsibilities of the Travel Agent

- Avoid exaggeration, misrepresentation, or puffery.
- Caution the client against reliance on pictures or sketches in a brochure (they may give a distorted view of reality). This also helps avoid the risk of being successfully sued for misrepresentation.
- Ensure that any specific requests, or special needs, of the client have been adequately addressed (special meal requests, nonsmoking rooms, etc.).
- Check all tickets, vouchers, and travel documents carefully to ensure accuracy before issuing them to a client.
- Ensure that cancellation insurance was offered (or that a signed waiver was obtained from the client).
- Ask the client to request in writing anything that is unusual and could be questioned later.
- If a client travels despite any risks that you have explained, (for example, travel to a dangerous locale), confirm your advice to the client in writing.
- Ensure that all necessary travel documentation is in place (client's passport is valid and other materials have been obtained: travel cards or visas, consent letters for travel by unaccompanied children, certificates of vaccination, etc.).

TRAVEL AGENCY INVOICE REQUIREMENTS

Upon selling travel services a travel agency must promptly provide the customer with a statement, invoice, or receipt setting out the following information:

1. Name and address of customer who purchased the travel services;

2. Date of the booking and date of the first payment;

3. Amount of payment, any balance owing, and the date when the balance should be paid;

4. Any taxes, fees, and service charges;

5. The business name, registration number, address, and phone number of the travel agent;

6. Brief description of travel services contracted, including destination, dates of travel, and supplier;

7. If known, name of any person or business involved in providing travel services to the client;

8. Confirmation of whether the customer wishes to purchase travel insurance;

9. Serial number of the receipt, invoice, or statement.

Sample Invoice

ASTOR TRAVEL SERVICES
1240 Bay Street, Suite 302
Toronto, Ontario M5R 2A7 CANADA

Invoice No.:	00123
Booking Date:	Oct. 18/99
Invoice Date:	Dec. 1/99
Agent:	Valerie
Terms:	Upon receipt

To: Mr. Chaud Chien
     123 Main Street
     Maintown, Province
     M4B 1A3

DESCRIPTION OF SERVICES

Air only (Regent Holidays) to Amsterdam				
Dates: August 6 to September 4				
Fare:	$759.00	× 3	=	$2,277.00
Dutch tax	22.00	× 3	=	66.00
Accommodation (Red Seal Tours)				
Hotel Terminus, Amsterdam, triple with bath				
August 7 to 8, 1 night	66.00	× 3	=	198.00
September 3 to 4, 1 night	66.00	× 3	=	198.00
Cruise Dutch Lowlands (Canadian Holidays)				
Triple/standard accommodation	765.00	× 2	=	1,530.00
August 8 to 12	573.75	× 2	=	573.75
Accommodation (Holiday House)				
Hotel Hofstetter, Munich, triple with bath				
August 18 to 21, 3 nights	75.00	× 3	=	225.00
Flexipass (Rail Europe)				
14 days travel in 1 month	714.00	× 3	=	2,142.00
"Majestic Europe" (Globus/Gateway Tours)				
August 21 to 30, 9 days	1,057.50	× 3	=	3,172.50
Voyageur Deluxe package insurance				
Policy S-1102370E	183.00	× 3	=	549.00
Total booking				10,931.25
Less deposit (paid October 18, 1999, by cheque)				3,741.25
Total due by June 5				$14,672.50 CAD

Reg. No. 5202542

ADVERTISING REQUIREMENTS

1. You must ensure that any advertising with respect to travel services is not false, misleading, or deceptive.

2. Any advertisement must include the registered name, address, and registration number of the registrant.

3. An advertisement for the sale of travel must not include a residential address or telephone number.

4. If the advertisement refers to the price of travel services, the price must include all fees, service charges, and taxes. The ad must state that the price includes GST and transportation taxes or that the price does not include those items.

5. The price will be noted in Canadian funds unless otherwise stated.

THE LITIGATION PROCESS

Even when you have done everything possible to avoid lawsuits, an unhappy client is probably a fact of life at some time or other.

Once you have tried everything possible to satisfy any reasonable request (including requesting price adjustments, refunds, or substituted travel vouchers from the wholesaler), your next step will be to obtain legal counsel. It is best to get your lawyer involved in the early stages of settling a dispute. Choose a lawyer who has had experience appropriate to the situation at hand. Perhaps, at that stage, the matter can be resolved with the legal advice obtained and without going to court. Consider your lawyer as a means of *avoiding* lawsuits, not simply defending them. (This is especially important if you or your agency, and not the wholesaler, caused the dispute.)

A client may have grounds to sue if there has been misrepresentation (whether innocent, fraudulent, or negligent) or if needed information was not provided to the client. Normally, but not always, legal actions will be based on a contract and the person will seek damages (but not necessarily just the return of monies paid by the client!) for breaching the contract. Damages may be awarded by a judge if the loss was reasonably foreseeable and if it was a direct result of the breach, provided it is within the monetary jurisdiction of the court selected. It is also possible for someone travelling for pleasure to recover damages for the loss of enjoyment.

The aggrieved client has the right to take legal action against any relevant party (this could include the tour operator, hotel, airline, government bodies, travel agency, and the travel counsellor, among others). However, travel agents will generally not be liable personally since they are acting as agents and not principals of their agency, assuming that the counsellor acted within the approved scope of authority. The other side of the coin is that the agency, because of its principal/agent relationship, may also be liable for something that you as an agent have said or not said to the client.

Even in the absence of a contract, the client who has incurred damage may still have the right to recover damages based on a negligent misstatement. For example, the client may nonetheless try to sue you or your agency if you recklessly provide information that later proves to be inaccurate and, relying on that information, the client used a different agent to book the trip. You may still be liable. In some cases, if there has been a breach of the Canadian Criminal Code you may even be criminally liable and, if found guilty, punished with a fine, jail, or both (in cases of criminal fraud, for example).

The best way to avoid legal problems is to be truthful and accurate and to inform the client about all relevant information. Obtain the client's approval in writing (including the client's signature) for any special details or foreseeable difficulties.

What to Do When a Problem Arises

After receiving notice of a problem, ask the client to put it in writing so that you have the facts straight before consulting a lawyer. The next step is to provide a timely written response, based on the legal advice.

Upon receipt of the Court Claim (or Statement of Claim), provide a copy to your lawyer immediately, in order to either settle the claim or to file a timely defence. There is limited time available to prepare and file with the Court a Defence (or Statement of Defence). Any out-of-court settlement with your client will need to be provided in writing, and a written release of further liability must be obtained from the client. This should not be negotiated without a lawyer.

After the Defence has been filed and served, and after any pre-trial motions, a disclosure process called Discovery will begin. At that point, you may be called as a witness and asked to give sworn testimony before a court-designated official (called a Special Examiner). You may then be cross-examined on this initial testimony at the trial, which may occur much later. It is therefore important, for consistency, that your records be as complete and accurate as possible, and that you remember the facts clearly. It is very important that your testimony at Discovery and during the trial are consistent.

During the trial, both sides will be entitled to examine and cross-examine the witnesses, and to introduce evidence. After a closing statement by each party, a decision will be made by the judge, based on the facts as presented and the law. Trial decisions are generally appealable to a higher level of court.

CONSUMER PROTECTION

Like any other businesses, travel suppliers must operate under the rules of the marketplace. Some businesses will survive and others will fail—our free market system inevitably produces business casualties. Travel businesses may fail for all types of reasons, some internal (poor organization, inadequate service, overpricing, failure to carve out a market niche, etc.), and others external (economic recession, changing tastes and attitudes, government or political interference, etc).

However, the government is beginning to recognize that it must play a role in the travel marketplace, in order to protect consumers when a travel business closes. A travel business failure means, at best, a lot of unhappy customers who risk losing their vacations and, at worst, passengers stranded in some far, out-of-the-way location with no means of returning home or of paying for an extended stay.

In Ontario, to ensure consumer protection, travel agencies must adhere to the following guidelines. Travel agencies must

- Obtain a certificate of registration from the Travel Industry Council of Ontario to operate (which is revocable for failure to comply with legislative requirements);
- Keep detailed records of financial transactions;
- File a bond of $5,000;
- Maintain a trust account for all funds received from the public for travel services to be supplied; and
- File annual financial statements along with an auditor's report.

Each travel agency is required to register in Ontario and to contribute to a compensation fund. Compensation fund payments are made half-yearly, starting with an initial payment of $2,000, and thereafter $3 for every $10,000 of sales volume, including commissions, generated during the previous half year.

The compensation fund is available to pay for claims made by travellers with losses who have first sought compensation directly from the travel suppliers, but who have either been refused or told the supplier is unable to pay. In order to qualify for payment from the fund, the following requirements must be met:

1. The client who has paid for travel services is entitled to compensation to the extent that the service was not provided as required, either due to refusal by the supplier to reimburse a client or due to the bankruptcy or insolvency of the supplier. However, no compensation will be paid to a client who received "travel services or alternative travel services" and is claiming compensation for the "cost, value, or quality" of the service rather than for the failure to provide the service.

2. The client is not entitled to compensation if advised before paying that the money was for either a nonrefundable deposit or a reasonable service charge.

3. The compensation fund must first determine the eligibility and amount of any claim for compensation before directing payment of any claim. While the decision is final, a hearing must be held where it asserts that any part of a compensation claim is not eligible for payment. No client has an absolute right to payment of a claim.

4. The client must provide notice of the claim within six months of the supplier's refusal or failure to pay.

The maximum total amount of claims for compensation as a result of the refusal or inability to pay by a supplier, is $1,500,000. If the total of claims against the supplier exceeds that amount, the various claims are proportionately reduced.

Provision is made for a traveller preparing for imminent departure from Canada where immediate funds are needed to alleviate suffering or inconvenience. Compensation up to $3,500 per client is available.

Finally, provision is also made for immediate payment of funds to a client who is stranded. Payment can be made for travel and any necessary accommodation, to alleviate suffering or inconvenience.

Similarly, in British Columbia, client monies received by a travel agent are deemed to be trust funds and a compensation fund, called the Travel Assurance Fund, was created. Each retail travel agency or travel wholesaler must contribute. The fund is available to compensate persons for direct economic loss due to insolvency or bankruptcy of an agent or wholesaler; for a client's failure to collect money that a court has ordered an agent or wholesaler to pay, provided that the client has already tried to collect the money unsuccessfully; and under other prescribed circumstances. Application for compensation must be made to the Registrar of Travel Services within one year after the loss occurred.

Emergency payments may also be authorized for stranded clients or for clients who did not get adequate advance notice of the inability or refusal to supply a travel service for which payment was made (or, arrangements may be made to supply alternate service, and paid for by the fund). There is also a requirement in B.C. that each travel agency file annual financial statements with the Registrar.

EXERCISES — *Legal Responsibilities*

1. Should I make it clear to the client exactly which supplier is providing hotel accommodation? Why or why not?

    _____

    _____

2. Can I be liable for not offering insurance to my clients?

    _____

    _____

3. If a supplier or a travel agency fails to complete a booking or to complete it correctly, the only penalty is loss of commission. True or false?

    _____

4. If your answer to number 3 was "false," what other penalty could be faced by the supplier or agency?

    _____

    _____

5. If an agency implies it has agreed to do something without specifically saying so, can it still be liable?

    _____

    _____

6. Can a travel counsellor find protection from all potential liabilities in the small print of a brochure or on a booking form?

    _____

    _____

7. Can an agency be found liable for a client who takes the agency's advice (which turns out to be inaccurate) but does not actually book with that agency?

    _____

    _____

8. Is it true that when a claim is verified, the travel counsellor, rather than the travel agency, is usually found liable?

    _____

    _____

9. How can the travel agent best avoid legal complications?

    _____

    _____

10. If you make a booking with ABC Tours in the United States directly, what advice may you want to give to your client?

    _____

    _____

11. If you have made a booking with an Ontario tour operator and it goes out of business, would your client lose all of the money he or she paid?

    _____

    _____

A LEGAL PERSPECTIVE

Tour Operators Are Not to Blame In These Cases

by Paul Unterberg

This column often cites cases where agents or operators are taken to court by irate consumers and found guilty of some infraction of the law. Not this week.

Chantal Pouliot does not have fond memories of the Dominican Republic. She bought from retailer Thomas Cook a Royal Vacances package to the popular Caribbean island and stayed in the Riviera Beach Hotel at Barahona.

Pouliot herself chose this destination. It was not suggested by either Thomas Cook or tour operator Royal Vacances. Upon returning from her vacation, Pouliot felt ill and went to the hospital where it was discovered she had contracted malaria during her vacation.

Because the plaintiff's long recovery period caused her to be absent from work for some time, she lost a lot of salary. Pouliot sued the retailer and the tour operator, claiming the tour operator should have told her the hotel was in a high-risk zone. The tour operator replied it had never been told by either the Canadian or Dominican government that malaria existed in that particular zone.

The Honourable Mr. Justice Jean-Louis Lamoureaux stated that based on the evidence one could not conclude the defendants were liable in this matter (in their testimony, the defendants noted it was Pouliot who

---

Can't guarantee that travellers won't get sick

---

chose the destination, and that she didn't inquire as to the necessity of protecting herself against any particular disease).

The court ruled that neither a travel agent nor a tour operator can guarantee that travellers will not get sick and that there was no evidence the Dominican Republic was a high-risk zone for malaria. The case was dismissed.

Noisy Neighbours

David Cameron and Jacques Desrosiers bought from Tourbec an Air Transit package to Cancun, Mexico, at the end of February 1995. On their return they complained that because they travelled to Cancun during the American spring break, the hotel and beaches were overrun with noisy students, most of them drunk (and apparently requiring no sleep!).

The Honourable Mr. Justice Gilles Trudel stated that the tour operator could not know there would be raucous American students in Cancun during that particular spring break. He also noted that the tour operator had no control over the hotel rooms reserved by other operators.

The judge acknowledged that the plaintiffs had suffered major inconvenience, but ruled it was not the fault of Transat or Tourbec. Again, case dismissed.

Canadian Travel Press, July 1996

Reprinted courtesy of Canadian Travel Press

PERSPECTIVE

When Is A Tour Operator Liable?

by Paul Unterberg

Sylvain and Celine St.-Pierre had been to the Hotel Decameron in Juan Dolio in the Dominican Republic in 1993. They didn't like their stay at all because the water wasn't clear and there were many sea urchins. However, during that trip, many people said how nice it was at the Boca Chica resort.

The next year, in September, they reserved at the Boca Chica resort and in November paid the full amount of their stay. When they arrived in January, the Royal Vacances representative told them

---

'That was exactly the place they wanted to avoid'

---

the Boca Chica resort was overbooked and sent them to the Hotel Decameron in Juan Dolio. That was exactly the place they wanted to avoid. Their room was tiny. The cupboards were too small and it was of dubious cleanliness. Celine didn't go swimming at all.

The Honourable Mr. Justice Gilles Trudel stated that if the plaintiffs had known they were going to Juan Dolio they never would have booked the trip. He ordered tour operator Royal Vacances to pay $500 in damages to each of the plaintiffs. Since the retailer, Boislard-Poirier, had not committed any fault, he was exonerated of all blame.

"All Inclusive" Includes Tips

Antonio Da Costa and his father bought from a local tour operator a package advertised as "all inclusive." In the tour operator's publicity it was specified that it included barbecues, Mexican Fiestas, Caribbean evenings, other evening activities, etc. Everything was supposed to be included. When the Da Costas arrived at the hotel, however, they were required to pay $20 each for "tips."

The Honourable Mr. Justice Jean-Louis Lamoureux stated that since this was supposed to be an all inclusive package and since no exceptions had been specified, it was the tour operator's duty to pay the tips. Therefore, he ordered the operator to reimburse each of the passengers $20.

Holy Week In Hell

The Gauthier family bought from retailer Travelaide a Mirabelle Tours package to the Dominican Republic. The week reserved was from April 4 to 11 at the Boca Chica Hotel in Santo Domingo. Everything was supposed to be included, meaning water sports, horseback riding, bicycles, an excursion to another island, lounge chairs on the beach and a whole series of activities and services.

Although they were supposed to leave at 3 p.m., they didn't leave until 2.40 a.m. They arrived at the hotel at 8 a.m., but were told their room was not yet available. Although there were five of them, they finally got one room at 6 p.m. and didn't get another until the next day. Even then, they didn't get the second room until 6 p.m. Obviously during that time, they weren't able to go to the beach, etc.

The next morning, the Mirabelle representative informed them that they had come during the worst possible week. All the local population has a big holiday during Holy Week and the beach is packed with cars, Red Cross tents and soldiers. The representative told the tourists it would be better not to go to the beach, but to stay in the hotel. The open areas of the hotel were barricaded.

Since no one could go to the beach, the swimming pool's water soon became murky.

The same day a note was delivered to their rooms saying that the Dominican Republic Minister of Tourism had prohibited the use of jet skis and other water vehicles during Holy Week. The government decree also ordered that all discos be closed on Good Friday. For the same reason, they were not able to take the excursion to the private island because there were too many people there already.

In his decision, the Honourable Mr. Justice Pierre Verdy stated that it was the tour operator's responsibility to tell the clients that Holy Week was a very special time and it was part of the defendant's duty (both Travelaide as a retail agent and the tour operator) to warn travellers of the particular situation during that week and of the major inconveniences which they would suffer. Their failure to do so rendered them liable in damages to the passengers.

He ordered them to reimburse approximately half the cost of the package.

Study Points to Mistakes

Norway's travel operators apparently have been spending "vast amounts" of money on offering the wrong products in the wrong markets, a Norwegian Tourist Board (NORTRA) study has determined.

"The study reveals that the French market is the one that is willing to pay most for a holiday in Norway," according to a summary report.

"Second on the list is Great Britain. Both these countries are growth markets for the Norwegian tourist trade while Germany—long held to be the major market for tourism—is not. Travel operators have so far channeled most of their marketing resources into enticing Germans to Norway."

The source of the information is a German firm, IPK International, which has looked also at market potential in Sweden, Denmark and the Netherlands.

"Its results indicate that the tourism industry has been backing the wrong horse," the summary says.

"Foreign tourists want round trips, a sector given low priority so far. They also want fjord and action holidays. Recreational holidays, organized bus tours and farm holidays are definitely out."

NORTRA Marketing Director Terje Raanas acknowledges the need to "restructure our marketing programs" suggesting that his organization will rely more on market-based information rather than signals from Norwegian operators.

Reprinted courtesy of Canadian Travel Press

15

Travel Documents and Other Travel Requirements

Each traveller crossing an international border is required to carry proper documentation, which will depend on the person's citizenship, country of residence, countries through which the client will pass, and the country of destination.

Failure to check the documents a passenger needs for a particular trip could mean refusal to admit him or her into the desired destination, or even a refusal to allow the client to board the plane at the outset of the journey.

It is the responsibility of travel agents to advise their clients of the required documentation.

PASSPORTS

A *passport* is an official document issued by the properly appointed public officials of a country to its citizens, in order for its citizens to leave and return to the country of their citizenship. Each country that issues passports will have its own requirements. A Canadian passport, for example, is issued for five years and is nonrenewable (when it expires, the citizen must apply for a new passport). A U.S. passport is issued for ten years and is also nonrenewable.

A Canadian passport can be obtained by mail from the Canadian Passport Office in Ottawa or in person at any of the regional offices. There are two types of applications, *Form A* for Canadian citizens over 16 years of age, and *Form B* for Canadian citizens under 16 who will be travelling without a parent accompanying them (otherwise, children under 16 will travel on the accompanying parent's passport).

A letter of consent from the nontravelling parent may be required when only one parent is accompanying the child, in order to avoid the possibility of a child abduction by either parent. Check carefully in advance for the exact requirements if only one parent will be travelling with the child; without the proper documentation, a client may be refused permission to leave the country with a child under 16 years of age.

Besides the adult and child passports, a third type of passport available is a *business passport*, which provides double the number of pages, at an increased fee, for frequent travellers.

Application forms for Canadian passports contain detailed instructions about their completion and application fees. Applications must be completed in ink, not pencil, and must be signed by the applicant.

The following items must accompany the completed application form:

1. Correct application fee (payable in cash, if applying in person, or by certified cheque, bank draft, or money order, if applying by mail).

2. Two identical passport photographs (of a size and type permitted), each signed by the applicant on the front and by a guarantor on the back.

3. A fully completed guarantor's form, provided in the application package. An approved list is included of the types of occupations that are allowed for persons to serve as guarantors; the guarantor must be a Canadian citizen and must have known the applicant for at least two years prior to submission of the passport application.

4. Original proof of citizenship of the applicant (for example, a birth certificate or a certificate of citizenship).

Replacement passports can be issued in the event of theft or loss. When travelling outside Canada, replacement passports can be obtained through the Canadian embassy, consulate. or high commission (as appropriate).

On the following pages, you will find extracted material from the Canadian Passport Office, with some commonly asked questions and answers.

VISAS AND TOURIST CARDS

A *visa* is a permit issued to enter and leave a country other than a person's country of citizenship. Usually, the only visa needed is the stamped entry in the passenger's passport, on arrival. However, in certain places, separate visas are required and must be paid for prior to arrival.

Visas are usually issued depending on the purpose of the travel, and include a *tourist visa*, issued to a person just visiting the country (no business activity can be undertaken) and a *business visa*, which allows a traveller to engage in business within the country.

A third type of visa required by certain countries is a *transit visa*, which permits travel through a country in order to get to a destination in another country. This visa is generally not necessary when the passenger is merely changing planes in a country—known as *TWOV* or *transit without visa*.

A fourth type of visa is a *tourist card*, similar to but distinct from a tourist visa. For example, a tourist card is required when visiting Mexico; it is available from Mexican government tourist offices, consulates, embassies, and servicing airlines. The Tourist Card is presented to immigration authorities when arriving at the airport in Mexico.

Some visa applications will require passport-style photographs and a fee. A list of current visa and entry requirements for each country can be found in the *Travel Information Manual* (*TIM*) published by the International Air Transport Association.

You
Asked Us!

Toronto
Suite 300
74 Victoria Street
Office Hours: 08:00–17:00

North York
Suite 380, 3rd floor
Joseph Shepard Bldg.
4900 Yonge Street
Office Hours: 08:00–17:00

Scarborough
Suite 828
200 Town Centre Court
Office Hours: 08:45–16:30

Hamilton
Suite 330
Standard Life Building
120 King Street West
Office Hours: 08:45–16:30

London
Suite 201
2nd floor
400 York Street
Office Hours: 08:45–16:30

Windsor
Suite 1010
Bank of Commerce Building
100 Ouellette Avenue
Office Hours 08:45–16:30

Thunder Bay
Suite 302
Royal Insurance Building
28 Cumberland St. North
Office Hours: 08:45–16:30

Brampton
Suite 305
Brampton Civic Centre
150 Central Park Drive
Office Hourse: 08:45–16:30

St. Catharines
6th Floor
43 Church Street
Office Hours: 08:45–16:30

Kitchener
Suite 630
The Galleria
101 Frederick Street
Office Hours: 08:45–16:30

WHO can obtain a Canadian passport?
Anyone who is a Canadian citizen.

WHERE can I get an application?
At passport offices, post offices, travel agencies and Government of Canada InfoCentres. **Form A** is for adults. **Form B** is for children under the age of 16. **Form B-1** is used to add a child to a parent's valid passport and is available only at passport offices.

PLEASE READ AND FOLLOW THE APPLICATION INSTRUCTIONS THOROUGHLY AND CAREFULLY.

WHICH countries require Canadian passports when I am travelling abroad?
MOST countries outside of North America require a passport for you to obtain entry. If you are uncertain, check with your travel agent or contact the Embassy, Consulate or High Commission for the countries you are planning to visit.

WHAT is the fee for a Canadian passport?
The current fee for a 24-page passport (ADULT or CHILD), is $60.00, payable when you apply by: cash, certified cheque or money order. Make cheques payable to: Receiver General for Canada. A 48-page passport is also available for a fee of $62.00.

HOW long does it take to process a passport?
Normal processing time for ALL in-person services is 5 working days.

IS there a "fast" passport service offered by the Passport Office?
No. However, in verifiable cases of travel emergency, staff at passport offices will make every effort to provide a passport to the traveller. In such cases, APPLICANTS MUST APPLY IN PERSON AT THE NEAREST PASSPORT OFFICE.

Airline tickets (a photocopy is acceptable) will be required upon application.

WHERE can I apply?
You are encouraged to APPLY IN PERSON (or have a member of your immediate family who resides at the same residence submit your application for you) during scheduled hours of service. In the Ontario Region you may apply at one of the locations listed in this brochure. For other passport office locations in Canada call 1-800-567-6868.

CAN a third party PICK UP my passport on my behalf?
YES! You can authorize your travel agent or another person to pick up your passport for you by providing their name and your signature on your passport pick up slip which was given to you when you applied in person. The person picking up the passport must present valid identification.

WHAT is the procedure when I apply in person?

Our larger offices have a convenient "Take-A-Number" system. Waiting times may vary at each office. Lunch hours are often a peak period.

CAN I apply by mail?

Yes. Mail-in service is available for persons who may find it difficult to appear in person at a passport office in or near their community. Mail applications to PASSPORT OFFICE, Ottawa, Canada K1A 0G3.

DO I have to show proof of Canadian citizenship and other identification?

YES. Your original documentary evidence of Canadian citizenship is required when you apply, as indicated on the application.

PHOTOCOPIES of citizenship documents are NOT ACCEPTED. When applying in person, be prepared to submit an extra piece of valid signed identification, such as a valid driver's license or credit card.

HOW do I obtain passports for my children?

1. Children under the age of 16 may have their OWN passport. Application Form B is required. For the protection of the child, both parents' signatures are required on the application.

   Two photographs and proof of Canadian citizenship are required, as indicated on the application.

2. Another option is to include your child's name in ONE parent's valid passport. The child (under the age of 16) must travel with that parent. A Form B-1 is required. It is available at passport offices only. Both parents' signatures are required on the B-1 application form.

   Photographs are NOT required for children being included in a parent's passport. Proof of Canadian citizenship and the valid passport to which the child is being added must be submitted.

PLEASE NOTE: Problems regarding UNAVAILABILITY of a parent's signature should be addressed directly to the Passport Office where you are applying.

WHAT is required if the custody of my children is subject to separation or divorce?

You are required to show ALL legal documents related to mobility of or access to the children.

WHERE can I get travel advisory information about safety when visiting other countries?

Consular Services provide emergency travel information only on a 24-hour basis. Call 1-800-267-6788.

You Asked Us!

HEALTH REGULATIONS

Vaccinations may be needed for certain diseases when travelling to specific infected areas. A record of travel vaccinations is kept in an *International Certificates of Vaccination* booklet, which the passenger needs to present when arriving at immigration if travelling to those specific locations of concern. For certain diseases for which there is no preventative vaccine (for example, malaria), it may be necessary to obtain a prescription for medication.

The diseases for which current vaccinations are most often required are as follows:

Smallpox—one injection, valid for three years beginning eight days after vaccination.

Yellow fever—one injection, valid for ten years beginning ten days after vaccination.

Cholera—two injections one week apart, valid for six months beginning six days after vaccination.

The various health requirements of a particular country can be verified by checking the current *Travel Information Manual*, referred to elsewhere in this chapter.

DEPARTURE TAXES

Each country may have its own departure (or arrival) taxes. In some countries (for example, France) the tax varies depending on the airport and on whether the departure is international or domestic.

In the United States a tax, called a *local facilities charge*, is imposed by the individual airports directly to cover costs of the airport's operations. There is a similar tax at some Canadian airports (such as Vancouver).

CUSTOMS RESTRICTIONS

Customs refers to the regulation by a government over the importation of goods into that country. Usually an arriving traveller is permitted to bring in personal belongings (clothing and the like) accompanying the traveller exempt from any duty or taxes. However, a country may charge its own residents for items purchased out of that country that fall outside any approved exemptions.

Restrictions may also apply on other goods, regardless of where the traveller lives. Usually there are strict limits on the amounts of alcohol and tobacco products that can be imported without duty; and pornographic items, firearms, and explosives may be prohibited altogether.

Rates of duty on other items, for which no exemption can be claimed, will depend on the type of good and the value. Valuable items taken with the passenger when travelling (for example, jewellery or cameras) should be pre-registered with customs before departure in order to avoid problems when returning.

There may also be specific restrictions on plants or animals, or possibly an outright prohibition on their importation (in order to prevent introduced foreign pests and diseases).

Canadian customs grants the following personal exemptions:

Personal Exemptions for Residents of Canada

Residents, temporary residents, and former residents of Canada returning to live in Canada may claim goods free of duties under one of the following exemptions:

Exemption Amount (Limit)	Minimum Absence from Canada
$750	7 days
$200	48 hours
$50	24 hours

- You may claim only one of the above exemptions on one trip, and you cannot combine your exemption with other travellers.
- You cannot claim the $50 exemption if the total value of all goods you are importing is more than $50. Alcohol and tobacco products are not eligible under the $50 category.
- You may include alcohol and tobacco products only in your $200 or $750 exemptions (see limits below) if these goods accompany you when you arrive in Canada.
- You may include unaccompanied goods, excluding alcoholic beverages and tobacco products, only in your $750 exemption.
- You may import goods not eligible for a personal exemption (which are not prohibited, restricted, or controlled), but you must pay any duties, provincial fees, and taxes that apply.

Personal Exemptions for Visitors to Canada

If you are a visitor to Canada, you may bring in the following items free of duties:
- Durable personal effects you need for the visit, as long as you will not be leaving any articles in Canada (alcohol and tobacco products are also allowed—see limits below);
- Gifts to residents of Canada for their personal use, not exceeding $60 per gift (gifts cannot include alcoholic beverages, tobacco products, or advertising matter).

Alcoholic Beverages and Tobacco Products: Quantities and Age Limits

1.14 litres (40 oz.) of liquor, 1.5 litres of wine, or 24 × 355 ml (12 oz.) bottles or cans of beer or ale (8.5 litres)—You must be 18 years of age or older to import alcoholic beverages into the provinces of Alberta, Manitoba, and Quebec. You must be 19 years or older to import alcoholic beverages into all other provinces.

200 cigarettes, 50 cigars or cigarillos, 400 grams of manufactured tobacco, 200 tobacco sticks, and 200 grams of manufactured tobacco—You must be 18 years of age or older to import tobacco products into the provinces of Prince Edward Island, Quebec, Manitoba, Saskatchewan, Alberta, the Yukon Territory, and the Northwest Territories. You must be 19 years or older to import tobacco products into all other provinces.

Restricted or Controlled Goods

Goods such as firearms, other weapons, drugs, and articles made or derived from endangered species may be restricted or controlled, or may require a special admission permit. If you are bringing in such goods, tell the customs officer during your personal interview.

You must declare all goods that you are bringing in or having shipped to Canada, that you purchased, received as gifts, or acquired in any manner while outside Canada, including goods purchased at duty-free shops, whether or not you claim them as part of your exemption. A customs officer may examine your goods.

Revenue Canada may seize any goods you do not declare, or any goods you falsely declare. You may also face prosecution.

The various exemptions cannot be combined on one trip. Also, there is a special flat rate of duty on the first $300 of dutiable goods, equal to 20%. Finally, there may be certain classes of goods that will either be non-dutiable or have reduced rates. The North American Free Trade Agreement and the rules of the European Economic Community have both served to reduce import duties within their respective areas of operation.

CURRENCY RESTRICTIONS

Currency restrictions may apply in the importation or exportation of a particular country's currency. For example, Kenya does not allow the exportation of any of its currency. It may also be necessary to make a declaration to customs if leaving with more than a specific amount of a country's currency (for example, the U.S. has this requirement).

TRAVEL INFORMATION MANUAL (TIM)

One of the best available sources of information on travel documents required by individual countries is the *Travel Information Manual* (*TIM*), published monthly by IATA. The *TIM* is generally also available on most airline computer systems. The manual will give current information on items such as passports, visas, health, and departure taxes. Check the excerpts from the *TIM* on pages 213 to 220 and answer the following questions:

1. A couple are planning a two-week stay in San Jose, Costa Rica. One person holds a Canadian passport, while the other holds a British passport.

    a. What documentation (passports/visas) do the passengers need for this trip?

    b. What are the health regulations/restrictions, if any, for entering Costa Rica?

    c. Assuming that departure is from Vancouver, B.C., will the passengers have to pay any airport taxes to or from Costa Rica?

    d. One passenger might be interested in taking her dog on the vacation. Give some advice on the procedure required.

e. Provide brief details of items the travellers are allowed to bring with them into Costa Rica?

_____

_____

f. Provide a basic description of the kinds of people who might be refused admission into Costa Rica.

_____

_____

2. In your own words, what is a tourist card?

_____

_____

3. Do the passengers below need visas to enter the following countries?

a. Canadian passport holder travelling to Costa Rica for two months

_____

b. British passport holder travelling to Costa Rica for two months

_____

c. Canadian passport holder travelling to Saudi Arabia for two weeks

_____

d. Canadian passport holder travelling to Israel for four weeks

_____

e. Thai passport holder travelling to Israel for thirty days

_____

4. What important admission-related restrictions do you think you might mention to the following passengers?

a. Traveller to Israel

_____

_____

_____

b. Traveller to India

_____

_____

_____

c. Traveller to Saudi Arabia

_____

_____

_____

Passport	Bureau des
Office	passeports

File No.

PASSPORT APPLICATION FORM A
(APPLICANTS AGE 16 AND OVER)

PROTECTED INFORMATION WHEN COMPLETED

1. NAME
NAME TO APPEAR IN PASSPORT

Surname

First Name

Middle Name(s) (optional)

FORMER SURNAME(S)

Surname at Birth

Former Name (if changed)

Date of departure, if known

2. PERSONAL INFORMATION

Date of Birth
Year   Month   Day

Place of Birth
City   Province   Country

Sex   Male   Female

Marital Status
Single   Married   Widowed   Divorced   Separated

Hair Colour   Eye Colour   Height   Weight   Occupation

Permanent Address
No.   Street   Apt.   City   Province   Postal Code

Telephone
Area Code   Home   Area Code   Business   Extension

Mailing Address
No.   Street   Apt.   City   Province   Postal Code

3. PREVIOUS CANADIAN PASSPORTS — In the last 5 years has a Canadian passport, certificate of identity or refugee travel document been issued to you?

Write yes or no

IF YES, indicate   Number   Date of Issue   and include it with your application.

If it has been lost, contact the Passport Office to obtain form PPT 203 that must be completed.

4. YOUR CHILDREN UNDER 16 — Complete only if you want their names in your passport. If the space is inadequate, attach a separate sheet. Photographs of children listed are not required. Evidence of citizenship for each child must be submitted.

Surname	First Name	Date of Birth Year	Month	Day	Place of Birth City	Country	Sex

A) Permanent address of children
No.   Street   Apt.   City   Province   Postal Code

B) Do the names of the children now appear in any valid Canadian passport, certificate of identity or refugee travel document?
Write yes or no
IF YES, include it with this application. If lost, complete and submit form PPT 203.

C) Has the custody of the children been the subject of a separation agreement or court order?
Write yes or no
IF YES, include all legal documents referring to custody of, mobility of or access to the children.

D) Is the other parent aware of this application?
Write yes or no
Provide details and signature of the other parent below.

Name

Telephone
Area Code   Home

Address
No.   Street   Apt.

Area Code   Business   Extension

City   Province   Postal Code

Signature of Other Parent

If the signature is missing, explain:

FOR OFFICIAL USE ONLY — SEE OVER

	In	Seen	Out
Birth	☐	☐	☐
Citizenship	☐	☐	☐
Naturalization	☐	☐	☐
Birth Abroad	☐	☐	☐
Passport	☐	☐	☐
Marriage	☐	☐	☐
Separation	☐	☐	☐
Divorce	☐	☐	☐
Change of Name	☐	☐	☐
Adoption	☐	☐	☐
Other (specify)	☐	☐	☐

Submitted by:

Examined   Signature

Guarantor check   Name

Written   Identification

Received by:

Inspection   Signature

Finishing   Name

Final inspection   Date

Docs. received   Identification

Canada

An agency of the Department of Foreign Affairs and International Trade
Un organisme du ministère des Affaires étrangères et du Commerce international

PPT 044 (96-12)

5. CITIZENSHIP – You must provide one of the documents below (an original only – photocopies or notarized photocopies are not acceptable):

	If you were **born in Canada**		If you were **born outside Canada**

☐ certificate of birth in Canada, or

_____   _____
Registration Number   Date of Issue

☐ record of birth in Quebec, or

_____   _____
Issued by   Date of Issue

☐ certificate of Canadian citizenship.

_____   _____
Certificate Number   Date of Issue

☐ certificate of Canadian citizenship, or

☐ certificate of naturalization, or

☐ certificate of retention of citizenship, or

☐ certificate of registration of birth abroad.

_____   _____
Certificate Number   Date of Issue

A) Was a certificate of Canadian citizenship issued to you after February 14, 1977?

Yes ☐ ▶ Go to question 6.

No ☐   ▶ Complete B and C.

B) Are you now or have you ever been a citizen of a country other than Canada?

Write yes or no ____ ▶ IF YES, indicate ☐ by birth   ☐ by naturalization

Country _____   Effective Date _____

C) Did you reside outside Canada for periods of more than 3 months before February 15, 1977?

Write yes or no ____ ▶ IF YES, give dates. If naturalized in Canada, indicate absences after you were naturalized.

From	To	From	To

6. MARRIAGE DATA — If the space is inadequate, attach a separate sheet.

Date of Marriage	Spouse's Name in Full	Spouse's Date of Birth	Spouse's Country of Birth	Spouse's Citizenship Before marriage	At present

7. PERSON TO NOTIFY IN CASE OF EMERGENCY — It is in your own interest to provide this information and we recommend that you provide the name of someone who would not normally accompany you.

Name _____ Relationship _____ Telephone _____

Area Code / Home

Address _____

No. / Street / City / Province / Postal Code / Area Code / Business / Extension

> **WARNING TO ALL APPLICANTS AND GUARANTORS** — Section 57(2) of the Criminal Code reads "Every one who, while in or out of Canada, for the purpose of procuring a passport for himself or any other person or for the purpose of procuring any material alteration or addition to any such passport, makes a written or an oral statement that he knows is false or misleading (a) is guilty of an indictable offence and liable to imprisonment for a term not exceeding two years; or (b) is guilty of an offence punishable on summary conviction."

8. DECLARATION OF APPLICANT

I solemnly declare that:

(i) the statements made in this application are true,

(ii) the photographs enclosed are a true likeness of me,

(iii) I am a Canadian citizen, and

(iv) I have known my guarantor personally for at least two years (or completed form PPT 132 "Declaration in Lieu of Guarantor").

Dated _____
Year / Month / Day

at _____
City / Province

Signature of Applicant _____

9. DECLARATION OF GUARANTOR — No fee is chargeable for this declaration. Before this declaration is signed, items 1-8 must be completed.

I,

Name of Guarantor _____

a Canadian citizen residing in Canada, declare that to the best of my knowledge and belief all the statements made in this application are true. I make this declaration from my knowledge of the applicant whose name is

Name of Applicant _____

whom I have known personally for _____ years
(Write Number of years)

and whose photograph I have certified on the back.

Occupation according to instruction 9 _____

Business address (include name of firm or organization) _____

No. / Street

City / Province / Postal Code

Telephone _____
Area Code / Home

_____
Area Code / Business / Extension

Dated _____
Year / Month / Day

at _____
City / Province

Signature of Guarantor _____

★ Passport Bureau des
Office passeports

File No. _____

PASSPORT APPLICATION FORM B
(FOR A CHILD UNDER 16)

PROTECTED INFORMATION
WHEN COMPLETED

1. CHILD'S NAME

NAME TO APPEAR IN PASSPORT

Surname

First Name

Middle Name(s)
(optional)

FORMER SURNAME

Former Surname
(if changed)

Date of departure, if known

2. CHILD'S PERSONAL INFORMATION

Date of Birth | Year | Month | Day

Place of Birth | City | Province | Country

Sex | Male | Female | Height | Weight | Hair Colour | Eye Colour

Permanent Address | No. | Street | Apt. | City | Province | Postal Code

Mailing Address | No. | Street | Apt. | City | Province | Postal Code

3. PREVIOUS CANADIAN PASSPORTS — Does the child's name appear in any Canadian passport, certificate of identity or refugee travel document issued in the last 5 years?

Write yes or no ▶

IF YES, indicate ☐ included in parent's document ☐ issued own document

Number

Date of Issue

and include it with the application.

If it has been lost, contact the Passport Office to obtain form PPT 203 that must be completed.

4. INFORMATION ABOUT PARENTS AND CUSTODY

Parent Applying | Other Parent

A) Name (mother's maiden name)

B) Particulars of Birth | Year | Month | Day | Country | Year | Month | Day | Country

C) Particulars of Marriage | Year | Month | Day | Present Marital Status | Year | Month | Day | Present Marital Status

D) Address | No. | Street | Apt. | No. | Street | Apt.

City | Province | Postal Code | City | Province | Postal Code

E) Telephone | Area Code | Home | Area Code | Home

Area Code | Business | Extension | Area Code | Business | Extension

Write yes or no

F) Is the child on interim or probationary adoption?   IF YES, include a letter of authorization from the appropriate authority.

Write yes or no

G) Has custody of the child been the subject of a separation agreement or court order?   IF YES, include all legal documents referring to custody of, mobility of or access to the child.

Write yes or no

H) Is the other parent aware of the application?   Have the other parent sign where indicated below.

Signature of Other Parent

If the signature is missing, explain:

FOR OFFICIAL USE ONLY   SEE OVER

	In	Seen	Out
Birth	☐	☐	☐
Citizenship	☐	☐	☐
Passport	☐	☐	☐
Marriage	☐	☐	☐
Separation	☐	☐	☐
Divorce	☐	☐	☐
Change of Name	☐	☐	☐
Adoption	☐	☐	☐
Other (specify)	☐	☐	☐

Submitted by:

Examined

Guarantor check

Written

Inspection

Finishing

Final inspection

Docs. received

Signature

Name

Identification
Received by:

Signature

Name

Date

Identification

Canadä ★

An agency of the Department of
Foreign Affairs and International Trade

Un organisme du ministère des
Affaires étrangères et du Commerce international

♺ PPT 046 (96-12)

5. CITIZENSHIP OF CHILD – You must provide one of the documents below (an original only – photocopies or notarized photocopies are not acceptable):

If your child was **born in Canada**

☐ certificate of birth in Canada, or

Registration Number   Date of Issue

☐ record of birth in Quebec, or

Issued by   Date of Issue

☐ certificate of Canadian citizenship.

Certificate Number   Date of Issue

If your child was **born outside Canada**

☐ certificate of Canadian citizenship

Certificate Number   Date of Issue

6. PERSON TO NOTIFY IN CASE OF EMERGENCY — It is in your child's interest to provide this information and we recommend that you provide the name of someone who would not normally accompany the child.

Name   Relationship   Telephone
Area Code   Home

Address
No.   Street   City   Province   Postal Code   Area Code   Business   Extension

WARNING TO ALL APPLICANTS AND GUARANTORS — Section 57(2) of the Criminal Code reads "Every one who, while in or out of Canada, for the purpose of procuring a passport for himself or any other person or for the purpose of procuring any material alteration or addition to any such passport, makes a written or an oral statement that he knows is false or misleading (a) is guilty of an indictable offence and liable to imprisonment for a term not exceeding two years; or (b) is guilty of an offence punishable on summary conviction."

7. DECLARATION OF APPLICANT (PARENT OR LEGAL GUARDIAN)

I,

Name of Applicant

solemnly declare that I am the _____ of the child
(Relationship)

Name of Child

and that:

(i) the statements made in the application are true,
(ii) the photographs enclosed are a true likeness of the child,
(iii) he/she is a Canadian citizen, and
(iv) I have known my guarantor personally for at least two years (or completed form PPT 132 "Declaration in Lieu of Guarantor").

Dated
Year   Month   Day

at
City   Province

Signature of Applicant (parent or legal guardian)

8. DECLARATION OF GUARANTOR — **No fee is chargeable for this declaration.** Before this declaration is signed, items 1-7 must be completed.

I,

Name of Guarantor

a Canadian citizen residing in Canada, declare that to the best of my knowledge and belief all the statements made in this application are true. I make this declaration from my knowledge of the applicant whose name is

Name of Applicant (parent or legal guardian)

whom I have known personally for _____ years
(Write Number of Years)

and from my knowledge of

Name of Child

whose photograph I have certified on the back.

Occupation according to instruction 8

Business address (include name of firm or organization)

No.   Street
City   Province   Postal Code

Telephone
Area Code   Home
Area Code   Business   Extension

Dated
Year   Month   Day

at
City   Province

Signature of Guarantor

PPT 046 (96-12)

Mexico Tourist Card

PARA EL LLENADO DE ESTA FORMA UTILICE LETRA DE MOLDE.
FOR THE FILLING OF THIS FORM USE CAPITAL LETTERS.
REMPLIR CETTE FORME EN CARACTERES D'IMPRIMERE.

121 No. A   9676395

NOMBRE   FIRST NAME   PRENOM.

APELLIDOS
SURNAMES
NOMS DE FAMILLE

| SEXO SEX SEXE | EDAD AGE AGE | SOLTERO (A) SINGLE CELIBATAIRE | 1 | CASADO (A) MARRIED MARIE (E) | 2 | DIVORCIADO (A) DIVORCED DIVORCE (E) | 3 | VIUDO (A) WIDO W(ER) VEUF (VE) | 4 |

| 0 | PROFESIONAL O TECNICO PROFESSIONAL OR TECHNICIAN PROFESSIONNEL OU TECHNICIEN - | 1 | GERENTE ADMINISTRADOR O FUNCIONARIO DE CATEGORIA DIRECTIVA. MANAGER, ADMINISTRATOR, OR ADMINISTRATIVE OFFICIAL DIRECTEUR, ADMINISTRATEUR OU FONCTIONNAIRE ATTACHE DE DIRECTION | 2 | EMPLEADO DE OFICINA PUBLICA O PRIVADA EMPLOYEE OF PUBLIC OR PRIVATE OFFICE EMPLOYE DE BUREAU PUBLICOU PRIVE | 3 | COMERCIANTE O VENDEDOR MERCHANT OR SELLER COMMERCANT OU VENDEUR |
| 4 | AGRICULTOR GANADERO PESCADOR, ETC. FARMER, LIVESTOCK-RAISER FISHER, ETC. AGRICULTEUR, FERMIER, PECHEUR, ETC | 5 | CONDUCTOR DE MEDIO DE TRANSPORTE, DRIVER OF VEHICLE, CHAUFFEUR DE VEHICULES DE TRANSPORT | 6 | OBRERO WORKER OUVRIER | 7 | SERVICIOS PERSONALES PERSONAL SERVICES SERVICES DE PERSONNEL | 8 | MIEMBRO DE LAS FUERZAS ARMADAS MEMBERS OF ARMED FORCES MEMBERS DES FORCES ARMEES | 9 | ESTUDIANTE, AMA DE CASA RENTISTA, JUBILADO, MENOR STUDENT, HOUSEWIFE BOND- HOLDER, RETIRED, MINOR ETUDIANT, MAITRESSE, DEMAISON RENTIER, RETRAITE, MINEUR |

LUGAR DE NACIMIENTO
PLACE OF BIRTH
LIEU DE NAISSANCE

NACIONALIDAD ACTUAL
PRESENT NATIONALITY
NATIONALITE ACTUELLE

DOMICILIO PERMANENTE

PERMANENT ADDRESS

DOMICILE PEMANENT

PASAPORTE
PASSPORT   **No.**
PASSEPORT

EXPEDIDO EN
ISSUED AT
D LIVRE A

DESTINOS PRINCIPALES EN LA REPUBLICA MEXICANA.
MAIN DESTINATIONS IN THE MEXICAN REPUBLIC.
DESTINATIONS PRINCIPALES OU GRANDG AXES

a)_____   b)_____   c)_____
CIUDAD   CIUDAD   CIUDAD
CITY   CITY   CITY
VILLE   VILLE   VILLE

MEDIO DE TRANSPORTE
MEANS OF TRANSPORTATION
MOYEN DE TRANSPORT

1   2   3   4   5   6

OTROS
OTHERS   7
AUTRES

PARA USO OFICIAL   FOR OFFICIAL USE OFFICIEL

AUTORIZADO PARA PERMANECER EN EL PAIS
AUTHORIZED TO REMAIN IN MEXICO
AUTORISE A SEJOURNER DANS LE DAYS

DIAS QUE PIENSA PERMANECER EN MEXICO
NUMBER OF DAYS THAT YOU ARE PLANNING TO
STAY IN MEXICO
COMBIEN DE JOUPS PENSEZ VOUS RESTER AU
MEXIQUE

* AUTORIZACION
PERMIT   **No.**
AUTORISATION

DE FECHA
DATE
DATEE LE

ENTRADA

* UNICAMENTE PARA NACIONALIDADES QUE REQUIEREN
AUTORIZACION ESPECIAL DE LA SECRETARIA DE GOBER-
NACION

* ONLY FOR NATIONALITIES WHICH REQUIRE SPECIAL PER-
MISSION FROM THE MINISTRY OF THE INTERIOR.

* SEULEMENT POUR LES NATIONALITIES CE QUI ONT BE-
SOIN D'AUTORISATION SPECIALE DU MINISTERE DE
L'INTERIEUR.

SELLO Y FECHA OFNA. EXPEDIDORA

SI EL EXTRANJERO ENTRO AL PAIS ACOMPAÑADO DE UN MENOR O ES RESPONSABLE DE UN
VEHICULO CON MATRICULA EXTRANJERA ANOTESE EN LA PARTE SUPERIOR.

INDIQUE CON UNA "X" EN LO REFERENTE A: SEXO, EDO. CIVIL, TRANSPORTE Y PROFESION U OCUPACION PRINCIPAL
MARK WITH "X" INFORMATION REGARDING: SEX, MARITAL STATUS, TRANSPORTATION AND PROFESSION OR PRINCIPAL OCCUPATION.
MARQUER D'UNC CROIX CE QUI CONCERNE: SEXE, ETAT CIVILE, TRANSPORT ET PROFESSION OU POSTE PRINCIPAL.

Department of National Health and Welfare or Travel Information Offices

Information on health requirements may be obtained from each country's Health Department.

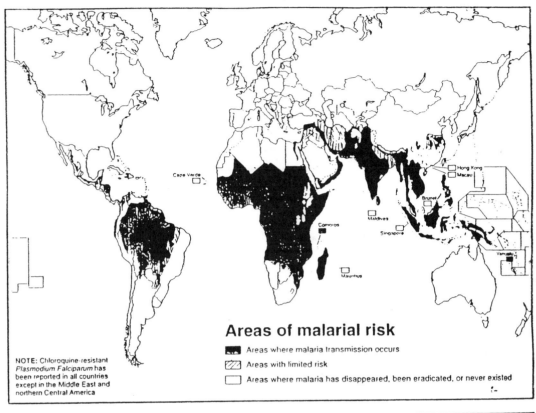

Areas of malarial risk

- Areas where malaria transmission occurs
- Areas with limited risk
- Areas where malaria has disappeared, been eradicated, or never existed

NOTE: Chloroquine-resistant *Plasmodium Falciparum* has been reported in all countries except in the Middle East and northern Central America

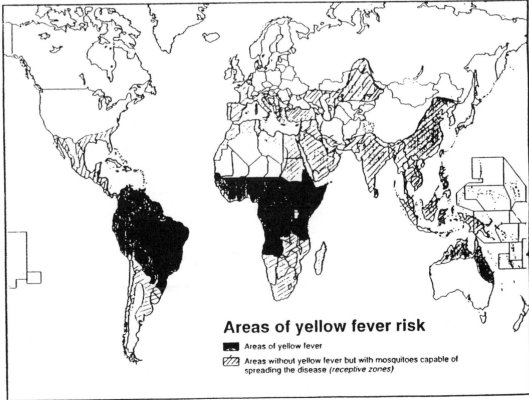

Areas of yellow fever risk

- Areas of yellow fever
- Areas without yellow fever but with mosquitoes capable of spreading the disease (*receptive zones*)

International Certificate of Vaccination or Revaccination Against YELLOW FEVER

This is to certify that Je soussigé(e) certifie que		Date of birth Né(e) le	Sex Sexe
Whose signature follows Dont la signature suit			

Has on the date indicated been vaccinated or revaccinated against yellow fever
A été vaccine(e) ou revacciné(e) contre la fiévre jaune á la date indiquée

Date	Signature and professional Status of vaccinator — Signature et qualité professionnelle du vaccinateur	Origin and batch no of vaccine — Origine du vaccin employé et numéro du loi	Official stamp of vaccinating centre — Cachet officiel du centre de vaccination	
1			1	2
2				
3			3	4
4				

Travel Information Manual

■ COSTA RICA

Geographical information:
Capital - San José (SJO).

1. **Passport:** Required, except for holders of:
   1. expired passports issued to nationals of Costa Rica;
   2. National Identity Card ("Cedula de Identidad") issued by Costa Rica;
   3. Laissez-Passer issued by the United Nations;
   4. Military Identity Card (with movement order) issued by the U.S. Forces;
   5. the following documents issued to nationals (including minors) of Canada and U.S.A.:
      a. expired passports, or
      b. Certified birth certificate accompanied by:
         1. driver's license containing holder's photograph, or
         2. official identification containing holder's photograph.
   6. proof of permission to enter, issued by Immigration Department to stateless persons and refugees;
   7. expired British passport endorsed "British Dependent Territories Citizen" issued in Hong Kong.
   Validity: passports must be valid for at least 6 months.
   Admission and transit restrictions:
   The Government of Costa Rica refuses admission to:
   — gypsies of any country;
   — visitors without sufficient funds.
   The following fashions are prohibited:
   long and unkempt hair and beards, indecent clothing.

2. **Visa: Warning:** *Non-compliance with the entry regulations will result in fines up to CRC 30,000.-.*
   Visa required, except for:
   1. nationals of Costa Rica;
   2. passengers mentioned under 1. "Passport" 3.;
   3. for a stay of max. 90 days **22**:
      a. nationals of: Argentina, Austria, Belgium, Brazil, Canada, Denmark, Finland, Germany, Hungary, Israel, Italy, Japan, Korea Rep., Liechtenstein, Luxembourg, Netherlands, Norway, Panama, Paraguay, Poland, Portugal, Romania, Spain, Sweden, Switzerland, Trinidad & Tobago, Uruguay, U.S.A. **24**;
      b. holders of British passports with on the front cover "United Kingdom of Great Britain and Northern Ireland" or "Jersey" or "Guernsey and its dependencies" or "Isle of Man" or if a passport is endorsed "British Citizen", "British National (Overseas)" or "British Dependent Territories Citizen" (may be expired if issued in Hong Kong).
      However if holding passport issued in Bermuda or Cayman Islands, visa exemption is for a stay of max. 30 days;
   4. for a stay of max. 30 days **22**:
      nationals of: Antigua & Barbuda, Australia, Bahamas, Bahrain, Barbados, Belize, Bolivia, Bulgaria, Chile, Colombia, Czech Rep., Dominica, El Salvador, France, Grenada, Guatemala, Guyana, Honduras, Iceland, Ireland Rep., Jamaica, Kenya, Kuwait, Mexico, Monaco, New Zealand, Oman, Philippines, Qatar, Russian Fed., San Marino, Saudi Arabia, Singapore, Slovak Rep., South Africa (not applicable if holding passport issued in Transkei or Venda), St. Kitts-Nevis, St. Lucia, St. Vincent & the Grenadines, Suriname, Turkey, United Arab Emirates, Vatican City, Venezuela and holders of Taiwan (Rep. of China) documents;
   5. holders of a tourist card for a stay of max. 90 days issued to nationals of Canada and U.S.A. over 16 years of age **24** holding documents as stated under 1."Passport" 5.;
   6. nationals of Peru holding:
      a. diplomatic, official and service passports;
      b. special passports provided holding written proof of a diplomatic mission from the "Cancilleria de Costa Rica";
   (TWOV)
   (Not applicable to stateless persons)
   7. those **21 25** continuing their journey to a third country within 48 hours, provided holding confirmed tickets and other documents for their next destination and without leaving the airport;

8. those **23 25** continuing their journey to a third country by **same flight** without leaving the aircraft or the airport transit area. However nationals of China (People's Rep.) and Cuba need transit visa authorized by the Dirección General de Migración.

   Merchant Seamen: there are no special facilities for merchant seamen. They have to comply with the normal entry/transit regulations applicable to their nationality.
   Issue: of Tourist Cards:
   For nationals of Canada and U.S.A holding documents as stated under 1. "Passport" 5., for a stay of max. 90 days.
   Tourist cards (each passenger must hold his own card) can be obtained against a fee of USD 2.- from:
   a. Costa Rican consulates; or
   b. offices of one of the airlines at the airports of: Amsterdam, Aruba, Barranquilla, Caracas, Curaçao, Panama and Port of Spain; or
   c. on arrival in Costa Rica.
   If the Tourist Card is issued by an airline, the card must be validated and signed by the issuing employee. No passport photograph is required. Airlines can also issue these tourist cards for transportation on flights of other airlines. A tourist card must be used within 90 days after date of issuance and may be revalidated every 30 days up to a maximum of 6 months.
   Tourist Card must **not** be issued to:
   1. those coming under commercial contract (e.g. professional boxers, professional football teams, professional dancers, personnel of foreign firms sent out for a permanent appointment in Costa Rica, etc.);
   2. immigrants;
   Additional information:
   1. Visas issued by consuls of Costa Rica must be used within 30 days after date of issue. (Nationals U.S.A.: within 90 days.)
   2. All passengers other than those mentioned in 1. "Passport" 1. through 3. must hold all documents required for next destination.
   3. Temporary visitors (even if holding a visa) must hold return or onward tickets and sufficient funds. **Exempt** are:
   — alien residents (holding residence visa or re-entry permit) and holders of diplomatic and official passports who are accredited to Costa Rica;
   — those holding visa showing they are exempt from exit ticket;
   — holders of a visa and United Nations "Laissez-Passer".
   Re-entry permit: Alien residents of Costa Rica who want to return must be in possession of a re-entry permit before leaving the country.
   Exit permit: Required when leaving the country for all passengers (except for those mentioned under 2. "Visa" 3.) who stayed in Costa Rica more than 30 days. For passengers staying less than 30 days no exit permit is required, provided they are in possession of a disembarkation card. The permit is issued by the "Ministerio de Seguridad" ("Ministry of Security").
   Notes:
   21 Not applicable to those nationals who need -in addition to their visa- the copy of an authorization cable sent by the Dirección General de Migración (valid 30 days after issuance). Moreover, a deposit of CRC 90,000.— is required.
   The above is applicable to all passengers, **except for:**
   a. those who are visa exempt according to 2. "Visa" 1. through 5.;
   b. nationals of Andorra, Belarus, Croatia, Cyprus, Dominican Rep., Ecuador, Egypt, Estonia, Greece, India, Indonesia, Latvia, Lithuania, Malaysia, Malta, Morocco, Nicaragua, Peru, Slovenia, Thailand, Ukraine and Zimbabwe;
   c. alien residents of the U.S.A.;
   d. those being alien resident of a country which nationals are visa exempt for entry Costa Rica.
   e. nationals of Cuba residing in one of the countries mentioned in 2. "Visa" 3. a and b.
   22 Extension of stay can be arranged on arrival. Passenger must obtain an exit visa from the Immigration Department at least three days before leaving Costa Rica.

23 This is the only possibility to transit without visa for those needing a visa and authorization cable for entry into the country (see Note 21 above), except for nationals of China (People's Rep.) who need authorized transit visa.
If transit for such passengers deviates from this TWOV facility, passenger must hold a transit visa and confirmed onward tickets indicating onward travel within the next 8 hours.
Non-compliance with the above will result in deportation of passenger while a fine of USD 1000.— per passenger will be imposed on transporting carrier.
24 If holding passport issued by the governments of Marshall Islands, Micronesia or Palau Islands: visa, copy of authorization cable (sent by Dirección General de Migración) and deposit of CRC 90,000.- required.
25 TWOV is only applicable for refugees residing in one of the countries mentioned under 2. "Visa" 3. and 4.

3. **Health:** No vaccinations are required to enter Costa Rica from any country.

   Recommended:
   Malaria prophylaxis. Malaria risk - almost exclusively in the benign (P. vivax) form - is moderate throughout the year in the cantons Matina, Limón and Talamanca (Limón Province) and Los Chiles (Alajuela Province). Lower transmission risk exists in 15 cantons in the provinces of Guanacaste, Alajuela and Heredia. Negligible or no risk of malaria transmission exists in the other 69 cantons of the country (see Terms & Definitions).
   Recommended prophylaxis in risk areas: CHL.

4. **Tax: Embarkation Tax** is levied when leaving Costa Rica on:
   a. nationals of Costa Rica: CRC 1,944.— and USD 44.— (or equivalent in CRC);
   b. alien residents of Costa Rica: USD 64.-;
   c. non-residents staying longer than 24 hours: CRC 2.900.— (or USD 16.50);
   d. transit passengers continuing within 24 hours: CRC 210.— (or USD 2.-).
   Place of payment: Airport of departure in Costa Rica.
   Exempt are:
   1. holders of diplomatic passports;
   2. members of U.S. Government agencies.

5. **Customs:**
   Import: free import
   1. 3 litres of alcoholic beverages for passengers older than 18 years;
   2. 500 grammes of elaborated tobacco or 400 cigarettes or 50 cigars;
   3. a reasonable quantity of perfume for personal use.
   Additional information: Costa Rica is member of the CITES (see Terms & Definitions).
   Pets: cats and dogs subject to quarantine up to 6 months. Require "Permiso de Importación" ("Import Permit") issued by Salubridad Pùblica Veterinaria ("Veterinary Health Dept.") de Costa Rica, San José, C.R. and a good health and rabies vaccination certificate. All documents must be authenticated and visaed by nearest Costa Rican Consulate. Certificates must be issued by Government Veterinarian. Parrots require "Permiso de Importación" ("Import Permit") issued by Ministerio de Agricultura y Ganadería ("Ministry of Husbandry") de Costa Rica, San José, C.R. Must have been in possession of owner at least six months. Also required government veterinarian certificate stating that parrots come from area free of psittacosis, ornithosis and salmonella and any other contagious diseases. This certificate must be visaed and authenticated by nearest Costa Rican Consulate.
   Baggage clearance: baggage is cleared at the first airport of entry in Costa Rica.
   Exempt: baggage of transit passengers, provided the passengers do not leave the transit area.

6. **Currency:**
   Import: allowed.
   local currency (Costa Rican Colon-CRC): no restrictions.
   foreign currencies: no restrictions, but only US Dollars are accepted for exchange.
   Export: allowed.
   local currency (Costa Rican Colon-CRC) and foreign currencies: no restrictions.

INDIA

Geographical information:
Capital - Delhi (DEL).

1. **Passport:** Required, except for holders of:
   1. Identity-emergency certificate (visa required at all times);
   2. Laissez-Passer issued by the United Nations;
   3. Seaman Book, provided travelling on duty;
   4. documents for stateless persons issued by U.N. or I.C.R.C., provided holding a landing permit for India.

Admission restrictions: The government of India refuses admission to:
1. nationals of Afghanistan, even if they hold a visa for India, if their ticket or passport shows evidence of transit or boarding in Pakistan;
2. holders of British passports - even if of Indian origin - who are forcibly sent to India and irrespective whether they require an entry visa or not.
   Despite this admission restriction, carriers often try to bring such passengers back to India. However, if the passenger himself at the moment of disembarkation refuses to enter India, the authorities will not force him to enter India, but on the contrary will force him to continue his journey by same flight without leaving the airport.
3. nationals of India holding other citizenship in addition to Indian citizenship.

2. **Visa: Warning:**
   1. *Any passenger, not acceptable to the local Immigration authorities due to invalid documents, will be deported to point of origin on the same or first available flight whichever is practical;*
   2. *Without specific permission of the Indian civil authorities it is not permitted to land at any (air)port in India any person against his wishes. All airlines are advised to satisfy themselves that their passengers will disembark voluntarily;*
   3. *Nationals of Pakistan, holding valid entry visa for India, are not allowed to embark/disembark via Calcutta, even if their entry visa shows Calcutta. They must embark/disembark at the airports of Mumbai or Delhi or Amritsar (also by rail/road).*
   4. *Nationals who are refused entry in any other country and who are deported back to India must only be deported back to station of origin, being the station of embarkation in India.*

Visa required, except for:
1. nationals of India;
2. nationals [21] of Bhutan and Nepal for a stay of max. 3 months;
3. nationals [21] of Maldives for a stay of max. 90 days. The period of 90 days shall include any prior period of stay during a period of six months immediately before the date of entry;
4. nationals of Argentina, Denmark and Vietnam, provided holding diplomatic, official or service passports for a stay of max. 90 days;
5. children under 16 years (irrespective of nationality) holding international passport with parents of Indian origin holding an Indian passport, for a stay of max. 90 days, provided holding certificate from the Indian High Commission stating the age, date of birth, nationality of the child, passport details of the child and that child has Indian parents (this certificate is also required if child is accompanied by one or both parents);
6. holders of a re-entry permit issued by a consulate of India abroad. Prior authorization has to be arranged before departure from India, which might be in the form of an endorsement stamp in passport reading "No objection to return". This stamp is not a substitute for the required re-entry permit;

(TWOV)
(Not applicable to stateless persons and refugees)
7. those holding confirmed onward ticket for next destination on first available connection. Leaving the airport transit area is not allowed.

Merchant Seamen: must travel on duty and hold Letter of Guarantee of shipping company (see Terms & Definitions).
1. If arriving by air in order to board ship:
   — visa not required for those mentioned in 2. "Visa" 1., 2. or 3.;
   — any other nationality: visa required.
2. If arriving by ship in order to board aircraft:
   — visa not required for those mentioned in 2. "Visa" 1., 2. or 3.;
   — any other nationality: visa required.
3. If in direct transit to abroad: visa not required for:
   — those mentioned in 2. "Visa" 1., 2. or 3.;
   — those holding confirmed onward ticket for next destination on first available connection. Leaving the airport transit area is not allowed.

Issue: By embassies/consulates of India abroad.

Additional information:
1. — **Individual tourists** - if not visa exempted in 2. "Visa" 2. or 3. - should preferably apply for a tourist visa and not for an ordinary visa, to avoid problems on departure - see under "Exit permit". They will also be entitled to special facilities. Four passport photos are required on arrival for passengers entering on an ordinary visa.
   — **Tourist groups** of nationals of Sri Lanka or any other nationality not visa exempted in 2. "Visa" 2. or 3. arriving by air for a stay of a specified period:
   Travel agency (approved by the Indian Ministry of Tourism) should obtain prior permission from the Immigration Officer in charge.
   The representative of the local travel agency will be held responsible for accompanying the group at all times during their stay in India. Permission to enter the country will be granted only upon submission of the name of the group, the number of passengers, details of the itinerary (incl. port of departure) and passport number, date of birth and nationality of each passenger.
2. All tourists, including nationals of India, not residing in India, must pay hotel bills in freely convertible currencies e.g. AUD, DEM, GBP or USD.
3. **Restricted areas:**
   A special permit is required for foreigners [22] who want to visit undermentioned areas.
   This permit can be issued by either Ministry of Home Affairs or Foreigners Registration Offices located in Calcutta, Chennai, Delhi, and Mumbai or the Indian diplomatic missions abroad, unless otherwise stated in the text below.
   Tourist groups shall consist of 4 to 20 persons.
   Assam: Kaziranga, Manas National Park, Gauhati City, Kamakhya Temple.
   Permits are issued for a stay of 10 days to those travelling in groups.
   Meghalaya: Shillong.
   Permits are issued for a stay of 7 days to those travelling in groups.
   West Bengal:
   — Darjeeling and adjoining areas (Tiger Hill, Lebong Race Course Jorabunglow, Ghoom and Kurseong).
   Permits are issued (also by Home Dept. of West Bengal) for a stay of 15 days to those travelling individually or in groups;
   — Sandakphu and Phalut areas in Darjeeling and wild life sanctuaries at Mahananda and Simchal and Jaldapara, Chapramari and Goruari in Jalpaiguri District.
   Permits are issued (also by the Home Dept. of West Bengal) for a stay of 7 days to those travelling in groups only.
   Andaman and Nicobar Islands:
   — Municipal area of Port Blair and Havelock Island:
   Permits for 15 days and nights visits are issued to those travelling individually or in groups;
   — Jolly Bouy, See North Cinque, Red Skin, Neil Is.:
   Permits for day visits only, are issued to those travelling in groups.
   Issue of permits also by Immigration Officer at Port Blair.
   Lakshadweep: Bangaram, Suheli and Tilkam Islands.
   Permits for a stay of 7 days are issued to those travelling in groups, only by the Ministry of Home Affairs and the Administrator of Lakshadweep.
   Sikkim (protected area):
   — Gangtok, Rumtek and Phodang.
   Permits for 7 days are issued to those travelling individually or in groups,
   — Zongry and West Sikkim.
   A 15 days permit is issued to groups coming for trekking.
   — Pamayangtse.
   A 2 days permit is issued to groups coming for trekking.
   Permits are issued exclusively by the Ministry of Home Affairs.
   Manipur (protected area):
   Imphal, Loktak Lake, Moirang INA Memorial, Kaibil Deer Sanctuary and Waillye Lake and Konyom War Memorial.
   Permits for 3 days will be issued to groups only, and exclusively by the Ministry of Home Affairs.

Re-entry permit: To be obtained before departure by alien residents of India who want to return.

Exit permit: Holders of an entry visa or an entry permit must obtain an **Income Tax Clearance** or a **Tax Exemption Certificate** before departure.
Income Tax Clearance or Tax Exemption Certificate is not required for the following groups of passengers:
1. holders of diplomatic passports;
2. holders of tourist, transit or courtesy visas;
3. those who do not need a visa to enter India.
   In case their stay exceeds 90 days in India, passengers arriving with a visa of more than 90 days have to register **and** give notice of their proposed departure after they have completed 90 days stay in India. However, if such passengers register themselves with the Police authorities they must report their departure to the Registration Officer of the district in which they are registered and get their registration certificate endorsed to this effect. The endorsed certificate has to be handed in at the (air) port of departure.
   Nationals of Pakistan must get themselves registered irrespective of duration of stay.

Notes:
[21] Provided they are neither missionaries nor persons intending to take up employment or business/professional activities.
[22] Not required for nationals of:
— Bhutan travelling by air to/from Bhutan via Bagdodra;
— Nepal travelling by air to/from Kathmandu.
However, if surface travel is involved and mentioned nationals travel via restricted areas, they require a "pass" issued by either the Foreigners Regional Registration Office (located in each major Indian city) or Superintendent of police (located in each Indian district) or the diplomatic representation of India in Bhutan or Nepal.

3. **Health:** Required - except for passengers transiting India by the same aircraft - vaccination against:
yellow fever [31], if arriving within 6 days after leaving or transiting infected areas or endemic areas (see General Health Information) or Trinidad & Tobago.
Exempt are: children under 6 months.

Recommended:
Malaria prophylaxis. Malaria risk exists throughout the year below 2000 m. in the whole country excluding parts of the States of Himachal Pradesh, Jammu & Kashmir and Sikkim. Highly chloroquine- resistant P. falciparum reported (see Terms & Definitions).
Recommended prophylaxis: C plus P.

Notes:
[31] Persons without valid yellow fever certificate - if required - are subject to **quarantine** for max. 6 days. If such persons refuse to pay the costs involved, the transporting carrier will be charged.

4. **Tax:** No airport tax is levied on passengers upon embarkation at the airport (see Terms & Definitions).
5. **Customs:**
Import: free import
(Import by non-residents, however, is only permitted if they enter India for a stay of not less than 24 hours and not more than 6 months, provided they visit India not more than once a month)
   a. persons of 17 years and older: 200 cigarettes or 50 cigars or 250 grammes of tobacco; one bottle (0.95 litre) of alcoholic liquor;
   b. medicines in reasonable quantities;
   c. 2 ounces of perfume and 1/4 litre of toilet water;
   d. travel souvenirs up to a value of INR 600.- [51] (tourists of Indian origin INR 3,000.- [51]) subject to re-exportation. Persons under 12 years are allowed 1/4 of the value admitted to adults.

Additional information:
1. India is member of the CITES (see Terms & Definitions).
2. Firearms: It is advisable to obtain a possession licence in advance (or hold proof of exemption) in order to avoid delay and inconvenience on arrival.
3. A Tourist Baggage Re-Export Form (TBRE) will be issued upon arrival to tourists for re-exportation of their expensive items duty free.

Pets: combined health and rabies certificate issued by a veterinary surgeon of the country of origin not later than 1 week before arrival.
Baggage clearance: baggage is cleared at the first airport of entry in India.

Notes:
[51] Goods in excess of the maximum permitted amount will be subject to an import duty of 80%.

Currency:
Import: allowed.
1. foreign currencies [61]: unlimited, however if the total value in cash exceeds USD 5,000.-, or exceeds USD 10,000.- (or equivalent) in traveller's cheques, it must be declared;
2. from Saudi Arabia, special banknotes (Haj notes), issued by the Reserve Bank of India, without limit.

Prohibited: local currency (Indian Rupee-INR).

Export: allowed.
1. special banknotes (Haj notes), issued by the Reserve Bank of India up to the amount brought in.
2. local currency (Indian Rupee-INR) by passengers proceeding to:
   a. Nepal: no limit (excl. notes of denominations of INR 100.- or higher);
   b. Bangladesh, Pakistan or Sri Lanka: up to INR 20.- per person;
   c. other destinations: **prohibited.**
3. foreign currencies [61]: up to the amount imported and declared.

Notes:
[61] Foreign currencies include currency notes, traveller's cheques, cheques, drafts etc. (Re)exchange only through banks and authorized money changers.

■ INDONESIA

Geographical information:
Capital - Jakarta (JKT).

1. **Passport:** Required, except for holders of:
   1. Emergency Certificate issued by Indonesian Immigration Office;
   2. Laissez-Passer issued by the United Nations;
   3. Seaman Book or Seafarer's Identity Document, provided travelling on duty. See also "Special restrictions" 1.;
   4. Hong Kong Document of Identity (DI) or Certificate of Identity (CI), issued to residents of Hong Kong;
   5. Stateless persons holding documents stating their status issued by the country in which they reside.

   Validity: Passports must be valid at least 6 months after date of entry. Not applicable to nationals and alien residents of Indonesia.
   Special restrictions:
   1. The Indonesian authorities do not recognize:
      a. loose-leaf seaman certificate presented by merchant seamen instead of a Seaman Book;
      b. passports and seaman books issued by the Government of Israel. These passengers must obtain a travel affidavit from a representation of Indonesia.
   2. Passengers, other than nationals of Indonesia, who wish to travel to the Indonesian province of **Irian Jaya** must obtain a special permit "Surat Jalan" after arrival in Indonesia from the "Dinas Intel Pam Pol MABAK" in Jakarta or other regional police headquarters in Biak or Jayapura. It normally takes about 2 days to obtain such a permit.
      Upon arrival in Irian Jaya visitors must report to the local police office.
      Exempt from the special permit are holders of diplomatic passports or of a special permit issued by the Indonesian Ministry of Information (for reporters).
2. **Visa: Warning:** *Non-compliance with the entry/transit regulations will result in fines for carriers of USD 1,000.- per passenger. Moreover, passenger will be refused entry and deported by same aircraft.*
   Visa: required [21], except for:
   1. nationals of Indonesia holding a valid passport of the Republic of Indonesia *(avoid serious difficulties for passengers and carriers concerned! Refuse transportation to nationals of Indonesia holding a passport which is either expired or declared invalid!);*
   2. those under *a. b.* and *c.* below for a stay of max. 60 days, see also "2. Visa - Issue":
      a. holders of British passports (irrespective of endorsement in passport regarding their status);
      b. nationals of: Argentina, Australia, Austria, Belgium, Brazil, Brunei, Canada, Chile, Denmark, Egypt, Finland, France, Germany, Greece, Hungary, Iceland, Ireland (Rep.), Italy, Japan, Korea Rep. (South), Kuwait, Liechtenstein, Luxembourg, Malaysia, Maldives, Malta, Mexico, Monaco, Morocco, Netherlands, New Zealand, Norway, Philippines, Saudi Arabia, Singapore, Spain, Sweden, Switzerland, Thailand, Turkey, United Arab Emirates, U.S.A., Venezuela, Yugoslavia Fed. Rep.;
      c. holders of Taiwan (Rep. of China) passports endorsed with code **"MFA"** or **"M"**. **Warning:** if passport is endorsed with code **"OM"** or **"X"** (in which case a visa is required), arriving and departing is only allowed via the airports of Denpasar Bali (Ngurah Rai), Jakarta (Soekarno-Hatta) or Medan (Polonia);
      d. nationals of any country [22] coming to Indonesia for conference purposes provided holding on arrival a documentary proof of approval from the Indonesian Government which can also be valid for touristic purposes;
   3. holders of a re-entry permit issued by Indonesia;

   (TWOV)
   4. transit passengers [22] continuing their journey to a third country within 8 hours by the same or another aircraft without leaving the airport, provided holding tickets with reserved seats and other documents for their onward journey.

   Merchant Seamen: must travel on duty and hold Letter of Guarantee of shipping company (see Terms & Definitions).
   If arriving by air in order to board ship, or if arriving by ship in order to board aircraft, or if in direct transit to abroad:
   visa not required for nationals of Indonesia.
   Any other nationality need visa at all times (max. validity 5 days), to be obtained prior to arrival from any Indonesian representation abroad. Moreover:
   — ship has to be in the harbour upon seaman's arrival;
   — seaman must be met at airport by shipping agent. Shipping company is responsible for immediate transportation to the ship or aircraft;
   — prior telex information to station manager of transporting airline is required.
   Issue:
   1. By any Indonesian representation abroad;
   2. On arrival of a landing/entry permit to those described under 2. "Visa" 2. on following conditions:
      a. no extension possible;
      b. the passenger must hold on arrival tickets and other documents for the return/onward journey. Purchase of a ticket is also accepted;
      c. they must hold at least USD 1,000.- or a valid credit card;
      d. they must arrive via:
      — the airports of: Ambon (Pattimura), Balikpapan (Sepinggan), Bandung (Husein Sastranegara), Batam (Hang Nadim), Biak (Frans Kaisiepo), Bali (Ngurah Rai), Jakarta (Soekarno-Hatta), Kupang (El Tari), Manado (Samratulangi), Mataram (Selaparang), Medan (Polonia), Padang (Tabing), Pekan-Baru (Simpangtiga), Pontianak (Soepadio), Surabaya (Juanda), Ujung Padang (Hadanuddin) and:
      — the seaports of: Bali (Benoa/Padang Bai), Jakarta (Tanjung Periok), Batam (Batu Ampar/Sekupang), Bitung (Bitung), Medan (Belawan), Ambon (Ambon), Semarang (Tanjung Mas), Surabaya (Tanjung Perak), Tanjung Pinang (Tanjung Pinang);
      e. they can depart from all Indonesian airports/seaports provided there is an immigration office available in that airport/seaport.
      Warning: Passengers exceeding their visa free stay not more than 60 days will be fined IDR 25,000.- per day. If not complying with this obligation imprisonment of max. 1 year is involved and/or a fine of max. IDR 5,000,000.- must be paid.
      If exceeding stay is more than 60 days imprisonment of max. 5 years is involved or passenger will be fined max. IDR 25,000,000.-.

   Additional information:
   1. nationals of China (People's Rep.) may entry/departure only via:
      — the airports of Bali (Ngurah Rai), Jakarta (Halim/Soekarno-Hatta), Medan (Polonia); and
      — the seaports of Jakarta (Tanjung Periok), Medan (Belawan), Surabaya (Tanjung Perak).
      They must hold return/onward ticket.
   2. holders of Hong Kong Certificate of Identity having a social culture visa are not allowed to arrive at Surabaya/Juanda Airport. **Exempt** are: those holding a business or tourist visa, travelling in a group of minimum 5 persons.
   3. government officials accredited to Indonesia must hold official visas to proof their status.

   Minors: All children, even when included in their parent's passports, must hold separate visas. A person is considered a minor until/including 10 years in domestic travel and until/including 12 years in international travel.
   Re-entry permit: Required for returning alien residents (to be obtained before departure from the Indonesian Immigration Office). Admission cards (KIM), Residential Cards (SIB/SKK) and cards of Temporary Admission are not considered re-entry permits.
   Notes:
   [21] — A tourist visa valid for 4 weeks can be extended only once for 2 weeks (total stay 6 weeks);
   — A visitors' visa (visa kunjungan) valid for:
   4 weeks can be extended to a maximum of 8 weeks;
   5 weeks can be extended twice to a maximum stay of 3 months.
   [22] Not applicable to nationals of Portugal and South Africa, who need a visa at all times.
3. **Health:** Required - except for transit passengers not leaving the airport - vaccination against:
   yellow fever, if arriving within 6 days after leaving or transiting [31] infected areas or countries situated in endemic areas (see General Health Information).

   Recommended:
   Malaria prophylaxis. Malaria risk exists throughout the year in the whole country except in Jakarta Municipality, big cities and the main tourist resorts of Java and Bali. P. falciparum highly resistant to chloroquine, and resistant to sulfadoxine/pyrimethamine reported. *P. vivax* resistant to chloroquine reported in Irian Jaya. (See Terms & Definitions).
   Recommended prophylaxis in risk areas:
   C plus P;
   In Irian Jaya: MEF.
   Notes:
   [31] Not required for those not leaving the airport in the areas concerned.
4. **Tax:**
   A. **Airport Tax:** is levied on air passengers as follows:
   If departing from:
   1. Jakarta (Soekarno-Hatta) and Den Pasar (Bali Island) on
      a. international flights: . . . . IDR 50,000.-;
      b. domestic flights: . . . . IDR 11,000.-;
   2. all other airports:
      a. international flights: . . . . IDR 20,000.-;
      b. domestic flights: . . . . IDR 9,900.-.

   10% VAT will be added to all domestic taxes.
   Place of payment: Airport of departure.
   Exempt are:
   1. children under 2 years;
   2. transit passengers in possession of through tickets and continuing their journey the same day (not applicable in Jakarta unless passengers stay within customs area/ transit room);
   3. officials on duty - with a travel order - of the Directorate General of Air Communications;
   4. official guests of the Indonesian government.

   B. **Fiscal Tax** of IDR 1,000,000.- is levied on passengers (incl. nationals of Indonesia) of any age when leaving for abroad.
   Place of payment: airport of departure in Indonesia.
   Exempt are:
   1. those (incl. nationals of Indonesia) who live abroad permanently and who:
      a. have stayed in Indonesia less than 6 months;
      b. have not undertaken any business activities in Indonesia.
      This exemption is valid only once in any 12 months' period.
   2. nationals of Indonesia being air/sea crew and travelling on duty;
   3. diplomatic or consular officials of foreign states and their dependants (provided not conducting business or profession).
5. **Customs:**
   Import: free import by adults only
   1. tobacco products (no limitations for diplomats):
      50 cigars or 200 cigarettes or 100 grammes of tobacco.
   2. 1 litre of liquor;
   3. a reasonable quantity of perfume;
   4. personal goods up to a value of USD 250.- per passenger or USD 1,000.- per family.

   Additional information:
   — Indonesia is member of the CITES (see Terms & Definitions).
   — (video) cameras, portable radio cassette recorder, binoculars and sport equipment may be imported by tourists provided also exported upon departure.

   Warning:
   1. Passengers **not** entering on a tourist visa have to pay duties for photo and film cameras unless this equipment is registered in their passport by the Indonesian Customs on former occasion. Importation of electronic equipment is not permitted at all.
   2. Film pre-recorders, video tapes, video laser disc, records and computer software must be screened by censor board.

   Prohibited:
   1. any kind of the following goods without a licence: Chinese medicines and printings, narcotics, fire arms and ammunition, pornography, fresh fruit, cordless telephone;
   2. any commercial or merchandised goods as part of baggage. Infringements will be charged IDR 25,000.- per piece. The use of cardboard boxes as baggage must be dissuaded.

   Pets: birds (other than parrots and parakeets), cats and dogs must be accompanied by health certificate (**and** photo copy) issued in country of origin within 5 days prior to shipment stating that the animals are free from disease and have not been in a Yellow Fever infected area for a period of at least 5 days prior to shipment.
   Inspection upon arrival at the airport for which carrier's office must previously be advised so that a veterinarian will be available at the airport.
   Furthermore, pets must be accompanied by:
   1. Import licence, to be obtained prior to arrival from Ministry of Agriculture, Jalan Salkemba Raya 16, 2nd floor, attn: Kesehatan Hewan (Animal Health); and
   2. copy of animal passport; and
   3. copy of passport of owner; and
   4. certificate from the Dept. of Agriculture, Directorate General of Farming, which may be issued by consular sections of embassies abroad.
      Cats, dogs, monkeys: Additional rabies inoculation certificate showing that vaccination was effected within 1 year prior to departure.

   Prohibited:
   1. Parrots and parakeets;
   2. Birds, cats, dogs, monkeys and other animals are stictly prohibited in the districts of Bali West Nusa Tenggara, East Nusa Tenggara, Irian Jaya, Madura, Maluku, Timor Timur, West Kalimantan, and the small islands surrounding the main island of Sumatra. Failure to comply will result in the immediate destruction of the animal concerned.

   Export: free export
   1. 1000 gr. of tobacco or 50 cigars or 200 cigarettes for persons of 21 years and older;
   2. less than 2 litres of alcoholic beverages in opened bottles;
   3. personal goods up to a value of IDR 1,000,000.-.

   Baggage clearance: (applicable to Airports of Denpasar Bali (Ngurah Rai - DPS), Jakarta (Soekarno Hatta Int'l - CGK) or Medan (Polania - MES) only).
   Baggage must be cleared at first airport of entry or first transit.
   Exempt:
   1. baggage of passengers arriving at DPS, CGK or MES and connecting with the same aircraft to DPS, CGK or MES, in which case baggage will be cleared at final destination.
   2. baggage of passengers transiting Indonesia with a destination outside Indonesia.
6. **Currency:**
   Import and
   Export:
   local currency (Indonesian Rupiah-IDR): up to IDR 50,000.- and must be declared to customs;
   foreign currencies: unlimited.

■ **ISRAEL**

Geographical information:
Capital - Jerusalem (JRS).

1. **Passport:** Required, except for holders of:
   1. Laissez-Passer issued by Israel;
   2. Laissez-Passer issued by the United Nations;
   3. Military Identity Card issued to U.S. military personnel based in Europe;
   4. Seaman Book, provided travelling on duty;
   5. Laissez-Passer issued to stateless persons and refugees.
   Validity: It is recommended that non-Israeli passengers hold passports that are valid for at least 6 months after period of intended stay.
   Additional information:
   1. Passengers intending to proceed from Israel to Arab countries other than Egypt and Jordan should see to it that their passport does not contain Israeli visa or stamps since no passenger is allowed to enter other Arab countries with such passports. Passengers who after a 3 months' stay in Israel are permitted to stay for a longer period, will obtain the extension stamp in their passport; it is not possible to have it stamped on a separate sheet;
   2. Travellers may:
   a. enter Jordan over land directly from occupied territory, but must hold a visa for Jordan, to be obtained from a representation of Jordan abroad, otherwise entry will be refused. The Jordanian authorities will **NOT** permit a recross to occupied territory;
   b. enter occupied territory overland directly from Jordan. The Israeli authorities will permit a recross to Israeli territory;
   3. A former national of Israel holding a foreign passport must show a written proof from the Israeli authorities abroad that he has given up his Israeli nationality. Failing to do so, such passenger will be considered a national of Israel, and so, he may have to get a new Israeli passport or have his original passport renewed, get a release from the army (if required) and conform to any other Israeli regulations when leaving Israel after his visit;
   4. Officially recognized Palestinian passports issued by the Palestinian autonomy are accepted for entry Israel. Other Palestinians still need an Israeli Laissez-Passer.

2. **Visa:** Warning: *Non-compliance with the entry regulations may result in deportation of passenger.*
   Visa: required, except for:
   1. nationals of Israel;
   2. a max. stay of 3 months:
   a. holders of normal British passports (irrespective of endorsement in passport regarding national status);
   b. nationals of: Argentina, Austria, Bahamas, Barbados, Belgium, Bolivia, Brazil, Canada, Chile, Colombia, Costa Rica, Cyprus, Czech Rep., Denmark, Dominican Rep., Ecuador, El Salvador, Fiji, Finland, France, Greece, Guatemala, Haiti, Hungary, Iceland, Ireland Rep., Italy, Jamaica, Japan, Korea Rep., Lesotho, Liechtenstein, Luxembourg, Malawi, Malta, Mauritius, Mexico, Monaco, Mongolia, Netherlands, Norway, Panama, Paraguay, Philippines, Portugal, Slovenia, Spain, Swaziland, Sweden, Switzerland, Trinidad & Tobago, Uruguay, Vanuatu;
   c. holders of normal passports being nationals of:
   Australia, Central African Rep., New Zealand, San Marino, South Africa, St. Kitts-Nevis, Suriname, U.S.A.;
   d. nationals of Germany if born after January 1, 1928. Those born before January 1, 1928 may enter on expired visa provided stamped in valid passport. However, loose leaf visa (not stamped in passport) are valid for the period as indicated thereon;
   e. diplomatic or service passports: nationals of Albania, Bulgaria, Burkina Faso, Honduras, Latvia, Liberia, Madagascar, Nicaragua, Peru, Sierra Leone, Slovak Rep., Thailand, Turkey, Ukraine and Venezuela;
   f. diplomatic or official passports: nationals of Lithuania;
   3. holders of a re-entry permit issued by Israel;
   (TWOV)
   4. those 📶 continuing their onward or return journey within 24 hours (extension possible) by same or first connecting aircraft, provided holding confirmed onward/return reservations.
   Passengers are not allowed to leave the airport.
   Merchant Seamen: must travel on duty and hold Letter of Guarantee of shipping company (see Terms & Definitions).
   1. If arriving by air in order to board ship (ship must be in an Israeli harbour): visa not required:
   — if nationality of seaman is mentioned in 2. "Visa" 1., 2.a., b., c., d. and 3.;
   — for any other nationality 📶 provided seaman: is met at airport by shipping company. Shipping agent is responsible for immediate transportation to the ship; — spends the night aboard his ship;
   2. If arriving by ship in order to board plane: visa not required:
   — if nationality of seaman is mentioned in 2. "Visa" 1., 2.a., b., c., d. and 3.;
   — for any other nationality 📶 provided procedure is completely arranged by shipping agent;
   3. If in direct transit to abroad: visa not required:
   — if nationality of seaman is mentioned in 2. "Visa" 1., 2.a., b., c., d. and 3.;
   — for any other nationality 📶 provided continuing within 24 hours and holding onward reservations.
   Issue:
   1. by a diplomatic or consular mission of Israel in: Argentina (Buenos Aires), Australia (Canberra, Sydney), Austria (Vienna), Azerbaijan (Baku), Belarus (Minsk), Belgium (Brussels), Bolivia (La Paz), Brazil (Brasilia, Rio de Janeiro, Sao Paulo), Bulgaria (Sofia), Cameroon (Yaounde), Canada (Montreal, Ottawa, Toronto), Chile (Santiago), China (People's Rep.) (Beijing, Shanghai), Colombia (Bogota), Congo Kinshasa (Kinshasa), Costa Rica (San José), Cote d'Ivoire (Abidjan), Cyprus (Nicosia), Czech Rep. (Prague), Denmark (Copenhagen), Dominica (Santo Domingo), Ecuador (Quito), Egypt (Alexandria, Cairo), El Salvador (San Salvador), Eritrea (Asmara), Ethiopia (Addis Ababa), Fiji (Suva), Finland (Helsinki), France (Marseille, Paris), Georgia (Tbilisi), Germany (Berlin, Bonn, Cologne, Munich), Greece (Athens), Guatemala (Guatemala), Honduras (Tegucigalpa), Hong Kong (Hong Kong), Hungary (Budapest), India (Delhi, Mumbai), Ireland (Dublin), Italy (Milan, Rome), Japan (Tokyo), Jordan (Amman), Kazakstan (Almaty), Kenya (Nairobi), Korea Rep. (Seoul), Latvia (Riga), Mexico (Mexico City), Morocco (Rabat), Myanmar (Yangon), Nepal (Katmandu), Netherlands (The Hague), New Zealand (Wellington), Nigeria (Lagos), Norway (Oslo), Panama (Panama City), Paraguay (Asuncion), Peru (Lima), Philippines (Manila), Poland (Warsaw), Portugal (Lisbon), Romania (Bucharest), Russian Fed. (Moscow), Senegal (Dakar), Singapore (Singapore), South Africa (Capetown, Johannesburg, Pretoria), Spain (Madrid), Swaziland (Mbabane), Sweden (Stockholm), Switzerland (Bern, Geneva), Thailand (Bangkok), Turkey (Ankara, Istanbul), U.S.A. (Atlanta, Boston, Chicago, Houston, Los Angeles, Miami, New York, Philadelphia, San Francisco, Washington), Uruguay (Montevideo), Uzbekistan (Tashkent), Venezuela (Caracas), Vietnam (Hanoi), Ukraine (Kiev), Zimbabwe (Harare).

2. upon arrival for those holding confirmation from Israeli Ministry of Interior.
   Fee: for holders of
   — normal passports: USD 80.—;
   — diplomatic and service passports: free of charge.
   Facility is not applicable to nationals of:
   — Honduras holding normal, consular, official, duty or special passports;
   — Jordan (all passport types);
   — Lithuania holding normal, consular, duty or special passports;
   Additional information: Visitors must hold onward/return tickets and sufficient funds for maintenance.
   Re-entry permit:
   — Required before leaving the country for alien residents of Israel who want to return again. Re-entry permits are issued by the Ministry of Interior.
   — Nationals of Jordan and stateless persons holding an Israeli Laissez-Passer must obtain a re-entry permit from an Israeli consulate abroad before returning to Israel.
   Notes:
   📶 Not applicable to:
   a. nationals of:
   — an Arab League country (see Terms & Definitions) other than Egypt;
   — Iran and Zimbabwe;
   Except those transiting by same flight or first connecting aircraft within 24 hours, without leaving the airport and holding a passport and confirmed onward reservations;
   b. stateless persons and refugees.

3. **Health:** No vaccinations are required to enter Israel from any country.

4. **Tax:** No airport tax is levied on passengers upon embarkation at the airport (see Terms & Definitions).

5. **Customs:**
   Import: free import
   1. 250 cigarettes 🗝 or 250 grammes of other tobacco products 🗝;
   2. 2 litres of wine 🗝 and 1 litre of other alcoholic beverages 🗝;
   3. gifts;
   4. 1/4 litre of Eau de Cologne or perfume.
   Residents:
   gifts up to the amount of USD 150.— excl. the articles stated in note 🗝 and the quantities under 1., 2. and 4. above.
   Non-residents: gifts up to the equivalent of USD 125.— in ILS excl. the articles stated in note 🗝 and the quantities under 1., 2. and 4. above.
   Moreover, for their personal use and provided re-exported: one video camera, one photo camera, one movie camera, one tape recorder and up to a value of USD 125.—: films and video cassettes.
   These articles are subject to high deposits which can be paid in cash or by **Visa** credit card only.
   Flowers, plants, seeds: health certificate required.
   Prohibited: fresh meat, bananas and pineapples. Fruits and vegetables from the African continent and especially from South Africa.
   Additional information: Israel is member of the CITES (see Terms & Definitions).
   Pets: cats, dogs and birds, provided:
   1. accompanied by:
   — a written declaration of the owner stating that the animals have been in his/her possession for at least 90 days prior to arrival in Israel;
   — a health certificate issued by a government veterinary officer in the country of origin within 5 days prior to export, stating that the animals were examined and found healthy and free from infectious and contagious diseases. The veterinary health certificate must also state that the cat/dog was vaccinated against rabies, not more than a year and not less than a month prior to arrival in Israel;

2. max. 2 of each type are imported.
   Veterinary import permit if:
   — more than 2 of each type are imported at a time, or
   — arriving unaccompanied by their owner.
   Quarantine in case of non-compliance with the veterinary requirements or suspicion of disease.
   Refusal or destruction in case the animal(s) arrive(s) without the documents required.
   Prohibited: Dogs and cats under the age of 3 months.
   Export: free export
   No limit for tobacco products and alcoholic beverages. Export permit for antiquities. It is advisable to have the camera empty on departure. Loaded cameras will be retained by the airport authorities and placed in a sealed box aboard the aircraft on which the passenger is travelling. The camera will be returned to the passenger at his destination.
   Baggage clearance: baggage is cleared at the first airport of entry in Israel.
   Transfer of baggage from plane to plane without clearance is possible in some cases, but it is strongly advised to contact the carrier for more information about these possibilities.
   Notes:
   🗝 For persons over 17 years only.
   🗝 Not including television sets, cameras, movie cameras, tape recorders and typewriters.

6. **Currency:**
   Import: allowed.
   RESIDENTS:
   local currency (New Israeli Sheqel-ILS): no restrictions;
   foreign currencies: not more than exported;
   NON-RESIDENTS:
   local currency and foreign currencies: unlimited.
   Export: allowed.
   RESIDENTS:
   foreign currencies: up to USD 3,000.-
   local currency: not more than the equivalent amount of USD 200.- in ILS.
   NON-RESIDENTS:
   local currency: apply to local bank before departure from Israel;
   foreign currencies: up to the amount imported. Foreign currencies exchanged upon arrival into local currency can be reconverted up to the equivalent of USD 500.— per passport.

■ MEXICO

Geographical information:
Capital - Mexico City (MEX).

1. **Passport:** Required, except for holders of:
   1. the following documents:
      a. Proof of citizenship for nationals of Canada [12], Japan [12], Mexico [11] and U.S.A. [12];
      b. U.S. Alien Registration Receipt Card (form I-551) with additional official photo identification (e.g. driver's licence);
      c. Canadian Alien Resident Card issued to permanent residents;
   2. "Certificado a Petición de Partes" ("certificate of application for exit") of Mexican consulate issued to stateless persons residing outside Mexico;
   3. "Documento de Identidad y Viaje" ("Identity and Travel Document") issued in Mexico to stateless persons residing in Mexico;
   4. identity documents and travel documents for stateless persons issued in Canada, U.S.A. and Western Europe, provided coming for touristic stay of max. 60 days and holding permit obtained by foreign representation of Mexico prior to arrival;
   5. "Permiso Previo del Instituto Nacional de Migracion" issued to stateless persons not mentioned in 1. "Passport" 4. [13];
   6. Laissez-Passer (provided with visa) issued by the United Nations;
   7. Seaman Book, provided travelling on duty.

Minors: (applicable to minors aged until/incl. 15 years)
   1. Mexican minors must hold a notarized letter of consent [14], signed by both parents or the parent not accompanying the minor, even if holding their own passport. However, if minor is holding own passport and article 421 is stamped on page 3 (or it is the actual page 3), a letter of consent is not required. Minors under 12 years travelling alone should be met at the airport of arrival by an adult.
   2. Minors being nationals of Canada or U.S.A.:
   a. travelling alone require one of the following documents together with a notarized letter of consent [14] signed by both parents:
      a valid passport or an original (or notarized copy of the) birth certificate or a notarized affidavit.
   b. travelling with one parent require:
      a valid passport or an original (or notarized copy of the) birth certificate or a notarized affidavit [14].
      Together with the above mentioned documents they must hold:
      —if the parents are divorced: a court order of child custody; or
      —if one of the parents is deceased: a death certificate; or
      —if the other parent is not travelling: a notarized letter of consent [14] signed by the parent not accompanying the minor.
      —if their birth certificate shows that the minor has only one parent, it will be sufficient to hold only (notarized copy of) birth certificate.
   3. All other alien minors travelling alone not mentioned in 1. "Passport" - Minors 2. above require a valid passport and:
   a. if the parents are divorced: a court order of child custody; or
   b. if one of the parents is deceased: a death certificate; or
   c. a notarized letter of consent [14] signed by both parents.
      If minor has only one parent it is recommended to hold birth certificate together with passport.
   4. Minors with
      — Mexican mother and father being national of the U.S.A. or vice versa; or
      — Mexican mother and father being national of Canada or vice versa:
      need to hold a notarized letter of consent [14] signed by both parents or the parent not accompanying the minor, even if holding their own passport.

Notes:
[11] As proof of Mexican citizenship one of the following Mexican documents can be accepted: expired passport, matricula consular, birth certificate with consular registration, certificate of nationality issued by a Mexican consulate abroad, certificate of military duty, voter's certificate, certificate of baptism.
[12] One of the following documents is accepted as proof of citizenship, provided coming for touristic purposes:
   — certificate of Canadian citizenship;
   — notarized copy of county or state issued birth certificate;
   — county or state issued original birth certificate with raised seal;
   — Voter's Registration Card ;
   — Naturalization Certificate (applicable only to nationals of U.S.A.);
   — notarized affidavit.

If any of above-mentioned documents does not contain a photo, then document must be accompanied by an official photo identity, such as a driver's licence. Photocopies are not accepted.
Other documents are not accepted as proof of citizenship, e.g. an expired passport, driver's licence, any document with an expired notary seal.
Minors, up to incl. 15 years, travelling either with both parents or only one parent are not required to hold a separate photo identity.
[13] Stateless persons entering Mexico for tourist, social or business purposes must hold Form FM3 and re-entry permit, both issued by Mexican consulate or embassy in the country of origin.
[14] The notarized letter of consent for minors of all nationalities can be an original, facsimile or photocopy. However, the **stamp must be an original** even if the letter is a facsimile or photocopy. The letter of consent has no set validity period but is good for a single entry only.

2. **Visa: Warning:**
   1. — *All visitors must hold tickets* [21] *and documents for their onward or return journey and sufficient funds for maintenance during their stay in Mexico;*
      — *nationals of countries not stated under 2. "Visa" - Issue must obtain a consular visa abroad at (or nearest to) their home country.*
      Non-compliance with the entry regulations will result in fines for carrier from USD 850.- to a maximum of USD 1800.- and deportation of visitor to home country at carrier's expense;
   2. *several nationalities need,* **in addition to their visa,** *also a previous permit or a Tourist Card/form FMT. For issuance of these documents see 2. "Visa" - Issue.*

Visa required, except for:
   1. nationals of Mexico holding form FME issued either by the airline upon departure or on arrival;
   2. alien residents, including government officials accredited to Mexico, holding form FME, issued by the airline upon departure, and form FM2/FM3;
   3. Tourist Card/form FMT with consular stamp issued by Mexican Embassy/Consulate in place of residence for nationals of: Belize, Bosnia Herzegovina, Croatia, Ecuador, El Salvador, FYROM (Former Yugoslav Rep. of Macedonia), Jamaica, Yugoslavia Fed. Rep.;
   4. Tourist Card/form FMT with consular stamp issued by Mexican Embassy/Consulate in Jamaica to nationals of Bahamas. Alien residents of Bahamas must apply to Embassy/Consulate in U.S.A. or Venezuela;
   5. Tourist Card/form FMT issued by airlines [22], [23] (for conditions see below) for a stay of max. 30 days:
   a. San Marino;
   b. normal, consular or special passports: Venezuela;
   6. Tourist Card/form FMT issued by airlines [22], [23] (for conditions see below) for a stay of max. 90 days:
   a. Argentina, Costa Rica, Greece, Hungary, Iceland, Poland, Portugal, Slovenia, Spain;
   b. France. However, visa exemption is not applicable if holding passports issued in French Guiana, French Polynesia, French West Indies, New Caledonia or Reunion; see 2. "Visa" - Issue 1;
   c. holders of British passports endorsed "British National (Overseas)";
   d. normal, diplomatic, official and service passports: Chile;
   e. normal, diplomatic and official passports: Korea Rep.;
   f. diplomatic, official or service passports: Bolivia, Brazil, China (People's Rep.), Cyprus, Czech Rep., Germany, Japan, Morocco, Nicaragua, Panama, Romania, Slovak Rep., Switzerland, Trinidad and Tobago and Venezuela;
   g. diplomatic or official passports: Canada, Denmark, Guyana, Indonesia, Italy, Malaysia, Norway, Peru, Philippines, Slovenia, St.Vincent & Grenadines (for max. 30 days), Sweden and Uruguay;
   h. diplomatic passports: Honduras, Russian Fed., Turkey and Ukraine;
   i. consular, diplomatic and official passports: Guatemala;
   7. holders of form FME issued by airlines for a stay of max. 90 days:
      diplomatic, official and service passports: Ecuador;
   8. Tourist Card/form FMT issued by airlines [22], [23] (for conditions see below) for a stay of max. 180 days:
   a. Andorra, Australia, Austria, Belgium, Finland, Ireland (Rep.), Israel, Liechtenstein, Luxembourg, Monaco, New Zealand, Singapore, U.S.A.;
   b. Netherlands (including passports issued in Aruba). If passport issued in the Netherlands Antilles (Bonaire, Curaçao, Saba, St. Eustatius, Sint Maarten) see 2. "Visa"-Issue 5;

   c. holders of British passports [21]:
      — endorsed "British Citizen"or "British Dependent Territories Citizen"; or
      — issued in Bermuda;
   d. diplomatic or official passports: Colombia;
   e. normal, consular, service and special passports: Canada, Denmark, Italy, Norway, Sweden and Uruguay;
   f. normal, consular and special passports: Germany, Japan and Switzerland;
   g. diplomatic passports: Cuba;
   h. alien residents of Canada, Japan and U.S.A. coming directly from country of residence, provided holding an alien residents card and an official photo identification e.g. driver's licence;

Tourist Card/form FMT issued by airlines:
Airlines are authorized to issue Tourist Card/ form FMT to tourists mentioned under 2. "Visa" item 5., 6. and 7. above, who must hold tickets [21] and documents for their onward or return journey and sufficient funds for maintenance during their stay in Mexico;
   9. nationals of Canada and U.S.A. coming for business purposes of max. 30 days (extension possible) and holding form FMN. This form can be issued by travel agencies, airlines or on arrival;
(TWOV)
   10. (facility not applicable to those mentioned in 2. "Visa" - Issue 1. They need transit visa. Non-compliance will result in fines of USD 1000.-.)
      Those [24] continuing their journey to a third country within 24 hours by same or first connecting flight without further intermediate landings in Mexican territory, and provided holding confirmed onward tickets and other documents for their next destination. Leaving the airport is not allowed.
      All passengers (except nationals of U.S.A.) travelling to/from Cuba must continue within 12 hours.
      Airline employees travelling on tickets "subject to load" are NOT accepted for transit without visa;
   11. nationals of India continuing their journey to a third country by same aircraft provided not leaving the airport transit area;

Merchant Seaman: must travel on duty and hold Letter of Guarantee of shipping company (see Terms & Definitions).
   1. If arriving by air in order to board ship: Foreign Merchant Seamen cannot be provided with tourist card/form FMT. They must obtain form FM 6 from a Mexican consulate abroad. The nationalities mentioned in 2. "Visa" - Issue 1. through 5. require previous authorization from the Mexican government.
      It is required that:
      — either seamen hold FM 6 issued by consulate:
      — or shipping company must provide advance information of seaman as shown below, to its shipping agency in Mexico, at least 36 hours prior to arrival of seaman. The shipping company should obtain authorization from Mexican immigration that form FM 6 will be issued on arrival of seaman. Shipping company should inform station manager of transporting airline in Mexico accordingly. Fee of Form FM 6 issued on arrival: USD 8.-.
      Advance information to be sent:
      Passenger's name (also state "seaman"); nationality; complete itinerary; name of ship to board; name of shipping company and name of their handling agent in Mexico. Do not embark your passenger to Mexico unless telex message (O.K. for travel) is received from station manager Mexico of transporting airline. (copy of "O.K. for travel" telex to be stapled to passenger's ticket).
   2. If arriving by ship in order to board aircraft:
      foreign merchant seamen can obtain their FM 6 from the seaport immigration authorities.
   3. If in direct transit to abroad: visa not required for:
      — the nationals listed in 2. "Visa" 1., 2. and 3.;
      — those mentioned in 2. "Visa" 8. provided complying with conditions mentioned therein.

Issue:
   1. The following nationals need, **in addition to their visa,** also a previous permit or tourist card/form FMT from the Mexican Embassy/Consulate in country of residence:
      — Afghanistan, Bangladesh, Bolivia, Brazil, Cambodia, China (People's Rep.) (not applicable if holding diplomatic, official or service passports), Colombia, Cuba (not applicable if holding diplomatic passports), Dominican Rep., France (only if holding passports issued in French Guiana, French Polynesia, French West Indies, New Caledonia or Reunion), India, Iran, Iraq, Korea (Dem. People's Rep.), Libya, Malaysia, Nicaragua, Pakistan, Panama (only applicable if holding normal passports), Paraguay, Peru, Sri Lanka, Vietnam;

— Jordan, Lebanon, Syria, Turkey (not applicable to holders of diplomatic passports), Yemen Rep. However, if holding visa issued by Mexican Embassy in Saudi Arabia and holding visa for a third country (if required), then previous permit or tourist card/form FMT is not required;

2. nationals of Haiti need, **in addition to their visa**, also a tourist card/form FMT with consular stamp only to be obtained from the Mexican embassy in Haiti;

3. nationals of Guatemala (holding normal passports only) and South Africa need, **in addition to their visa**, also a tourist card/form FMT stamped by Mexican consulate in (or nearest to) their home country;

4. nationals of Honduras being of Chinese origin need, **in addition to their visa**, also a previous permit issued by the "Secretaria de Gobernacion" located in Mexico;

5. visas and Tourist Card/form FMT with consular stamp may only be issued to the nationals mentioned below by the Mexican Embassy/Consulate established in:

— Africa and Western Europe:
Algeria, Benin (Rep.), Botswana, Burkina Faso, Burundi, Cape Verde Isl., Cameroon, Central African Rep., Chad, Comores Isl., Congo (Brazzaville), Congo (Kinshasa), Côte d'Ivoire, Djibouti, Egypt, Ethiopia, Gabon, Gambia, Ghana, Guinea Rep., Equatorial Guinea, Guinea-Bissau, Kenya, Lesotho, Liberia, Malawi, Mali, Morocco, Madagascar, Mauritius, Mauritania, Mozambique, Namibia, Niger, Nigeria, Rwanda, Senegal, Seychelles, Somalia, Sudan, Tanzania, Togo, Uganda, Zimbabwe;

— Asia, Australia, New Zealand or Papua New Guinea:
Brunei, Bhutan, Fiji, Indonesia, Kiribati, Laos, Maldives, Mongolia, Myanmar, Nauru, Nepal, Papua New Guinea, Philippines, Solomon Isl., Samoa Western, Thailand, Tonga, Tuvalu, Vanuatu and to holders of U.S. "Trust Territories of the Pacific Islands" passport issued in Micronesia.

— Asia, Western Europe, Australia, New Zealand or Papua New Guinea:
Bahrain, Kuwait, Oman, Qatar, Saudi Arabia, United Arab Emirates.

— Eastern Europe:
Armenia, Azerbaijan, Belarus, Bulgaria, Czech Rep., Georgia, Kazakstan, Kyrgyzstan, Moldova (Rep. of), Poland, Romania, Russian Fed., Slovak Rep., Tajikistan, Turkmenistan, Ukraine, Uzbekistan.

— Western Europe:
Albania (also by Mexican Embassy/Consulate in Yugoslavia Fed. Rep.), Angola, Cyprus, Malta.

— Jamaica:
Antigua & Barbuda, Dominica, St. Kitts-Nevis, St. Lucia, St. Vincent & the Grenadines and to holders of British passports issued in: Cayman Isl., Leeward Isl., Montserrat or Turks & Caicos Isl ; holders of U.S. passports issued in U.S. Virgin Isl.

— U.S.A.:
holders of British passports issued in Bermuda.

— Venezuela:
Barbados, Grenada, Guyana, Suriname;

— Jamaica, U.S.A. or Venezuela:
holders of Dutch passports issued in Netherlands Antilles (Bonaire, Curaçao, Saba, St. Eustatius, Sint Maarten).

Additional information:

1. A cash deposit may be required for nationals of countries not stated under 2. "Visa" - Exemptions (refundable upon departure). Amounts vary according to nationality and period of stay.

2. Tourist Card/form FMT only grant a visa exemption to holder himself. Children and Infants mentioned in holder's passport should each have their own Tourist Card/ form FMT. On the Tourist Card/ form FMT of the father or the mother, a notation should appear as to the number of minors that travel with them.
Tourist Card/form FMT may be completed by passenger himself in handwritten block letters but the issuing carrier must always stamp and sign the box "SELLO Y FECHA OFICINA EXPEDIDORA" ("Stamp and date of issuing office") both on the original and on the copy of the Tourist Card/form FMT.

Tourist Card/form FMT is printed in Spanish, English and French and can be completed in Spanish, English or French. Airlines can also issue Tourist Card/form FMT for transportation on flights of other airlines as long as carriers involved are authorized to issue Tourist Card/form FMT to the nationality concerned as per 2. "Visa" -Issue of Tourist Card/form FMT by airlines.
No passport photos required for nationals to whom airlines are authorized to issue Tourist Card/form FMT.
Do not fail to issue Tourist Card/form FMT to eligible passengers. Airline staff can issue Tourist Card/form FMT to passengers who misplaced or lost their form prior to check by Immigration.

3. Visas in expired passports or Seaman Books are not valid.

Minors: Mexican minors, leaving Mexico and being under 18 years without holding own passport and travelling alone or with one parent, need:
a. affidavit signed by both parents or by the other parent who is not travelling with the minor; or
b. if the parents are divorced: a court order of child custody; or
c. if one of the parents is deceased: a death certificate.

Re-entry permit: Returning alien residents need to hold both a form FME as well as a form FM2/FM3.

Notes:

21 The following passengers are allowed to enter Mexico on one-way tickets:
a. nationals of Canada, Japan and U.S.A.;
b. those holding British passports endorsed "British Citizen", provided they hold either Tourist Card/form FMT or visa.

22 Provided travelling for touristic purposes.

23 Those who intend to stay longer than indicated, must obtain a consular visa abroad in addition to the Tourist Card/ form FMT.

24 Stateless persons and refugees need to hold Form FM3 if being in transit.

3. **Health:** Required - except for transit passengers not leaving the airport - vaccination against:
yellow fever, if arriving within 6 days after leaving or transiting **31** infected and endemic areas (see General Health Information).
Exempt are: children under 6 months of age.

Recommended:
Malaria prophylaxis. Malaria risk - almost exclusively in the benign (P. vivax) form - exists throughout the year in some rural areas that are not often visited by travellers. The states most affected are (in decreasing order of importance): Oaxaca, Chiapas, Sinaloa, Michoacán, Nayarit, Guerrero, Tabasco, Quintana Roo, Chihuahua, Campeche, Hidalgo. (See Terms & Definitions).
Recommended prophylaxis in risk areas: CHL.
Notes:
31 Not required for those not leaving the airport in the areas concerned.

4. **Tax:** Airport tax is levied on passengers departing from Mexico:
a. on domestic flights:
— within buffer zone: . . . . . . MXN 87.89;
— outside buffer zone: . . . . . MXN 91.89;
b. on international flights: USD 18.- (embarkation tax of USD 15.- and Immigration tax of USD 3.-).
Place of payment: airport of departure in Mexico (if not already included in ticket).
Exempt are:
1. children under 2 years;
2. holders of a diplomatic passport;
3. transit passengers complying with the TWOV conditions.

5. **Customs:**
Import: free import
1. (only for persons over 18 years:) 400 cigarettes **or** 50 cigars **or** 250 grammes of pipe tobacco;
2. (only for persons over 18 years:) 3 litres of wine or liquor (alcoholic beverages);
3. a reasonable quantity of perfume, eau-de-cologne and lotions for personal use;
4. a photo or movie or video camera. One additional camera for passengers residing outside Mexico;
5. 12 rolls of film or video cassettes;
6. goods up to USD 300.-.

Additional information:
1. Goods imported in addition to the categories above are dutiable, but exempt from import licence, provided the total value of these additional goods is max. USD 500.- and the value of goods of the same character (e.g. leather goods) included therein is max. USD 100.-. Excluded from these additional goods are articles considered unnecessary luxury goods, e.g. ivory, cutglass, porcelain, electrical appliances etc.
2. Firearms and ammunition require import permit, to be obtained from Secretaría de la Defensa ("Secretary of Defence"), Estado Mayor 6a. Sección, Lomas de Sotelo, Mexico D.F.
3. Mexico is member of the CITES (see Terms & Definitions).

Prohibited:
— any uncanned foodstuff (e.g. pork) and derivatives.
Import of canned food is permitted, except for pork and derivatives.
For full information contact the nearest representation of Mexico.
— earth, plants, parts of them, flowers, fruits, seeds or materials of vegetable origin used as containers, packing or in the manufacture of handicrafts.

It is allowed to import seeds and plants of varieties and species that are beneficial to the nation, having first secured authorization from the Ministry of Agriculture.
Pets: all pets require veterinary health certificate, issued no longer than 10 days before arrival. For dogs and cats also a rabies vaccination certificate is required. Birds including parrots require veterinary health certificate.
Import permit from Ministry of Agriculture is required for pet birds accompanying passengers, except for birds destined to Merida and Campeche.
Export: free export of tobacco products and alcoholic beverages.
Prohibited: Export of archaeological relics.
Baggage clearance: baggage is cleared at the first airport of entry in Mexico. It is strongly advised to inform the passenger about this before embarking. All baggage has to be labeled accordingly.

6. **Currency:**
Import: allowed.
local currency (Nuevo Peso-MXN): up to an equivalent of USD 10,000.-. Higher amounts must be declared;
foreign currencies: any amount must be declared on arrival. Exchange into local currency is only allowed at authorized banks. Non-residents can exchange amounts as necessary for their own expenses.
Only freely convertible currencies will be accepted by the banks.
Export: allowed.
RESIDENTS and Mexican nationals:
local currency (Nuevo Peso-MXN): up to an equivalent of USD 10,000.-;
foreign currencies: unlimited.
Airport exchange offices will sell a minimum of USD 1,000.- and up to USD 3,000.- per trip abroad.
Additional amounts for business trips, medical purposes etc. must be obtained from the Banco de Mexico.
NON-RESIDENTS other than Mexican nationals:
local currency: up to an equivalent of USD 10,000.-;
foreign currencies: unused amounts previously declared upon arrival.

SAUDI ARABIA

Geographical Information: Capital - Riyadh (RUH).
Saudi Arabia is a member state of the Gulf Cooperation Council (see Terms & Definitions).

WARNING FOR PILGRIMS!

1. Pilgrims arriving (either on special pilgrim flights or on normal scheduled flights) on:
   — foreign carriers: must enter Saudi Arabia via Jeddah only. (Some carriers do not accept pilgrims during the pilgrimage season at all. Please consult transporting carrier);
   — Saudi Arabian Airlines: must enter Saudi Arabia via Jeddah or Medina only. This regulation is applicable both outside and during the pilgrim season.

   Moreover, pilgrims performing "Umrah" (visiting holy places outside the normal pilgrim season) must hold tickets for return- or onward transportation.
   Umrah visas will be converted into Haj visas upon arrival during pilgrimage dates.
2. Haj pilgrims or pilgrims performing "Umrah" arriving in Jeddah are required to produce a vaccination certificate for meningitis. The date of vaccination should be not more than 3 years and not less than 10 days from the date of arrival in Saudi Arabia.
   If a pilgrim arrives without the required health documents he will either be vaccinated at the airport or will be quarantined. No charges.
3. All pilgrims must carry an identity card fixed on a wrist band containing information about their health condition.
   This card will be provided by Ministry of Haj to Hajis originating in Saudi Arabia. If originating abroad the card will be provided by Haj organizers.
4. All pilgrims must be in possession of return tickets with confirmed reservations. Offices making reservations for Haj passengers are requested to add "PILGRIM" in their reservation messages.
   Moreover, pilgrims, especially those not holding pilgrim passes, should hold a cheque in ARI for payment of their Haji arrangements.
5. As baggage of pilgrim and non-pilgrim passengers are handled at different terminals, it is essential that the baggage of pilgrims arriving by normal scheduled flights (no pilgrim charters) is provided with a special "Pilgrim" label or sticker.
   For foodstuffs included in their baggage: see 5. Customs.
6. **1999 Pilgrimage Dates:**
   HAJ period starts from January 18, 1999 and ends midnight of March 21, 1999 for those coming to Jeddah. However, for those coming to Medina the period ends at midnight March 17, 1999 (First Phase).
   Carriers bringing in pilgrims with HAJ-visa after above mentioned date will be fined!
   Pilgrims start leaving the country from April 1, 1999, 04.00 hours local time (Second Phase).
   Final leaving date for pilgrims is April 26, 1999.
   Note that:
   1. pilgrim visas are worded in Arabic only;
   2. the religious group of the Quadyani will be refused entry.
7. On their way to Holy Places pilgrims are not allowed to visit other places than those which figure in their pilgrimage (e.g. Medina and/or Makkah, formerly spelled "**Mecca**") to leave the airport on **which they are waiting for a connecting flight either into or out of Saudi Arabia.**
8. The governments in some countries with a large Moslem population issue special pilgrim passes to Moslem pilgrims. If such pilgrim passes cannot be obtained, normal passports stating legally that the holder is going on pilgrimage to Makkah are acceptable. In such a case, however, it is necessary that either the passport or another official certificate states that the passenger concerned is of the Moslem faith.

1. **Passport:** Required, except for:
   1. holders of Laissez-Passer issued by the United Nations;
   2. holders of a Seaman Book, provided travelling on duty;
   3. Moslem pilgrims holding pilgrim passes, tickets and other documents required for their return or onward journey (see section Geographical Information - WARNING FOR PILGRIMS 1.).

   Validity: Passports of alien non-residents must be valid for at least 6 months upon entry.

   Admission and transit restrictions: The Government of Saudi Arabia refuses admission and transit to:
   a. nationals of Israel;
   b. those arriving in apparent intoxicated state. The delivering carrier will be held responsible and their regular operations to Saudi Arabia might be jeopardized due to violation of the Islamic laws.
   c. those who do not comply with the Saudi Arabian requirements regarding general appearance and behaviour such as:
   — women exposing legs or arms, or wearing too thin or too tight clothes;
   — men wearing shorts exposing legs;
   — men and women displaying affection in public in any manner.

   Additional information: Housemaids or wives travelling unaccompanied, joining their husband, must:
   — be met at the airport by sponsor or husband; and
   — have confirmed onward reservations up to their final destination in Saudi Arabia.
   Non-compliance may result in deportation.

2. **Visa: Warning:**
   1. *Non-compliance with the entry requirements will result in a fine of SAR 3,000.-.*
   2. *Transit passengers are only allowed to make one transit stop in Saudi Arabia. They must proceed to another country on a non-stop flight, so without making another landing in Saudi Arabia. Exempt are holders of diplomatic passports with a transit visa for Saudi Arabia.*

   Visa required, except for:
   1. nationals of Saudi Arabia;
   2. holders of a Bahrain, Kuwait, Oman, Qatar or United Arab Emirates passport;
   3. holders of a re-entry permit;
   4. holders of a "Landing Permit" issued by the Saudi Arabian Ministry of Foreign Affairs;

   (TWOV)
   5. those [24] continuing to a third country by same or first connecting aircraft (maximum connecting time for Dhahran, Jeddah and Riyadh 12 hours), provided:
      — not leaving the transit lounge at the airport (very limited catering facilities in Dhahran, Jeddah and Riyadh transit lounges); and
      — onward flight does not make another landing in Saudi Arabia; and
      — holding tickets with confirmed onward reservations and other documents for an onward destination.
      To avoid uncomfortable overnights, e.g. in case of missed connections, it is recommended to hold a transit visa for Saudi Arabia.
      Those holding a transit visa can be hosted in a hotel by the transporting carrier, provided this carrier holds the responsibility of their stay until they travel on the first connecting flight.

   Merchant Seamen: must travel on duty and hold prior approval to enter from Immigration Authorities and Letter of Guarantee of shipping company (see Terms & Definitions). Merchant seamen are only allowed to land at Dhahran and Jeddah airports [23].
   1. If arriving by air in order to board ship: visa not required:
      — if nationality of the seaman is mentioned in 2. "Visa" 1. and 2.;
      — for any other nationality [21] [22] provided their ship is either already in the harbour or will arrive within about 24 hours after the arrival of the seaman and the seaman is met by the agent of the shipping company.
      The station manager of the arriving airline in Saudi Arabia is informed prior to arrival of:
      — name of seaman, ship and shipping company and name, address and telephone number of its agent;
      — flight number and date of arrival and if seaman arrives on Thursday or Friday emphasize this, thus enabling the station manager of the delivering airline to take the necessary measures in time (on one of the preceeding working days).
      A copy of the telegram/telex/letter must be attached to the seaman's ticket, to enable checking by boarding point.
   2. If arriving by ship in order to board aircraft: visa not required:
      — if nationality of the seaman is mentioned in 2. "Visa" 1. and 2.;
      — for any other nationality [21] [22] provided procedure is completely arranged by shipping agent;
   3. If in direct transit to abroad: visa not required:
      — if nationality of the seaman is mentioned in 2. "Visa" 1. and 2.;
      — for those using TWOV-facility per 2. "Visa" 5.

   Issue: by a representation of Saudi Arabia in Afghanistan (Kabul), Algeria (Algiers), Australia (Canberra), Austria (Vienna), Bahrain, Belgium (Brussels), Chad (N'Djamena), Denmark (Copenhagen), Egypt (Cairo), Ethiopia (Addis Ababa), France (Paris), Germany (Bonn), Ghana (Accra), Greece (Athens), Guinea (Conakry), India (Delhi), Indonesia (Jakarta), Iran (Tehran), Iraq (Baghdad, Basra), Italy (Rome), Japan (Tokyo), Jordan (Amman), Kazakstan (Almaty), Kuwait, Lebanon (Beirut), Libya (Benghazi, Tripoli), Malaysia (Kuala Lumpur), Morocco (Rabat), Netherlands (the Hague), Nigeria (Lagos), Pakistan (Karachi), Senegal (Dakar), Singapore, Somalia (Mogadishu), Spain (Madrid), Sudan (Khartoum), Sweden (Stockholm), Switzerland (Berne), Syria (Damascus), Thailand (Bangkok), Tunisia (Tunis), Turkey (Ankara), United Kingdom (London), U.S.A. (Washington D.C. and New York City), Venezuela (Caracas) and the United Nations (New York).

   A pilgrim visa is worded in the Arab language only. Business and visitors' visas are half Arab/half English.
   It may take considerable time to obtain a visa. In order to avoid the possibility of refusals visa applicants should preferably write to the consulate acting for their home country, thereby stating the number of entries into Saudi Arabia, included in their itinerary. Muslims cannot obtain a visitor's visa during the pilgrimage season (for periods see section Geographical Information - WARNING FOR PILGRIMS **5.**). The issue of such a visa to non-Muslims may be suspended during said period.
   Passengers must arrive in Saudi Arabia within the period of validity of the visa, which commences on the date of issue. Visas are valid for one entry only, unless otherwise specified.
   Visas show the period of validity and of permitted stay in Saudi Arabia.

   Additional information:
   1. If applying for a visa, passport must be valid for at least 6 months.
   2. If arriving within the validity of the entry visa then validity of the visa will start from the day of travelling.
   3. Visitors must hold:
   a. all documents required for their next destination;
   b. return or onward tickets that are not refundable in Saudi Arabia.
   This requirement is not applicable to:
   — merchant seamen travelling on duty with a seaman book;
   — passengers travelling with tickets issued against a government order;
   — family members joining expatriate staff stationed in Saudi Arabia;
   — passengers holding a re-entry permit, residence visa or a working visa for Saudi Arabia, **unless** working as a servant in the house.

   Re-entry permit: Required, to be obtained before leaving Saudi Arabia by all alien residents who wish to return, except for members of the United States armed forces who are already registered in Saudi Arabia.
   Exit permit: Exit permit is required for nationals and alien residents of Saudi Arabia leaving from an airport in Saudi Arabia, except for members of the United States armed forces who are already registered in Saudi Arabia. One passport photo is required.
   Issuance: by the Chief of Police about three days after application.
   Notes:
   [21] Not applicable to nationals of: Albania, Armenia, Azerbaijan, Belarus, Bulgaria, China (People's Rep.), Cuba, Czech Rep., Georgia, Hungary, Kazakstan, Korea (Dem. People's. Rep.), Kyrgyzstan, Moldova (Rep. of), Mongolia, Poland, Romania, Russian Fed., Slovak Rep., Tajikistan, Turkmenistan, Ukraine, Uzbekistan, Vietnam, Yugoslavia Fed. Rep.;
   [22] Also applicable to the wife of the captain, even if not holding Seaman Book or visa in passport, provided escorted by husband and holding legal documents proving her marital status.
   [23] Seamen being nationals of Saudi Arabia are allowed to land at any airport.
   [24] Not applicable to residents of Burkina Faso, Mali, Niger and Nigeria who always need a transit visa.

3. **Health:** Required - except for transit passengers not leaving the airport - vaccination against:
   yellow fever, [32] if arriving within 6 days after leaving or transiting [31] countries any parts of which are infected areas (see General Health Information).
   Meningitis, which is required for:
   a. Hajis and Umrah passengers (see also section Geographical Information - WARNING FOR PILGRIMS **2.**); and
   b. nationals of Burkina Faso, Mali, Niger and Nigeria, arriving from Burkina Faso, Cameroon, Central African Rep., Chad, Congo (Kinshasa), Ethiopia, Gambia, Ghana, Guinea Rep., Mali, Niger, Nigeria and Sudan.
   The date of vaccination should be not more than 3 years and not less than 10 days from the date of arrival in Saudi Arabia. If arriving without meningitis vaccination certificate, passenger will be vaccinated upon arrival or quarantined.
   Angina (Diphteria), which is only required for Hajis and Umrah passengers coming from C.I.S. countries (see Terms & Definitions). If arriving without a vaccination certificate, these passengers will be vaccinated upon arrival. Suspected cases will be subject to quarantine and those who have been associated to suspected cases will be under strict supervision.
   Nationals of C.I.S. countries will obtain penicellin or erythromycin on arrival.

   The immigration officer must be informed of the number of passengers on each flight, flight number and date of arrival for further handling of vaccination on arrival.

   Recommended:
   Malaria prophylaxis. Malaria risk - mainly in the malignant (P. falciparum) form - exists throughout the year in most of the Southern Region (except in the high-altitude areas of Asir Province) and in certain rural areas of the Western Region. Chloroquine-resistant P. falciparum reported (see Terms & Definitions).
   Recommended prophylaxis in risk areas: C plus P.
   Notes:
   [31] Not required for those not leaving the airport in the countries concerned.
   [32] **Quarantine:** Persons without valid yellow fever certificate - if required - will be vaccinated upon arrival and are subject to quarantine.

4. **Tax:** No airport tax is levied on passengers upon embarkation at the airport (see Terms & Definitions).

5. **Customs:**
   Import: free import
   1. (irrespective of age) 600 cigarettes or 100 cigars or 500 grammes of tobacco (any excess prohibited);
   2. a reasonable quantity of perfume;
   3. a reasonable amount of cultured pearls for personal use.

   Additional information:
   1. Nothing can be imported free of duty as passenger's baggage, except clothes and strictly personal effects.
   2. No foodstuffs may be imported except: fruits, nuts, sweets prepared under hygienic conditions, honey and other foodstuffs in an "easy-to-open can" which can easily be inspected. Consult the Consulate for restrictions regarding foodstuffs from cholera infected areas (see General Health Information).
   3. Customs charges are even on photographic cameras, typewriters, etc. If these articles are re-exported within 90 days, customs charges may be refunded. It is advisable not to put a film in a camera.
   4. Saudi Arabia is member of the CITES (see Terms & Definitions).

   Warning: Import ban (also for passenger's baggage) until further notice!
   — All kinds of edible goods, like dairy products, vegetables, meat, fish, fruits, baby food, carbonated water etc.;
   — live animals and birds (including pets) and
   — all types of palm trees or derivatives of palm trees

   from or in transit via:
   1. Armenia, Azerbaijan, Belarus, Bulgaria, Czech Rep., Germany (only former East Germany), Georgia, Hungary, Kazakstan, Kyrgyzstan, Moldova (Rep. of), Poland, Romania, Russian Fed., Slovak Rep., Tajikistan, Turkmenistan, Ukraine, Uzbekistan, Yugoslavia Fed. Rep. or any other country announced (or still to be announced) by the World Health Organization;
   2. (unless accompanied by a certificate issued by the official Department of the country concerned, stating that the radiation does not exceed the normal international levels. Examination will be conducted on arrival to verify radiation percentage.) Austria, Belgium, Brazil, Denmark, Finland, France, Germany (not applicable for former East Germany), Greece, Ireland Rep., Italy, Netherlands, Norway, Portugal, Spain, Sweden, Turkey and United Kingdom.

   Prohibited (also for transit passengers): alcoholic beverages, firearms or other lethal weapons; drugs of narcotic nature, except medicines for personal use and provided holding prescription; pork products; natural pearls.

   Pets:
   1. Dogs:
   a. Watch dogs, hunting dogs, seeing-eye dogs for the blind and hearing dogs for deaf persons. The purpose of use of such dogs must be shown in a veterinary certificate.
   To be obtained prior to arrival: basic permission from the Saudi Arabian Consul in the country of origin. To be inserted in the veterinary certificate.
   b. Other dogs (whether as baggage or as cargo): prohibited in case of import or transit if leaving the airport, but the possibility exists that the authorities above grant incidental exemptions from this prohibition.
   Non-compliance will result in serious consequences. Moreover the dog will be returned by first available flight.
   2. Cats: must be accompanied by 2 veterinarian health certificates and a rabies inoculation certificate, stating inoculation between 12 months and 30 days prior to arrival.
   3. Birds: Health certificate and import permit required.

   Prohibited: live chickens, turkeys, pigeons, ducks, geese and parrots.
   Baggage clearance: baggage is cleared at the airport of final destination in Saudi Arabia, provided this is an international airport.
   Exempt: baggage of transit passengers with a destination outside Saudi Arabia.

6. **Currency:**
   Import: allowed
   local currency (Saudi Arabian Rial-SAR) and foreign currencies (other than Israeli Sheqel): unlimited.
   Prohibited: Israeli Sheqel.
   Export: allowed
   local currency (Saudi Arabian Rial-SAR) and foreign currencies: unlimited.

■ ST. LUCIA

Geographical information:
Capital - Castries (SLU).
Independent St. Lucia is one of the Windward
Islands which form the southern part of the
Lesser Antilles that stretch in a semi-circle
from Venezuela to Puerto Rico.

1. **Passport:** Required, except for holders of:
   1. Proof of identity e.g. Birth Certificate or driver's license issued to nationals of St. Lucia;
   2. Proof of Citizenship issued to nationals of Canada and U.S.A. provided:
      — presented together with a photo identity (e.g. birth certificate and driver's license or Voters Registration Card and driver's license).
      — their stay is not exceeding 6 months;
      — holding return/onward tickets and other documents required for their next destination.
      For U.S. minors below the age of 12 holding certified copy of birth certificate no additional photo identification is required;
   3. Seaman Book, provided travelling on duty;
   4. travel documents issued to stateless persons and refugees.
   Validity: nationals of Canada, Great Britain (regardless of endorsement in passport), St. Lucia and U.S.A. may enter on expired passport provided holding photo identity and birth certificate.

2. **Visa:** Required, except for:
   1. nationals of St. Lucia;
   2. nationals of Canada, Germany and U.S.A. for a stay of 6 months;
   3. nationals of Chile, Haiti and South Africa holding normal passports for a stay of max. 90 days (extension possible for max. 90 days);
   4. holders of British passports 21 (irrespective of endorsement in passport);
   5. nationals 21 of: Albania, Antigua and Barbuda, Argentina, Armenia, Australia, Austria, Azerbaijan, Bahamas, Bangladesh, Barbados, Belarus, Belgium, Belize, Bolivia, Botswana, Brazil, Brunei, Bulgaria, Cameroon, Costa Rica, Cyprus, Czech Rep., Denmark, Dominica, Dominican Rep., Ecuador, El Salvador, Estonia, Fiji, Finland, France, Gambia, Georgia, Ghana, Greece, Grenada, Guatemala, Guyana, Honduras, Hungary, Iceland, India, Indonesia, Iran, Ireland (Rep.), Israel, Italy, Jamaica, Japan, Kazakstan, Kenya, Kiribati, Korea Rep., Kuwait, Kyrgyzstan, Lesotho, Liechtenstein, Lithuania, Luxembourg, Malawi, Malaysia, Maldives, Malta, Mauritius, Mexico, Moldova (Rep. of), Nauru, Netherlands, New Zealand, Nicaragua, Nigeria, Norway, Pakistan, Panama, Papua New Guinea, Peru, Philippines, Poland, Portugal, Russian Fed., Samoa (Western), San Marino, Seychelles, Sierra Leone, Singapore, Slovenia, Solomon Is., Spain, Sri Lanka, St. Kitts-Nevis, St. Vincent and the Grenadines, Suriname, Swaziland, Sweden, Switzerland, Tajikistan, Tanzania, Thailand, Tonga, Trinidad & Tobago, Tunisia, Turkey, Turkmenistan, Tuvalu, Uganda, Ukraine, Uruguay, Uzbekistan, Vanuatu, Venezuela, Zambia, Zimbabwe and holders of Taiwan (Rep. of China) documents;
   6. holders of a re-entry permit issued by St. Lucia;
   (TWOV)
   7. those continuing their journey to a third country by same aircraft without leaving the airport.
   However, if being national of a communist country a transit visa is required.
   Merchant Seamen: must travel on duty and hold Letter of Guarantee of shipping company (see Terms & Definitions).
   1. If arriving by air in order to board ship: visa not required:
      — if nationality of seaman is mentioned in 2. "Visa" 1., 2., 3., 4. and 5.;
      — for any other nationality provided: - seaman is met at airport by shipping agent. Shipping company is responsible for immediate transportation to the ship; - prior telex information (with name of seaman and ship, flight number and date of arrival) to station manager of transporting airline is required. Copy of the message to the station manager/shipping agency should be attached to the ticket;
   2. If arriving by ship in order to board plane: visa not required:
      — if nationality of seaman is mentioned in 2. "Visa" 1., 2., 3., 4. and 5.;
      — for any other nationality provided the shipping agency concerned should be informed about name of crew member, name and arrival date of the ship and in-

tended date and flight of departure. Copy of the message to the station manager/shipping agency should be attached to the ticket;
   3. If in direct transit to abroad: visa not required:
      — if nationality of seaman is mentioned in 2. "Visa" 1., 2., 3., 4. and 5.;
      — for any other nationality provided continuing to a third country by same aircraft without leaving the airport.

Issue:
1. by representations of St. Lucia abroad (in Australia: by the Department of Foreign Affairs in Canberra and its Passport Offices in the State Capitals) **or** by British Consulates in countries where there is no such representation;
2. on arrival of transit visa provided passenger is in possession of a ticket to the final destination;
3. on arrival without reference for a stay of max. three months provided holding:
   a. sufficient funds for return journey to country of origin; or
   b. a suitable guarantee that these expenses can be covered; or
   c. return or onward tickets and all required documents for next destination.
Nationals of communist countries cannot apply for visa issue on arrival.
Additional Information:
1. Visitors must hold documents for the next destination and either return/onward tickets or sufficient funds for maintenance and the return to their home country.
2. Visitors may be required to make a cash deposit equal to the cost of their return passage.
3. Businessmen coming to solicit business or to represent a foreign company and salesmen coming to advertise a product must pay on arrival a non-refundable amount of XCD 150.-. This does not apply to those owning business in St. Lucia.
Re-entry permit: Required for all alien residents and to be obtained prior to their departure from St. Lucia.
Notes:
21 Visa exemptions are normally for a stay of 28 days, after which extensions may be requested from the Police Department.

3. **Health:** Required - except for transit passengers not leaving the airport - vaccination against:
   yellow fever; if arriving within 6 days after leaving or transiting 31 infected areas (see General Health Information).
   Exempt are: children under 1 year.
   Notes:
   31 Not required for those not leaving the airport in the areas concerned.

4. **Tax: Departure Tax** is levied on all passengers embarking for all destinations abroad:
   a. for residents : XCD 35.-;
   b. for alien non-residents: XCD 40.-.
   Place of payment: Airport of departure.
   Exempt are:
   1. passengers transiting by same or connecting aircraft within 24 hours;
   2. children under 12 years;
   3. government employees travelling on duty;
   4. diplomats;
   5. Voluntary Service Overseas (VSO) peace corps workers.

5. **Customs:**
   Import: free import
   1. 200 cigarettes or 250 grammes of tobacco products;
   2. 40 oz. of wine or spirits.
   Additional information: St. Lucia is member of the CITES (see Terms & Definitions).
   Pets: Cats and dogs can only be imported from Anguilla, Antigua and Barbuda, Australia, Barbados, Dominica, Great Britain and Northern Ireland, Ireland Rep., Jamaica, Montserrat, New Zealand, St. Kitts-Nevis, St. Vincent and the Grenadines.
   Health certificate required. Moreover, a permit must be obtained in advance from the Government Veterinarian in St. Lucia. By most airlines only accepted if shipped as cargo.
   Baggage clearance: baggage is cleared at the airport of entry in St. Lucia.
   Exempt: baggage of transit passengers, which is cleared at the airport of final destination in or outside St. Lucia. However 1 to 10 per cent of this baggage still risks to be subject of coincidental clearance.

6. **Currency:**
   Import and
   Export: local currency (East Caribbean Dollar-XCD) and foreign currencies: no restrictions.

Appendix A:
Agency Forms

Working in a travel agency entails a lot of paperwork that must be correctly filled out. Here are some general guidelines to remember:

1. For certain forms and records, there are legal requirements for accuracy and for what information must be included (for example, an agency invoice).

2. There are many details involved when handling a travel reservation, and the correct use of a well-designed form ensures important facts will not be forgotten.

3. Because a travel agent receives so much information, handling details in an organized fashion is very important.

Many forms used in the travel industry will be designed by an agency to suit the needs of their particular business. Other forms will be produced by the individual service supplier (for example, coupons or tickets).

In addition, you should become familiar with the industry's standard forms in general use, such as the UCCCF (universal credit card charge form). In the travel industry, one standardized form has been adopted by all of the credit card companies for that method of payment.

Under the Travel Industry Act of Ontario, full disclosure must be provided on invoices. The following details must be set out on each invoice:

1. Full name, address, and phone number of the travel agency;

2. Name and address of each passenger;

3. Full cost of the travel arrangements, broken down into its components;

4. Date and amount of deposits or installments paid;

5. Balance due and when it must be paid;

6. Name of each travel supplier;

7. Complete travel data;

8. Details of insurance (and signature line for a waiver);

9. Any entry requirements;

10. Form of payment used.

There are a number of additional documents used when air travel is involved using scheduled airlines, which are authorized for use by IATA:

1. Standard 4 coupon tickets;

2. Miscellaneous charges orders (MCOs);

3. Cash and credit card refund notices (CRNs, CCRNs);

4. Ticket exchange notices (TENs);

5. Tour orders.

AGENCY FORMS

The following are examples of forms that might be used by a travel agency:

Vacation contact sheet—Each agent in a travel agency should keep a central list (daily) of all client prospects for follow-up purposes and any other agency use (see example on page 224).

Booking/reservation form—A booking/reservation form should be completed for each client, to summarize all relevant information (see example on page 225).

Cruise line data and reservation sheet—This is a booking/reservation form used specifically for booking cruises (see example on page 226).

Customer inquiry record—For future contact reference, consider keeping a customer inquiry record of prospects who seek information or are supplied with brochures (see example on page 227).

Personal travel profile—This is a useful way of recording preferences of frequent travellers or regular clients (see example on page 228).

Itinerary—When providing travel vouchers, tickets, etc., it is a good idea to have a detailed travel itinerary form included, setting out in date order each travel component reserved, with departure/arrival times and any special information (for example, air flight numbers, hotel names, and bed and room types). An example of a typed itinerary has been included on page 229. In some agencies, the itinerary would simply be typed on letterhead rather than using a preprinted agency form. However, a sample of a preprinted form has also been included (see page 230).

Car/hotel voucher—In cases where a car or hotel accommodation has been independently reserved (not part of a tour package), obtain confirmation of the booking from the supplier and complete a voucher that clearly sets out the necessary reservation information; the client can present it on arrival. Use of a voucher should help avoid misplaced reservation information (see example on page 231).

Costing sheet—This is useful for calculating costs of various travel services (see example on page 232).

Invoice—The detailed requirements of the Travel Industry Act must be followed when preparing client invoices in Ontario. Two types of sample invoices have been included in this chapter, one a blank invoice form (see page 233) and the second a typed invoice (see page 234).

Receipt—The client should be given a receipt for each payment made (see example on page 235).

The following two agency forms will help you keep an office record of particular hotels and ships inspected by the agent. The information can then be passed on to a client who is considering that accommodation.

Hotel description form—(see example on page 236).

Checklist for shipboard inspections—(see example on pages 237 and 238).

The following industry/supplier forms are also included:

Application for insurance—(see example on page 239).

Insurance waiver—(see example on page 240).

Universal credit card charge form—(see example on page 241).

Tour order—(see example on page 242 and instructions on page 243).

Vacation Contact Sheet

VACATION CONTACT SHEET							
				AGENT:			
				DATE:			
TODAY'S DATE	PROSPECT	PHONE/ WALK-IN	SOURCE	# PAX	DESTINATION	TRAVEL DATE	COMMENTS

Booking/Reservation Form

BOOKING / RESERVATION FORM

DATE	AGENT	INVOICE NUMBER	RECORD LOCATOR	CLIENT #

PASSENGER	AGE	HOME #	BUS. #
		ADDRESS	
		HOME #	BUS. #
		ADDRESS	
		HOME #	BUS. #
		ADDRESS	
		PASSPORT	
		VACCINATION	
		VISA	
		INSURANCE	

FROM	TO	CA	FT#	CL	DATE	DEP	ARR	DATE	STATUS	SIGN	AMOUNT

HTL/CAR RENTAL	CITY	IN	OUT	# NTS	RATE	STAT	SIGN	AMOUNT

SPECIAL REMARKS:

AMOUNT	_____
AIR TAX	_____
HTL TAX & SER. CHRG	_____
INSURANCE	_____
OTHER	_____
TOTAL AMOUNT	_____
DEPOSIT PAID	_____
BALANCE DUE	_____

FARE BASIS	INSURANCE OFFERED	METHOD OF PAYMENT:
TICKET # _____	☐ DECLINED	CASH CHEQUE CREDIT CARD
TICKET # _____	☐ ACCEPTED	
TICKET # _____	INITIALS _____	NO. _____

© International Institute of Travel

Cruise Line Data and Reservation Sheet

Cruise Line Data and Reservation Sheet
Bold Face type is information essential before making a call to the reservation department of a cruise company.

1. Name of Client _____   Date : _____
2. Address _____   Zip Code : _____
3. Telephone : (Home) _____ (Business) _____

4. Total Number of Party _____   Comprised of : _____ Adults _____ Children (Age)
5. Name of Party Members _____ A or C
   _____ A or C
   _____ A or C
   _____ A or C

6. New _____ Repeat _____   Last Travelled _____   Source _____
7. Departure Date _____   Alternate Departure Date _____   Total Vacation Days _____
8. Prior Vacations _____   Successful / Unsuccessful
   _____   Successful / Unsuccessful
   _____   Successful / Unsuccessful
9. Special Interests / Destinations: _____

• • • • • • • • • • • • • • • •

10. Line: _____   Ship: _____   Sailing Date: _____
11. Alt. Line: _____   Alt. Ship: _____   Alt. Sailing Date: _____
12. Accommodations:

	Requested	**Offered**
A. Type, Category, Cabin No., or Description (bed type)		
B. Price (Cruise only)		
C. AIR ALLOWANCE .... Air / Sea .... Air / Sea City		
D. Option Date		
E. Deposit Amount		
F. Cancellation Insurance...... (Offered) (Declined)		
G. Port & Departure Taxes		
H. Extras (Pre-post cruise pkg.)		
I. Amt. Final Payment from Client .... When Due at Line		
J. Form of Payment		
K. Commission		
L. Net Due to Line		

13. Citizenship _____   Special Diet / Occasion _____
14. Dining Room Sitting: 1st _____   2nd _____   Smoking: Yes: _____ No: _____
15. Table For: _____ (Number)   Seated With: _____

• • • • • • • • • • • • • • •

16. Reservations Made By : _____ Date : _____   17. Air/Sea Only
   Booking #: _____   Flight Nos. _____ / _____
   Offered By: _____   Departure Times: _____ / _____
   Accepted By: _____   Arrival Times: _____ / _____
   Gift Order Sent: _____   Seat Assign: _____ / _____

18. Documents Received: _____   Delivered: _____

16-6   © International Institute of Travel

© International Institute of Travel

Customer Inquiry Record

	COUNSELLOR #	FOLLOW-UP DATE

Name	Date
Address	Taken by
Telephone (H)	(B)

Destination(s) _____

Type of Holiday _____

Number of Persons in Party _____   Adults _____   Children, ages _____

Approx. Departure Date _____   Duration of Trip _____   Days _____

Type of Accommodation _____   ( ) Deluxe   ( ) F-Class   ( ) Modest

Specific Interests _____

_____

Maximum Budget (if any)   per person _____   in total $ _____

MATERIAL RELEASES (maximum 3 pieces)   ( ) MAILED   ( ) PICKED UP

1. _____   Date released _____

2. _____   By _____

3. _____   Date followed up _____

By _____

REMARKS

_____

_____

_____

_____

_____

_____

Personal Travel Profile

PERSONAL TRAVEL PROFILE

PERSONAL TRAVEL PROFILE (Confidential)

NAME : _____   TRAVELS WITH :   BIRTHDAY:

ADDRESS : _____   _____ _____

_____   _____ _____

CITY : _____   _____ _____

POSTAL CODE : _____

Phone - Home : _____   Office : _____ Fax : _____

PREFERRED AIRLINE / SEATING / FREQUENT FLYER _____

_____

SPECIAL REQUESTS _____

_____

CREDIT CARDS _____

_____

TRAVEL HISTORY

DATE	DESTINATION	VALUE	REMARKS

Sample Itinerary

ASTOR TRAVEL SERVICES ✈

1240 Bay Street, Suite 302
Toronto, Ontario M5R 2A7 CANADA

For our valued clients

Mr. Chien, Mr. Chat, Mr. Cheval

Aug 06	Depart Toronto—Air Transat Flight #1234	7:20 p.m.
	Arrive Amsterdam	10:00 a.m. Aug 07
	Seats 21A/B/C confirmed	
Aug 07–08	Reservation—Hotel Sofitel, Amsterdam	1 night
	Triple room with bath—voucher (Red Seal)	
	Includes continental breakfast	
Aug 08–12	Cruise on board Ms Moselle, (as per itinerary)	4 nights
	Seascape Deck, KD Rhine Line	
	Embarkation 3 hours prior	
	Cabin—3 sharing	
	All charges included except drink and shore excursions	
	Disembark Aug 12—3:00 p.m.	
Aug 12–18	On own using Eurail Pass. Be sure to validate on Aug 12	7 nights
Aug 18–21	Reservation—Hotel Hofstetter, Munich	3 nights
	Use prepaid voucher (Holiday House)	
	All taxes and continental breakfast included	
Aug 21–30	"Majestic Europe" Tour as per Globus/Gateway Itinerary	
Sep 03–04	Reservation—Hotel Sofitel, Amsterdam	1 night
Sep 04	Depart Amsterdam—Air Transat Flight #435	12:30 p.m.
	Arrive Toronto	4:15 p.M.
	Please checkin at Schiphol Airport 2 hours prior to flight.	

Note: Please check in Terminal One, Air Transat desk 2 hours prior to departure.
Reconfirm return flight reservations 72 hours prior.
Valid passport is required for entry.

Reprinted courtesy of Astor Travel Services

(Note: No client file is complete until a detailed itinerary is included. Make sure all important details are included, particularly flight details, terminal number/name, check-in times, documentation, and reconfirmation of flights.)

Itinerary

ASTOR TRAVEL SERVICES

1240 Bay Street, Suite 302
Toronto, Ontario M5R 2A7 CANADA
(416) 924-9597

_____

PAX NO. 1 _____   PAX NO. 3 _____

PAX NO. 2 _____   PAX NO. 4 _____

	TIME	DATE	AIRLINE
LEAVE			
ARRIVE			

	TIME	DATE	AIRLINE
LEAVE			
ARRIVE			

	TIME	DATE	AIRLINE
LEAVE			
ARRIVE			

SPECIAL NOTES _____

_____

_____

_____

_____

_____

_____

_____

_____

Car/Hotel Voucher

ASTOR TRAVEL SERVICES _____

1240 Bay Street, Suite 302
Toronto, Ontario M5R 2A7 CANADA

CONFIRMATION NO. _____

DATE CONFIRMED _____

BOOKED THROUGH _____

PLEASE PROVIDE _____   PARTY OF _____

WITH _____

FROM _____   TO _____   NTS/DAYS _____   MEALS _____

RATE $ _____   DEPOSIT _____

REMARKS _____

TO _____   _____

ADDRESS _____   TELEPHONE _____

_____   CDW/LDW _____   ALI _____

_____   PAI _____   PEP _____

☐ Unlimited Mileage   ☐ KM / MLS Free   Each Additional @ _____   TAX _____

☐ Hotel has been GUARANTEED for late arrival. Please cancel by _____ to avoid penalties.

Reprinted courtesy of Astor Travel Services

Costing Sheet

COSTING SHEET

Date: _____

To: _____
_____
_____
_____

Attention: **ACCOUNTING**

Client: _____ # in Party _____
_____ File # _____
_____
_____

Destination / Land Arrangements _____
_____

Departure Date _____ Duration _____

Rate Calculation:
FLIGHTS / CRUISES / OTHER

Each Adult	_____	x _____	_____	_____
	_____	x _____	_____	_____
	_____	x _____	_____	_____
	_____	x _____	_____	_____
	_____	x _____	_____	_____
Each Child	_____	x _____	_____	_____
	_____	x _____	_____	_____
	_____	x _____	_____	_____
	_____	x _____	_____	_____
	_____	x _____	_____	_____
	_____	x _____	_____	_____
Discounts	_____	x _____	_____	_____
	_____	x _____	_____	_____
Hotel	_____	x _____	_____	_____
Car Rental	_____	x _____	_____	_____
Insurance	_____	x _____	_____	_____
	_____	x _____	_____	_____

COMMISSIONABLE AMOUNT

Tax - Canadian Departure	_____ x _____	_____
Tax - Other Departure / Country	_____ x _____	_____
Tax - Other (Non Comm)	_____ x _____	_____

TOTAL GROSS RATE

Deposit Paid _____ (_____)

Commission Rate _____ (_____)

Balance Due (Net to Operator)   Total _____

Form of Payment _____

Cardholder _____

Authorization _____

© International Institute of Travel

Invoice

INVOICE

ASTOR TRAVEL SERVICES ✈
1240 Bay Street, Suite 302,
Toronto, Ontario M5R 2A7 CANADA

BOOKING AGENT	DATE	NUMBER
		1421

CLIENT NAME & ADDRESS	TRAVEL DATE	SUPPLIER

DETAILS OF SALE	QUANTITY	UNIT PRICE	TOTAL
	BALANCE DUE		
	DATE DUE		

FORM OF PAYMENT	CREDIT CARD AUTHORIZATION
REMARKS	

NOTES:

Under the Travel Industry Act in Ontario, the following are the basic requirements for the invoice:

1. Full name, address, and phone number of the travel agency must be shown;

2. The name(s) and full addresses of all client's who are travelling must be provided;

3. Full cost of the trip must be detailed. Show a breakdown of the base rate, service charges and taxes. Indicate any charges that must also be paid locally;

4. Clearly indicate the date and amount of deposit and installment payments made and the final payment date and amount owing at that time;

5. Indicate the name of all the suppliers of travel arrangements;

6. Show the complete travel data, including destination, departure and return dates, flight times, number of nights, name of hotel, type of room, ticket numbers for airline tickets, etc.;

7. Provide all details of travel insurance purchased, premium costs, policy number and name of insurance company. Have space for signatures if client declines insurance; and

8. Outline entry requirements required for the trip.

Reprinted courtesy of Astor Travel Services

Sample Invoice

ASTOR TRAVEL SERVICES
1240 Bay Street, Suite 302
Toronto, Ontario M5R 2A7 CANADA

To: Mr. Chaud Chien
123 Main Street
Maintown, Province
M4B 1A3

Invoice No.:   00123
Booking Date: Oct. 18/99
Invoice Date: Dec. 1/99
Agent: Valerie
Terms: Upon receipt

REMARKS:

Valid Canadian Passport required.

DESCRIPTION OF SERVICES

Air only (Regent Holidays) to Amsterdam
Dates: August 6 to September 4

Fare:	$759.00	× 3	=	$2,277.00
Dutch tax	22.00	× 3	=	66.00

Accommodation (Red Seal Tours)
Hotel Terminus, Amsterdam, triple with bath

August 7 to 8, 1 night	66.00	× 3	=	198.00
September 3 to 4, 1 night	66.00	× 3	=	198.00

Cruise Dutch Lowlands (Canadian Holidays)

Triple/standard accommodation	765.00	× 2	=	1,530.00
August 8 to 12	573.75	× 2	=	573.75

Accommodation (Holiday House)
Hotel Hofstetter, Munich, triple with bath

August 18 to 21, 3 nights	75.00	× 3	=	225.00

Flexipass (Rail Europe)

14 days travel in 1 month	714.00	× 3	=	2,142.00

"Majestic Europe" (Globus/Gateway Tours)

August 21 to 30, 9 days	1,057.50	× 3	=	3,172.50

Voyageur Deluxe package insurance

Policy S-1102370E	183.00	× 3	=	549.00

Total booking   10,931.25

Less deposit (paid October 18, 1999, by cheque)   3,741.25

Total due by June 5 $14,672.50 CAD

Reg. No. 5202542

Sample Receipt

Date: Receipt Number: **00001**

Received from:

The sum of _____ /100

$ _____

Details of the transaction _____

_____

_____

Signature _____

Hotel Description

<table>
<tr><td colspan="2" align="center">HOTEL DESCRIPTION</td></tr>
<tr><td></td><td>Date of Visit_____</td></tr>
</table>

Hotel name _____
Age of hotel _____
Renovated _____
Number of floors _____
Lobby area _____
Dining area _____
Hotel rooms _____
(beds/room amenities/balcony) _____
Cots/cribs _____
Laundry facilities _____
Kitchen _____
Radio/TV _____
Beauty/barber shop _____
Room service _____
Babysitting _____
Ice machines _____
Shuttle service _____
Parking _____
Sports _____
Beach _____
Handicap facilities _____
Lounge chairs _____
Spa _____
Check-in/check-out times _____
Credit cards _____
Lounge _____
Entertainment _____
Shopping _____
Golf nearby _____
Tennis _____
Social director _____
Games rooms _____
Meeting facilities _____

Sun Destinations
Pool _____   Jacuzzi_____   Pool bar _____
Pool towel service _____   Kiddie pool_____   Activities_____

General Comments _____

Checklist for Shipboard Inspections

CHECKLIST FOR SHIPBOARD INSPECTIONS

NAME OF SHIP _____
DATE OF INSPECTION _____
INSPECTED BY _____
IN PORT _____
AT SEA _____

Instructions: Identify each stateroom, restaurant or other facility in the space provided and make appropriate comments.

1. Passengers' accommodations	Cabin ____	Cabin ___	Cabin ____	Cabin ____
Size of room				
Berth arrangement (upper/lower/sofa, etc)				
Furniture comfort & arrangement				
Windows and portholes (sealed at sea)				
Floor covering				
Decor				
Self-controlled air temp				
Television / radio				
Lighting				
Drawer space				
Bathroom facilities				
Convenience Items				
Clothes hangers				
Clothes hooks				
Writing shelf				
Night light				
Reading light				
110V. elec. for hair blowers				
Refrigerator				
Potable water				
Bottle opener				
Clothes line				
2. **Cabin Service**				
Promptness				
Courtesy				
Professionalism				
Efficiency				
Food and beverages				
Quality				
Quantity				
Eye appeal				
Hot/cold				

3. Entertainment	Professional	Movies	Semi-professional	Crew sponsored
Quality				
Frequency				
Variety				
Audience reaction				

Checklist for Shipboard Inspections

4. Restaurant		**7. Theatre**	
Seating Arrangement		Obstruction of view	
Table for two		Air conditioning	
four		Acoustics	
six		Lighting	
eight		Seating comfort	
twelve		Accessibility	
Cleanliness			
Lighting		**8. Passageway**	
Air Conditioning		Lighting	
Seating comfort		Hand rails	
Noise level		Ashtrays	
Service		Floor covering	
Promptness		Width	
Courtesy		Height	
Professionalism			
Efficiency		**9. Service areas**	
Food		Shops	
Quality		Drug store	
Quantity		Beauty & barber shops	
Eye appeal		Photo shop	
Served hot (cold)		Tour office	
Special diets available		Purser's office	
5. Lounges & other public rooms		**10. Miscellaneous**	
Seating arrangements		Medical facilities	
Seating comfort		Chapel facilities	
Cleanliness		Casino	
Lighting		Slots only	
Air conditioning		Full casino	
Acoustics		Gymnasium	
Dance areas		Sauna	
Bar accessibility		Indoor Pool	
View of sea		Children's playroom	
6. Lido and deck areas		**11. Pier: facilities**	
Size		Lighting	
Spaciousness		Heating	
Shaded areas		Ventilation	
Deck chairs		Cleanliness	
Food and beverage services		Baggage handling areas	
Deck surface		Customs inspection facilities	
Pool features		Parking facilities (indoor-outdoor)	
Hand rails			

Application for Insurance

PROPOSITION D'ASSURANCE / INSURANCE APPLICATION		

RBC INSURANCE ASSURANCES RBC
Member of Royal Bank Financial Group*
Membre du Groupe Financier Banque Royale*

SIÈGE SOCIAL / HEAD OFFICE:
P.O. Box 97, Station A, Mississauga, Ontario L5A 2Y9
1-800-265-6896
SUCCURSALES / BRANCHES:
SAINT-LAURENT · CALGARY · BURNABY

N° DE POLICE / POLICY NO.
D- **VOID** 9 -E

ASSURÉ (NOM DE FAMILLE) / INSURED (FAMILY NAME)	(PRÉNOM AU COMPLET / FIRST NAME IN FULL)	DATE DE NAISSANCE (MM JJ AA) / DATE OF BIRTH (MM DD YY)
CONJOINT ASSURÉ (NOM DE FAMILLE) / INSURED SPOUSE (FAMILY NAME)	(PRÉNOM AU COMPLET / FIRST NAME IN FULL)	DATE DE NAISSANCE (MM JJ AA) / DATE OF BIRTH (MM DD YY)
NOM COMPLET DES ENFANTS ASSURÉS / FULL NAME OF INSURED CHILDREN		DATE DE NAISSANCE (MM JJ AA) / DATE OF BIRTH (MM DD YY)
NOM COMPLET DES COMPAGNONS DE VOYAGE ASSURÉS / FULL NAME OF INSURED TRAVELLING COMPANIONS		DATE DE NAISSANCE (MM JJ AA) / DATE OF BIRTH (MM DD YY)
ADRESSE DU DOMICILE / HOME ADDRESS	BÉNÉFICIAIRE « SUCCESSION » SAUF STIPULATION CONTRAIRE BENEFICIARY "ESTATE" UNLESS OTHERWISE STATED	PARENTÉ / RELATIONSHIP

DATE DE DÉPART PRÉVUE / SCHEDULED DEPARTURE DATE			DATE DE RETOUR PRÉVUE / SCHEDULED RETURN DATE			DATE DE LA PROPOSITION / DATE OF APPLICATION		
MM	JJ / DD	AA / YY	MM	JJ / DD	AA / YY	MM	JJ / DD	AA / YY

DURÉE DU VOYAGE (INCLUANT LE JOUR DE DÉPART ET LE JOUR DE RETOUR) LENGTH OF TRIP (INCLUDING DAY OF DEPARTURE AND DAY OF RETURN)	POINT DE DÉPART / DEPARTURE POINT	DESTINATION PRINCIPALE / PRINCIPAL DESTINATION	SIGNATURE (ASSURÉ OU REPRÉSENTANT AUTORISÉ) SIGNATURE (INSURED OR AUTHORIZED REPRESENTATIVE)

CE FORMULAIRE NE CONSTITUE UN CONTRAT D'ASSURANCE QU'UNE FOIS REMPLI ET LA PRIME REQUISE PAYÉE
THIS FORM DOES NOT CONSTITUTE AN INSURANCE CONTRACT UNTIL IT IS COMPLETED AND THE REQUIRED PREMIUM HAS BEEN PAID

Catégorie d'assurance / Class of Insurance			Capitaux et sommes assurés par personne Principal Sums & Sums Insured per Person		N° de personnes x No. of Persons	Prime par personne Premium per Person	Prime / Premium	
		✓	AVANT LE DÉPART BEFORE DEPARTURE	APRÈS LE DÉPART AFTER DEPARTURE				
Forfait Package	Supérieur - jusqu'à 74 ans Deluxe - up to age 74		$	ILLIMITÉ / UNLIMITED	X	$		
			$	ILLIMITÉ / UNLIMITED	X	$	PT	
			0 $	ILLIMITÉ / UNLIMITED	X	$		
	Supérieur - de 75 à 84 ans Deluxe - age 75 to 84		$	ILLIMITÉ / UNLIMITED	X	$		
			$	ILLIMITÉ / UNLIMITED	X	$	TT	
			0 $	ILLIMITÉ / UNLIMITED	X	$		
	Non médical Non-Medical		$	ILLIMITÉ / UNLIMITED	X	$		
			$	ILLIMITÉ / UNLIMITED	X	$	NT	
			0 $	ILLIMITÉ / UNLIMITED	X	$		
	Standard Standard		$	$	X	$		
			$	$	X	$	IT	
			0 $	MAXIMUM 400 $ MAXIMUM $400	X	$		
Assurances frais médicaux d'urgence Emergency Medical Insurances	Frais médicaux classiques Classic Medical			□ INDIVIDUELLE / SINGLE □ FAMILIALE / FAMILY	X	$	HME	
	Frais médicaux standard Standard Medical				X	$	MED	
	VacanSanté° Privilège TravelCare°·HealthSelect°	IMPORTANT LE QUESTIONNAIRE MÉDICAL DOIT ÊTRE REMPLI MEDICAL QUESTIONNAIRE MUST BE COMPLETED		COUVERTURE INDIVIDUELLE SINGLE	X	$	HSP	
	VacanSanté° Or TravelCare°· Gold				X	$	MEG	
	VacanSanté° Argent TravelCare°· Silver				X	$	MES	
	VacanSanté° Bronze TravelCare°· Bronze				X	$	MEB	
	Annuelle Voyages multiples Multi-Trip Annual		OPTION 10 JOURS 10 DAY PLAN	□ INDIVIDUELLE / SINGLE	X	$	ANN	
			OPTION 30 JOURS 30 DAY PLAN	□ FAMILIALE / FAMILY	X	$		
Assurance Visiteurs au Canada Visitors to Canada Insurance	Régime standard I Standard Plan I		MAX 25 000 $ MAX $25,000	□ INDIVIDUELLE / SINGLE □ FAMILIALE / FAMILY	X	$		
	Régime standard II Standard Plan II		MAX 50 000 $ MAX $50,000	□ INDIVIDUELLE / SINGLE □ FAMILIALE / FAMILY	X	$	HMV	
	Régime supérieur Deluxe Plan		MAX 150 000 $ MAX $150,000	□ INDIVIDUELLE / SINGLE □ FAMILIALE / FAMILY	X	$		
Annulation et interruption de voyage Cancellation & interruption			AVANT LE DÉPART/BEFORE DEPARTURE $	APRÈS LE DÉPART/AFTER DEPARTURE $	X	$	TCI	
Bagages et effets personnels Baggage & Personal Effects			$	MAXIMUM 2 000 $ PAR PERSONNE OU FAMILLE MAXIMUM $2,000 PER INDIVIDUAL OR FAMILY	X	$	BFB	
Dommages au véhicule de location Rental Car Physical Damage			DU / FROM MM JJ/DD AA/YY	AU / TO MM JJ/DD AA/YY	MAXIMUM 50 000 $ $50,000 MAXIMUM	X	$	CAR
Accident de vol Flight Accident				$	X	$	AF	

CARTE DE CRÉDIT / CREDIT CARD: □ VISA □ MASTERCARD □ AMERICAN EXPRESS □ DINERS CLUB EN ROUTE

				PRIME TOTALE TOTAL PREMIUM	

N° DE CARTE DE CRÉDIT / CREDIT CARD NO.

MONTANT / AMOUNT $

TAXE DE VENTE (s'il y a lieu)
SALES TAX (if applicable) **VOID**

BUREAU N° / OFFICE NO.	CONSEILLER / COUNSELLOR	DOSSIER / DOCKET	EXPIRATION MM AA / YY	AUTORISATION / AUTHORIZATION	**TOTAL**

*Registered trade-marks of Royal Bank of Canada. RBC Travel Insurance Company, licensee of trade-marks.
*Marques déposées de la Banque Royale du Canada. Compagnie d'assurance voyage RBC, licenciée de ces marques.

Formule / Form # 88256 (000/06)

COPIE POUR RAPPORT/VÉRIFICATION / REPORTING/AUDIT COPY

Note: RBC Travel Insurance Company issues their policies using automated systems, capturing information relevant to each policy holder from this manual.

Insurance Waiver

INSURANCE WAIVER

Date of departure _____   Date _____

I have been offered the following travel insurance and I have declined the purchase of

☐   Trip cancellation   ☐   Baggage

☐   Travel accident/sickness   ☐   Flight insurance

                                           ☐   All of the above

I, the undersigned, will not hold this travel agency and/or its agents responsible for any expenses incurred by me resulting from cancellation of my trip, accident, sickness, or stolen or damaged baggage.

Name of agency:

Agent's signature_____   Client's signature _____

Universal Credit Card Charge Form

THE UNIVERSAL CREDIT CARD CHARGE FORM

I ACKNOWLEDGE RECEIPT OF TICKET(S) AND OR COUPONS RELATED CHARGES DESCRIBED HEREON. PAYMENT IN FULL TO BE MADE WHEN BILLED OR IN EXTENDED PAYMENTS IN ACCORDANCE WITH STANDARD POLICY OF COMPANY ISSUING CARD AND AS REFLECTED IN APPLICABLE TARIFFS. J'ACCUSE RÉCEPTION DES BILLETS OU COUPONS CORRESPONDANT AUX DÉBITS CI-CONTRE. LE PAIEMENT POURRA ETRE EFFECTUE SOIT INTEGRALEMENT DES LA FACTURATION SOIT EN VERSEMENTS ECHELONNES AUX CONDITIONS FIXÉES PAR LA SOCIÉTÉ ÉMETTRICE DE LA CARTE ET STIPULÉES AUX RÉGLEMENTS TARIFAIRES APPLICABLES. X ⑬	UNIVERSAL CREDIT CARD CHARGE FORM / BORDEAU DE DÉBIT UNIVERSAL - CARTES DE CRÉDIT AIRLINE CODE CODE Cie AéR. ⑪ DATE OF ISSUE/DATE D'ÉMMISSION	1.CONTRACTOR INVOICE COPY FACTURE DU CONTRACTANT IF EXTENDED PAYMENT APPLICABLE, CIRCLE NO. OF MONTHS. ENTOURER LE NOMBRE DE MENSUALITÈS, EN CAS DE PAIEMENTS ÉCHELONNÉS. 3 6 9 12 ___	DATE AND PLACE OF ISSUE ⑫
NAME OF PASSENGER IF OTHER THAN CARDHOLDER NOM DU PASSAGER SAUF S'IL EST TITULAIRE DE LA CARTE ⑭	ONTARIO NO. N D'OTATO	CONNECTION OF PASSENGER WITH SUBSCRIBER RELATION ENTRE PASSAGER ET SOUSCRIPTEUR	⑩ APPROVAL CODE RÉF. DE L'ACCORD
COMPLETE ROUTING / ITINERAIRE COMPLET FARE BASIS / BASE TARIFAIRE	CARRIER / TRANSPORTEUR	AIRLINE/ CieAER. FORM SERIAL NO. /N DU BILLET ⑧	LIEU ET DATE D'ÉMISSION
⑨		**TICKETS NOT TRANSFERRABLE NO CASH REFUNDS BILLETS INCESSIBLES AUCUN REMBOURSEMENT EN ESPÈCES**	
FARE/TARIF ⑤ TOTAL ⑦ ROUTE CODE / INDICATIF DU PARCOURS TAX/TAXE ⑥ ÉQUIV.AMT. PO CONTRE VAL.VERSEE ⑮		② ③ ④ CREDIT CARD NAME/CODE NOM OU CODE DE LA CARTE ①	

BOX

(1)   Use the official credit card codes (AX, VI, CA, ER, etc.) which are universally recognized.

(2, 3, 4)   This information will be imprinted off the client's credit card (the credit card number, expiry date and name on the card). The credit card is used on an imprinter.

(5)   Base Price of package (exclusive of taxes and service charges).

(6)   Total taxes and service charges.

(7)   Total charges on the credit card (base price + taxes and service charges).

(8)   Print the full name of the tour company / wholesaler.

(9)   Complete details of arrangements booked. Include name of tour operator, accommodation arrangements, number of days, locator number, car, insurance, etc.

(10)   Make sure that you have received authorization from the credit card issuer for the credit card amount. The agent is liable for accepting of the payment, if accepting without authorization. The code to be used will be given with the authorization.

(11)   Date of issue (must correspond to the deadlines for payment).

(12)   Validate with agency information.

(13)   Make sure your client signs the form.

(14)   Indicate the name of passenger if different from the name on the credit card.

(15)   If the credit card payment is in foreign currency, convert into CAD and show the equivalent amount in Canadian dollars here, together with the rate of exchange.

Tour Order

3050 968 461

AUDIT COUPON
COUPON COMPTABILITE

BILL TO: NAME OF TOUR OPERATOR / FACTURER A (NOM DE L'ORGANISATEUR) (2)

TOUR NAME / DESIGNATION DU CIRCUIT (5)

TOUR CODE / CODE CIRCUIT (3)
IIT

DATE OF ISSUE / DATE D'EMISSION

PASSENGER NAME / NOM DU PASSAGER (4)

(NOT TRANSFERABLE / INCESSIBLE)

PTY OF / Nbre pers (6)

PRESENT TO / REMETTRE A (7)

COUPON	AT / A (8)	VALUE / VALEUR (9)
1		
2		
3		
4		

TOTAL TOUR COST / PRIX TOTAL DU CIRCUIT (16)

LESS DEPOSIT / MOINS DEPOT (17)

FINAL PAYMENT / SOLDE (18)

EQUIV AMT PAID - CONTRE-VALEUR VERSEE (19)

COMM. RATE / CODE COMMISSION (20)

FORM OF PAYMENT / MODE DE PAYMENT (21)

PLACE OF ISSUE-AGENCY/AGENCE - LIEU D'EMISSION VALID ONE YEAR FROM DATE OF ORIGINAL ISSUE VALABLE UN AN A COMPTER DE LA DATE DE PREMIERE EMISSION (1)

AIR TICKET NUMBER(S) / BILLET(S) D'AVION No's (22)

ISSUED IN EXCHANGE FOR / EMIS EN ECHANGE DE (23)

DATE AND PLACE OF ORIGINAL ISSUE DATE ET LIEU DE PREMIERE EMISSION (24)

TOUR FEATURES / PARTICULARITES (10)

HOTEL DETAILS / A L'INTENTION DE L'HOTEL (11)

☐ SINGLE / CH. I PERS. ☐ DOUBLE / CH. 2 PERS. ☐ OTHER / AUTRE ☐ TWIN / CH. 2 LITS

COMMISSION % (20)

ISSUED BY / EMIS PAR

ROUTE CODE / CODE DE PARCOURS

ENCODE/CODE-CENTRE DE TRAITMENT

CPN / COUPON

AIRLINE / CIE AER.

FORM

SERIAL NUMBER / No DU BILLET

CK / CONTROLE (25a)

(25b)

NUMBER OF NIGHTS
NOMBRE DE NUITEES (12)

IN DATE / DU (13a)

OUT DATE / AU (13b)

DEPARTURE FLIGHT / DATE
DATE (DE) DEPART DU VOL (15)

ARRIVAL FLIGHT / DATE
DATE (D') ARRIVEE DU VOL (14)

3050968461 2 O

O

DO NOT MARK OR WRITE IN THE WHITE AREA ABOVE / NE RIEN INSCRIRE DANS LA PARTIE BLANCHE CI-DESSUS

How to Complete a Tour Order

Box 1   "Place of Issue" should be validated using a validating machine and the agency's IATA plate. The box will then contain the name and IATA number of the issuing agency.

Box 2   "Bill To: Name of Tour Operator" should indicate the name of the operator of the tour.

Box 3   "Tour Code" is found in the terms and conditions section of the supplier's tour brochure.

Box 4   Full name of the passenger (the correct order is surname/initial and title, for example, Lincoln/A Mr.).

Box 5   "Tour Name" is found in the supplier's tour brochure.

Box 6   "Party Of" is used to indicate the total number of persons who are together on the tour.

Box 7   "Present To" will include the name of the supplier(s), one per line (maximum of four per tour order).

Box 8   "At" refers to the city where the supplier's service will commence. A coupon is presented to each supplier at the beginning of service to be supplied. Any unused coupons should be marked "VOID" in this area.

Box 9   "Value" should set out in the published currency used in the tour brochure, the value of the service to be supplied by each supplier.

Box 10   "Tour Features" include destination cities, and arrival and departure dates.

Box 11   "Hotel Details" describe the type of accommodation being prepaid (single, double, or twin beds).

Box 12   "Number of Nights" on tour.

Box 13a "In Date" is the arrival date at prepaid accommodation.

Box 13b "Out Date" is the departure date from prepaid accommodation.

Box 14   "Arrival Flight/Date" includes the airline code, the flight number of the first flight, and the date of arrival.

Box 15   Fill in the airline code, the flight number of the last flight and the date of departure in the "Departure Flight/Date Box"

Box 16   "Total Tour Cost" for all parties travelling together (complete this information on this tour order only— do not include amounts from any other orders for the same tour).

Box 17   "Less Deposit" is any deposit paid.

Box 18   "Final Payment" is the gross amount minus any deposit.

Box 19   "Equiv. Amt. Paid." If the tour is published in foreign currency, convert into CAD and show the equivalent Canadian amount together with the rate of exchange.

Box 20   "Comm. Rate" is the rate of the agent's commission (usually 10%).

Box 21   "Form of Payment" will indicate cash, cheque, or the credit card name and number.

Box 22   "Air Ticket Numbers" are printed here for all passengers included on this tour order.

Box 23   "Issued in Exchange For" includes the numbers of any prior tour orders being exchanged (or an MCO number, if applicable).

Box 24   "Date and Place of Original Issue" includes the same information as the original tour order, in the event of an exchange.

Box 25a/b The "Issued By" box and the box in the lower right hand corner of the tour order are both completed by using a validating machine and a Carrier Identification Plate for the IATA carrier that issues the tour order.

Appendix B:
Worldwide Accommodation

GOLF RESORTS (A SAMPLING OF U.S. GOLF RESORTS)

The Boulders Resort—Carefree, Arizona
Arizona Biltmore—Pheonix, Arizona
Camelback Inn Resort—Scottsdale, Arizona
The Phoenician—Scottsdale, Arizona
Scottsdale Princess—Scottsdale, Arizona
La Costa Resort—Carlsbad, California
Carmel Valley Ranch—Carmel Valley, California
Hyatt Grand Champions Resort—Indian Wells, California
Marriott's Desert Springs—Palm Desert, California
Doubletree Resort—Palm Springs, California
Rancho Las Palmas Resort—Rancho Mirage, California
The Peaks—Telluride, Colorado
Turnberry Isle Resort—Aventura, Florida
Amelia Island Plantation—Amelia Island, Florida
Boca Raton Resort & Club—Boca Raton, Florida
Bonaventure Resort & Spa—Ft. Lauderdale, Florida
Radisson Inverrary Resort—Ft. Lauderdale, Florida
Indian River Plantation—Hutchinson Island, Florida
The Villages of Grand Cypress—Lake Buena Vista, Florida
Doral Golf Resort & Spa—Miami, Florida
Naples Beach Hotel & Golf Club—Naples, Florida
Quality Inn Golf Resort—Naples, Florida
Hyatt Regency Grand Cypress—Orlando, Florida
The Breakers—Palm Beach, Florida
PGA National Resort & Spa—Palm Beach, Florida
Palm-Aire Resort & Spa—Pompano Beach, Florida
Ponte Vedra Inn & Club—Ponte Vedra Beach, Florida
Resort at Longboat Key Club—Sarasota, Florida
Ponce de Leon Golf Resort—St. Augustine, Florida

Saddlebrook Resort—Tampa, Florida
Lake Lanier Islands Hilton Resort—Atlanta, Georgia
The Cloister—Sea Island, Georgia
Hilton Waikoloa Village—Kamuela, Hawaii
Kauai Marriott Resort—Kalapaki Beach (Kauai), Hawaii
The Kapalua Villas—Kapalua (Kauai), Hawaii
Four Seasons Resort Hualalai—Kona Coast, Hawaii
Turtle Bay Hilton Golf & Tennis Resort—Kuilima Point (Oahu), Hawaii
Sun Valley Resort—Sun Valley, Idaho
Indian Lakes Resort—Bloomingdale, Illinois
The Inn At Eagle Creek Resort—Findlay, Illinois
Oak Brook Hills Hotel & Resort—Oak Brook, Illinois
Samoset Resort—Rockport, Maine
Turf Valley Resort—Ellicott City, Maryland
The Mirage—Las Vegas, Nevada
The Sagamore—Bolton Landing, New York
Athenaeum Hotel—Chatauqua, New York
Nevele Hotel Resort—Ellenville, New York
Concord Resort Hotel (temporarily closed for renovation)—Kiamesha Lake, New York
Kutsher's Country Club—Monticello, New York
Fripp Island Resort—Fripp Island, South Carolina
Palmetto Dunes Resort—Hilton Head Island, South Carolina
Sea Pines Resort—Hilton Head Island, South Carolina
Plantation Resort—Myrtle Beach, South Carolina
Woodstock Inn—Woodstock, Vermont
The Greenbrier—White Sulphur Springs, West Virginia

TENNIS RESORTS (A SAMPLING OF U.S. TENNIS RESORTS)

Marriott's Grand Hotel—Point Clear, Alabama
The Wigwam Resort—Litchfield Park, Arizona
Arizona Biltmore—Phoenix, Arizona
Hyatt Regency at Gainey Ranch—Scottsdale, Arizona
Marriott's Mountain Shadows—Scottsdale, Arizona
The Phoenician—Scottsdale, Arizona
Radisson Resort—Scottsdale, Arizona
Scottsdale Princess—Scottsdale, Arizona
Enchantment Resort—Sedona, Arizona
Canyon Ranch Spa—Tucson, Arizona
The Lodge at Ventana Canyon—Tucson, Arizona
Sheraton el Conquistador Resort—Tucson, Arizona
Westward Look Rook—Tucson, Arizona
Fairfield Bay Resort—Greers Ferry Lake, Arkansas
Arlington Resort Hotel & Spa—Hot Springs City, Arkansas
La Jolla Beach & Tennis Club—La Jolla, California
Newport Beach Hotel & Tennis Club—Newport Beach, California
The Inn at the Racquet Club—Palm Springs, California
The Inn at Spanish Bay—Pebble Beach, California
The Ritz Carlton—Rancho Mirage, California

The Aspen Club Lodge—Aspen, Colorado
The Broadmoore—Colorado Springs, Colorado
The Snowmass Lodge & Club—Snowmass, Colorado
Boca Raton Resort & Club—Boca Raton, Florida
Inverrary Resort—Ft. Lauderdale, Florida
The Villas of Grand Cypress—Lake Buena Vista, Florida
Turnberry Isle Resort—Miami, Florida
Registry Resort—Naples, Florida
The Breakers—Palm Beach, Florida
PGA National Resort & Spa—Palm Beach, Florida
Ritz Carlton—Palm Beach, Florida
The Colony Beach & Tennis Resort—Sarasota, Florida
Resort at Longboat Key Club—Sarasota, Florida
Palm-Aire Resort & Spa—Pompano Beach, Florida
The Cloister—Sea Island, Georgia
Jekyll Island Club Hotel—Jekyll Island, Georgia
The Royal Lahaina Resort—Kaanapali Beach (Maui), Hawaii
Kauai Marriott Resort & Beach Club—Kalapaki Beach (Kauai), Hawaii
Hilton Waikoloa Village—Kamuela, Hawaii
The Orchid at Mauna Lani—Kamuela, Hawaii
Ritz Carlton—Kapalua (Maui), Hawaii
Turtle Bay Hilton Golf & Tennis Club—Kuilima Point (Oahua), Hawaii
Sun Valley Resort—Sun Valley, Idaho
Seaview Resort—Atlantic City, New Jersey
The Sagamore—Bolton Landing, New York
The Pines Resort Hotel—Fallsburg, New York
Montauk Yacht Club—Montauk, New York
Kutsher's Country Club—Monticello, New York
Kiawah Island Resort—Charleston, South Carolina
Hilton Head Island Beach—Hilton Head Island, South Carolina
Island Club of Hilton Head—Hilton Head Island, South Carolina
Sea Pines Resort—Hilton Head Island, South Carolina
John Newcombe's Tennis Ranch—New Braunfels, Texas
Topnotch at Stowe Resort—Stowe, Vermont
Sugarbush Inn—Warren, Vermont

SPA HOTELS (A SAMPLING OF U.S. SPA HOTELS)

Olympia Spa Golf Resort—Dothan, Alabama
Sheraton Crescent Hotel—Phoenix, Arizona
Camelback Inn Resort—Scottsdale, Arizona
The Phoenician—Scottsdale, Arizona
Scottsdale Hilton Resort—Scottsdale, Arizona
Enchantment Resort—Sedona, Arizona
Canyon Ranch Spa—Tucson, Arizona
Omni Tucson National Golf Resort & Spa—Tucson, Arizona
Palace Hotel—Eureka Springs, Arkansas
Arlington Resort Hotel & Spa—Hot Springs City, Arkansas
Majestic Hotel & Spa—Hot Springs City, Arkansas
Westwood Marquis Hotel—Beverly Hills, California
Silver Rose Inn & Spa—Calistoga, California

Desert Hot Springs Spa Hotel—Desert Hot Springs, California
Givenchy Hotel & Spa—Palm Springs, California
The Palms—Palm Springs, California
Sonoma Mission Inn & Spa—Sonoma, California
The Aspen Club Lodge—Aspen, Colorado
The Peaks—Telluride, Colorado
Sanibel Harbour Resort & Spa—Fort Myers, Florida
Pier House Resort & Caribbean Spa—Key West, Florida
Doral Golf Resort & Spa—Miami, Florida
Lido Spa Resort—Miami Beach, Florida
Palm-Aire Resort & Spa—Pompano Beach, Florida
Ihilani Resort & Spa—Ko'olina (Oahu), Hawaii
Canyon Ranch—Lenox, Massachusetts
Gurney's Inn Resort & Spa—Montauk, New York
Woodlands Resort & Inn -Charleston, South Carolina
Lake Austin Spa Resort—Austin, Texas
Green Valley Resort—St. George, Utah

DUDE RANCHES (A SAMPLING OF U.S. DUDE RANCHES)

Saguaro Lake Ranch Resort—Mesa, Arizona
Grapevine Canyon Ranch—Pearce, Arizona
Lazy K Bar Guest Ranch—Tucson, Arizona
White Stallion Ranch—Tucson, Arizona
Flying E Ranch—Wickenburg, Arizona
Merv Griffin's Wickenburg Inn—Wickenburg, Arizona
Rancho De Los Caballeros—Wickenburg, Arizona
Scott Valley Resort—Mountain Home, Arkansas
Alisal Guest Ranch—Solvang, California
T-Lazy 7 Guest Ranch—Aspen, Colorado
Colorado Trails Ranch—Durango, Colorado
Aspen Lodge—Estes Park, Colorado
White Pine Ranch—Gunnison, Colorado
Sylvan Dale Ranch—Loveland, Colorado
Don K Ranch—Pueblo, Colorado
Vista Verde Guest & Ski Touring Ranch—Steamboat Springs, Colorado
Teton Ridge Ranch—Tetonia, Idaho
Double JJ Resort—Rothbury, Michigan
Lone Mountain Ranch—Big Sky, Montana
Double Arrow Lodge—Seeley Lake, Montana
Rancho Encantado Resort—Santa Fe, New Mexico
Arrowhead Dude Ranch—Parksville, New York
Dixie Dude Ranch—Bandera, Texas
Pack Creek Ranch—Moab, Utah
Cody's Ranch Resort—Cody, Wyoming
Hidden Valley Ranch—Cody, Wyoming
Lazy L&B Ranch—Dubois, Wyoming
Lost Creek Ranch—Jackson Hole, Wyoming
Moosehead Ranch—Jackson Hole, Wyoming
Spotted Horse Ranch—Jackson Hole, Wyoming
Crossed Sabres Ranch—Wapiti Valley, Wyoming

CASINO HOTELS (A SAMPLING OF U.S. CASINO HOTELS)

Bally's Park Place Casino Resort—Atlantic City, New Jersey
Caesar's Atlantic City—Atlantic City, New Jersey
Claridge Casino Hotel—Atlantic City, New Jersey
The Grand—Atlantic City, New Jersey
Harrah's Casino Hotel—Atlantic City, New Jersey
Merv Griffin's Resorts Casino Hotel—Atlantic City, New Jersey
Trump's Castle—Atlantic City, New Jersey
Trump Taj Mahal Casino—Atlantic City, New Jersey
Aladdin Hotel & Casino—Las Vegas, Nevada
Ballys Casino Resort—Las Vegas, Nevada
Bellagio Hotel—Las Vegas, Nevada
Caesar's Palace—Las Vegas, Nevada
Circus Circus Hotel & Casino—Las Vegas, Nevada
Excalibur Hotel & Casino—Las Vegas, Nevada
Flamingo Hilton Las Vegas—Las Vegas, Nevada
Golden Nugget Hotel & Casino—Las Vegas, Nevada
Hacienda Hotel & Casino—Las Vegas, Nevada
Harrah's Las Vegas—Las Vegas, Nevada
Imperial Palace Hotel & Casino—Las Vegas, Nevada
Mandalay Bay & Four Seasons Hotel—Las Vegas, Nevada
MGM Grand Hotel & Casino—Las Vegas, Nevada
The Mirage—Las Vegas, Nevada
New York, New York Hotel & Casino—Las Vegas, Nevada
Sahara Hotel & Casino—Las Vegas, Nevada
Showboat Hotel—Las Vegas, Nevada
Venetian Hotel—Las Vegas, Nevada
Harrah's Casino Hotel—Laughlin, Nevada
Circus Circus Hotel/Casino—Reno, Nevada
Flamingo Hilton Reno—Reno, Nevada
Harrah's Casino Hotel—Reno, Nevada
Sands Regency Hotel Casino—Reno, Nevada

ALL-INCLUSIVE RESORTS (CARIBBEAN)

Bushiri Bounty Beach Resort—Aruba
Tamarijn Aruba Beach Resort—Aruba
Club Med Village—Eleuthera Island, Bahamas
Club Fortuna Beach—Grand Bahama Island, Bahamas
Breezes—New Providence Island, Bahamas
Sandals Royal Bahamian—New Providence Island, Bahamas
Club Med Village—Paradise Island, Bahamas
Paradise Island Fun Club—Paradise Island, Bahamas
Club Med Columbus Isle—San Salvador Island, Bahamas
Almond Beach Club—Barbados
Club Rockley—Barbados
Island Inn Hotel—Barbados
Sandals—Barbados
Coco Point Lodge—Barbuda
The K Club—Barbuda

Harmony Club—Bermuda
Spanish Bay Reef—Grand Cayman, Cayman Islands
Pirates Point Resort—Little Cayman, Cayman Islands
Delta Las Brisas Club Resort—Guardalavaca, Cuba
Delta Sierra Mar Club Resort—Santiago de Cuba, Cuba
Club Varadero Super Clubs Resort—Varadero Beach, Cuba
Caribbean Village Club on the Green—Playa Dorado, Dominican Republic
Heavens—Playa Dorado, Dominican Republic
Jack Tar Village—Playa Dorado, Dominican Republic
Paradise Beach Club—Playa Dorado, Dominican Republic
Bayside Hill Resort & Beach Club—Puerto Plata, Dominican Republic
Caribbean Village Luperon—Puerto Plata, Dominican Republic
Puerto Plata Beach Resort & Casino—Puerto Plata, Dominican Republic
Caribbean Village Bavaro—Punta Cana, Dominican Republic
Club Med—Punta Cana, Dominican Republic
Hotel Cayacoa Beach—Samana Peninsula, Dominican Republic
Caribbean Village Decameron—San Pedro De Macoris, Dominican Republic
Caribbean Village Tropics—San Pedro De Macoris, Dominican Republic
Hamaca Beach Hotel & Casino—Santo Domingo, Dominican Republic
La Source—Grenada
Club Med Caravelle—Guadeloupe
Trelawny Beach Hotel—Falmouth, Jamaica
Breezes—Montego Bay, Jamaica
Jack Tar Village—Montego Bay, Jamaica
Sandals—Montego Bay, Jamaica
Sandals Royal Jamaican—Montego Bay, Jamaica
Grand Lido—Negril, Jamaica
Hedonism II—Negril, Jamaica
Poinciana Beach Resort—Negril, Jamaica
Sandals—Negril, Jamaica
Swept Away Resort—Negril, Jamaica
Boscobel Beach Hotel—Ocho Rios, Jamaica
Club Jamaica Beach Resort—Ocho Rios, Jamaica
Couples Jamaica—Ocho Rios, Jamaica
Sandals Dunn's River—Ocho Rios, Jamaica
Sandals Ocho Rios—Ocho Rios, Jamaica
Fern Hill Club—Port Antonio, Jamaica
Braco Village Resort—Runaway Bay, Jamaica
Breezes Runaway Bay—Runaway Bay, Jamaica
Club Med Buccanneer's Creek—Martinique
Jack Tar Village Beach Resort & Casino—St. Kitt's
Club Med—St. Lucia
Club St. Lucia—St. Lucia
Jalousie Plantation Resort—St. Lucia
Rendezvous—St. Lucia
Sandals Halcyon Beach—St. Lucia
Le Sport—St. Lucia
Great Bay Beach Hotel & Casino—St. Maarten
Canouan Beach Hotel—Canouan Island, St. Vincent & The Grenadines
Club Med Turkoise—Providenciales Island, Turks & Caicos Islands
The Windmills Plantation—Salt Cay, Turks & Caicos Islands

A SELECTION OF DELUXE HOTELS OF THE WORLD

U.S.A.

Arizona Biltmore—Scottsdale, Arizona
Marriott's Camelback Inn Resort—Scottsdale, Arizona
The Phoenician—Scottsdale, Arizona
The Ritz Carlton—Scottsdale, Arizona
Scottsdale Princess—Scottsdale, Arizona
Canyon Ranch Spa—Tucson, Arizona
La Costa Resort & Spa—Carlsbad, California
Carmel Valley Ranch—Carmel, California
Quail Lodge Resort—Carmel, California
Hyatt Grand Champions Resort—Indian Wells, California
The Beverly Hills Hotel—Los Angeles, California
Four Seasons Hotel—Los Angeles, California
Hotel Bel-Air—Los Angeles, California
The Peninsula Beverly Hills—Los Angeles, California
The Regent Beverly Wilshire—Los Angeles, California
Givenchy Hotel & Spa—Palm Springs, California
The Inn at Spanish Bay—Pebble Beach, California
The Lodge at Pebble Beach—Pebble Beach, California
Rancho Bernardo Inn—Rancho Bernardo, California
Mission Hills Resort—Rancho Mirage, California
Rancho Las Palmas Resort—Rancho Mirage, California
The Ritz Carlton—Rancho Mirage, California
Hotel Del Coronado—San Diego, California
Loews Coronado Bay Resort—San Diego, California
Campton Place Hotel—San Francisco, California
The Clift—San Francisco, California
The Donatello—San Francisco, California
Fairmont Hotel & Tower—San Francisco, California
The Mandarin Oriental—San Francisco, California
The Mark Hopkins—San Francisco, California
The Palace Hotel—San Francisco, California
The Renaissance Stanford Court Hotel—San Francisco, California
The Ritz Carlton—San Francisco, California
Four Seasons Biltmore—Santa Barbara, California
Sonoma Mission Inn & Spa—Sonoma, California
The Broadmoor—Colorado Springs, Colorado
The Peaks at Telluride—Steamboat Springs, Colorado
Hotel Du Pont—Wilmington, Delaware
Four Seasons Hotel—Washington, D.C.
The Madison Hotel—Washington, D.C.
Mayflower Hotel—Washington, D.C.
The Ritz Carlton -Washington, D.C.
The Watergate Hotel—Washington, D.C.
The Willard—Washington, D.C.
Boca Raton Resort & Club—Boca Raton, Florida
Harbor Beach Resort—Ft. Lauderdale, Florida

Pier Sixty Six—Ft. Lauderdale, Florida
Ocean Reef Club—Key West, Florida
Buena Vista Palace Resort & Spa—Lake Buena Vista, Florida
Walt Disney World Swan And Dolphin—Lake Buena Vista, Florida
Doral Golf Resort—Miami, Florida
Grand Bay Hotel—Miami, Florida
Hyatt Regency Coral Gables—Miami, Florida
Mayfair House Hotel—Miami, Florida
Turnberry Isle Resort & Club—Miami, Florida
Fountainbleau Hilton—Miami Beach, Florida
Ritz Carlton—Naples, Florida
Hyatt Regency Grand Cypress—Orlando, Florida
The Peabody—Orlando, Florida
Four Seasons Ocean Grand—Palm Beach, Florida
Ritz Carlton—Palm Beach, Florida
The Resort At Longboat Key Club—Sarasota, Florida
The Grand Hotel—Atlanta, Georgia
Ritz Carlton—Atlanta, Georgia
The Gastonian—Savannah, Georgia
The Cloister—Sea Island, Georgia
Mauna Kea Beach Hotel—(Hawaii Island, The Big Island), Hawaii
The Orchid at Mauna Lani—(Hawaii Island, The Big Island), Hawaii
Hilton Waikoloa Village—Kamuela (Hawaii Island, The Big Island), Hawaii
Mauna Lani Bay Hotel—Kohala Coast (Hawaii Island, The Big Island),
    Hawaii
Four Seasons Resort Hualalai—Kona Coast (Hawaii Island, The Big Island),
    Hawaii
Kona Village Resort—Kona Coast (Hawaii Island, The Big Island), Hawaii
Hyatt Regency Kauai Resort & Spa—Poipu Beach (Kauai), Hawaii
Princeville Hotel—Princeville (Kauai), Hawaii
The Lodge at Koele—Lanai City (Lanai), Hawaii
Hotel Hana Maui—Hana (Maui), Hawaii
Ritz Carlton—Kapulua (Maui), Hawaii
Aston Wailea Resort—Wailea (Maui), Hawaii
Four Seasons Resort—Wailea (Maui), Hawaii
Renaissance Wailea Beach Resort—Wailea (Maui), Hawaii
Halekulani—Honolulu (Oahu), Hawaii
Hyatt Regency Waikiki Resort—Honolulu (Oahu), Hawaii
The Royal Hawaiian—Honolulu (Oahu), Hawaii
Sheraton Moana Surfrider—Honolulu (Oahu), Hawaii
Ihilani Resort & Spa—Ko'olina (Oahu), Hawaii
Ali'i Tower at the Hilton Hawaiian Village—Waikiki (Oahu), Hawaii
Chicago Hilton—Chicago, Illinois
The Fairmont Hotel—Chicago, Illinois
Four Season Hotel—Chicago, Illinois
The Palmer House—Chicago, Illinois
The Sutton Place Hotel—Chicago, Illinois
The Ritz Carlton—Chicago, Illinois
Hotel Intercontinental—New Orleans, Louisiana
The Pont Chartrain—New Orleans, Louisiana

Saint Louis Hotel—New Orleans, Louisiana
Westin Canal Place—New Orleans, Louisiana
Windsor Court Hotel—New Orleans, Louisiana
The Copley Plaza—Boston, Massachusetts
Four Seasons Hotel—Boston, Massachusetts
Le Meridien—Boston, Massachusetts
The Regal Bostonian—Boston, Massachusetts
The Ritz Carlton—Boston, Massachusetts
The River Place—Detroit, Michigan
Harrah's Casino Hotel—Lake Tahoe, Nevada
Luxor—Las Vegas, Nevada
MGM Grand Hotel—Las Vegas, Nevada
The Mirage—Las Vegas, Nevada
The Grand—Atlantic City, New Jersey
Trump Plaza Hotel—Atlantic City, New Jersey
The Sagamore—Bolton Landing, New York
The Carlyle—New York, New York
Hotel Intercontinental—New York, New York
Hotel Plaza Athenee—New York, New York
The Lowell—New York, New York
The Peninsula—New York, New York
The Pierre—New York, New York
The Plaza Hotel—New York, New York
The Ritz Carlton—New York, New York
The St. Regis Hotel—New York, New York
The Waldorf Astoria—New York, New York
Cincinnatian Hotel—Cincinnati, Ohio
Omni Netherland Plaza—Cincinnati, Ohio
The Heathman Hotel—Portland, Oregon
River Place Hotel—Portland, Oregon
The Bellevue Hotel—Philadelphia, Pennsylvania
The Rittenhouse Hotel—Philadelphia, Pennsylvania
The Adolphus Hotel—Dallas, Texas
Hotel Crescent Court—Dallas, Texas
Mansion of Turtle Creek—Dallas, Texas
La Colombe D'or—Houston, Texas
Houstonian Hotel—Houston, Texas
The Homestead—Hot Springs, Virginia
Alexis Hotel—Seattle, Washington
Four Seasons Olympic Hotel—Seattle, Washington
The Greenbrier—White Sulphur Springs, West Virginia

Canada

Banff Springs Hotel—Banff, Alberta
The Rimrock Resort Hotel—Banff, Alberta
Hotel Macdonald—Edmonton, Alberta
Jasper Park Lodge—Jasper, Alberta
Chateau Lake Louise—Lake Louise, Alberta
Four Seasons—Vancouver, British Columbia
Hotel Vancouver—Vancouver, British Columbia

Pan Pacific Vancouver Hotel—Vancouver, British Columbia
The Sutton Place Hotel—Vancouver, British Columbia
Waterfront Centre Hotel—Vancouver, British Columbia
The Westin Bayshore—Vancouver, British Columbia
The Empress Hotel—Victoria, British Columbia
Chateau Laurier—Ottawa, Ontario
Four Seasons Hotel—Toronto, Ontario
Hotel Inter-Continental—Toronto, Ontario
The King Edward Hotel—Toronto, Ontario
The Sutton Place Hotel—Toronto, Ontario
Westin Harbour Castle—Toronto, Ontario
Le Chateau Montebello—Montebello, Quebec
Bonaventure Hilton—Montreal, Quebec
Loews Hotel Vogue—Montreal, Quebec
Marriott Chateau Champlain—Montreal, Quebec
The Ritz Carlton Kempinski Hotel—Montreal, Quebec
Chateau Frontenac—Quebec City, Quebec
Hotel Saskatchewan Radisson Plaza—Regina, Saskachewan

Mexico

Acapulco Princess—Acapulco
Las Brisas—Acapulco
Pierre Marques—Acapulco
Villa Vera Hotel & Racquet Club—Acapulco
Caesar Park Cancun Beach & Golf Resort—Cancun
Camino Real—Cancun
Fiesta Americana Coral Beach—Cancun
The Ritz Carlton—Cancun
Presidente Intercontinental—Guadalajara
Fiesta Americana—Merida
Camino Real—Mexico City
Four Seasons Hotel—Mexico City
Hotel Marquis Reforma—Mexico City
Hotel Nikko Mexico—Mexico City
Sheraton Maria Isabel—Mexico City
Camino Real—Puerto Vallarta
Sheraton Buganvilias Resort—Puerto Vallarta
The Westin Brisas Resort—Zihuatanejo

Central America

Cariari Hotel & Country Club—San Jose, Costa Rica
Camino Real—San Salvador, El Salvador
Westin Camino Real—Guatemala City, Guatemala
Caesar Park—Panama City, Panama

South America

Alvear Palace Hotel—Buenos Aires, Argentina
Caesar Park—Buenos Aires, Argentina

Park Hyatt—Buenos Aires, Argentina
Park Tower—Buenos Aires, Argentina
Sheraton Buenos Aires—Buenos Aires, Argentina
Llao Llao Hotel & Resort—San Carlos De Bariloche, Argentina
Belem Hilton—Belem, Brazil
Belo Horizonte Othon Palace Hotel—Belo Horizonte, Brazil
Caesar Park Hotel Ipanema—Rio de Janeiro, Brazil
Copacabana Palace Hotel—Rio de Janeiro, Brazil
Hotel Intercontinental—Rio de Janeiro, Brazil
Le Meridien Copacabana—Rio de Janeiro, Brazil
Rio Othon Palace Hotel—Rio de Janeiro, Brazil
Sheraton Rio Hotel—Rio de Janeiro, Brazil
Caesar Park Hotel—Sao Paulo, Brazil
The Maksoud Plaza—Sao Paulo, Brazil
Sheraton Mofarrej Hotel—Sao Paulo, Brazil
Hotel Carrera—Santiago, Chile
Sheraton San Cristobal—Santiago, Chile
Cartagena Hilton—Cartagena, Colombia
Excelsior Hotel—Asuncion, Paraguay
Hotel Resort & Casino Yacht & Golf Club Paraguay—Asuncion, Paraguay
Sheraton Lima Hotel & Casino—Lima, Peru
Tamanaco Inter-Continental Hotel—Caracas, Venezuela
Melio Puerto La Cruz Hotel—Puerto La Cruz, Venezuela

Europe

Bristol Hotel—Salzburg, Austria
Hotel Kobenzl—Salzburg, Austria
Ambassador Hotel—Vienna, Austria
Ana Grand Hotel—Vienna, Austria
Hotel Bristol Wien—Vienna, Austria
Hotel Imperial Wien—Vienna, Austria
Hotel Inter-Continental—Vienna, Austria
Vienna Plaza—Vienna, Austria
Brussels Hilton—Brussels, Belgium
Le Meridien—Brussels, Belgium
Royal Windsor Hotel—Brussels, Belgium
Sheraton Hotel—Brussels, Belgium
Cyprus Hilton—Limassol, Cyprus
D'Angleterre Hotel—Copenhagen, Denmark
Inter-Continental—Helsinki, Finland
Hotel Du Cap-Eden Roc—Antibes, France
Carlton Inter-Continental—Cannes, France
Hotel Majestic—Cannes, France
Negresco Hotel—Nice, France
Le Bristol—Paris, France
Le Grand Hotel Inter-Continental—Paris, France
Hotel De Crillon—Paris, France
Hotel George V—Paris, France
Hotel Lancaster—Paris, France
Hotel Plaza Athenee—Paris, France

Hotel Ritz—Paris, France
Brenner's Park Hotel & Spa—Baden-Baden, Germany
Grand Hotel Esplanade—Berlin, Germany
Kempinski Hotel Bristol—Berlin, Germany
Excelsior Hotel Ernst—Cologne, Germany
Hotel Im Wasserturm—Cologne, Germany
Hotel Breidenbacher Hof—Dusseldorf, Germany
Steigenberger Parkhotel—Dusseldorf, Germany
Arabella Grand Hotel—Frankfurt, Germany
Hotel Hessicher Hof—Frankfurt, Germany
Hamburg Marriott—Hamburg, Germany
Vier Jahreszeiten Hotel—Hamburg, Germany
Der Europaeische Hof/Hotel Europe—Heidelberg, Germany
Hotel Koenigshof—Munich, Germany
Hotel Palace—Munich, Germany
Kempinski Hotel Vier Jahreszeiten Munchen—Munich, Germany
Munich Park Hilton—Munich, Germany
Athenaeum Inter-Continental—Athens, Greece
Athens Hilton—Athens, Greece
Grande Bretagne Hotel—Athens, Greece
Budapest Hilton—Budapest, Hungary
Kempinski Hotel Corvinus Budapest—Budapest, Hungary
Berkeley Court Hotel—Dublin, Ireland
The Davenport Hotel—Dublin, Ireland
Westbury Hotel—Dublin, Ireland
Grand Hotel Quisisana—Capri, Italy
Grand Hotel—Florence, Italy
Hotel Excelsior—Florence, Italy
Excelsior Hotel Gallia—Milan, Italy
Four Seasons—Milan, Italy
Grand Hotel Et De Milan—Milan, Italy
Hotel Principe Di Savoia—Milan, Italy
Milan Hilton—Milan, Italy
Cavalieri Hilton—Rome, Italy
Le Grand Hotel—Rome, Italy
Hotel Eden—Rome, Italy
Hotel Excelsior—Rome, Italy
Hotel Hassler—Rome, Italy
Bauer Grunwald—Venice, Italy
Hotel Cipriani—Venice, Italy
Hotel Danieli—Venice, Italy
Hotel Gritti Palace—Venice, Italy
Hotel Inter-Continental—Luxembourg City, Luxembourg
Hermitage Hotel—Monte Carlo, Monaco
Hotel De Paris—Monte Carlo, Monaco
Loews Monte Carlo Hotel—Monte Carlo, Monaco
Amstel Inter-Continental—Amsterdam, The Netherlands
Amsterdam Hilton—Amsterdam, The Netherlands
Amsterdam Marriott—Amsterdam, The Netherlands
The Grand Westin Demeure—Amsterdam, The Netherlands
Hotel Okura Amsterdam—Amsterdam, The Netherlands

Des Indes Inter-Continental—The Hague, The Netherlands
Grand Hotel—Oslo, Norway
Hotel Continental—Oslo, Norway
Radisson SAS Scandinavia Hotel—Oslo, Norway
Marriott Warsaw Hotel—Warsaw, Poland
Madeira Palacio Hotel—Funchal (Madeira Island), Portugal
Hotel Ritz Inter-Continental Lisboa—Lisbon, Portugal
Meridien Lisboa—Lisbon, Portugal
Hotel Metropol—Moscow, Russia
Kempinski Hotel Baltschug Moskau—Moscow, Russia
Hotel Regency—Belgrade, Serbia
Hotel Princesa Sofia—Barcelona, Spain
Husa Palace—Barcelona, Spain
Le Meridien—Barcelona, Spain
Rey Juan Carlos I—Conrad International—Barcelona, Spain
The Ritz—Madrid, Spain
Don Carlos—Marbella, Spain
Gran Hotel Bahia Del Duque—Tenerife Island, Spain
Grand Hotel—Stockholm, Sweden
Basel Hilton—Basel, Switzerland
Drei Koenige Am Rhein—Basel, Switzerland
Bellevue Palace Hotel—Berne, Switzerland
Hotel D'Angleterre—Geneva, Switzerland
Hotel Des Bergues—Geneva, Switzerland
Hotel President Wilson—Geneva, Switzerland
Le Richemond—Geneva, Switzerland
Palace Hotel—Gstaad, Switzerland
Beau-Rivage Palace—Lausanne, Switzerland
Hotel Le Lausanne Palace—Lausanne, Switzerland
Grand Hotel National—Lucerne, Switzerland
Palace Hotel—Lucerne, Switzerland
Villa Principe Leopoldo—Lugano, Switzerland
Le Montreux Palace—Montreux, Switzerland
Badrutt's Palace Hotel—St. Moritz, Switzerland
Carlton Hotel—St. Moritz, Switzerland
Kulm Hotel—St. Moritz, Switzerland
Baur Au Lac—Zurich, Switzerland
Dolder Grand Hotel—Zurich, Switzerland
Eden Au Lac—Zurich, Switzerland
Ankara Hilton Sa—Ankara, Turkey
Sheraton Ankara Hotel—Ankara, Turkey
Hyatt Regency—Istanbul, Turkey
Swallow Hotel—Birmingham, England (U.K.)
The Chester Grosvenor—Chester, England (U.K.)
The Berkeley—London, England (U.K.)
Churchill Inter-Continental—London, England (U.K.)
Claridge's—London, England (U.K.)
The Connaught—London, England (U.K.)
The Dorchester—London, England (U.K.)
Four Seasons Hotel—London, England (U.K.)
Grosvenor House—London, England (U.K.)

Le Meridien Piccadilly—London, England (U.K.)
Park Lane Hilton—London, England (U.K.)
The Ritz—London, England (U.K.)
The Savoy—London, England (U.K.)
Balmoral Hotel—Edinburgh, Scotland (U.K.)
The Caledonian—Edinburgh, Scotland (U.K.)

Middle East

Forte Grand Diplomat—Manama, Bahrain
Le Royal Meridien—Manama, Bahrain
The King David Hotel—Jerusalem, Israel
Dan Hotel—Tel Aviv, Israel
Amman Marriott Hotel—Amman, Jordan
Forte Grand Amman—Amman, Jordan
Hyatt Regency—Jeddah, Saudi Arabia
Inter-Continental—Jeddah, Saudi Arabia
Hyatt Regency—Riyadh, Saudi Arabia
Inter-Continental Hotel—Abu Dhabi, United Arab Emirates

Africa

Alexandria Renaissance Hotel—Alexandria, Egypt
Cairo Nile Hilton—Cairo, Egypt
Cairo Ramses Hilton—Cairo, Egypt
Le Meridien—Cairo, Egypt
Semiramis Inter-Continental—Cairo, Egypt
New Stanley Hotel—Nairobi, Kenya
Mount Kenya Safari Club—Nanyuki, Kenya
Royal Mansour Hotel—Casablanca, Morocco
La Mamounia Hotel—Marrakech, Morocco
Hyatt Regency—Rabat, Morocco
Mount Nelson Hotel—Cape Town, South Africa
Royal Hotel—Durban, South Africa
The Carlton—Johannesburg, South Africa
Sandton Sun & Towers—Johannesburg, South Africa
The Palace—Sun City, South Africa

Asia

Beijing Hilton—Beijing, China
China World Hotel—Beijing, China
The Great Wall Sheraton—Beijing, China
White Swan Hotel—Guangzhou, China
Grand Hyatt—Hong Kong, China
Island Shangri-La—Hong Kong, China
Mandarin Oriental—Hong Kong, China
The Peninsula—Hong Kong, China
The Regent—Hong Kong, China
The Ritz Carlton—Hong Kong, China
Garden Hotel—Shanghai, China

Shanghai Hilton—Shanghai, China
Welcomgroup Mughal Sheraton—Agra, India
The Oberoi—Bangalore, India
The Oberoi—Bombay, India
The Oberoi Grand—Calcutta, India
Taj Bengal—Calcutta, India
Le Meridien—Delhi, India
Hyatt Regency—New Delhi, India
The Oberoi—New Delhi, India
The Taj Mahal—New Delhi, India
Four Season Resort—Bali Island, Indonesia
The Oberoi—Bali Island, Indonesia
Jakarta Hilton International—Jakarta, Indonesia
The Regent—Jakarta, Indonesia
Shangri-La Hotel—Jakarta, Indonesia
Hotel Hankyu International—Osaka, Japan
Hyatt Regency—Osaka, Japan
Osaka Hilton—Osaka, Japan
Akasaka Prince Hotel—Tokyo, Japan
Ana Hotel—Tokyo, Japan
Century Hyatt—Tokyo, Japan
Dai-Ichi Hotel—Tokyo, Japan
Deluxe Plaza Inter-Continental—Tokyo, Japan
Four Seasons Chinzan-So—Tokyo, Japan
Hotel Nikko—Tokyo, Japan
Hotel Okura—Tokyo, Japan
Imperial Hotel—Tokyo, Japan
Palace Hotel—Tokyo, Japan
Royal Park Hotel—Tokyo, Japan
Grand Hyatt Seoul—Seoul, South Korea
Renaissance Hotel—Seoul, South Korea
Ritz Carlton—Seoul, South Korea
Seoul Hilton—Seoul, South Korea
Seoul Plaza Hotel—Seoul, South Korea
The Shilla—Seoul, South Korea
Mandarin Oriental—Macau City, Macau
Hotel Nikko—Kuala Lumpur, Malaysia
Kuala Lumpur Hilton International—Kuala Lumpur, Malaysia
Parkroyal Penang—Penang Island, Malaysia
Penang Mutiara Beach Resort—Penang Island, Malaysia
Avari Hotel—Lahore, Pakistan
Inter-Continental—Manila, Philippines
Mandarin Oriental—Manila, Philippines
The Manila Hotel—Manila, Philippines
The Peninsula—Manila, Philippines
Shangri-La Hotel—Manila, Philippines
Ana Hotel—Singapore City, Singapore
Goodwood Park Hotel—Singapore City, Singapore
Hyatt Regency—Singapore City, Singapore
Marina Mandarin—Singapore City, Singapore

The Oriental—Singapore City, Singapore
The Pan Pacific Hotel—Singapore City, Singapore
Raffles Hotel—Singapore City, Singapore
Shangri-La Hotel—Singapore City, Singapore
Grand Formosa Regent Hotel—Taipei, Taiwan
Grand Hyatt—Taipei, Taiwan
The Sherwood—Taipei, Taiwan
Taipei Hilton—Taipei, Taiwan
Dusk Thani Hotel—Bangkok, Thailand
Grand Hyatt Erawan—Bangkok, Thailand
Hilton International—Bangkok, Thailand
The Landmark—Bangkok, Thailand
The Mansion Kempinski—Bangkok, Thailand
The Oriental—Bangkok, Thailand
The Regent—Bangkok, Thailand
Shangri-La Hotel—Bangkok, Thailand
The Sukhothai—Bangkok, Thailand
The Regent—Chiang Mai, Thailand
Amanpuri—Phuket Island, Thailand
Banyan Tree—Phuket Island, Thailand

South Pacific

Adelaide Hilton—Adelaide, Australia
Conrad International Treasury Casino—Brisbane, Australia
The Heritage Hotel—Brisbane, Australia
Cairns Hilton—Cairns, Australia
The Reef Hotel Casino—Cairns, Australia
Hyatt Hotel—Canberra, Australia
The Beaufort—Darwin, Australia
The Pan Pacific Hotel—Gold Coast, Australia
Sheraton Mirage—Gold Coast, Australia
Hayman Island Resort—Hayman Island, Australia
The Hotel Como—Melbourne, Australia
Sheraton Towers Southgate—Melbourne, Australia
The Windsor—Melbourne, Australia
Burswood Resort Hotel—Perth, Australia
Ana Hotel—Sydney, Australia
Hotel Nikko Darling Harbour—Sydney, Australia
Inter-Continental—Sydney, Australia
The Landmark Hotel—Sydney, Australia
The Observatory Hotel—Sydney, Australia
Park Hyatt—Sydney, Australia
The Regent—Sydney, Australia
The Ritz Carlton—Sydney, Australia
Sheraton on the Park—Sydney, Australia
Kaimbu Island Resort—Fiji Islands
Carlton Hotel—Auckland, New Zealand
Stamford Plaza—Auckland, New Zealand

Appendix C:
Sea Transportation

CRUISE LINES

A large number of companies operate cruises. Below is a list of the better-known cruise lines and their specialties or a short description.

Abercrombie and Kent	Specialized cruises for experienced passengers
Alaska Sightseeing Tours	Specialize in Alaska cruising
Amazon River Cruises	Specialize in Amazon river cruising
American-Canadian Caribbean Line	Caribbean cruises
American Family Cruises	Family-oriented cruises
American Hawaii Cruises	Cruising the Hawaiian islands
Bergen Line	Scandinavian cruises
Carnival Cruise Lines	Very popular "fun ships"
Celebrity Cruise Line	Elegant, yet casual
Commodore Cruise Line	Caribbean, South America, and Mexico cruises
Costa Cruise Lines	European flavour; top-notch service and food
Crystal Cruises	Luxurious
Cunard Line	Traditional; excellent service (for example, QE II)
Delta Queen Steamboat	Paddle-wheeled river steamboats
Diamond Cruises	Luxury cruises on ships using unique twin-hull design
Discovery Cruises	One-day "cruises to nowhere"
Disney Cruise Lines	Cruising combined with a visit to Disney World
Dolphin Cruise Lines	Activity-oriented cruises

Epirotiki Lines	Mediterranean cruises
ETA/Sea Escape	Gambling cruises (overnight) to the Bahamas
French Country Waterways	French river cruises
Galapagos Network	Galapagos Island cruises
Hilton International Nile Cruises	Nile River cruises
Holland America Line	Premium-level cruises
KD German Rhine Line	Rhine River cruises
Majesty Cruise Line	Bahamas, Bermuda, and Mexico cruising
Norwegian Cruise Line	Official cruise line of pro sport NBA and NFL
Oceanic Cruises	State-of-the-art ships
Odessa America	Russian flavour with good value
Orient Lines Inc.	Destination cruises to Australia, New Zealand, Africa, India, South America, Antarctica, Greek Isles
Paquet French Cruises	French flavour
Pearl Cruises	European ambiance
Premier Cruise Line	Family vacations
Princess Cruises	Richly appointed ships; known as the "love boats"
Regal Cruises	High quality (member of Chaine des Rotisseurs, the world's oldest gourmet society)
Regency Cruises	Elegant, European style
Renaissance Cruises	All cabins are outside suites; elegant
Royal Caribbean Cruise Line	Excellent food and value; modern ships
Royal Cruise Line	Deluxe cruises oriented to experienced passengers
Royal Olympic Cruise Line	Greek style
Royal Viking	Traditional elegance
Seabourn Cruise Line	The ultimate in deluxe cruises
Seawind Cruises	International flavour with quality food
Seven Seas Cruise Line	Small ships, personal service; luxurious
Silversea Cruises	Deluxe cruises, yet good value
Special Expeditions	Unusual cruises (for example, the Amazon River)
Starlite Cruises	Sailing ships
St. Lawrence Cruises	St. Lawrence River cruises
Sun Line	European service and unique itineraries
Tall Ship Adventures	Utilizes "tall ship" sailing crafts
Windjammer Barefoot Cruises	Fun-oriented, laid-back style, few formalities; French Polynesia and the Caribbean
Windstar Cruises (Club Med)	High-tech ships and exceptional service
World Explorer Cruises	Cultural and educational cruises

FERRIES

The following is a list of some of the more popular ferry services utilized by travellers.

United States

Alaska Marine Highway	Services various Alaskan ports, including Ketchikan, Juneau, Sitka, and Skagway
California	Service to Catalina Island, and between San Francisco and Sausalito
New York	New York State ferry services (Lake Champlain, Staten Island)
Washington	Washington State ferry services

Canada

British Columbia Ferry Corporation	Services B.C. ports (for example, service between Tsawwassen on the mainland and Swartz Bay on Vancouver Island)
Marine Atlantic	Service between the various Atlantic provinces of Canada and between Nova Scotia and the U.S.A.
Ontario	Service to and from Manitoulin Island
Societie des traversiers due Quebec—Travquebec	Ports of Quebec

Mexico

Mexico	Service between Mazatlan and La Paz

South America

Brazil	Service between Rio de Janeiro and Niteroi

U.K. and EUROPE

Adriatica	Service between Italy and Croatia, and between Italy and Greece
B&I Lines	Service between the U.K. and Ireland
Baltic Shipping Company	Baltic Sea
Baltrum Line	German ports
Belfast Car Ferries	Service between England and Northern Ireland
Bornholmstraffieken	Danish ports
British Ferries	Service between Italy and Turkey

Brittany Ferries	Service between France and the U.K.
Caremar	Service between Italy and Sicily, and between Italy and Ischia
Ceres Hydrofoil Joint Service	Greek ports
Cie Nationale Algérienne	Service between France and the Balearic Islands, France and Spain, and France and Algeria
Cie Trasmediterranée	Service between France and the Balearic Islands
Cie Tunisienne	Service between France and Tunisia
Comanav Casablanca	Service between France and Morocco
Compania Transmediterranea, S.A.	Service between Barcelona, Spain, and the Balearic Islands
Corsica Ferries	Service between Italy and Corsica
DFDS	Between Norway and Denmark, and between the U.K. and Scandinavia
DFDS Prinzenlinien	Service between Germany and the U.K.
DSB	Danish ports;
Emeraude Lines	Service between France and the U.K. Channel Islands
Finnjet Line	Service between Germany and Finland
Grand Traghetti	Service between Italy and Sicily
Greece	Various inter-island ferry services available
Hardanger	Norwegian ports
Hellenic Mediterranean	Service between Italy and Greece
Isle Of Man Steam Packet Co. Ltd	Service between England and the Isle of Man
Iltour	Service between France and the U.K. islands of Jersey and Guernsey
Jahre Line	Between Germany and Norway
KD German Rhine Line	German ports
MRF—More Og Romsdal Flykesbatar	Norwegian ports
Naviganzione Lago Maggiore	Italian and Swiss ports
North Sea Ferries	Service between the U.K. and Holland
P&O Ferries	Service to Orkneys and Shetland Islands
Polish Baltic Shipping Co.	Between Germany and Denmark, and between Germany and Poland

RD Vendee — Inter Isles	France
Scan Line	Between Norway and Denmark
Sea Link	Service between U.K. and the European continent
Shetland	Service to the Shetland Islands in the U.K.
Silja, Viking Lines	Between Sweden and Finland
Skagerrak Express	Between Norway and Denmark
Smyril Line	Iceland
SNCM	Service between France and Sardinia, France and Corsica, France and Algeria, and France and Tunisia
Stena Line	Scandinavian ports
Tirrenia	Service between Italy and Sardinia, Italy and Sicily, Italy and Capri. and Italy and Malta
Torremar	Service between Italy and Elba
Townsend Thoresen	Service between France and the U.K., and between Belgium and the U.K.
TT Saga Line	Between Germany and Sweden
Turkish Maritime Line	Service between Italy and Turkey
Ventouris Ferries	Service between Italy and Greece
Zealand Steamship Co.	Service between Holland and the U.K.

Asia

Hong Kong	Star Ferry
Philippines	Aboitiz Shipping Corporation Escano Lines, Inc. Gothong Lines, Inc. Si-Kat Ferries, Inc. Sulpicio Lines, Inc. Sweet Lines, Inc. Williams Lines, Inc. WG&A Philippines

FREIGHTERS

Lykes Brothers Steamship Company
Ivaran Lines
Compagnie Polynesienne
Freighter World Cruises
Sea the Difference
Blue Star North America

CRUISE PORTS

The following is a list of the world's major cruise ports, subdivided by area:

North America (and Hawaii)

Anchorage, Alaska
Boston, Massachusetts
Charleston, South Carolina
Ft. Lauderdale (Port Everglades), Florida
Honolulu, Hawaii
Juneau, Alaska
Los Angeles, California
Miami, Florida
New Orleans, Louisiana
New York City, New York
Palm Beach, Florida
Port Canaveral, Florida
Portland, Oregon
San Diego, California
San Francisco, California
Seattle, Washington
Seward, Alaska
Sitka, Alaska
St. Petersburg, Florida
Tampa, Florida
Vancouver, British Columbia

Caribbean and Bermuda

Anguilla
Antigua—St. John's
Aruba—Oranjestaad
Bahamas—Nassau, Freeport, Bimini, San Salvador
Barbados—Bridgetown
Barbuda
Bequia
Bermuda—St. George's, Hamilton
British Virgins—Virgin Gorda, Tortola, Norman Island, Peter Island
Cayman Islands—Grand Cayman
Costa Rica
Curacao—Willemstad
French Guiana—Devil's Island
Grenada—St. George's
Guadeloupe—Point-a-Pitre

Jamaica—Ocho Rios, Montego Bay

Martinique—Fort de France

Mexico—Playa del Carmen, Cozumel

Montserrat—Plymouth

Nevis

Panama—San Blas Islands, Cristobal (Caribbean), Balboa (Pacific)

Puerto Rico—San Juan

Saba

St. Bartholomey

St. Croix—Christiansted

St. Eustatius

St. John

St. Kitts

St. Lucia

St. Maarten—Philipsburg

St. Thomas—Charlotte Amalie

Venezuela—La Guaira (Caracas), Isla Margarita

Mexico Pacific

Acapulco

Cabo San Lucas

Ensenada

La Paz

Manzanillo

Mazatlan

Puerto Vallarta

Zihuatanejo/Ixtapa

South America

Belem, Brazil

Buenos Aires, Argentina

Callao, Peru

Cartagena, Columbia

Fortaleza, Brazil

La Guaira (Caracas), Venezuela

Montevideo, Uruguay

Natal, Brazil

Punta Arenas, Chile

Recife, Brazil

Rio de Janeiro, Brazil

Salvador Bahia, Brazil

Santos, Brazil

Valparaiso, Chile

Europe

Amsterdam, Netherlands

Antwerp, Belgium

Barcelona, Spain

Bari, Italy

Bremerhaven, Germany

Calais, France

Cherbourg, France

Copenhagen, Denmark

Corfu, Greece

Dover, U.K.

Genoa, Italy

Gibraltar

Gothenburg, Sweden

Hamburg, Germany

Helsinki, Finland

Istanbul, Turkey

Kusadasi, Turkey

Lisbon, Portugal

Malaga, Spain

Marseille, France

Monte Carlo, Monaco

Naples, Italy

Nice, France

Ostend, Belgium

Palermo, Italy

Palma, Mallorca

Piraeus, Greece

Rotterdam, Netherlands

Southampton, U.K.

Stockholm, Sweden

St. Petersburg, Russia

Valletta, Malta

Venice, Italy

Africa

Abidjan, Cote d'Ivoire

Canary Islands

Capetown, South Africa

Casablanca, Morocco

Conakry, Guinea

Dakar, Senegal

Dar es Salaam, Tanzania

Durban, South Africa
Freetown, Sierra Leone
Lagos, Nigeria
Mombasa, Kenya
Monrovia, Liberia
Port Said, Egypt
Tunis, Tunisia

Asia

Bangkok, Thailand
Hong Kong
Kobe, Japan
Macau
Madras, India
Manila, Philippines
Mumbai, India
Nagasaki, Japan
Pusan, South Korea
Shanghai, China
Singapore
Tokyo, Japan

Australia & Pacific Islands

Auckland, New Zealand
Cairns, Australia
Easter Island
Fiji Islands
Honolulu, Hawaii
Papeete, Tahiti
Sydney, Australia
Tonga

Appendix D:
Tour Operators

The following is a list of many, but not all, of the tour operators in Canada and the U.S.A. It is impossible to provide a complete list as it is constantly changing. Also, there are many other very small tour operators who concentrate on small local markets for their business.

Tour Operators	Destinations
Air Canada Vacations	California, Hawaii, Florida, Georgia, Texas, Colorado, Nevada, Canada, Bermuda, Caribbean, Bahamas, Mexico
Air Transat Holidays	U.K., Europe, Caribbean, Bahamas, Mexico, Nevada, Florida
Alba Tours	Italy, Mexico, Caribbean, Bahamas
American Express Vacations	Europe, Caribbean, U.S.A., Canada, Mexico, South America, China, Japan, India, Hawaii, New Zealand, Australia
Australian Pacific Tours Ltd.	Australia
Blue Danube Holidays	Eastern Europe, Austria, Switzerland
Brendan Tours	U.K., Europe, East Africa, Egypt, South America
Canadian Holidays	California, Caribbean, Bahamas, Florida, Hawaii, Nevada, Mexico, Canada
Canadian Swan International	China
Chinapac International	China, Hong Kong, Southeast Asia
China Travel Service (Canada) Inc.	China, Hong Kong, Singapore, Southeast Asia

CIT Canada Inc.	Western Europe
Classic Hawaii	Hawaii
Collette Tours Canada Ltd.	Canada, U.S.A., Europe, South America
Conference Travel and Tours	China, Southeast Asia, India, Pakistan, Middle East, South Africa, East Africa
Conquest Tours	East Africa, India, Hong Kong, China, Southeast Asia, Greece, Israel, Jordan, Russia, Scandinavia, South America, Caribbean, Bermuda, Bahamas, Mexico, Costa Rica, California, Florida, Canada
Contiki Holidays	U.S.A., Canada, Europe, Australia, New Zealand
Cultural Tours	Philippines, Japan, China, Hong Kong, Sri Lanka, Southeast Asia, South Africa
DER Tours	U.K., Europe, China, Hong Kong, Southeast Asia
Domenico Tours	U.S.A., Canada, Caribbean, Europe
East African Travel Consultants Inc.	East Africa
En Route Holidays Limited	U.S.A.
Fun Sun Tours	U.S.A., Mexico, Central America
G.A.P. Adventures	Central America, South America, Galapagos Islands
Gateways International	Central America, South America
Gem Tours	South America, Portugal, Spain, Tunisia, Morocco
General Tours	Russia, Europe, Scandinavia, China, Japan, India, Middle East, East Africa
Girassol	Spain, Portugal, Africa
Globus/Cosmos Tourama	Africa, U.S.A., Canada, Mexico, South America, Galapagos Islands, Europe, Russia, Scandinavia, Middle East, Turkey, Japan, Southeast Asia, Australia, New Zealand, India
GM Tours	Greece, Middle East
Gogo Tours	Various
Goway Travel Ltd.	Australia, New Zealand, Pacific Islands, Southeast Asia, Hong Kong, India, South Africa
Grecian Tours	Greece, Egypt
Hanover Holiday Tours Ltd.	U.S.A., Canada
Hillcrest Tour Group Ltd.	U.S.A., Canada
Hola Sun	Cuba, Mexico, Florida

Holiday House Ltd.	Europe, Florida, Caribbean
Holland America/Westours	Alaska, Canadian Rockies, Mexico, Caribbean
Horizon Holidays Limited	Canada, U.K., Bermuda, Ireland, Portugal, Australia, New Zealand, Southeast Asia
Insight International Tours	Europe, the Balkans, Russia, Scandinavia
Intours Corporation	Ukraine, Russia
Islands in the Sun	Caribbean, U.K., France, Greece, New Zealand, Tahiti
Isram Group	Middle East, Europe, Africa, China, Japan
J&O (Japan & Orient) Pacific Tours	Japan, China, South Pacific
Jade Tours	China, Hong Kong, Japan, Southeast Asia
Jetset Tours (North America) Ltd.	Europe, U.K., China, Japan, Australia, New Zealand, South Pacific
Jet Vacations	U.S.A., Europe, Middle East, Africa, Australia, New Zealand, South Pacific
JM Sun Spree Vacations	Japan, Philippines, Southeast Asia
Just Tours Inc.	Greece, Spain, Israel, Egypt, Turkey
Kentours	Eastern Europe
Kompass Express	Europe, Egypt, Africa
Latin World Tours	South America
Magna Holidays Inc.	South America, Caribbean
Mandarin Tours	South America, Australia, New Zealand, India, China, South Africa
Marco Polo Holidays	China, Japan, Philippines, Southeast Asia
Maupintours	U.S.A., Canada, Europe, South America, Middle East, India, Japan, South Pacific
Mayflower Tours	U.S.A., Canada
Mirassol Vacations Inc.	South America, Galapagos Islands
MTI Vacations, Inc.	U.S.A., Mexico, Caribbean
Nordic Tours Ltd.	Africa, Seychelles, Turkey, Middle East
Olson-Travelworld	U.K., Europe, Scandinavia, Middle East, Africa, China, Japan, India, Southeast Asia, South Pacific, South America
Olympic Holidays	Greece, Turkey, Cyprus, Middle East
Orient Express Travel & Tours	India, Pakistan, Nepal, Maldives

Pacific Bestours Inc./ Global Bestours Inc.	Eastern Europe, Africa, China, Japan, Australia, South Pacific
Pan Pacific Holidays	Hong Kong, Japan, Southeast Asia
Pathway Tours Inc.	Canada, U.S.A.
Qantas Vacations	Hong Kong, Australia, New Zealand, Southeast Asia, Fiji
Quest Nature Tours	Canada, South America, Galapagos Islands, Africa
Red Seal Tours	U.S.A., Caribbean, Canada
Regent Holidays	Florida, Caribbean, Mexico, Colombia, Panama, Venezuela
Romantic Holidays	South America, Portugal, Spain, Canary Islands, Morocco
Safna Vacations Ltd.	Africa, Turkey, India, Pakistan, Seychelles, Hong Kong, Southeast Asia
Shalom-K-Tours	Israel
Signature Vacations	Florida, Nevada, Canada, Bahamas, Caribbean, Mexico
Silkway Tours	Australia, Papua New Guinea, South Pacific Islands
Sita World Travel Inc.	Africa, Middle East, India, Pakistan, Sri Lanka, Seychelles
South American Tours International	South America, Easter Island
South Pacific Tours	Australia, New Zealand, Papua New Guinea, Pacific Islands
Standard Tours	U.S.A., Canada
Sunflight Holidays	Florida, Bahamas, Caribbean, Mexico
Sunquest Vacations	U.S.A., Mexico, Caribbean, U.K., Western Europe, Israel, Canada
Taj Tours	India, Pakistan, Sri Lanka, Hong Kong, Thailand
Tauk Tours	U.S.A., Canada
Tourcan Vacations Inc.	Greece, Middle East, Africa, India, Pakistan, Sri Lanka, Seychelles, Hong Kong, Southeast Asia
Tour East Holidays	Switzerland, Holland, Eastern Europe, Middle East, Southeast Asia, China, Hong Kong, Japan, Russia, Scandinavia, Turkey
Tradewind Tours	Australia, New Zealand, Philippines, Southeast Asia
Trafalgar Tours	U.K., Ireland, Europe, Middle East, Canada
Travel Impressions, Inc.	U.S.A., Caribbean, South America

Trek Holidays	Central America, South America, Galapagos Islands, France, Greece, Turkey, Israel, Africa, Australia, New Zealand, Southeast Asia, India, Tibet
Trentway Tours	Canada, U.S.A.
Unitours Inc.	Europe, Middle East, Japan
Wild Africa Safaris	Africa
Wings of the World	Mexico, South America, Galapagos Islands, Africa, Seychelles, India, Sri Lanka, Hong Kong, China, Japan, Southeast Asia, Australia, New Zealand, Papua New Guinea, Pacific Islands
World Expedition Monde	Belize, Ecuador, Africa, Turkey, Southeast Asia

Index

Credits

Chapter 4   pp. 50–51,pages from *Official Hotel Guide* reproduced courtesy of Cahners Travel Group; pp. 52, page from *CTG Business Travel Planner* reproduced courtesy of Cahners Travel Group; pp. 53, page from *Star Service* reproduced courtesy of Cahners Travel Group.

Chapter 5   pp. 64, page from *Avis Worldwide Directory* reproduced courtesy of Avis Inc.

Chapter 6   pp. 81, 83–98, VIA Rail material reproduced courtesy of VIA Rail; pp. 101–111, Amtrak material reproduced courtesy of Amtrak. Amtrak Schedules in effect through May 20/2000. pp. 120–131 material reproduced courtesy of Rail Europe; p. 114, Thomas Cook Timetable reproduced by permission of Thomas Cook Publishing.

Chapter 8   pp. 150–151, Plan of the Nieuw Amsterdam reprinted with permission of Cruise Lines International Association, 2000 *Cruise Manual*.

Chapter 14   pp. 196–197, article reprinted courtesy of Canadian Travel Press.

Chapter 15   pp. 206–209, passport application forms reproduced courtesy of Ministry of Foreign Affairs and International Trade and the Passport Office; pp. 210–212, Mexico Tourist Card, maps of areas of malarial risk, and International Certificate of Vaccination reproduced from the *Travel Information Manual* courtesy of International Airline Publications.

Appendix A   p. 239, insurance application form reproduced courtesy of RBC Travel Insurance Company.